CW01637764

Hymns and Hymnody

Hymns and Hymnody

Historical and Theological Introductions

Volume 3: From the English West to the Global South

Edited by
Mark A. Lamport
Benjamin K. Forrest
and Vernon M. Whaley

James Clarke & Co

James Clarke & Co
P.O. Box 60
Cambridge
CB1 2NT
United Kingdom

www.jamesclarke.co
publishing@jamesclarke.co

Paperback ISBN: 978 0 227 17722 8
PDF ISBN: 978 0 227 90723 8

British Library Cataloguing in Publication Data
A record is available from the British Library

First published by James Clarke & Co, 2020

Published by arrangement
with Cascade Books

Dedications

From Mark—To my wonderful aunt, Kay Sutton, longtime church organist; and dear friend, Mark E. Fitzgerald (1955–98), gifted classical organist/pianist. Lovers of music offered in praise of God and the mission of his church.

From Benjamin—To my grandparents, Bill and Joyce Seal, who began, many years ago, a legacy of worship that has extended from their example to a generation of grandchildren who know, love, and worship Jesus. Thank you for your prayers and faithful example!

From Vernon—To my friend, pastor, and co-worker in ministry, Dr. Robert J. Morgan—Thank you for renewing my love of the hymns by faithfully telling their story.

Contents

Part 8: Twentieth Century

Part 9: Twenty-First Century

List of Tables

List of Figures

About the Editors, Introduction Contributors and Editorial Advisory Board

EDITORS

Mark A. Lamport (PhD, Michigan State University) is a graduate professor in the United States and Europe. He is coeditor of *Encyclopedia of Christianity and the Global South* (2 vols., 2018); *Encyclopedia of Martin Luther and the Reformation* (2 vols., 2017); *Encyclopedia of Christianity in the United States* (5 vols., Selected: "Notable Books of 2016"); *Encyclopedia of Christian Education* (3 vols., Winner, Booklist Editors' Choice: Adult Books, 2016).

Benjamin K. Forrest (EdD, Liberty University) is Professor of Christian Education and Associate Dean at the College of Arts and Sciences at Liberty University. He is coeditor of *A Legacy of Preaching* (2 vols., 2018), *Biblical Leadership: Theology for Everyday Leaders* (2017), and *Biblical Worship: Theology unto the Glory of God* (forthcoming).

Vernon M. Whaley (PhD, University of Oklahoma) is Dean of the Liberty University School of Music. His publications include *Exalt His Name* (2018), *Worship Through the Ages* (2012), *The Great Commission to Worship* (2011), and *The Dynamics of Corporate Worship* (2001).

INTRODUCTION CONTRIBUTORS

Robin A. Leaver studied at Clifton Theological (now Trinity) College, Bristol, England, and holds a doctorate from the Rijksunversiteit Groningen, the Netherlands. He is Professor Emeritus, Westminster Choir College, Princeton, and Visiting Professor, Yale Institute of Sacred Music, New Haven, and

Queen's University, Belfast, Northern Ireland. Leaver has an international reputation for research and writings in the areas of church music, theology, liturgy, and hymnology, especially in Luther and Bach studies.

Pedrito U. Maynard-Reid (ThD, MDiv, MA, Andrews University; MTh, Fuller Theological Seminary; BTh, Northern Caribbean University; LRSM, Royal Schools of Music; LTCL, ATCL, Trinity College London) is Assistant to the President for Diversity and Professor of Biblical Studies and Missiology at Walla Walla University. He is a specialist in music and worship, with special emphasis on African American, Caribbean, and Hispanic.

Paul Westermeyer is Professor Emeritus of Church Music, Luther Seminary, St. Paul, Minnesota. He received his PhD from the University of Chicago and studied under Martin E. Marty. Westermetey books include *The Church Musician*; *Te Deum: The Church and Music*; the *Hymnal Companion to Evangelical Lutheran Worship;* and the essays from 1850 to 1900 in *Church Music in the United States.*

EDITORIAL ADVISORY BOARD

Kimberly Hope Belcher (PhD, MTS, Theology—Liturgical Studies, University of Notre Dame, Notre Dame, Indiana) is the Tisch Family Assistant Professor of Theology at the University of Notre Dame, where her research includes sacramental and liturgical theology and ritual studies. She is especially interested in ecumenical dialogue and serves as a Catholic representative in the US Catholic-Methodist dialogue.

Alexandra Buckle (PhD, University of Oxford) is Lecturer in Music at St. Hilda's College, Oxford. She works on late medieval English music, with a special focus on institutions, iconography, and patrons. Buckle has published widely on fifteenth- and sixteenth-century English music and articles can be found in *Early Music*; *Plainsong and Medieval Music*; *Journal of Liturgical Studies*; and *BBC History Magazine.* Alexandra was on the committee for the reinterment of King Richard III at Leicester Cathedral in March 2015 and her research guided the ceremony. Alexandra enjoys speaking about her research in more popular outlets, on the radio, and has twice acted as a music consultant for English Heritage.

Jeremy Dibble (MA, Trinity College, Cambridge; PhD, Southampton University; FRSCM, FGCM) is a Professor of Music at Durham University. He has published monographs on C. Hubert H. Parry (Oxford University

Press), Charles Villiers Stanford (Oxford University Press), and John Stainer (Boydell Press), as well as numerous articles on church music, hymnody, and organ music of the Victorian and Edwardian eras. He is the musical editor of the *Canterbury Dictionary of Hymnology.*

Margot E. Fassler (PhD, Cornell) has recently published the textbook *Music in the Medieval West* and its *Anthology* (New York, 2014); the edited volume (with Katie Bugyis and Andrew Kraebel) *Medieval Cantors and Their Craft: Music, Liturgy, and the Shaping of History, 800–1500* (York, 2016); and the co-authored two-volume study (with Jeffrey Hamburger, Eva Schlotheuber, and Susan Marti) *Liturgical Life and Latin Learning at Paradies bei Soest, 1300–1425: Inscription and Illumination in the Choir Books of a North German Dominican Convent* (Munster, 2016). Fassler is a fellow of the Medieval Academy of America and of the American Academy of Arts and Sciences, and is currently Vice President of the Medieval Academy of America.

C. Michael Hawn (DMA, Music Education and Voice, Southern Baptist Theological Seminary; MCM, Musicology and Voice, Southern Baptist Theological Seminary; BME, Wheaton College) is University Distinguished Professor of Church Music and Director of the Sacred Music Program at Perkins School of Theology, Southern Methodist University. He conducts research in hymnody and publishes widely in this field, especially in the area of non-Western congregational song.

Joseph Herl (PhD, University of Illinois; MMus, North Texas State University) is Professor of Music at Concordia University, Nebraska. His 2004 book *Worship Wars in Early Lutheranism* was awarded the Roland Bainton Prize of the Sixteenth Century Society and Conference. More recently, he was coeditor of a historical companion to the *Lutheran Service Book.*

Lim Swee Hong (PhD, Drew University, New Jersey; MSM, Southern Methodist University, Texas) is Deer Park Associate Professor of Sacred Music and Director, Master of Sacred Music program at Emmanuel College of Victoria University in the University of Toronto, Canada. He is also the Director of Research for the Hymn Society in USA and Canada.

Pedrito U. Maynard-Reid (ThD, MDiv, MA, Andrews University; MTh, Fuller Theological Seminary; BTh, Northern Caribbean University; LRSM, Royal Schools of Music; LTCL, ATCL, Trinity College London), is Assistant to the President for Diversity and Professor of Biblical Studies and Missiology at Walla Walla University. He is a specialist in music and worship, with special emphasis on African American, Caribbean, and Hispanic.

David W. Music (DMA/MCM, Southwestern Baptist Theological Seminary) is Professor of Church Music in the School of Music at Baylor University. He served as editor of *The Hymn* (1991–96) and has written extensively on congregational song and sacred choral music.

Stephen Michael Newby (DMA, Music Composition, The University of Michigan at Ann Arbor; MM, The University of Massachusetts at Amherst) is Associate Professor of Music at Seattle Pacific University in Seattle, Washington. His recent publications include areas of theology of multiethnic music and worship, oratorio, and musical theater works based upon the prophet Hosea, Civil Rights and Underground Railroad movements.

Iain Quinn (PhD, Historical Musicology, University of Durham; MM, Yale University; BM, University of Hartford) is Assistant Professor of Organ and Coordinator of Sacred Music at Florida State University. Publications include editions of Barber, Czerny, Elgar, and Goss, and books *The Highest Walks of Art—The Development of an English Organ Sonata* and *Saint or Siren? The Organist in Victorian Literature.*

Lester Ruth (PhD, University of Notre Dame; ThM, Candler School of Theology; MDiv, Asbury Theological Seminary) is the Research Professor of Christian Worship at Duke Divinity School. Prior to Duke, he taught at Asbury Theological Seminary and Yale Divinity School. His current research explores the non-musical aspects of the history of contemporary worship.

Jo-Michael Scheibe (BA/M.M, California State University at Long Beach; DMA, University of Southern California) chairs the Thornton School of Music's department of Choral and Sacred Music at the University of Southern California. He is in frequent demand nationally and internationally as a clinician, conductor, and adjudicator for choruses at the university, community college, community, and secondary levels. Future engagements include international presentations in Shanghai, Bangkok, and Salzburg; national concerts at Orchestra Hall in Chicago and Carnegie Hall in New York City.

Bryan D. Spinks (DD, University of Durham) is the Bishop F. Percy Goddard Professor of Liturgical Studies and Pastoral Theology at Yale Institute of Sacred Music and Yale Divinity School. His areas of specialism include Church of the East, Syrian Orthodox and Reformed worship as well as Anglican rites. His most recent book is *Do This in Remembrance of Me: The Eucharist from the Early Church to the Present Day* (2013).

Martin Tel (DMA, University of Kansas; MA, Calvin Theological Seminary; MM, University of Notre Dame) is the Director of Music at Princeton Theological Seminary where he directs the seminary choirs, facilitates the music ministry for daily worship, and offers courses in church music. His research focuses on psalmody and congregational song.

Karen B. Westerfield Tucker (PhD/MA, Theology/Liturgical Studies, University of Notre Dame; MDiv, The Divinity School, Duke University) is Professor of Worship at the School of Theology, Boston University, where she teaches courses in the areas of liturgical studies and church music. Her publications take up such topics as Methodist/Wesleyan liturgical history and theology, worship and ecumenism, and hymnody.

Mel R. Wilhoit (DMA, Southern Baptist Theological Seminary) served as Professor of Music and Department Chair at Bryan College, Dayton, Tennessee, for over thirty years. His popular and scholarly works on music have appeared in numerous traditional and online publications.

EDITORIAL CONSULTANTS

Jonathan L. Best (PhD, St. Thomas University, Miami, Florida) teaches online courses in religion and theological writing for St. Thomas University, and operates an editing company—Best Academic Editing. His book *A Postmodern Theology of Ritual Action?* is scheduled to be published by Pickwick in 2019. He explores theological and philosophical issues related to uncertainty, transition, and being in-between at www.liminaltheology.org.

Ron J. Bigalke (PhD, University of Pretoria; PhD, MTS, Tyndale Theological Seminary; MDiv, Luther Rice University; MApol, Columbia Evangelical Seminary) is Georgia State Minister for Capitol Commission, and Research Associate, New Testament Department, University of Pretoria, mission and ethics project.

Mark D. Eckel (ThM, Grace Theological Seminary; PhD, Southern Baptist Theological Seminary) is Professor of Leadership, Education, and Discipleship, Capital Seminary and Graduate School, Washington, DC. Numerous publications include reviews, articles, curricula, books, and hundreds of essays at www.warpandwoof.org.

Benjamin D. Espinoza (MA, Asbury Theological Seminary) is a writer on Christian education, church history, and practical theology. He has several years of diverse ministry experience, and has contributed essays and reviews to *Christian Education Journal, Religious Education, Common Ground Journal, YouthWorker Journal,* and many others. He serves on the board of the Society for Children's Spirituality: Christian Perspectives.

Bryce F. Hantla (EdD, Southeastern Baptist Theological Seminary; MA, North Carolina State University) is Director of Institutional Research and Accreditation as well as Associate Professor for Christian Education and English at the College of Biblical Studies-Houston.

D. Joshua Pruden (MA, Northland International University) is a part-time freelance writer and lover of all things theology and research. He has experience in teaching English as a second language and is a regular preacher at his church, Christ the King, Edmonton.

Moriah Wilson (MA in Music Education) is a classically trained musician and has studied both piano and voice. Her publications include an honors thesis titled "The Suzuki Method: Influences of Shinichi Suzuki on Japanese Music Education."

Introduction to Volume 3
From the English West to the Global South

Pedrito U. Maynard-Reid

Although some basics have remained the same in hymnody and worship music from the nineteenth century until today, these forms of music have experienced many and varied changes during the last two centuries. The speed of change has been as rapid as the speed of social and economic changes in the last two hundred years. In these years, we have moved from the beginning of the industrial revolution, to a technological age, with no end in sight as to the content of change or its speed. Worship music and liturgy has, and is, experiencing the same phenomena.

What has been constant is the need to make worship in general, and music in particular, relevant to the time and context. Although there has always been push-back, those who were in the camp of relevancy have always won the "worship wars."

An example of the "constants" in the nineteenth century is the effect of the age of Romanticism on hymnody. Prior to this, the focus was on congregational melodic line singing. The classical romanticist harmonization and the growth of the secular part-song influenced the rise of harmonization in congregational singing. Further constants are the effects of the Second Great Awakening as well as the rise and popularity of the Layman's Revival, which inspired the need for songs that were simple (with simple harmonic structures), based on popular melodies, easy to memorize, emotional, and evangelistic. There was a renaissance in creativity that matched the age, and a movement away from the inflexibility that dominated traditional music.

The twentieth century saw this revolution continue. Hymnody matched the rapid changes brought about by the major wars; the decolonization of nations; ecumenism; new missional emphasis of denominations and para-church organizations; and significant social, moral, and theological changes, all unseen since the birth of Christianity. In all of these cases, cutting-edge hymn and worship songwriters created liturgical works that were attuned to the times—times in which there was more global awareness and greater diversity in music. These were times in which it was recognized that music was not a "universal language," but a "universal phenomenon" with varied expression (instrumentation, complexity of rhythmic structures and notation, language, and styles).

This is not to say that there were not intense efforts to keep the status quo and to resist the changing times. The growth of Southern gospel is a case in point. Yet even that genre grew out of a need to be relevant to the yearnings of white, cultural southern, conservative Christians, who sought to recapture their identity after the Civil War in the nineteenth century, and the civil rights movements in the twentieth through the twenty-first centuries.

Among the basic and major changes in hymnody and worship liturgy are changes in worldview (a move from a Greek and Eurocentric philosophical grounding), globalization, and social constructs that rejected centuries of Christian teachings and values.

The influence of the Greek worldview and the stress on individualism in the nineteenth century impacted the music of the church. The majority of gospel hymns and songs emphasized the personal dimensions of Christianity. They were self-focused and subjective. The stress was on the "I," "me," "mine." At that time and into the twentieth century the vast majority of Christians lived in the Global North. Today more than 70 percent of Christians domicile in the Global South, where the worldview is communal. Thus, there has been a shift from the individualistic stress to a more communal emphasis and engagement. Whereas the new revival songs of previous generations highlighted personal salvation and liberation from personal sins, many of the songs of the Global South and decolonized peoples celebrate, or make clarion calls for, political and social liberation. The liberative calls of the Old Testament prophets has taken precedence over the seeming individualistic Pauline corpus in the music of the twenty-first century. Conversion and repentance are not only for the individual, but also for nations and communities. There is a theology of righteousness, justice, holiness, and ethics, which is communal, social, and political.

The move away from Eurocentric Christianity saw a move toward a worldview of holism. Whereas the western philosophical assumptions dichotomize the human person, the eastern/Global South makes no such distinction. The body/matter is not evil and the soul good; the secular is not bad and the sacred virtuous. Worship music of previous centuries emphasized the cognitive over the experiential and emotive. Today, the emotive is an integral part of music enterprise. It is because of this shift that the charismatic dimension of Pentecostalism has dominated the worship landscape of the twentieth century.

The shift is also pronounced as the distinction between what is secular and what is sacred is minimized. For example, there is celebration in some quarters, and chagrin in others that Bob Marley's reggae hit, "One Love," is now in some hymnals. The same chagrin is expressed as unstructured popular dance has become an important part of the hymnic and sacred song liturgical event. Others celebrate this shift as a return to holistic worship in which the whole being is given over to God, and expresses itself in rhythmic praise, as the body joins the mouth and the mind in praise and worship.

The greatest change in hymnody and worship songs since the second half of the twentieth century is in the content. The content has represented the rapidly changing social worldview. And just as the technological renaissance of the twenty-first century is going at a speed beyond our imagination, so the shifts in theology and traditional morality are shifting. As goes the theology so goes the content of hymnody.

Science, technology, urbanization, globalization, and other changes in the world have forced the social issues that have driven these new understandings of Scripture upon us. The hymns of the nineteenth and early twentieth centuries were inadequate responses to today's concerns.

The modern conception of humanity that rejects the superiority of maleness and whiteness, and promotes equity and inclusiveness, has not only affected translations of Scripture, but stimulated the retuning of old hymns and creation of new worship musical lyrics that are sensitive to feminism and other excluded and marginalized peoples. Language that includes all and demeans none—whether they be of a different race or gender, disabled, of different national origin, or age—is now in vogue. Language that sees God as only male, or highlights oppressive structures or perpetuates them, are eliminated more and more from the worship liturgy.

The globalization of Christianity and the death of European colonization has possibly brought about the greatest change since the nineteenth century when even Christians sang "Rule Britannia, Britannia Rules the World." No longer are the hymns that were staples in the menu of Christian worship for centuries, relevant or dominant in the decolonized churches and movements of the world. *The Constitution on the Sacred Liturgy* that was produced by Vatican II in 1963, and the rise of societies like ethnomusicology and ethnodoxology, promoted music and worship that were inculturated in the indigenous patterns of the varied cultures. The metaphors, the musical patterns, the rhythmic structures, were no longer dependent on centuries of European culture, but fresh new texts and musical innovations (which, for many of these cultures, were millennial old) were arising.

The changes were not limited to the Global South. Even within the dominant culture of the developed western world there were rejections of the past and its hymnody as the primary source of worship. The new songs, as was noted earlier, reflected the culture of the times. The old hymns are slowly dying out. The need for hymnals are lessened with technological advances (projection and personal digital devices, for example), and the creation of the Christian Copyright Licensing International (CCLI), which has changed the delivery of worship music. And as in the wider society, the turnover in worship music is significant. It has been called the "binge and purge cycle." The praise and worship parallels the top charts of popular culture.

At the same time, ecumenism has affected worldwide worship music. Hymnals and worship song collections have become more diverse and inclusive. Worshipers are no longer surprised or at a loss when having a liturgical experience in Jamaica, Walla Walla, Helsinki, or Bangkok, they find themselves singing hymns of Luther, songs from Zimbabwe, and Hispanic rhythmic *coritos* from Puerto Rico.

Part 7

Nineteenth Century

Chapter 1

Oxford's Tractarian Movement

JEREMY DIBBLE

HISTORICAL BACKGROUND

IN THE CENTURIES AFTER the Reformation, the Church of England lost sight of its hymnody and while dissenters and nonconformists, particularly the Wesleyans and Methodists, began to develop a vibrant tradition of hymn-singing in their own churches during the eighteenth century, Anglicanism remained aloof in its attitude toward the potential of the hymn within the liturgy as an agency of religious proselytization and as a potent cultural catalyst. At the beginning of the nineteenth century the Anglican Episcopacy, keen to steer a centrist path to placate many of its middle- and upper-class worshipers (who were weary of doctrinal debate), endeavored to shape a practical, rational form of religion, free of extremes, a stance. This earned them the soubriquet "Latitudinarians," while provincial parishes, impressed by the zeal and optimism of the Methodists, were largely evangelical (or low church) in their approach to liturgy and the authority of the Bible. It was a different story, however, in England's ancient universities. Here, in an environment that was still semi-monastical, where clerics dominated academic life, there was much opposition to what was perceived as a secularization of the established church and the state, a vexed relationship at the best of times, particularly in areas such as church lands and other forms of financial income. The Church of England opposed many of the Whig reforms in parliament and was equally opposed to theological liberalism. What is more, opposition had also been fueled by other reforms such as the Catholic Emancipation Bill of 1829 and the 1832 Reform Act, and there were whiffs of change in the air regarding the very academic and social structures of the ancient universities, the rights of dissenters and even ecclesiastical reforms to the rights of employment clergymen had enjoyed for centuries.

Oxford University became a focal point for this opposition. John Keble's famous "National Apostasy" sermon of July 14, 1833, is often regarded as the beginning of so-called Tractarianism, more commonly known today as the Oxford movement. As Keble declared:

> The point really to be considered is, whether, according to the coolest estimate, the fashionable liberality of this generation be not ascribable, in a great measure, to the same temper which led the Jews voluntarily to set about degrading themselves to a level with the idolatrous Gentiles? And, if it be true anywhere, that such enactments are forced on the Legislature by public opinion, is Apostasy too hard a word to describe the temper of that nation?[1]

In consequence, several prominent Anglican clerics in Oxford—John Henry Newman, Richard Hurrell Froude, Edward Bouverie Pusey, Robert Wilberforce, Hugh James Rose, John Keble, and William Palmer—began to publish a series of tracts, ninety in total, from which the movement drew its name and in which practice doctrine and theology within the Church of England were closely examined. The first twenty tracts were published in 1833; an additional thirty followed in 1834, and the remaining forty were published over the next seven years until 1841, many of the latter being concerned with matters of doctrinal content and practice. The tract form of publication, which was inexpensive, made it eminently accessible to clergy, laity, and scholars alike and it meant that these writings were widely read and understood. Indeed, the publication of the first group of tracts proved so influential that a signed declaration by seven thousand clergymen was sent to the Archbishop of Canterbury expressing "deep attachment to the apostolic doctrine and liturgy and polity of the Church of England."[2] The laity also had their own petition and Keble led a deputation to Lambeth Palace on behalf of the poor.[3]

1. Keble, *Christian Year*, 549.
2. Reed, *Glorious Battle*, 8.
3. Lock, *John Keble*, 82.

The role of the tracts proved important for several reasons: first, they articulated a new sense of authority and order for the Church of England; second, they explored a new awareness of mystery within the liturgy; and third, there was a rediscovery of the significance of the Eucharist and its frequent participation as part of a recognition of the church's inherent sacramental richness and a desire to revive old Catholic practices and rites such as the "Real Presence" and confession. Adherence to Cranmer's *Book of Common Prayer* was also emphasized, but Newman also argued in his famous Tract 90, *Remarks on Certain Passages in the Thirty-Nine Articles,* that while the *Prayer Book* "was acknowledged on all hands to be of Catholic origin, our Articles also, the offspring of an uncatholic age, are, through God's providence, to say the least, not uncatholic, and may be subscribed by those who aim at being catholic in heart and doctrine."[4] This caused some consternation among the evangelical wing of the church, which was suspicious of what they perceived as the Oxford movement's propinquity to Romanism; but for many, this thinking was consistent with a new means of defining a *via media* between the Protestant Reformation and Romanists. While Oxford concerned itself with matters of theology, doctrine, liturgy, and the sacraments, Cambridge's sympathies to reform—through the Cambridge Camden Society and later the ecclesiologists—were reflected much more by the Romantic source from which the entire church revival flowed. This could be observed in translations of texts by the early fathers John Mason Neale and Benjamin Webb, in neo-gothic church architecture (which extended well beyond any medieval sentimentalism or nostalgia), the decoration of churches, stain glass, frescoes, and music, and in particular the rediscovery of plainsong and polyphony. Indeed, plainsong became an important focus for the ecclesiological movement who wanted to revive chanting both for the choir and congregation as a part of common liturgical practice. This was certainly the hope of Thomas Helmore, choirmaster and vice principal of St. Mark's College, Chelsea. Having shown considerable interest in the new editions of John Merbeck's sixteenth-century *Booke of Common Praier Noted* and William Dyce's ornate *Book of Common Prayer with Plain Song* (both issued in 1844), he looked to publish his own editions of *A Manual of Plain Song* (1850) and, more significantly, *The Hymnal Noted* (1854), which used many of Neale's translations. Although Helmore's work was highly significant as part of the nineteenth-century plainsong revival, in truth, this aspect of hymnody in general never gained any real traction. Nevertheless, the Oxford movement's attraction to hymnody, while sluggish to begin with, grew to be immensely enthusiastic, and by the 1850s,

4. Newman, *Tract 90*, 4.

there was a new momentum alive in English hymnody that ignited a major renaissance of creativity, both in words and music, and formed a tradition that still occupies a major place in the hymn-book literature of the Anglican communion.

In its zeal for reform, the Oxford movement had definite ideas about the role and presence of choirs. There was a dislike of the old "west gallery" tradition where organist and choir were placed in a gallery at the end of the church behind a curtain. The choir was too distant (and also prone to bad behavior), so the recommendation was to bring the choir, properly robed in cassocks and surplices, into the chancel; similarly, the preferred placing of the organ was also in the chancel if space was available on both the north and south sides. In making the choir a more central focus of worship, there were other factors in the new "order" that affected their deportment. Prayers in the vestry, formal processions to and from the choirstalls, and formal investiture of choristers all formed part of a new reverence, added to which the entire purpose of music was newly conceived to serve the liturgy. In this way, music for Matins, Evensong, and especially Choral Eucharist, assumed a more important role for it was not only harnessed to enhance the orders of service as laid out in the *Book of Common Prayer*, but also more specifically for the church's year from Sunday to Sunday and for major and minor feast days.

During the first thirty years of the nineteenth century, hymnody within Anglicanism had itself experienced some important changes. Until the end of the eighteenth century, the Anglican hierarchy had strictly controlled the singing of hymns in church both in what could be sung and when. Metrical psalms still proved to be the staple diet of most churches and cathedrals and little had changed in terms of their textual and musical scope since the *Old Version* published by Sternhold and Hopkins in 1562 (which borrowed heavily from the Genevan psalter), or its expansion by Thomas Ravenscroft in 1621, and the *New Version* first published Tate and Brady in 1696. The authority of the Church of England over hymn-singing remained inflexible during the eighteenth century; however, by 1830, it had weakened considerably as parishes began to take ownership of local tunes, words, and hymn-books. This is particularly evident in the work of Thomas Cotterill whose *Selection of Psalms and Hymns for Public and Private Use* (1810) proved popular and ran to many editions.

What is more, the Church of England began to covet the success and enthusiasm that the Methodists and other nonconformists were demonstrating with their fondness for hymn-singing and realized that the same thing would be a powerful agency for their own congregational mission. This was realized by various important episcopal figures such as Bishop

Reginald Heber whose *Hymns Written and Adapted to the Weekly Church Service of the Year* epitomized the growing concern for Anglican hymnody to reflect the church calendar. As a poet himself, influenced by the great swell of English Romantic poetry of the time by Wordsworth and Coleridge, Heber judiciously produced hymns for specific Sundays and Holy Days in the church year, relating the sensibility of his words and language to readings from the Epistles and Gospels. What is more, these hymns could be sung at places within the service (notably that of the Nicene Creed and the sermon) and not purely at the beginning or end, that is "outside" the liturgy, or at the point of the anthem as outlined by the *Book of Common Prayer*. Another figure was Henry Hart Milman, Professor of Poetry at Oxford and later Dean of St. Paul's Cathedral, whose own hymns were published in Heber's posthumous *Hymns* of 1827. Milman's enthusiasm from hymn-singing was witnessed by his introduction of Sunday evening services under the dome in St. Paul's in November 1858. Such was the popularity of these services, people flocked to the cathedral and many thousands were unable to gain entrance. Moreover, such were the numbers that crowded the space under the dome that the cathedral was forced to purchase additional chairs and finance the expansion of the organ.[5] In the same year as Heber's *Hymns* of 1827, John Keble, who was often perceived as the founder of Tractarianism (or the Oxford movement), published his seminal *Christian Year*. This was a series of poems for each Sunday of the Christian year and soon became a publication germane to Tractarian sensibilities and as a volume of poetical verse (Keble was Professor of Poetry at Oxford between 1831 and 1841), it was one of the most widely read volumes of the nineteenth century and many of his verses (such as "Sun of my soul, thou Saviour dear") have become permanent fixtures of the repertory. As Temperley has noted, the Tractarian "rediscovery" of the Roman Breviary, which Cranmer had deliberately omitted from the *Book of Common Prayer* after the Reformation, was a significant turning-point.[6] While there was reluctance in part from those who saw value in the Breviary's Latin texts, which were often perceived as "primitive" (indicated by John Chandler's *Hymns of the Primitive Church* of 1837), the translation of these texts into English became increasingly popular. Furthermore, because of their intrinsic relationship to the church year, to the liturgy and the daily office of morning and evening prayer, the texts were entirely appropriate to the Tractarian's desire for greater order, and because they could be sung in the vernacular (Latin, of course, was prescribed within the Anglican liturgy), there was no legal impedance.

5. Dibble, *John Stainer*, 146.

6. Temperley, *Music of the English Parish Church*, 263.

Added to which, these Latin hymns would symbolize a major restoration of those facets of the ancient church for which many Tractarians yearned. J. M. Neale, who like many Anglicans had originally nurtured a suspicion of hymnody, was quickly drawn to Tractarian translations of Latin hymns and, by way of research both in England and on the continent, soon became a national authority on the medieval hymn by way of criticizing what he believed were careless translations by earlier Tractarian translators. A landmark in this respect was his *Medieval Hymns and Sequences* of 1851, though his most significant publication was undoubtedly the *Hymnal Noted* (1851 and 1854). Following the footsteps of Heber and Keble, the *Hymnal Noted* was conceived as a hymnal to suit all the Sundays of the church year in which *all* the hymns were Latin translations that had been in use in England before the Reformation and were set to their original plainsong melodies (many of them from the ancient Sarum sources).[7] Plainsong may have represented the more extreme ideological stance of the Tractarian movement, but its larger process of antiquarian research led to the discovery of old German melodies and chorales that became the focus for Frances Cox's *Sacred Hymns from the German* (1841), Catherine Winkworth's influential *Lyra Germanica* (1855) and the *Chorale Book for England* (1863) edited by William Sterndale Bennett and Otto Goldschmidt.

THEOLOGICAL PERSPECTIVES

One of the major literary products of the Tractarians was the emergence of a rich seam of poetical invention. In part this was stimulated by the new wave of Romanticism in British poetry and literature during the first half of the nineteenth century, but it was also provoked by the Oxford movement's pursuit of a new sense of mystery within the liturgy and the traditional tenets of Christian faith such as the incarnation, the Annunciation, Advent, Christmas, Epiphany, Septuagesima, Ash Wednesday, Lent, Easter, Ascension, and the Trinity, not to mention the new and increased awareness of the sacraments, and in particular the centrality of the Eucharist. While these elements were self-evident, the Tractarians also saw a need for an updating the traditional feast days and calendar periods of the hymn book and how they could serve a new, modern industrial society. In this way, new categories were introduced to cater for children, for those in military service, for consecration, marriage, pilgrimage, for those at sea, for the elderly, for the poor, and for the sick and dying with the provision of new, specially focused poetry which, through its immediacy to contemporary experience,

7. Temperley, *Music of the English Parish Church*, 264.

had a greater relevance to the dangers and arduous work of modern life. Keble and Heber have already been mentioned for their groundbreaking contributions to Tractarian poetry and the way in which poetry had a place in the devotional life, but in their wake were a host of others who left their stamp on the repertory. One of Keble's and Pusey's close colleagues at Oxford was John Henry Newman whose literary gifts produced "Lead, kindly light," a hymn for guidance, and, after Newman had been received into the Roman Church, "Firmly I believe and truly" and "Praise to the holiest in the height" from his narrative poem *The Dream of Gerontius*. Newman was one of several prominent Tractarians to convert to Rome. Another was Frederick William Faber, who idolized Newman and was a friend of Wordsworth, who wrote a hymnbook in 1862 that contained such texts as "My God, how wonderful Thou art," "O come and mourn with me awhile," "Sweet Saviour, bless us ere we go," and "O Paradise, O Paradise." The high-church sensibility of Faber was also mirrored in another Roman convert and Newman follower, Edward Caswall, who made numerous translations from the Latin for his *Lyra Catholica, containing all the breviary and missal hymns* of 1850, which included "Come, Holy Ghost," "Jesus, the Very Thought of Thee," and "When Morning Gilds the Skies." Conversion to Roman Catholicism by Newman, Faber, Caswall, and Matthew Bridges only served to vindicate the opposition of those who perceived the Oxford movement's leanings toward Rome, a perception that erupted in the Papal Aggression in 1850 when the Roman Catholic hierarchy was reestablished in England. There were, however, many Anglican clergy who cleaved to the ideals of Tractarianism or whose poetry chimed with its principles. In this way clergyman-poets such as John Ellerton (who gave us three fine evening hymns: "The day thou gavest, Lord, is ended," "O strength and stay upholding all creation," and "Saviour again to Thy dear name we raise"), Henry Williams Baker ("O praise ye the Lord! Praise him in the height," "The King of love my shepherd is," "We love the place, O God," "Praise, O praise our God and King," "Let us with a gladsome mind," and "Lord, thy word abideth"), and Christopher Wordsworth (nephew of the poet) whose hymn collection *The Holy Year* (1862) contained 177 of his own poems that were widely set (including "Alleluia! Alleluia! Hearts to heaven and voices raise," "Gracious Spirit, Holy Ghost," "Hark, the sound of holy voices," "O day of rest and gladness," and "Songs of thankfulness and praise"). Women poets also made a significant contribution. Cecil Frances Alexander (née Humphreys), much influenced by the example of Keble, produced *Verses for Holy Seasons* (1846), *Narrative Hymns for Village Schools* (1853), *Poems on Subjects in the Old Testament* (Part I, 1854; Part II, 1857), and *Hymns Descriptive and Devotional* (1858). Known today as "Mrs. Alexander," she is best remembered for "All things bright and beautiful," "There is a green hill far away," and "Once in royal David's city," as well as "St. Patrick's Breastplate" ("I bind unto myself today"). Charlotte Elliott, best known perhaps for "Just as I am without one plea" authored two important collections, *The Invalid's Hymn Book* (1835) and *Hours of Sorrow Cheered and Comforted* (1836), related to her own illness and suffering, as did Francis Ridley Havergal in *Ministry of Song* (1869), which contained the popular "Take my life and let it be." And among the most popular of Christmas carols, "In the bleak mid-winter" and "Love came down at Christmas," are by the devout high-church Anglican Christina Rossetti (sister of the Pre-Raphaelite painter, Dante Gabriel) in which the mysteries of the incarnation find its *locus* within an altogether more familiar English environment.

CONTRIBUTION TO LITURGY AND WORSHIP

The exponential growth of hymn-singing and hymn-writing within the Church of England inevitably gave rise to a major spurt in the publication of hymn books, especially in the 1850s. Among the most popular were Kemble's *Selection of Psalms and Hymns* (1853), the Society for the Promotion of Christian Knowledge's *Psalms and Hymns* (1853), Mercer's *Church Psalter and Hymn Book* (1854), *The Salisbury Hymn Book* (1857) edited by Keble and Earl Nelson, and the *Congregational Hymn and Tune Book* edited by Richard Chope, which all went into mass production. Of these, Mercer's hymn book took, as Temperley has noted, a broader position in catering for a wider group of tastes, while Blew's *The Church Hymn and Tune Book* (1852) and the *Hymnal Noted* (1854) by Neale and Helmore, with their preference for medieval Latin hymns, accommodated the high-church wing.[8] While appealing to a wide congregation, Mercer's hymn book also possessed other important attributes. The music (as four-part harmony) for each hymn was printed with the words. This was not entirely new, since both Helmore and Blew did so in their hymn books, but while the latter appealed only to a small specialized congregation, Mercer's aspired to a much larger *tirage*. In addition, the musical editor of Mercer's, John Goss, organist of St. Paul's Cathedral (where the hymnal was commonly used for the populous evening Sunday evening services), brought it additional prestige. Chope acknowledged the Tractarian contributions of Keble, Milman, Christopher Wordsworth, Neale Isaac Williams, Faber, Caswall, Godfrey Thring, and William Walsham How, and, on the title page, he paid special tribute to the musical involvement of John Bacchus Dykes (precentor of

8. Temperley, *Music of the English Parish Church*, 297.

Durham Cathedral), W. T. Best (organist of St. George's Hall, Liverpool), George Cooper (organist of the Chapel Royal), E. J. Hopkins (organist of the Temple Church), E. G. Monk (organist of York Minster), and James Turle (organist of Westminster Abbey) from whom he commissioned tunes; there was also acknowledgement of the help and contribution of other eminent musicians and composers such Sterndale Bennett, Frederick Ouseley, and John Hullah.

The spirit of Mercer's hymnal ultimately proved to be the guiding light for the most successful of all English Tractarian hymn books, *Hymns Ancient & Modern*. Appearing in 1861 under the general editorship of Sir Henry Baker, its intention was to reach out to the full spectrum of Anglicanism, adhering to Keble's *dictum* that "if you wish to make a hymn book for the use of the Church, make it comprehensive."[9] Nevertheless, while there were metrical psalms and hymns by Isaac Watts and Charles Wesley that served the palate of the evangelicals, much of the hymn book's 273 items were occupied by ancient melodies, German chorales, and plainsong hymns, the musical part having been undertaken by its editor, W. H. Monk (organist of King's College, London) who was assisted by Ouseley.

One of the most compelling facets of the Tractarian hymn is that its Romantic literary disposition and motivation also found its natural home in *musical* Romanticism among composers who were entirely at ease with the contemporary idiom of modern harmonic chromaticism. What is more, the art of the Tractarian hymn and the industrial production of hymn books such as *Hymns Ancient & Modern* coincided with a major choral revival in England. This revival could be measured not only by the success of provincial choral festivals, the popularity of choral societies and, later, the competitive music festival (which sought to improve standards even further), but by the very grass roots that supported these ventures, the church choirs. The role of the choir in the service was, of course, to lead the singing, but during the nineteenth century this experience amounted to more than the pure rendition of a melody. For church choirs, many of them substantial in number, the social and religious involvement of hymn-singing was to sing in four parts, which in turn meant the enhanced experience of singing in *harmony*. An inevitable consequence of the choral desire to sing in harmony was the response of composers who soon began to adorn their tunes with the modern harmonic resources available in secular music from composers such as Schubert, Weber, Spohr, Mendelssohn, and Schumann. What is more, the hymn itself began to take on the identity of the secular part-song, a thoroughly Romantic idiom strongly associated with harmonic

9. Temperley, *Music of the English Parish Church*, 298.

invention and entirely given to the promotion of textual nuance. Owing to the enjoyment gained from the singing of hymns, often by large choirs with a capable organist, the experience itself took on the aura of a performance in which nuances (such as dynamics, which eventually found their way into later printed copies of the hymns) became an intrinsic part of the dramatic depiction of the poetic verse. A further dimension of this sense of "performance" was the presence of the organ, which not only provided support to the choir but would often furnish new, varied, and often extemporized harmonies in a climactic unison final verse; or in many cases, composers could incorporate unison parts of their hymn composition (as a contrast to the harmonic sections) in which the organ *had to* engage as an essential part of the larger expressive apparatus. The corollary of this aspect of hymn-singing was the emergence of hymns with elaborate printed organ parts. Hymns of this kind can be observed in contributions by Monk, Dykes, Stainer, Sullivan, and Hopkins. Dykes, who was surely the most archetypal of Tractarian hymnodists, produced throughout his life a catalogue of immensely varied settings in which his musical susceptibilities (as a Cambridge student he was a pupil of Thomas Attwood Walmisley, the professor of music) found a fertile home in the fecund environment of Tractarian verse. Besides Mendelssohnian part-song, his hymns could show the declamatory influence of cantata or oratorio, or the lyricism of Schubert song, and the creative (and often irregular) metres of the poetry would frequently give rise to the most interesting variety of musical forms (particularly those with refrains). The involvement of composers in the process of Tractarian hymnody was therefore to enhance even further the already well-accepted genre of religious poetry so that the hymn ultimately became an artistic entity in its own right. Not only were poets expected to show a literary flair in their choice of words and evocation of theological doctrine and mystery, composers similarly understood the hymn as a creative challenge in much the same way as they approached other musical idioms. In the hymn tunes of Dykes and Stainer, who exercised this practice *par excellence*, it was possible to perceive a process of organic "unity" in which, over and above the cohesion of melody and harmony, there existed a matrix of thematic motives through which well-established principles of "composition" became an integral feature of the form. Thus, for composers, the hymn became a serious object of creative attention and, in several cases, triggered the publication of "complete hymns" as the account of a life's work in the idiom.[10]

10. Stainer published his *Complete Hymns* in 1899. Hopkins followed in 1901 and Dykes posthumously in 1902.

NOTABLE HYMNS

The first edition of *Hymns Ancient & Modern* contained significant contributions by contemporary Tractarian authors and modern tunes by Monk, Ouseley, Henry Gauntlett, and John Bacchus Dykes and many of these became highly popular with congregations, notably Henry Francis Lyte's "Abide with me" with Monk's tune "Eventide," and all seven of Dykes's contributions including settings of William Whiting's "Eternal Father strong to save" (tune: "Melita"), Heber's "Holy, holy, holy, holy, Lord God Almighty" (tune: "Nicaea"), and Faber's "O come and mourn with me awhile" (tune: "St Cross"). *Hymns Ancient & Modern* outstripped the sales of all other hymn books during the 1860s so that, by 1868, there was demand for a supplement. For this expanded edition of 386 hymns, Monk asked Dykes for an additional seventeen tunes (the largest new contribution by any single composer) among which were three prominent Tractarian texts: Newman's "Lead, kindly light" (tune: "Lux Benigna"), "Praise to the Holiest" (tune: "Gerontius"), and Baker's "The King of Love my Shepherd is" (tune: "Dominus regit me"). A second edition of the hymnal was published in 1875 in which the number hymns expanded to 473 and Dykes's contribution of modern tunes, many of them with Tractarian texts, amounted to 56, almost one-eighth of the entire collection. A further supplement, which represented the apogee of the Tractarian hymn, appeared in 1889, with a significant contribution from John Stainer, organist of St. Paul's Cathedral as well as other prominent organist-composers such as E. J. Hopkins and Joseph Barnby.

Although Dykes's corpus of hymns are most representative of the Tractarian sensibility, or what is often referred to as the "High Victorian" hymn, one of the most enduring examples of the art may be found in John Stainer's *The Crucifixion: A Meditation on the Sacred Passion of the Holy Redeemer*. This was written in 1887 for his pupil William Hodge, the organist of St. Marylebone Parish Church, an ecclesiologist church with a large choir of more than thirty choristers and a dozen men. The text of *The Crucifixion* was provided by the young J. W. Sparrow Simpson, who later became a prominent commentator on Anglo-Catholicism. Intended for parish choirs who could not furnish the resources of the passions by J. S. Bach, *The Crucifixion* offered a practical alternative in its use of two soloists (tenor and bass), four-part choir, and organ part of modest difficulty. Shorter than a traditional passion narrative, the work was nevertheless comparable in the way it used congregational hymns to punctuate the structure of solo and choral numbers; in this way the hymns took on a reflective role similar to those of the Lutheran passion chorales, though locating the piece very much within the context of nineteenth-century Anglicanism. Stainer's six hymns, in particular "Cross of Jesus" and "All for Jesus," are amongst the finest of their type in the repertoire for their highly developed harmonic resource, the adroitness of their construction and the individual nature of their expressive Romantic sentiment.

BIBLIOGRAPHY

Adelmann, Dale. *The Contribution of Cambridge Ecclesiologists to the Revival of Anglican Choral Worship* 1839–62. Aldershot, UK: Ashgate, 1997.

Brilioth, Y. "The Anglican Revival." In *Studies in the Oxford Movement*. London: Longman, Green & Co. Ltd, 1933.

Chadwick, Owen. *The Spirit of the Oxford Movement*. Cambridge: Cambridge University Press, 1992.

Dibble, Jeremy. "Musical Trends and the Western Church: A Collision of the 'Ancient' and 'Modern.'" In *The Cambridge History of World Christianities c. 1815–1914*, edited by S. Gilley and B. Stanley, 121–35. Vol. 8. Cambridge: Cambridge University Press, 2006.

Dibble, Jeremy. *John Stainer: A Life in Music*. Woodbridge,UK: Brewer & Boydell, 2007.

Faber, G. *Oxford Apostles: A Character Study of the Oxford Movement*. London: Pelican, 1954.

Frere, W. H., and M. Frost, eds. *Historical Companion to Hymns Ancient & Modern*. London: William Clowes & Sons, 1909.

Gatens, William. *Victorian Cathedral Music in Theory and Practice*. Cambridge: Cambridge University Press, 1986.

Julian, John. *Dictionary of Hymnology*. London: John Murray, 1899; rev. 1907.

Keble, John. *The Christian Year, Lyra Innocentium and Other Poems together with His Sermon on "National Apostasy."* London: Oxford University Press, 1914.

Knox, E. A. *The Tractarian Movement 1833–1845*. London: Putnam, 1933.

Lock, W. *John Keble*. London: Methuen, 1923.

Newman, John Henry. *Tract 90, Remarks on Certain Passages in the Thirty-Nine Articles*. London: J., G. F. & J. Rivington, 1838.

Rainbow, Bernarr. *The Choral Revival in the Anglican Church*. Oxford: Oxford University Press, 1970.

Reed, J. S. *Glorious Battle: The Cultural Politics of Victorian Anglo-Catholicism*. Nashville: Vanderbilt University Press, 1996.

Tennyson, G. B. *Victorian Devotional Poetry: The Tractarian Mode*. Cambridge: Harvard University Press, 1981.

Sparrow Simpson, W. J. *The History of the Anglo-Catholic Revival from 1845*. London: George Allen & Unwin, 1932.

Temperley, Nicholas. *The Music of the English Parish Church*. Cambridge: Cambridge University Press, 1979.

Watson, J. Richard. *Canterbury Dictionary of Hymnology*. Norwich, UK: Canterbury Press, 2013.

Watson, J. Richard. *The English Hymn: A Critical and Historical Study*. Oxford: Oxford University Press, 1991.

Webb, C. C. J. *Religious Thought in the Oxford Movement*. London: S.P.C.K, 1928.

Chapter 2

Fanny Crosby

Songs of Salvation, Consecration, Service, and Heaven

Beverly A. Howard

HISTORICAL BACKGROUND

Frances (Fanny) Jane Crosby was born on March 24, 1820, in Bridgeport, Connecticut, the only child of John and Mercy Crosby. According to her definitive biographer, Edith Blumhofer, details of Crosby's childhood are from reminiscences she dictated as an elderly woman. Two events occurring in infancy shaped her destiny: her loss of vision and the death of her father.

The first event is the oft-told story of Crosby being blinded before she was two months old. Crosby had an eye infection and in the absence of a doctor, a stranger claiming medical expertise applied hot poultices to her eyes. Allegedly this treatment left her blind with only the ability to perceive light and dark, although it is possible that she was blind from birth.[1] Throughout her life, Crosby was adamant that she harbored no resentment toward this person, but rather "because I have always believed from my youth to this very moment that the good Lord, in His Infinite Mercy, by

1. Blumhofer, *Her Heart Can See*, 15.

this means consecrated me to the work that I am still permitted to do."[2] Thus, "a nameless man shaped an infant's destiny": a vulnerable infant who would eventually author more than eight thousand hymns, give song to nineteenth-century American evangelicals, and also become known as the "Queen of Gospel Song."[3]

The second formative event was that Crosby's father died before she was a year old. Because her mother, by necessity, worked to support the family, her grandmother, Eunice Paddock Crosby, was influential in Fanny's nurture and spiritual formation. Crosby recalls:

> My grandmother was a woman of exemplary piety; and from her I learned many useful and abiding lessons. She was a firm believer in prayer; and, when I was very young, taught me to believe that our Father in Heaven will always give us whatever is for our good; and therefore that we should be careful not to ask him anything that is not consistent with His Holy Will.[4]

Her grandmother provided emotional support for both young Fanny and her mother, instilling in them the view "that sometimes Providence deprived persons of some physical faculty in order that spiritual insight might more fully awake[n]."[5] In this nurturing home, Fanny learned Scripture, classic literature (Milton, Shakespeare, Bunyan), and hymns by Isaac Watts.[6]

Crosby's formal education began at the age of fifteen when she left home and enrolled in the New York Institution for the Blind where she was a student from 1835–45. The curriculum included academic studies (writing, grammar, literature, math, geography, reading), vocational training, and music lessons. In addition to singing, she learned to play piano, organ, guitar, and harp. Crosby had always exhibited an aptitude and passion for writing poetry, an ability that she honed while at the institution. Because the concept of educating the blind was a novel endeavor in the early 1800s, the school's directors exploited student progress for purposes of raising money, recruiting students, and raising public awareness of the institution. Thus, Crosby was frequently called upon to recite her poems before philanthropists, politicians, and the public. Conceived as a fundraising strategy, poems from her time at the institution were published in *The Blind Girl and Other Poems* (1844). A reviewer in the *New York Mirror* wrote that the

2. Crosby, *Memories of Eighty Years*, 19.
3. Blumhofer, *Her Heart Can See*, 15.
4. Crosby, *Memories of Eighty Years*, 12.
5. Blumhofer, *Her Heart Can See*, 16.
6. Blumhofer, *Her Heart Can See*, 17.

book justified "great modification of our pity for the blind. . . . Eyes could scarce do more."[7] The institution is also where she met her future husband, Alexander Van Alstyne, a talented musician. By 1846, Crosby transitioned from being a student to an instructor at the institution, teaching rhetoric, grammar, and American and Roman history to the younger students.[8]

Crosby left the institution upon her marriage to Van Alstyne in 1858, living briefly in Maspeth, New York, where her husband was a private music teacher and church organist. After living there a short time, they returned to New York City. Only later in life did Crosby reveal that she and Van Alstyne had a child who died in infancy. Details of their marriage are shrouded in mystery. Following their return to New York City, they maintained separate living arrangements for many years, apparently due to a rift in their relationship.

Crosby experienced an eclectic spiritual formation. She descended from Puritans, inheriting their strong Calvinist theology. When her mother took employment in North Salem, New York, Crosby became acquainted with the Society of Friends. As a child she attended the Presbyterian meetinghouse, Sunday school, and singing school, and would have been well-versed in psalter singing and hymns by Isaac Watts.[9] She attended her first Methodist meeting in 1835, which was her initial exposure to their ardent worship and hymn singing. As a student at the institution, Crosby worshiped with various Protestant congregations in New York City, including Eighteenth Street Methodist Church where she accompanied singing for Thursday evening religious classes.[10] She experienced a spiritual awakening in 1850 during the fall revival services at the Thirtieth Street Methodist congregation where the lines "Here, Lord I give myself away, 'Tis all that I can do" from the Isaac Watts hymn "Alas, and Did My Savior Bleed" moved her profoundly, resulting in her making a deeper spiritual commitment. As an adult, Crosby attended Plymouth Church where Henry Ward Beecher was pastor; Fourth Presbyterian Church, pastored by a distant cousin Howard Crosby; an Episcopal church; a Dutch Reformed Church; and Brooklyn Tabernacle.[11] Finally, in 1887, Crosby formally joined a church: Cornell Memorial Methodist Episcopal Church.

7. Blumhofer, *Her Heart Can See*, 64.

8. Blumhofer, *Her Heart Can See*, 71.

9. Blumhofer, *Her Heart Can See*, 23.

10. Blumhofer, *Her Heart Can See*, 106.

11. Blumhofer, *Her Heart Can See*, 113–15.

By mid-century, Crosby was an established secular poet who had interacted with the foremost entrepreneurial musicians and publishers.[12] Crosby and George F. Root (1820–95) composer and music teacher at the Institution, collaborated on secular songs and cantatas. However, it was Crosby's Sunday school hymn collaborations with tunesmith William B. Bradbury (1816–1868) that launched her career as a hymn writer. Before his death, Bradbury and Crosby collaborated on several Sunday school hymnals, including *Golden Censer* (1864) and *Bradbury's Fresh Laurels for the Sabbath School* (1868). Following his death, Crosby continued working with Bradbury's successors William Doane and Robert Lowry and publisher Biglow and Main. Under her own name and multiple pseudonyms assigned by her publishers, she contributed to *Bright Jewels* (1869), *Brightest and Best* (1875), and numerous others publications by Biglow and Main.[13] For a number of years, the publisher contracted Crosby to provide three new hymn texts per week, paying her a meager stipend.

Sunday school songs provided revivalists a model for early gospel songs (i.e., singable tunes with texts delivering a simple gospel message that were emotionally appealing). Crosby's collaborations with the famed evangelism team Dwight L. Moody (1837–99) and Ira D. Sankey (1840–1908) produced scores of gospel hymns disseminated widely, published in collections such as *Gospel Hymns and Sacred Songs* (1875). Sankey became a trusted friend and benefactor. Crosby also worked with Phoebe Palmer Knapp (1839–1908), a tunesmith active in the Methodist holiness movement. It was this collaboration that gave the world "Blessed Assurance, Jesus Is Mine."

After 1880, Crosby directed her energy toward working in the missions of New York City, particularly the Bowery Mission. For Crosby, reaching marginalized people was a gospel imperative. This work produced some of her most enduring hymns such as "Pass Me Not, O Gentle Savior," and "Rescue the Perishing." Crosby regularly spoke at meetings in various missions, prisons, and gatherings of the Women's Christian Temperance Union.

Owing to declining health, Crosby returned to her hometown of Bridgeport, Connecticut, in 1900, living out her final years with family.[14]

12. In addition to *The Blind Girl and Other Poems* (1844), two other published collections were *Monterey and Other Poems* (1853) and *A Wreath of Columbia's Flowers* (1858),

13. For a listing of over two hundred of Crosby's pseudonyms, see Blumhofer, *Her Heart Can See*, Appendix B.

14. Blumhofer details Mercy Crosby's second marriage in 1838 and the six children (half-siblings to Fanny) produced by that union.

Following a six-month illness, she died on February 12, 1915, succumbing to a massive stroke.

Crosby lived and worked in the midst of social upheaval in America. During the nineteenth century there was an astounding growth in population with overwhelming demographic shifts due to immigration. The Civil War and its aftermath further contributed to a fractured society. However, this was also a time of spiritual renewal and a boom in music publishing. Her evangelical faith, prodigious output, and associations with leading revivalists, pastors, musicians, and publishers all coalesced in Crosby achieving the status of "Queen of the Gospel Song."

THEOLOGICAL PERSPECTIVES

Succinctly stated, Fanny Crosby's hymns communicate a Christocentric theology, focusing on salvation through Christ's atoning blood, the assurance of Christ's presence now, the duty of Christian service, and eternal life. She rarely wrote texts concerned with cerebral church doctrines such as incarnation, trinity, baptism, communion, etc. Hers was an experiential theology evident in her Sunday school hymns and later gospel hymns. Crosby believed her texts captured the essence of historical Protestant faith viewed through an evangelical lens and "voiced a popular understanding of evangelical Christianity."[15]

One scholar offers four broad categories through which to examine Crosby's hymns: Salvation, Consecration, Service, Heaven. Within these categories, common topics emerge: "cleansing, rest, safety, intimacy with Christ, duty, readiness for Christ's return, and seeing Christ."[16] Her texts convey strong reliance on Scripture and biblical images, compassionate naming of the sinner, her belief of salvation being available to all, and a personal experience of salvation. Applying these four categories to selected Crosby hymns, this section of the essay explores her theological perspectives as sung and embraced by an entire generation.

Salvation

Crosby's understanding of atonement/salvation appears in many of her Sunday school hymns such as "All to Christ I Owe" and "Jesus, Keep Me Near the Cross." Using familiar language such as "ransom," "debt of sin,"

15. Blumhofer, *Her Heart Can See*, 283.

16. Blumhofer, *Her Heart Can See*, 253.

"washed in the blood," "flowing fountain," "pardon," "purchase of blood," and "paid," her texts resonate with ransom and penal atonement theories. "All to Christ I Owe" is typical of Crosby's comprehension of salvation as a debt sinful humanity owes to God but is paid, or satisfied, by Jesus' death.

Redeeming work is done;
The debt of sin is paid;
The precious Lamb of God;
My sacrifice is made. (Refrain)

I'll bow at Jesus' feet,
And plead his grace so free;
I'll wash me in his blood,
That blood was shed for me. (Refrain)

Yes, Jesus paid it all;
To him the glory be;
His love my pardon speaks,
And grace has set me free. (Refrain)

Refrain:
Jesus paid it all;
All to Him I owe!
Sin had left a crimson stain;
He washed it white as snow.[17]

Another atonement theory espoused in her texts is that of healing, i.e., through Christ humanity is healed from spiritual disease (sin). Images such as "healing stream" ("Jesus, Keep Me Near the Cross," st. 1), and "fount of healing" ("Come to the Fount of Healing," st. 1) support this theory. This aspect of salvation is explicit in Crosby's "There Is Healing at the Fountain" (st. 2):

There is healing at the fountain,
Come and find it, weary soul,
There your sins may all be covered;
Jesus waits to make you whole.[18]

In one of her most poignant hymns, "Pass Me Not, O Gentle Savior" (st. 1–3), a penitent pleading with Jesus for healing, confesses a "wounded, broken spirit" that can only find "relief" and "comfort" through grace.

Pass me not, O gentle Savior,

17. Lowry, *Bright Jewels for the Sunday School*, 139.

18. Excell, *Triumphant Songs*, 119.

Hear my humble cry,
While on others Thou art calling,
Do not pass me by.

Refrain:
Savior, Savior,
Hear my humble cry;
While on others Thou art calling,
Do not pass me by.

Let me at a throne of mercy
Find a sweet relief;
Kneeling there in deep contrition,
Help my unbelief. [Refrain]

Trusting only in Thy merit,
Would I seek Thy face;
Heal my wounded, broken spirit,
Save me by Thy grace. [Refrain][19]

Crosby hymns are replete with scriptural allusion and biblical images in expressing Christ's salvific action. "Praise Him, Praise Him," one of Crosby's popular Sunday school songs, features an exuberant text and tune exhorting all earth, highest archangels, and saints to praise Jesus for his redemptive acts. Each stanza, opening with the litany "Praise Him, praise Him, Jesus, our blessed Redeemer," issues a list of common biblical metaphors for Jesus, including shepherd, rock, hope of salvation, prophet, priest, and king.

Praise Him! praise Him! Jesus, our blessed Redeemer!
Sing, O earth, His wonderful love proclaim!
Hail Him! hail Him! highest archangels in glory,
Strength and honor give to His holy name!
Like a shepherd, Jesus will guard His children;
In His arms He carries them all day long:

Refrain:
Praise Him! praise Him! tell of His excellent greatness!
Praise Him! praise Him! ever in joyful song!

Praise Him! praise Him! Jesus, our blessed Redeemer!
For our sins, He suffered and bled and died;
He our Rock, our hope of eternal salvation,
Hail Him! hail Him! Jesus the crucified.
Sound His praises! Jesus who bore our sorrows,

19. Bliss and Sankey, *Gospel Hymns and Sacred* Songs, 28.

Love unbounded, wonderful, deep, and strong: [Refrain]

Praise Him! praise Him! Jesus, our blessed Redeemer!
Heavenly portals loud with hosannas ring!
Jesus, Savior, reigneth forever and ever;
Crown Him! Crown Him! Prophet and priest and King!
Christ is coming, over the world victorious,
Power and glory unto the Lord belong: [Refrain][20]

In addition to biblical images, Crosby quotes or alludes to Scripture to strengthen her texts. For example, the first stanza of "Though Your Sins Be as Scarlet" quotes Isa 1:18 (also "All to Him I Owe," cited above). One of her most enduring hymns, "To God be the Glory," proclaims the path to salvation through Christ's atoning death, alluding to John 3:16 in the first stanza. Other scriptural references in this hymn include "opened the life-gate that all may go in" (Matt 7:13–14) and "O come to the Father, through Jesus the Son" (John 14:6). In this text, redemption is immediate upon belief and is accomplished through "purchase" (st. 2), another reference to ransom atonement.

To God be the glory, great things he has done!
So loved he the world that he gave us his Son,
Who yielded his life an atonement for sin
And opened the life-gate that all may go in.

Refrain:
Praise the Lord! Praise the Lord!
Let the earth hear his voice!
Praise the Lord! Praise the Lord!
Let the people rejoice!
O come to the Father, through Jesus the Son,
And give him the glory! Great things he has done!

O perfect redemption, the purchase of blood!
To every believer the promise of God!
The vilest offender who truly believes,
That moment from Jesus forgiveness receives. [Refrain]

Great things he has taught us, great things he has done,
And great our rejoicing through Jesus the Son;
But purer and higher and greater will be
Our wonder, our rapture, when Jesus we see. [Refrain][21]

20. Lowry, *Bright Jewels for the Sunday School*, 82.

21. Lowry and Doane, *Brightest and Best*, 162.

During the nineteenth century, gospel hymnwriters illustrated a fundamental tonal shift when singing about the unconverted, or the sinner: the "God of Love and Mercy" replaced the "God of Wrath and Judgment."[22] This shift may be first noticed in Sunday school hymns of the era.

Several generations of children, perhaps including a young Fanny, sang the Calvinistic view of children as reprobates. Isaac Watts published a popular children's collection *Divine and Moral Songs* (1715) in which his hymns present God as a harsh judge of children with the promise of heaven counterbalanced with the threat of hell. One such hymn admonishes young liars that they will have their "portion in the lake / That burns with brimstone and with fire" if they are not vigilant in truth telling: "Lest I be struck to death and hell / Since God a book of reckoning keeps / For every lie that children tell."[23]

As Calvinism waned and the ideals of Romanticism swelled, the "concept of children as diminutive yet depraved sinners metamorphosed into that of innocent little angels, awaiting formative instruction."[24] Sunday school hymn collections provided children with accessible language and tunes to sing praise to God and learn about their loving friend in Jesus. In sharp contrast to the Watts text is one of Crosby's children's hymns, which is notable for its nurturing language: "watchful eye," "gentle power," "constant guide," "tender care."

> Dear Saviour, let they watchful eye,
> Protect me day by day,
> That from the precious fold I love,
> My heart may never stray.
> (Chorus)
>
> Make me humble, loving, dutiful;
> Make they how within me beautiful:
> Cleanse my heart from sin;
> Let no stranger in. —Chorus
>
> I want my Spirit's gentle power,
> My constant guide to be;
> I want Thy love thy tender care,
> To bind me close to thee. —Chorus[25]

22. Downey, "Revivalism," 116.

23. Watts, *Divine and Moral Songs*, 15.

24. Wilhoit, "Sing a Sankey," 104.

25. Lowry, *Bright Jewels*, 115, stanzas 1 and 2.

In her gospel hymns, Crosby continued using such tender language by referring to sinners as "lost," "wandering," "wounded," "weary," "oppressed." While these are all biblical metaphors, they are less harsh in contrast to earlier hymnists describing the sinner as "vile," "guilty," or even "a worm."[26] Although Crosby was clear that the unrepentant sinner risked their eternal soul, she used language that was compassionate, wooing the wayward soul to salvation as in stanzas 1, 2, and 4 of "Jesus Is Tenderly Calling Thee Home."

Jesus is tenderly calling thee home,
Calling today, calling today;
Why from the sunshine of love wilt thou roam
Farther and farther away?

Chorus:
Calling today,
Calling today;
Jesus is calling,
Is tenderly calling today.

Jesus is calling the weary to rest,
Calling today, calling today;
Bring Him thy burden and thou shalt be blest;
He will not turn thee away. [Chorus]

Jesus is pleading; O list to His voice,
Hear Him today, hear Him today;
They who believe on His name shall rejoice;
Quickly arise and away. [Chorus][27]

Crosby's hymns sang of salvation being available to all. Her Calvinist background would have taught a limited atonement; however, her encounter with Methodists opened her to the concepts of free will and free grace.[28] Both "All to Christ I Owe" (st. 2–3) and "To God be the Glory" (st.1), cited earlier, illustrate that salvation is by God's grace and free to all. The refrain to her hymn "Behold, behold the wondrous love" and stanza one of "Jesus, Keep Me Near the Cross" both unequivocally state this doctrine:

All praise and glory be unto Jesus
For He hath purchased a full salvation;
Behold how wondrous the proclamation,

26. Blumhofer, *Her Heart Can See*, 255.

27. Sankey, McGranahan, and Stebbins, *Gospel Hymns*, 42.

28. Blumhofer, *Her Heart Can See*, 254.

> Whosoever will may come![29]

And

> Jesus, keep me near the cross:
> there a precious fountain,
> free to all, a healing stream,
> flows from Calvary's mountain.[30]

With the notable exception of "To God Be the Glory," all the hymns cited thus far use first-person singular language. Nineteenth-century gospel hymns are noted for and frequently criticized for their ubiquitous first-person voice. Historically, hymn writers used first-person in devotional hymns in the medieval Roman church and pietistic streams of the Protestant church. However, it became standard for nineteenth-century evangelicals to express theology couched as "I," "me," or "mine." One of the lasting criticisms is that hymns celebrating the individual experience are not appropriate for a community in corporate worship. Several recent scholars have addressed Crosby's reliance on personal language in her texts. Based on the work of M. G. De Jong, one scholar concludes:

> The main aim of evangelical hymnody is to put into words "the longing for completeness." When singing or reading the hymn, the believer can imaginatively identify with the text, especially when it has a first-person character/narrator—thus aspects of salvation and accordingly the assurance thereof can be addressed.[31]

Thus, a person singing "Pass Me Not, O Gentle Savior," "Jesus, Keep Me Near the Cross," and "Redeemed, How I Love to Proclaim It" can engage more fully in the conversion experience.

According to De Jong, nineteenth-century commentators considered hymns as preserved personal testimony.[32] Author June Hadden Hobbs relates the background of "All the Way My Saviour Leads Me" as Crosby's testimony to God's providence at a time when she needed money. Crosby recorded in her memoirs:

> Not long after I prayed for the money, a gentleman came into the house, "passed the time of day," shook hands with me, and

29. Crosby and Sankey, "Behold, behold the wondrous love," https://hymnary.org/text/behold_behold_the_wondrous_love.

30. Lowry, *Bright Jewels,* 130.

31. Kruger, "Sweet Peace of Perfect Assurance," 138–50.

32. De Jong, "I Want to Be like Jesus," 461–93, 256–59.

> went out immediately. When I closed my hand after the friendly salutation, I found in it a five-dollar bill, which he had left there.
>
> I have no way to account for this, except to believe that God, in answer to my prayer, put it into the heart of this good man, to bring me the money. . .I have never had the least reason to doubt the practical usefulness of that promise that if we ask we shall receive.[33]

Crosby's subsequent testimony in song:

> All the way my Saviour leads me;
> What have I to ask beside?
> Can I doubt his tender mercy,
> Who through life has been my Guide?
> Heavenly peace, divinest comfort,
> Here by faith in Him to dwell!
> For I know whate'er befall me
> Jesus doeth all things well.[34]

Current scholarship includes feminist analysis of why Crosby and other women relied on first-person voice. Hobbs suggests that Crosby, aligning with other female hymnists of the era, used first-person to voice their feelings and experiences in a society where they were effectively silenced. According to Hobbs, Crosby's hymn "Redeemed, How I Love to Proclaim It" illustrates the poet's response to her situation. In stanza two Crosby recognizes her human inability to put her experience into words: "Redeemed and so happy in Jesus, / No language my rapture can tell." Hobbs posits that in the third stanza Crosby resolves her conflict as a woman and evangelical who feels compelled to share the gospel: she sings!

> I think of my blessed Redeemer,
> I think of Him all the day long;
> I sing, for I cannot be silent;
> His love is the theme of my song.[35]

Hobbs concludes that "the hymn testifies on her behalf and preserves her story while it erases her identity as an autonomous person."[36] However, Hobbs' argument is weakened by the fact that Crosby did have a voice: she spoke regularly for mission groups, temperance meetings, in prisons, and enjoyed the respect of evangelists, musicians, and the public alike.

33. Hobbs, *I Sing for I Cannot Be Silent*, 104–5.
34. Bliss and Sankey, *Gospel Hymns*, 60.
35. Sweney, O'Kane, McCabe, and Kirkpatrick, *Songs of Redeeming Love*, 7.
36. Hobbs, *I Sing for I Cannot Be Silent*, 114.

Consecration

This intense personal experience of salvation leads to a longing for intimacy and, ideally, consummate union with Christ. Crosby, and others, referred to this as consecration or holiness, which required prayerful devotion. Hymns cited above, such as "Jesus, Keep Me Near the Cross," "Pass Me Not, O Gentle Savior," and "All the Way My Savior leads me," all claim Christ's sufficiency as guide, comforter, sustainer, healer, lover, etc. The singer "rests" in Jesus or in the cross. Lines from "I Am Thine, O Lord" illustrate the desire of the singer to be drawn closer to Christ, being so dedicated to Christ's service that "my will is lost in Thine."

> I am Thine, O Lord, I have heard Thy voice,
> And it told Thy love to me;
> But I long to rise in the arms of faith
> And be closer drawn to Thee.
>
> Refrain:
> Draw me nearer, nearer blessed Lord,
> To the cross where Thou hast died;
> Draw me nearer, nearer, nearer blessed Lord,
> To Thy precious, bleeding side.
>
> Consecrate me now to Thy service, Lord,
> By the pow'r of grace divine;
> Let my soul look up with a steadfast hope,
> And my will be lost in Thine.[37]

"Blessed Assurance," arguably Crosby's most beloved hymn, assures the singer of salvation (st. 1). The refrain's reference to praising Jesus "all the day long" is a common theme for the believer desiring consecration. Both "perfect submission, perfect delight" (st. 2) and "lost in his love" (st. 3) denote the desired consummate union with Christ.

> Blessed assurance, Jesus is mine:
> O what a foretaste of glory divine!
> Heir of salvation, purchase of God;
> born of his Spirit, washed in his blood:
>
> Refrain:
> This is my story, this is my song,
> praising my Saviour all the day long.

37. Lowry and Doane, *Brightest and Best*, 60.

Perfect submission, perfect delight,
visions of rapture burst on my sight;
angels descending bring from above
echoes of mercy, whispers of love: [Refrain]

Perfect submission, all is at rest,
I in my Saviour am happy and blest—
watching and waiting, looking above,
filled with his goodness, lost in his love: [Refrain][38]

Service

Although many nineteenth-century gospel hymns appear to be self-focused, if not narcissistic, Crosby and other evangelicals envisioned the Christian life to include service to others. This was the gospel imperative: to rescue the prodigal. Famed evangelist Dwight L. Moody believed that "social renovation could only be effected by 'the moral and spiritual regeneration of individuals,' and 'that political, social, and economic reform must be an appendage of revivals.'"[39]

One of her early hymns, "To the Work, To the Work," illustrates Crosby's interest in addressing temporal as well as spiritual needs.[40] If taken literally, the second stanza exhorts the Christian worker to feed the hungry and lead them to Christ.

To the work! To the work!
Let the hungry be fed;
To the fountain of life let the weary be led;
In the cross and its banner our glory shall be,
While we herald the tidings,
"Salvation is free!"[41]

"Rescue the Perishing," perhaps one of Crosby's best hymns, was inspired by her work in New York City missions, becoming the "theme song of the home missions movement."[42] In contrast to consecration hymns with their passive language ("rest," "submission," etc.), service hymns are replete

38. Sweney, Kane, McCabe, and Kirkpatrick, *Gems of Praise*, 19.
39. Downey, "Revivalism," 116.
40. Blumhofer, *Her Heart Can See*, 271.
41. Lowry and Doane, *Pure Gold for the Sunday School*, 141.
42. Hobbs, *I Sing for I Cannot Be Silent*, 100.

with active verbs. The first stanza of this text commands Christians to rescue, care, snatch, weep, and lift those wandering on a wayward path.

> Rescue the perishing, care for the dying,
> snatch them in pity from sin and the grave;
> weep o'er the erring one, lift up the fallen,
> tell them of Jesus, the mighty to save.
>
> Refrain:
> Rescue the perishing,
> care for the dying;
> Jesus is merciful,
> Jesus will save.
>
> Though they are slighting Him, still He is waiting,
> waiting the penitent child to receive;
> plead with them earnestly, plead with them gently.
> He will forgive if they only believe. [Refrain]
>
> Down in the human heart, crushed by the tempter,
> feelings lie buried that grace can restore;
> touched by a loving heart, wakened by kindness,
> chords that are broken will vibrate once more. [Refrain]
>
> Rescue the perishing, duty demands it.
> Strength for thy labor the Lord will provide;
> back to the narrow way patiently win them,
> tell the poor wanderer a Savior has died. [Refrain][43]

Through her urban mission work, Crosby encountered humanity in all conditions: homeless, impoverished, addicted, abused. Throughout this text, she uses compassionate rather than condescending, judgmental language about those in need. The third stanza echoes Crosby's philosophy toward those she ministered to, as related in her autobiography:

Kindness in this world will do much to help others, not only to come into the light, but to grow in grace day by day. There are many timid souls whom we jostle morning and evening as we pass them by; but if only the kind word were spoken they might become fully persuaded.[44]

Christian service, in Crosby's view, is a duty, albeit daunting. Stanza four reiterates this but with assurances the Lord will provide the worker strength for the task.

43. Hobbs, *I Sing for I Cannot Be Silent*, 109.

44. Crosby, *Memories of Eighty Years*, 144.

Heaven

Heaven was real for Crosby, with the final stanza of many of her hymns referring to that much-anticipated future. One scholar notes that her hymns are formulaic with stanzas organized as:

1. exclamation of trust in Jesus, resulting in
2. confidence for daily life, but
3. yearning for union with him, and
4. looking forward to life in heaven.[45]

Crosby envisioned heaven as home, rest, union with Christ, reward for earthly labors, but most importantly for the blind Crosby, a place where she would "see" Jesus, as illustrated in "Some Day the Silver Cord Will Break."

> Some day the silver cord will break,
> And I nor more as now shall sing;
> But, O, the joy when I shall wake
> Within the palace of the King!
> And I shall see Him face to face,
> And tell the story—Saved by grace.[46]

CONTRIBUTION TO LITURGY AND WORSHIP

While Crosby intended her texts for para-church settings, those hymns became part of the sung theological canon of a generation. As recently as the 1950s, her hymns were standard repertoire in evangelical Protestant congregations, having worked their way into corporate worship during the twentieth century due, in part, to the music publishing boom of the nineteenth and early twentieth centuries, advent of recordings, and appeal of evangelistic crusades.

Despite their widespread popularity and sales among grassroots evangelicals, Crosby's hymns did not always pass critical inspection. John Julian, editor of *The Dictionary of Hymnology* (1891), noted "they are, with few exceptions, very weak and poor, their simplicity and earnestness being their redeeming features."[47] It is precisely their "simplicity and earnestness," the essence of a gospel hymn text, that captured the hearts of her generation.

45. Watkins, "Few Kind Words for Fanny Crosby," 256.
46. Alexander, *Alexander's Hymns No. 3*, 141.
47. Blumhofer, *Her Heart Can See*, 284.

Perhaps Crosby's most important contribution to the church's song is that she gave voice to grassroots American evangelicalism, continuing a pietistic line of devotional song. In all generations, new hymns and sacred songs appear, enjoy popularity, then wane or disappear entirely. Crosby's publisher Robert Lowry optimistically believed:

> The time has not yet come when Fanny Crosby's place among the hymn writers of Christendom may be determined; but it is safe to say that, of the many hymns which have come up from the throbbings of her warm heart, there will be found in the ultimate sifting no inconsiderable number which the world will not willingly let die.[48]

Today Crosby hymns are enjoying a resurgence among non-western composers who are providing new settings and recordings of some of her unpublished texts.[49] Crosby maintains a vibrant internet presence with Facebook pages and YouTube platform for recordings.

NOTABLE HYMNS

While most of her hymns have fallen into disuse, some of her iconic texts, such as "Blessed Assurance" and "To God Be the Glory" appear in recent hymnals. The following list includes some hymns still enjoying use.

> All the Way My Shepherd Leads Me
> Blessed Assurance
> I am Thine O Lord (Draw Me Nearer)
> Jesus, Keep Me Near the Cross
> Pass Me Not, O Gentle Savior
> Praise Him! Praise Him!
> Rescue the Perishing
> To God Be the Glory

Other texts providing further insight into her hymn writing include:

> A Wonderful Savior is Jesus My Lord
> Christ Has Risen! Hallelujah!
> Come, Poor Sinner, to the Blessed, Blessed Feast
> Hark! Ten Thousand Harps and Voices
> Hark the Voice of Jesus Crying, "Who Will Go and Work Today?"
> How Tranquil the Slumber, How Lovely the Night

48. Blumhofer, *Her Heart Can See*, 341.

49. Kimbrough and Young, *Blessed Assurance*.

Redeemed, How I Love to Proclaim it
Safe in the Arms of Jesus
Thou My Everlasting Portion (Close to Thee)
To the Work, To the Work, We Are Servants of God

BIBLIOGRAPHY

Alexander, Charles M., ed. *Alexander's Hymns No. 3* New York: Fleming H. Revell, 1915.

Bliss, P. P., and Ira D. Sankey, eds. *Gospel Hymns and Sacred Songs as Used by Them in Gospel Meetings*. New York: Biglow and Main, 1875.

Blumhofer, Edith L. *Her Heart Can See: The Life and Hymns of Fanny J. Crosby*. Grand Rapids, MI: William B. Eerdmans, 2005.

Crosby, Fanny J. *Memories of Eighty Years*. Boston: James H. Earle, 1906. https://archive.org/stream/memoriesofeightyoocros#page/n9/mode/2up.

De Jong, Mary G. "'I Want to Be like Jesus': The Self-Defining Power of Evangelical Hymnody." *Journal of the American Academy of Religion* 54.3 (1986) 461–93.

Downey, James C. "Revivalism, the Gospel Songs and Social Reform." *Ethnomusicology* 9.2 (1965) 115–25.

Excell, E. O., ed. *Triumphant Songs for Sunday Schools and Gospel Meetings*. Toronto: William Briggs, 1887.

Hobbs, June Hadden. *"I Sing for I Cannot Be Silent": The Feminization of American Hymnody, 1870–1920*. Pittsburgh: University of Pittsburgh Press, 1997.

Kimbrough, S. T., Jr., and Carlton R. Young, eds. *Blessed Assurance: Hymns of Fanny J. Crosby with familiar and new musical settings from Africa, Asia, Caribbean Region, Europe, North America, South America*. Singapore: Global Music and Media Productions, 2008.

Kruger, Daleen. "The Sweet Peace of Perfect Assurance: On Well-Being in the Hymn Texts of Fanny Crosby." *TD: The Journal for Transdisciplinary Research in Southern Africa* 10.2 (2014) 138–50.

Lowry, Robert, ed. *Bright Jewels for the Sunday School: a new collection of Sunday School songs written expressly for this work, many of which are the latest compositions of William B. Bradbury*. New York: Biglow and Main, 1869. https://hymnary.org/hymnal/BJSS1869.

Lowry, Robert, and William H. Doane, eds. *Brightest and Best*. New York: Biglow and Main, 1875. https://hymnary.org/hymnal/BB1875?.

———, eds. *Pure Gold for the Sunday School*. New York: Biglow and Main, 1872. https://hymnary.org/hymnal/PGSS1871?page=1.

Sankey, Ira D., James McGranahan, and George C. Stebbins, eds. *Gospel Hymns No. 5 with Standard Selections*. New York: Biglow and Main, 1887.

Sweney, Jno R., T. C. O'Kane, C. C. McCabe, and W. J. Kirkpatrick, eds. *Gems of Praise: Choice Collection of Sacred Melodies*. Philadelphia: Methodist Episcopal Book Room, 1876. https://hymnary.org/hymnal/GPCC1876.

———, eds. *Songs of Redeeming Love*. Chicago/Philadelphia: Cranston&Stowe/John J. Hood, 1882. https://hymnary.org/hymnal/SoRL1882.

Watkins, Keith. "A Few Kind Words for Fanny Crosby." *Worship* 51. 3 (1977) 248–59.

Watts, Isaac. *Divine and Moral Songs for Children.* Christian Classics Ethereal Library 15. Grand Rapids, MI: 1715, 1866. https://www.ccel.org/ccel/watts/divsongs.html.

Wilhoit, Mel R. "Sing a Sankey." In *Music and Theology in Nineteenth-Century Britain*, edited by Martin V. Clarke, 97–116. Surrey, England: Ashgate, 2012.

Chapter 3

William B. Bradbury

Singing of the Love of Jesus

JOANNA PEPPLE

HISTORICAL BACKGROUND

Jesus loves me, this I know,
For the Bible tells me so,
Little ones to Him belong,
They are weak but He is strong.

IT IS DIFFICULT TO read the above verses without hearing their familiar and endearing musical setting. The text "Jesus Loves Me" seems inextricably linked to its music, set by the New York composer William Bradbury (1816–68). This hymn has a rich history in the Protestant church, transcending denominational divides. Bradbury set this text with the intent of educating young children in church doctrine as well as in musicianship. Today children share an integral role in the worship ministry of many Protestant churches, and their involvement in music ministry is indebted to nineteenth-century church musicians in America who shared a common vision to educate children in the fundamentals of music. Through the education of children, they sought to revitalize music-making in the church, ultimately impacting musicianship in society. One of the founders of this movement was Lowell Mason (1792–1872), who had a direct influence on Bradbury. Bradbury went on to impact childhood education in America and children's hymnody through his role as a musical director, a hymn writer, and a publisher. His impact in children's hymnody, as well as in Protestant hymnody at large, resonates to this day.

The background of Lowell Mason and the Sunday school movement in America is significant to the story of William Bradbury, because Mason was instrumental through his foundational work in childhood music education in the church—work that Bradbury continued throughout his career. Mason is recognized throughout numerous historical accounts for his work and influence in the reform movement in American sacred music, particularly in the evangelical movement.[1] As a church musician passionate about music education in schools, he argued that church music could only be revitalized when efforts were made to teach music to children in schools.[2] Originally from Maine, Mason moved to Boston in 1827 and quickly began impacting the musical culture by directing the choir at the Bowdoin Street Church (1831–45), as well as serving as the president and music director of the Boston Handel and Haydn Society (1827–32).[3] During his early years at Bowdoin Street Church he worked with the children in singing classes and concerts, perhaps using some of his own publications that were intended for children: *The Juvenile Psalmist* (1829) for Sunday school, and *The Juvenile Lyre* (1831) for school education.[4]

In 1833, while Mason was still directing the choir at Bowdoin Street Church, he and George James Webb (1803–87) founded the Boston Academy of Music. They sought to teach music fundamentals to children and adults, with the ultimate aim of improving musicianship in the church.[5] In this same year Bradbury came into contact with Mason. Bradbury's family was also from Maine, and they moved to Boston in 1830, when he was fourteen years old.[6] In 1833 Bradbury enrolled at Mason's singing-school as well as at the Boston Academy of Music. Through his connection with Mason, Bradbury joined the choir at Bowdoin Street Church and was eventually invited to play the organ at the church.[7] Bradbury's relationship with Mason

1. Broyles, *Music of the Highest Class*, 62.

2. Pemberton, "Critical Days," 70.

3. Eskew et al., "Mason."

4. Eskew et al., "Mason."

5. Eskew et al., "Mason."

6. Wingard, "Life and Works," 24.

7. Wingard, "Life and Works," 24–26. Wingard relays an amusing story about Bradbury's brief time as an organist at Bowdoin Street Church: Mason accepted Bradbury into his prestigious Bowdoin Street Church Choir, and within a few months, Bradbury

in these impressionable years of his youth stayed with him as he continued to develop his own career in sacred music. Even though Bradbury was a part of a younger generation, Alan Wingard groups Bradbury with Mason and another hymn reformer of the older generation, Thomas Hastings (1784–1872), describing these three men as forming a "triumvirate . . . which did a great deal for church and vocal music in this country."[8]

William Bradbury was born as the middle child into a family of five children that had a rich lineage of American church reformers. On his mother's side Bradbury could trace ancestors to esteemed men such as Rev. John Cotton (1584–1652) and Rev. John Tufts (1689–1752).[9] After moving to Boston and completing music lessons at Lowell Mason's Boston Academy, he taught lessons and singing classes in Machias, Maine (1836–38), St. John's, New Brunswick (1838–40), and New York (1840–47).[10] In these teaching appointments he directed singing festivals for children while working as a singing-school teacher. During these festivals thousands of children would join together in singing. Bradbury's efforts in New York encouraged the New York public schools to incorporate music in their curriculums, just as Lowell Mason had advocated for the inclusion of music in the Boston public schools.[11]

Travelling in Europe with his wife and daughter between 1847 and 1849, Bradbury sought to satisfy his curiosity about how music was taught in schools in London, Leipzig, and Switzerland. He then wrote copious notes and observations about his experiences, many of which appeared in installments in the *New York Evangelist*.[12] Upon his return to the United States in 1849 he sought to use the methods and techniques that he observed in Europe in his American classes and private lessons, and he thus

---

was offered the position of church organist. Bradbury accepted despite his lack of extensive piano and harmony study. The Bowdoin organ was completely wooden and required double effort when playing, to both push the keys down and then pull them up again. Despite the difficult work, his wages were $25 a year. Bradbury argued that the double effort of pushing the keys down and pulling them up again demanded double pay, at $50 a year. This argument fell on deaf ears, however, and the trustees merely told him that his organ playing gave "the highest satisfaction" (27–28). Hence, Bradbury only lasted three months in this position before he found a better job.

8. Wingard, "Life and Works," 253.

9. Wingard, "Life and Works," 19, 21. Rev. Cotton was a Puritan leader in Boston, and Rev. Tufts was a Congregational minister in Newburyport, Massachusetts, the latter who is known in part for his developments in gathering music for printing.

10. Eskew, "Bradbury."

11. Eskew, "Bradbury."

12. Wingard, "Life and Works," 48–49.

openly advertised his European training.[13] One of the European pedagogical strategies that impressed him the most was the idea of teaching children to sing first, before encumbering them with the fundamentals of reading music. In other words, he advocated for a practice of action-based learning before explanations and exercises.[14]

Several years after returning to the United States, Bradbury demonstrated his passion not only for children, but also for music teachers. Sharing a common vision, he teamed with his former teacher Lowell Mason and George Frederick Root (1820–95) in 1853 to open the New York Normal Musical Institute, a music-teacher training school. Later, other normal musical institutes were opened in other cities.[15] In addition, Bradbury wrote and published numerous hymns and books for instructing children and adults in sound theology as well as basic musicianship. In 1854, he was involved in piano manufacturing with his brother, Edward G. Bradbur and F. C. Lighte.[16]

While he was continually compiling sacred music books and issuing hymns for children, Bradbury opened his own publishing firm in New York in 1861. This allowed him to publish his own tune books as well as the works of others.[17] The hymn books he published during this time were quite popular; some were referred to as "Sunday school hymnals," reflecting a growing need for instructional music in the church.[18] Table 3.1 lists Bradbury's numerous publications, most published in his lifetime, but a few appearing posthumously.[19]

Table 3.1: Bradbury Collections Listed Chronologically[20]

Date	Bradbury Collection
1841	*The Young Choir*
1843	*The School Singer, or Young Choir's Companion*
	Bradbury's Singing School for Ladies and Gentlemen

13. Karpf, "'Would That It Were So in America!'" 34.

14. Karpf, "'Would That It Were So in America!'" 31.

15. Karpf, "'Would That It Were So in America!'" 36.

16. Eskew, "Bradbury."

17. Eskew, "Bradbury."

18. Blumhofer, "Fanny Crosby," 220.

19. When Bradbury died in 1868, his publishing company, under Lucius Biglow and Sylvester Main, was renamed Biglow & Main. See Eskew, "Bradbury."

20. The contents of this table are taken from Wingard, "Life and Works," 488–92.

1844	*The Psalmodist*
	The Social Singing Book
1845	*The Young Melodist*
1847	*Flora's Festival*
	The New York Choralist
	The Sacred Choralist
1849	*Congregational Harmony*
	The Mendelssohn Collection, or Hastings and Bradbury's Third Book of Psalmody
	Musical Gems
1850	*The Alpine Glee Singer*
	Pocket Lesson
	Bradbury's Sabbath School Melodies
1851	*Psalmista*
1852	*The Metropolitan Glee Book, or Alpine Glee Singer, Volume Second*
	The Singing Bird, or Progressive Music Reader
	The Seasons, Part II, Summer
1853	*Daniel*
	The Shawm
1854	*The Singing Book for Boys' and Girls' Meetings*
1855	*The New York Glee and Chorus Book*
	Bradbury's Young Shawm
1856	*The Book of Cantatas*
	Esther, the Beautiful Queen
	The Musical Bouquet, and Institute Choir
	Bradbury's Sabbath School Choir
1857	*The Jubilee*
1859	*Cottage Melodies*
	The Festival Glee Book
	Oriola
1860	*Bradbury's Anthem Book*
	The Eclectic Tune Book
	Orio
1861	*Bradbury's Golden Chain*
	The Carol
1862	*Bradbury's Golden Shower*
	Golden Chain and Golden Shower

1863	*Pilgrims' Songs*
	The Key-Note
	Anniversary of Sunday Schools of Brooklyn, E. D.
1864	*The Golden Censer*
	The Devotional Hymn and Tune Book for Social and Public Worship
	Bradbury's Golden Trio
1865	*The Plymouth Sabbath School Collection of Hymns and Tunes*
	Praises of Jesus
	Selections of Choruses, No. 1
1866	*The New Golden Chain*
	The New Golden Shower
	Golden Chain and Shower (new)
	Bradbury's Golden Trio (new)
	The New Golden Trio, or Bradbury's Golden Series of Sabbath School Melodies
	Oriola (30th ed.)
	Temperance Chimes
	Golden Chain and Censer
	Golden Shower and Censer
	Golden Hymns
1867	*Bradbury's Fresh Laurels*
	The Clarion
	The Clariona
	Songs of Praise for Sabbath Schools
	The Temple Choir
1868	*Chapel Melodies*
1869	*Bright Jewels for the Sunday School*
	Laurels and Jewels for the Sunday School
	New Praise of Jesus
	The Victory
1870	*The New Golden Censer*
	The New Golden Chain and Censer
	The Bradbury Trio
	Sunday School Hymns
1886	*The New Flora's Festival*

THEOLOGICAL PERSPECTIVES

As was the case for Mason and many of the other hymn reformers in the nineteenth century, Bradbury's theology directed his musical decisions. He often collaborated regularly with poets such as Fanny Crosby, and at other times, he would find a poem that was particularly well-suited to an intimate hymn or a children's tune. In *Bradbury's Fresh Laurels for the Sabbath School: A New and Extensive Collection of Music and Hymns Prepared Expressly for Sabbath Schools, etc.* (1867), he wrote specifically about his passion and perspective in selecting appropriate music and texts:

> While the hymn is the text, containing often the essence of the Gospel that we wish to fasten upon the mind of the child, much depends upon the manner and medium through which such text is presented. How many of us have heard a beautiful hymn so miserably read as to lose all its beauty and attractiveness. How much worse then must it be to set a sprightly life-like "whole souled" hymn to a dull, low, stiff, slow, tame and *sleepy* tune; and how often this is done we need not remind our readers. The tune, while adapted to the hymn, should be so attractive, so musical, as to win the love of the child. Then, when thoroughly learned, it is never forgotten. Thus, through the medium of this tune, the hymn will be stereotyped upon the memory.[21]

A Crosby text serves as the opening hymn in this collection, sharing the same title as the collection itself: "Fresh Laurels for the Sunday School." The hymns in this collection are set in four-part harmony with simple rhythms and diatonic melodies. Bradbury's thoughts on the musical content and the need for attractive melodies to accompany the text reveal his deliberate commitment to creating melodies and harmonies that would be simple to learn yet enjoyable for a child to sing. These tunes and Sunday school hymnals became exceedingly popular during the latter half of the nineteenth century. During this time hymns found a wider market than even popular secular songs of the day. In essence, hymns *were* the popular music of this time.[22]

Bradbury's publications were not all for Sunday school use; some were intended specifically for the public schools. His *Singing Bird, or Progressive Music Reader: Designed to Facilitate the Introduction of Vocal Music in Schools and Academies* (1852) was intended to teach music fundamentals in the public school (see book cover in Figure 3.1). While some religious

21. Bradbury, *Bradbury's Fresh Laurels,* Preface.

22. Broyles, *Music of the Highest Class,* 62.

songs are sprinkled throughout this collection, most of the works are more instructive or secular in content. In the index, the songs are organized in categories such as "Rounds," "Sentences, and other Short Pieces," "Songs for opening or closing School," "Temperance Pieces," and others.

Stating his purpose for the collection at the beginning of the book, Bradbury wrote,

> The title of this work perhaps sufficiently explains its design. The plan, it will be perceived, is quite different from any of the author's former works. The *Singing Bird* is intended especially to render comparatively easy and pleasant the introduction of Vocal Music as a study, as well as a pastime, in school, and seminaries, and juvenile classes. By the new arrangement of the Elements, the pupil begins to sing by note, and in pleasing melodies, from the very first lesson, and the Elementary and Song department are so completely interwoven, that the pupil will not soon tire of study, as he reaps at every step an abundant reward for all his application in the pleasant songs that continually greet and cheer him.[23]

Bradbury is clear in representing *The Singing Bird* as a pedagogical text on singing. Since this work was published only a few years after his return from Europe, his idea of focusing on the singing first (rather than beginning with a course on fundamentals) is quite evident.[24] Throughout the text Bradbury intersperses instructions on conducting (or beating time), note reading, dynamics, scales, and other elements while singing simple tunes and songs. This style of pedagogy reveals the direct influence of his European training.

23. Bradbury, *Singing Bird,* Preface.

24. Karpf, "'Would That It Were So in America!'" 31.

Figure 3.1: Cover of Bradbury's *The Singing Bird* (1853).
Courtesy of the Warren D. Allen Music Library, Florida State University.

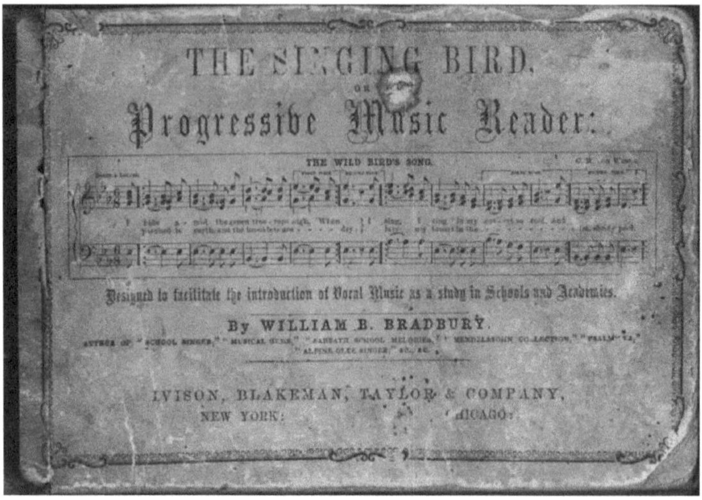

One such tune is based on the well-known aphorism "Try, Try, Again" (see Figure 3.2). In this example, Bradbury appears to be drilling the descending and ascending arpeggios with voices in unison at the beginning. Occasionally the voices move to three-part harmony, where the three upper voices move mostly in thirds, while the bass voice serves as a harmonic pedal. There is one unusual leap of a seventh in the soprano part. The other leaps are sixths. Brief scalar motives function as the foundation of the melody. Rhythmically, five different note values occur, adding variety to the piece.

Figure 3.2: "Try, Try, Again" from *The Singing Bird* (1853).[25]
Courtesy of the Warren D. Allen Music Library, Florida State University.

25. This is a printing error in the final measure of "Try, Try, Again" in Bradbury's *Singing Bird*. The final note in the bass voice should be G2.

These educational pieces for children reflect standard and functional voice leading, which allow for a greater focus on Bradbury's melodies. In this case, he was quite successful in using a familiar text and combining it with an attractive and memorable tune. In "Try, Try, Again," perhaps he was seeking to underscore a particular pedagogical lesson in intervals and arpeggios. Bradbury's strengths were in the composition of simple and attractive tunes, a necessity for teaching and educating.

Today Bradbury's best-known tune is "Jesus Loves Me." As a hymn tune writer and not a poet, he was largely dependent on finding good texts or collaborating with poets. Bradbury found the text for "Jesus Loves Me" in a novel coauthored by Susan and Anna Warner, titled *Say and Seal* (1860).[26] The words come from a song that Mr. Linden, a school teacher, sings to a dying little boy, while cradling the weak child in his arms. Anna Warner supplied the text of the song but no music.[27] The original text was specific to the Warner story but nevertheless quite similar to the version adapted today:

Table 3.2: Jesus Loves Me

[1]*Jesus loves me, this I know,* *For the Bible tells me so:* *Little ones to Him belong,* *They are weak, but He is strong.*	[3]*Jesus loves me, loves me still,* *Though I'm very weak and ill;* *From His shining throne on high* *Comes to watch me where I lie.*
[2]*Jesus loves me, He who died* *Heaven's gates to open wide;* *He will wash away my sin,* *Let his little child come in.*	[4]*Jesus loves me, He will stay* *Close beside me all the way.* *Then his little child will take* *Up to heaven for His dear sake.*[28]

Bradbury must have delighted in this mysterious song with no music when he read the novel, and he thus composed a tune for it. It appeared for the first time in *The Golden Shower* (1862), a Sunday school hymnal published after Bradbury had established his publishing firm (see Figures 3.3 and 3.4).[29]

26. Morgan, *Jesus Loves Me*, 49.
27. Morgan, *Jesus Loves Me*, 54–55.
28. Warner and Warner, *Say and Seal*, 2:115–16.
29. Wingard, "Life and Works," 207–8.

Figure 3.3: Cover of *The Golden Shower* (1862).
Courtesy of the Music Library, University of North Carolina, Chapel Hill.

Figure 3.4: "Jesus Loves Me" from *The Golden Shower* (1862).
Courtesy of the Music Library, University of North Carolina, Chapel Hill.

This melody is quite tuneful and has lasted for numerous generations. The intervals are primarily stepwise, with the greatest leap being a fifth. Whereas Bradbury was using more challenging intervallic relationships in his *Singing Bird* to teach certain theoretical concepts, that was no longer necessary here. He was not seeking to teach vocal technique and music reading through this hymn, but instead he was aiming to create an attractive and appealing melody that children would enjoy singing. His harmonization as shown in Figure 3.3 portrays standard voice leading, but it is not inventive. In the four-part harmony the tenor voice appears to be optional at times, as indicated by the smaller size of the note heads. What is remarkable is that Bradbury's tune remains intact to this day with almost no alterations, except perhaps a minor regularizing of rhythm in the penultimate measure. "Jesus Loves Me" is a song that children continue to sing at church and at home, over 150 years later.

CONTRIBUTION TO LITURGY AND WORSHIP

Bradbury participated actively in church worship during his lifetime by giving a voice to children's theological education and worship and writing frequently about the importance of melodic style. By selecting his own texts, Bradbury could also shape the theological bent that he wished to convey. His simple and appealing melodies likewise endear the listener and mirror the simple and trusting faith of a child. Even though his contribution to hymnody was through sounds and tones, he repeatedly explained his purpose in the preface of his numerous publications, and his theological perspective shines through in his musical style. Bradbury explained the reason for the attractive melodies presented in his *Oriola:* "Next to a good Superintendent, that which tends more than any thing [sic] else to make a Sunday school popular, is, doubtless, GOOD SINGING. . . . We believe in making the children so happy on Sabbath day, by the use of all proper means, that they shall look forward to it through the week as 'a delight.' It is the *Lord's* day; a sacred day, a happy day. Psalm cxviii. 24."[30]

Bradbury's musical compositions establish him as an influential figure in the Sunday school movement, particularly through his pedagogical perspectives on children, music, and the church. He contributed greatly to hymn writing through his practical work with children as a singing instructor and choirmaster, as well as through his publishing, writing, and composing. As a disciple of Lowell Mason, Bradbury became a successful advocate for music education in the church (Sunday school) as well as in the public schools.

30. Bradbury, *Oriola*, ii.

Without these musicians and the numerous lay workers, music education in American public schools would look very different today. Bradbury's visit to Europe, and in particular to Leipzig, held a formative influence in his pedagogical ideas about music education upon his return to the States. His harmonization of various children's tunes is simple, but the true ingenuity of Bradbury's hymn tunes lies in the memorable and winsome melodies that have left a lasting imprint in American hymnody. His philosophy that children's hymns should not only contain solid doctrine within a functional musical setting, but rather, that the music and melodies should "win the love of the child," is echoed again and again, as children continue to sing the beloved hymn "Jesus Loves Me," and adults and children alike appreciate the simple and attractive melodies of his other hymns.

NOTABLE HYMNS

Not all Bradbury's Sunday school tunes enjoyed such a long life as "Jesus Loves Me," yet some of his musical gems have transcended the centuries, such as "He Leadeth Me," "Just as I Am," "Savior, Like a Shepherd Lead Us," "Sweet Hour of Prayer," and "The Solid Rock" (see Table 3.3). These six hymns remain in Protestant hymnbooks to this day. They exhibit strong emotionalism and intimacy regarding the relationship between Jesus and the disciple, representative of the evangelical revivals occurring in American Protestant churches in the latter half of the nineteenth century.

While Bradbury did not write the texts to these hymns himself, he chose his texts from various writers, and his selection of texts reveals the theological perspectives he wanted to convey. For example, a study of the texts in these six hymns reveals significant use of first-person pronouns, such as I, me, my, us, and our. "Jesus Loves Me" contains thirty-three first-person pronouns throughout the four verses, and "He Leadeth Me" and "Savior Like a Shepherd Lead Us" are close behind, with twenty-eight and twenty-five, respectively. These personal pronouns encourage the perspective that one must cultivate a personal relationship with Jesus. The third verse of "He Leadeth Me" begins, "Lord, I would clasp thy hand in mine," giving a word picture of an intimate relationship that allows one to imagine the physical sense of holding hands. That same verse ends with the words, "Since 'tis my God that leadeth me," emphasizing the deep connection and relationship between the writer/singer and God. Furthermore, many themes throughout these texts include the words *sweet* or *blessed* (see especially "Savior Like a Shepherd" and "Sweet Hour of Prayer"), once again underlining the *sweet* and comforting relationship with Jesus.

Table 3.3: Bradbury Hymns Commonly Found in Contemporary Protestant Hymnbooks

Hymn Title	Bradbury Collection (first appearance)	Text Author	Key	Melodic Range
He Leadeth Me	*The Golden Censer*, 1864 (p. 105)	Joseph H. Gilmore	D major	D4 to E5 (authentic)
Jesus Loves Me	*Bradbury's Golden Shower*, 1862 (p. 68)	Anna Warner	E-flat major	Eb4 to Eb5 (authentic)
Just as I Am Original Tune: Woodworth	*The Mendelssohn Collection*, 1849 (p. 60)	Charlotte Elliot	C major	C4 to C5 (authentic)
Savior Like a Shepherd Lead Us	*Oriola*, 1859 (p. 64)	Dorothy Ann Thrupp (ed.)	E major	E4 to E5 (authentic)
Sweet Hour of Prayer	*Oriola*, 1859 (p. 248)	William W. Walford	D major	D4 to D5 (authentic)
The Solid Rock	*The Golden Censer*, 1864 (p. 83)	Edward Mote	G major	D4 to E5 (plagal)

Bradbury also wrote the music for "Just As I Am," but it was several years until the words and music known today appeared together. The tune first appeared in Bradbury's *Mendelssohn Collection, or Hastings and Bradbury's Third Book of Psalmody* (1849) with Elizabeth Scott's text "The God of Love will sure indulge" (see Figure 3.5), but the well-known text for "Just as I Am" was written by Charlotte Elliot in her *Invalid's Hymn Book* (1836). The earliest recorded instance of Bradbury's Woodworth tune and Elliot's text combined was in Bradbury's *Eclectic Tune Book* (1860).[31] There Bradbury's *Woodworth* tune has been moved to the tenor voice instead of the soprano voice in the *Mendelssohn Collection* (see Figures 3.5 and 3.6). Several of the tunes in his *Eclectic Tune Book* are in the tenor voice. Bradbury states in the preface that the hymns in the present book were the ones "most generally recommended" after lists of hymns were circulated to leading churches across the county.[32] This indicates that the combination of Bradbury's Woodworth tune and Elliot's "Just as I Am" text were already in circulation. It is interesting to note that the *Eclectic Tune Book* contains four different musical settings for Elliot's "Just as I Am," all by different composers, and only Bradbury's setting lasted into the modern era.

31. Glover, *Hymnal 1982 Companion*, 1296–98.

32. Bradbury, *Eclectic Hymn Book*, 2.

Figure 3.5: Bradbury's *Woodworth* Tune from *The Mendelssohn Collection* (1849). Courtesy of the Warren D. Allen Music Library, Florida State University.

Figure 3.6: "Just as I Am" from Bradbury's *Eclectic Tune Book* (1860). Courtesy of the Princeton Theological Seminary Library.

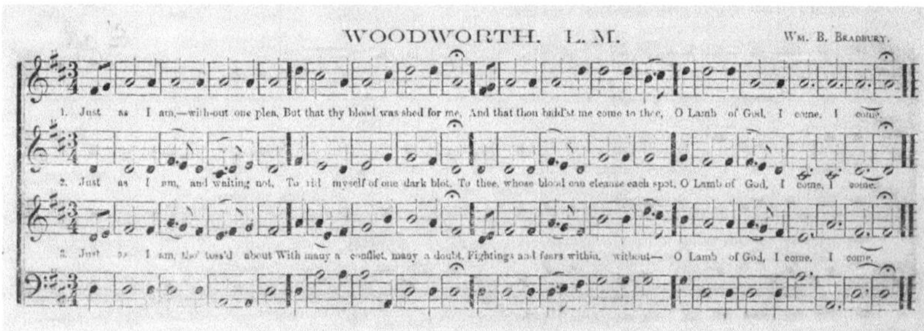

Aside from the texts chosen, Bradbury's use of keys and the musical content of his tunes also shed light on the utility and role his hymns were intended to serve (see Table 3.3). All the above hymns are in major keys, underlining their simplicity and joyful character. Melodic motion is primarily stepwise and diatonic throughout his tunes, with only small skips and leaps, allowing for ease of learning and memorizing the tunes. In many of the hymns Bradbury includes a fermata, emphasizing a high point in the melody. This is particularly evident in "Sweet Hour of Prayer" on the words *prayer* and *throne* (see Figure 3.7), and the idea of holding a high note in the melody for emphasis can also be found in "He Leadeth Me," "Jesus Loves Me," and "Savior Like a Shepherd." While the stepwise melodies make the tunes easy to learn, the held notes at the top of the melodic range make them more memorable, setting Bradbury's melodies apart from the "dull, low, stiff, slow, tame and *sleepy* tune" that he sought to avoid.

Figure 3.7: "Sweet Hour of Prayer" from *Bradbury's Golden Chain* (1864).[33] Used by permission of the University of Missouri-Kansas City Libraries, Dr. Kenneth J. LaBudde Department of Special Collections.

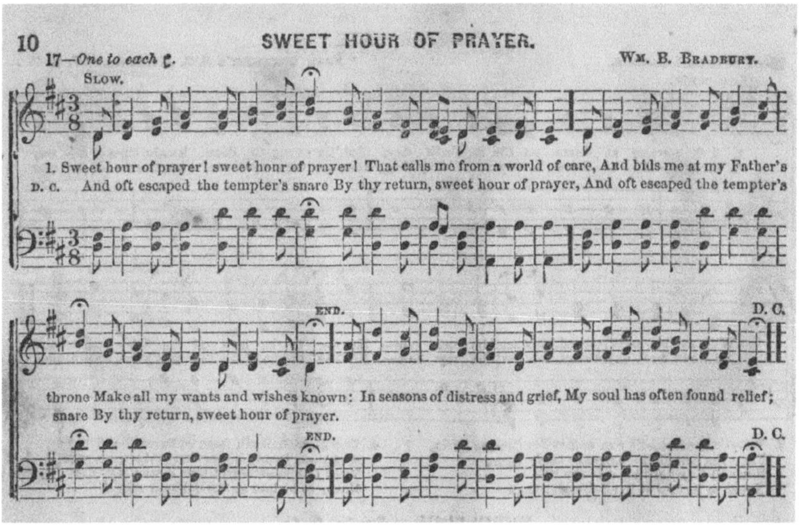

These hymns are mostly authentic tunes, with the melodic range spanning an octave above the tonic. Among these six hymns there are two exceptions: (1) "He Leadeth Me" is an authentic tune that reaches to the ninth (i.e., D4 to E5), with the E5 appearing twice in the chorus, and (2) "The Solid Rock" is the only plagal tune among the six Bradbury hymns that regularly appear in current Protestant hymnbooks. The text of "The Solid Rock" is also somewhat different from those of the other hymns that deal primarily with the theme of "Jesus and me" as a sweet and comforting relationship. While "The Solid Rock" is still about hope in Jesus, words such as "solid rock," "blood and righteousness," "darkness," and "stormy gale" paint more rugged word pictures than the others. The melodic motion in "The Solid Rock" is also less conjunct than some of Bradbury's other hymns (see Figure 3.8). For example, the opening motive of the verse begins with a heroic G-major arpeggio, supporting the message of the hymn about Christ's protection and strength. While many of Bradbury's hymns feature texts about the sweet personal relationship with Jesus, this tune suggests that he was also able to portray more triumphant theological precepts as well.

33. This image of "Sweet Hour of Prayer" from *Bradbury's Golden Chain* (1864) appears to be printed from the same plates as were used originally in his *Oriola* (1859).

Figure 3.8: "The Solid Rock" from *The Golder Censer* (1864). Courtesy of the Boston Public Library.

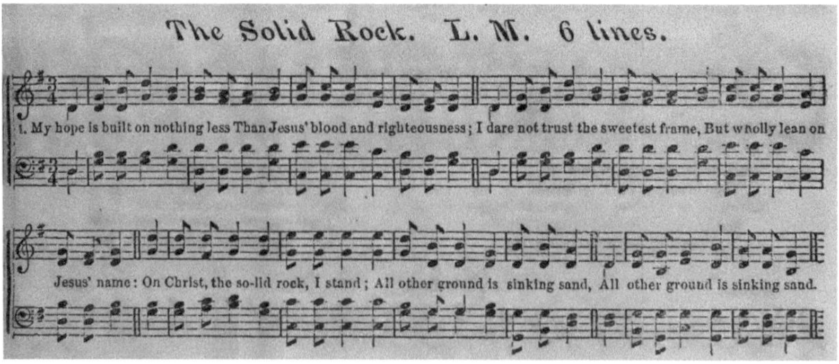

Harmonization throughout Bradbury's hymns is simple, diatonic, and conventional for the period and genre. The alto, tenor, and bass parts are not exceedingly interesting, allowing a greater focus on the winsome melodies. In Bradbury's *Oriola,* he wrote,

> The popular tune for children should be as simple as their own thoughts—sprightly as their own dispositions. Lambs require plenty of skipping room. They thrive best in the green fields. Let the children's songs, then by such as they can understand, appreciate and enjoy; such as they will love to sing both in the Sabbath School and at their homes. These will ever be to them a source of delight, and will render the [Sunday] school doubly attractive.[34]

Any part-writing in these hymns simply supports the melodies, and Bradbury's ultimate aim was to keep these children's tunes simple and accessible to young minds, in order to imprint theological truths in their hearts through the use of attractive melodies.

BIBLIOGRAPHY

Blumhofer, Edith L. "Fanny Crosby and Protestant Hymnody." In *Music in American Religious Experience,* edited by Philip V. Bohlman, Edith L. Blumhofer, and Maria M. Chow, 215–31. New York: Oxford University Press, 2006.

Bradbury, William B. *Bradbury's Fresh Laurels for the Sabbath School: A New and Extensive Collection of Music and Hymns Prepared Expressly for Sabbath Schools, etc.* New York: Biglow & Main, 1867.

———. *Bradbury's Young Shawm: A Collection of School Music.* New York: Mason Brothers, 1855.

34. Bradbury, *Oriola,* ii.

———. *The Clariona: A Collection of Hymns and Tunes for Sabbath Schools.* New York: Biglow & Main, 1867.

———. *The Eclectic Hymn Book.* New York: Mason Brothers, 1860.

———. *The Golden Censer: A Musical Offering to the Sabbath Schools, of Children's Hosannas to the Son of David.* New York: William B. Bradbury, 1864.

———. *The Golden Shower.* Philadelphia: J. C. Garrigues, 1862.

———. *The Jubilee: An Extensive Collection of Church Music for the Choir, the Congregation, and the Singing-School.* New York: Mason Brothers, 1858.

———. *Oriola: A New and Complete Hymn and Tune Book for Sabbath Schools.* 13th ed. Cincinnati: Moore, Wilstach & Baldwin, 1864.

———. *The Singing Bird, or Progressive Music Reader: Designed to Facilitate the Introduction of Vocal Music in Schools and Academies.* New York: Ivison, Blakeman, Taylor & Company, 1878.

Broyles, Michael. *Music of the Highest Class: Elitism and Populism in Antebellum Boston.* New Haven: Yale University Press, 1992.

Eskew, Harry. "Bradbury, William Batchelder." *Grove Music Online; Oxford Music Online.* https://doi.org/10.1093/gmo/9781561592630.article.A2248469.

Eskew, Harry, et al. "Mason." *Grove Music Online; Oxford Music Online.* Oxford University Press. https://doi.org/10.1093/gmo/9781561592630.article.17984.

Glover, Raymond F., ed. *Hymnal 1982 Companion.* Vol. 3B. New York: Church Publishing, 1994.

Karpf, Juanita. "'Would That It Were So in America!' William Bradbury's Observations of European Music Educators, 1847–49." *Journal of Historical Research in Music Education* 24.1 (2002) 5–38.

Morgan, Robert J. *Jesus Loves Me, This I Know: The Remarkable Story Behind the World's Most Beloved Children's Song.* Nashville: Countryman, 2006.

Pemberton, Carol A. "Critical Days for Music in American Schools." *Journal of Research in Music Education* 36.2 (1988) 69–82.

Teal, Mary D. "Letters of Thomas Hastings." *Notes* 34.2 (1977) 303–18.

Warner, Anna, and Susan Warner. *Say and Seal.* 2 vols. Philadelphia: J. B. Lippincott, 1860. Reprint, 1880.

Wingard, Alan Burl. "The Life and Works of William Batchelder Bradbury, 1816–1868." DMA, Southern Baptist Theological Seminary, 1973.

Chapter 4

John Bacchus Dykes

"Holy! Holy! Holy! Lord, God Almighty"

Iain Quinn

HISTORICAL BACKGROUND

In his 2012 book, *Freedom and the Arts,* Charles Rosen writes about how perceptions are sometimes formed and, to a certain extent, manipulated by its current context without a fair evaluation of the contemporary setting of an artist's work.[1] This is especially salient when considering the legacy

1. He says, "A museum, if is now generally realized, deforms and disfigures the works of art it contains. It wrenches the pictures and statues out of churches, palaces, and homes from which they drew their life and much of their significance, and exhibits them in an apparently neutral space, an intellectual void. Some of their functions have been wiped out; a good part of their meaning is lost. The walls have a color and texture different from the ones that originally set off the works of art, so that the harmony of the paint and the marble has be denatured, the space in which the art presents itself to the spectator has been altered. Although we may celebrate the uncanny aptitude of the objects in a museum to adapt to their new home, to present new aspects and even to convey some of the old meanings, historians deplore the inevitable loss that the institution entails. Nevertheless, we cannot do without museums; if they alter the meaning of the past beyond repair, they allow some of it to survive" (Rosen, *Freedom and the Arts*, 39).

of John Bacchus Dykes (1823–67) whose musical output remains one of ongoing discussion.

Dykes grew up in Hull on the northeastern coast of England where his father was a banker and his grandfather was a well-known evangelical vicar. He played the horn, violin, and piano, and read for a degree in classics at St. Catherine's College, Cambridge. His enthusiasm for classics continued for the rest of his life and while it appears he received little formal musical training while in Cambridge he took some lessons from Thomas Attwood Walmisley. He also joined the madrigal society while revitalizing the Cambridge University Musical Society, a point that was acknowledged in 1893 when the society celebrated its fiftieth anniversary. He made regular visits to the Three Choirs Festivals, which brought him into contact with Arthur Sullivan (1842–1900) and Samuel Sebastian Wesley (1810–76).

Ordained a priest in 1848 he was a curate in Malton, Yorkshire, for a year and then became a minor canon and precentor at Durham Cathedral in 1849. He was successful in establishing choir discipline, rehearsals for the lay clerks, and proper dress (surplices and cassocks).[2] During the extended illness of the cathedral organist, William Henshaw, Dykes often stepped in to assist with playing at services. Learning of the forthcoming publication of *Hymns Ancient and Modern*, he wrote to the music editor, W. H. Monk (1823–89) and submitted seven tunes for consideration. Monk was appointed organist at King's College, London, in 1849 and had the assistance of deacon Frederick Arthur Gore Ouseley for everything except the unbarred plainsong melodies, many of which were taken from Thomas Helmore's *Hymnal Noted* (Part 1, 1852; Part II, 1854). Dykes's tunes were well received and he ultimately contributed sixty tunes in various editions and in the 1868 appendix the largest number of new tunes were those of Dykes.[3] The chief contributors of new tunes to the first edition were Monk (17), Dykes (7), Ousleley (5), and Gauntlett (5). Despite shifting musical trends, thirty-one of his tunes were retained in the 1951 edition of *Hymns Ancient and Modern Revised*.[4] Together with Henry John Gauntlett (1805–1876), Dykes was the most prolific Victorian composer of hymn tunes.[5]

After thirteen years at the cathedral, he moved to become vicar of the neighboring parish of St. Oswald where he remained for the duration of his ministry. It was during this time that a now well-known heated exchange began with the Bishop of Durham (Baring), over the stipulations the bishop

2. Dibble, "John Bacchus Dykes."
3. Dibble, "John Bacchus Dykes."
4. Temperley, *Music of the English Parish Church*, 298.
5. Dibble, "John Bacchus Dykes."

made in the hiring of a curate. In order to license a curate in the parish, the bishop insisted that he would not "turn his back upon the congregation during the celebration of Holy Communion," or "be present at the burning of incense" despite the fact that incense was not used in any parish within the diocese. The bishop was fearful of a rise of popery in such a senior diocese of the region but Dykes took the matter to the Court of the Queen's Bench fearing it would be a betrayal of other clergy not to have acted against what he saw as an illegal action by the bishop. He published his views in an open letter to Baring, *Eucharistic Truth and Ritual* (1874). Ultimately he lost his case and it can be fairly suggested that the stress from the proceedings hastened his exhaustion and early death.

Temperley's view of Dykes as "the most important Tractarian composer of hymn tunes"[6] and Routley's summation of him as "the most famous hymn tune composer in English history"[7] draw attention not only to the consistent quality of Dykes's work but also the relative success he achieved in his own time; it is the latter point that bears consideration in relation to Rosen's commentary. In assessing Dykes or indeed Joseph Barnby (1838–96) or John Stainer (1840–1901) and the place of their works in liturgies from a twenty-first century viewpoint, there is too often an easy reliance on comparative analysis with other tune writers of different eras and too little attention devoted to the working situation that the composers and authors found themselves in.[8] The overarching tone of Fowler's *Life and Letters of John Bacchus Dykes*[9] communicates the formidable industry of Dykes's working life and his relative diffidence and kindness to others. His desire to write tunes to words where he genuinely felt there to be a lack of a fine melody with which to communicate the text is not tinged with any sort of overblown ambition. Rather, he saw his work as furthering the ministry of church musicians and to this end he met with considerable "success" in the modern sense. Of his writing, Dykes comments:

> I never think of setting a hymn that is worthily set, that would be a silly caprice, or vanity or presumption. But if a hymn does not appear to be worthily set, then I own, I am often induced, I may say, sometimes almost compelled, to try to do my best for it. . . .My own desire is this:—that each Hymn should be so set to

6. Temperley, *Music of the English Parish Church*, 250.

7. Routley, *Music of Christian Hymns*, 95.

8. An assessment of the critical voices writing about Dykes in the twentieth century can be found in Dibble, "John Bacchus Dykes."

9. Fowler, *Life and Letters of John Bacchus Dykes*.

> music (by whomsoever God wills to select for that purpose) that its power of influencing and teaching may be best brought out.[10]

Tastes shift and in the world of sacred and concerted music we can observe how the once popular choral work of Louis Spohr, *The Last Judgement* (1826), is now seldom heard and the organ music of Alexandre Guilmant (1837–1911), previously the second most performed composer in organ recitals after J. S. Bach, has also been relegated to a different league table of performance. As much as there is a canon of repertoire, there is equally a canon of performance both in terms of style and repertoire. When assessing the contributions of composers of the Victorian era it is critical to observe the seriousness with which composers of the church approached their craft and were typically cognizant of their place in history. When Ouseley wrote his second organ sonata in the early 1880s and included a classically inspired rondo as the last movement, he did so because he genuinely believed it to be an example of superior craftsmanship even if it already sounded quite dated by comparison with many other English sonatas of the era. Dykes was no different in wishing to achieve high artistic goals.

Dykes's tunes emerge in a post-Oxford movement culture that attempted to stimulate a congregational response and understanding of texts through a musical language that could highlight the greater meaning of Scripture. The use of word-painting in Dykes's tunes has been discussed at length by Harper[11] and it is Dykes's keen understanding of prosody that enables him to write a tune that captures the emotional aspect of the narrative so admirably. In this respect, Dykes has contributed tunes that appear a perfect marriage of music and text and it is an unfortunate fate of history that when texts are removed from hymnals amid sometimes-passing fashions, a fine tune is lost in the process, as has been the case with the majority of Dykes's work.

Beyond word painting that could often be as eloquent as it was simply achieved,[12] Dykes also drew on the part-song tradition and, whether knowingly or unknowingly, both his harmonic vocabulary and his freer use of typical form ("often treating the congregation as merely one element in a concert-like production"[13]) doubtless aided the larger popularity of his hymns. Instead of merely drawing attention to specific words, he achieved a higher artistic goal by setting words to a tune that could convey the larger sentiment of the text. Watson remarked,

10. Fowler, *Life and Letters of John Bacchus Dykes*, 42.
11. Harper, "Towards an Understanding," chapter 5.
12. See Harper, "Towards an Understanding," chapter 5.
13. Hutchings and Temperley, "John Bacchus Dykes."

> There was a musical and poetical education in every hymn book. This was a culture, not of the learned, but of the not-very-well-educated and not particularly privileged, for whom a hymn book would have been the dearest thing, apart from a Bible. To a repository of knowledge and an awareness of something beautiful. D. H. Lawrence valued it all his life; at home, he remembered many years later, hymn-singing was a way of spending an evening.[14]

The part-song aspect solicited an important commentary from Bernarr Rainbow in his seminal text *The Choral Revival in the Anglican Church*: "In style, those new tunes [in the 1868 Appendix] reflected the changed musical taste of the day. Many were more reminiscent of the part-song than of the stalwart classical hymn. But the emotional surge of such new tunes as Barnby's *Cloisters* appealed to the Victorian churchgoer, and won the day for the book."[15] It is the relative intransigence of the lower voices and the seemingly uneventful writing for inner voices that allowed for easy criticism by comparison to the choral harmonizations of Bach, although this was far from atypical for Dykes among his colleagues. Dykes's tune *St. Andrew of Crete* begins with eleven repetitions of the same note while "melody" is carried in the lower parts. However, as previously explained, what could be seen as harmonic stasis to the theorist was nonetheless intentional for the larger communication of the text. In this regard, it is important to note that the easy labelling of the Victorians as simple word-painters is found lacking when the musical sentiments conveyed in the whole hymn (music and text) are evaluated. This view of contextualization could also be applied when there is an intemperate examination of individual movements of Stainer's *The Crucifixion* rather than judging the balance of the whole work and the broader artistic statement.

Dykes's hymns are part of an important transition in the English hymn. The various challenges that one can see in earlier or even contemporary writers do not appear with any consistency in Dykes's writing. The sometimes perfunctory harmonizations of chants by Helmore (*Veni, Veni Emmanuel*), the angular writing of Havergal (*Dortmund, St. Chrysostom*) or the disjunct melodic line of Ouseley (*Contemplation*) are not seen in Dykes's work. A useful comparison between Ouseley and Dykes can be found in Ouseley's *Contemplation* when placed alongside Dykes's *Gerontius*, where Dykes uses significant leaps to both highlight the text as well as create an inner energy. Similarly, the sometimes awkward Bachian inner-voice activity

14. Watson, "Ancient or Modern," 2–3.

15. Rainbow, *Choral Revival in the Anglican Church*, 294.

seen in Havergal's *St. Chrysostom* finds greater fluidity and musical cogency in Dykes's *Melita* or in *O salutaris hostia*, where he alternates strictly homophonic sections with lines of constant passing notes or sustained harmonic tension. Both are examples of how the Victorian and ultimately Edwardian tunes could, at their best, provide aural color to the liturgy as well as capture a sense of drama in the text that could equally engage a congregation. Dykes's occasional use of a unison line in the tune *St. Cross* (1861) is a device later used by John Stainer in *The Crucifixion* (1887) hymn *Litany of the Passion* where in the final section the words "Crucified, I turn to thee, Son of Mary" are sung in unison at the octave and followed by the text "plead for me" in four-part harmony. Dykes was also not opposed to setting more unusual metres and the tunes *Lux Vera* (10.6.10.6) and *Dismissal* (8.7.8.7.4.7) are good examples of his flexibility in this regard.

There is a typical closeness of harmony in Dykes's hymn writing that Hutchings and Temperley note "tend[s] to hug the mediant and avoid striking leaps" of which *Strength and Stay* is a good example and in this respect there is a similarity of style with W. H. Monk's well-known *Eventide*. It is this sense of closeness that also draws the hymns toward the style of domestic music-making for the use of melodies within easy ranges and instantly memorable tunes is reminiscent of Mendelssohn's *Lieder ohne Worte* that were very familiar in many households. The relationship with past masters also has an interesting connection with organist-composers. As figures like W. T. Best, George Macfarren, and William Spark had looked to emulate classical models in their organ sonatas with references to Mozart and Beethoven[16] so too we see Dykes also imitating, perhaps unwittingly, Schubert with his use of appogiaturas.[17] This typically occurs on significant words that easily bring to mind the writing of the earlier era. It is this seemingly easy elegance with melody and harmony that, like the organist-composers, gives Dykes's hymns a welcome familiarity just as, in the concert world, the relationship between Handel and Mendelssohn's oratorios is paramount in understanding the success of the later composer with the public.

However, it is the same closeness that allows for a sustained tension in the building of harmony not least in the central lines of *Melita*. The dramatic impact of bolder harmonic gestures such as the movement from G minor to F in *Christus consolator* with an organ interlude to supply the transition is further seen in near Wagnerian levels in *Sanctuary*.[18] The more chromatic of the hymn tunes we associate with Dykes were in fact not contributed

16. See Quinn, *Genesis and Development*, chapters 1–3.

17. See Harper, "Towards an Understanding," 186–88.

18. Temperley, *Music of the English Parish Church*, 308.

to the first but the second edition of the hymn book, although there are a considerable number of hymns in which there is little chromatic motion, if any at all.[19]

THEOLOGICAL PERSPECTIVES

The composer's cousin, The Reverend George Huntington, wrote:

> I have been paying Cardinal Newman a visit. . . . I happened to mentioned his well-known hymn *Lead, kindly Light* which he said he wrote when a very young man, as he was becalmed on the Mediterranean, for a week, in 1832. I ventured to say, "It must be a great pleasure to you to know that you have written a hymn treasured wherever English-speaking Christians are to be found; and where are they not to be found?
>
> He was silent for some moments, and then said, with emotion, "Yes, deeply thankful, and more than thankful; then, after another pause, "But you see it is not the hymn, but the *tune*, that has gained the popularity! The tune is Dykes' and Dr. Dykes was a great master."[20]

Beyond being a supreme craftsmen, Dykes also had a reputation as being a considerate pastor. Chapter ten of Fowler's volume includes a large number of Dykes's *Spiritual Letters* and allows an insight into the thinking of a man who was otherwise seen unrelentingly occupied with the life of being a musically gifted priest. In his introduction to the chapter, Fowler writes:

> He had, by instinct, a very keen insight into human nature; he always seemed able, at a glance, to detect the secret springs of action; and his opinion on character was highly valued, and anxiously sought among his friends. This penetretative faculty it was which, under the guidance of God's Holy Spirit, and quicked by an ardent love of souls, fitted him, in a remarkable manner, for dealing with trouble consciences.[21]

A consideration of the theology behind Dykes's work requires both an evaluation of his personal upbringing and ministry as well as an assessment of the practical side of his work as a composer. Living and working around both Durham Cathedral and St. Oswald's required Dykes to think along

19. Hutchings, "In Praise of John Bacchus Dykes," 49.

20. Unknown, "Lux Benigna," 659.

21. Fowler, *Life and Letters of John Bacchus Dykes*, 237.

very pragmatic lines in terms of the needs of liturgy and there is no question that the larger share of his hymn tunes were written because of either a specific liturgical need or because he felt personally compelled to write them. A reading of his diary and letters is extremely valuable in evaluating the weekly life of Dykes, and by the standards of any era he was an unapologetic workaholic. He came from a large evangelical family that moved toward "ritualism." Hutchings's succinct commentary is borne out in the correspondence of Dykes:

> Because Dykes was a high churchman,[22] we should expect him to have waxed sentimental in setting verses about heaven, for many high churchmen of that time envisaged heaven as an existence in which holy souls participated in an eternal orgy of flamboyant music and ceremonial. But Dykes' letter to his wife and to his most intimate friends rarely mention matters of ritual or ceremonial [beyond the correspondence with the Bishop of Durham], not are there many passages upon theological points at all different from those one reads of evangelical clergy.
>
> He liked certain practices and symbols, now to be found in most parish churches, because they emphasised various tenets of evangelical piety. When in London, he preferred service in St. Andrew's, Wells Street, to that of St. Alban's, Holborn, where he "felt done to death by the so-called Gregorian music," though.
>
> He forbade his curate to use coloured stoles as "we are not ready for such things." It is clear that Dykes' high churchmanship was very little concerned with ceremonial and mysticism. If Dykes' ministry at St. Oswald's were to return, we should suppose that we had strayed into an evangelical congregation. Dykes' emotions are roused nearly always at an expression of devotion to God as Redeemer—the very core of Evangelical teaching.[23]

In many respects Dykes was a "man of his time" just as Stainer was and when we look at the late nineteenth century composer for the church, it is important to consider the consequence of the "popular" hymn and Dykes's place as a composer.

> His sympathies were with the tractarians, but he composed "as the spirit moved him," without conscious plan, as did the

22. Dykes embraced the "consubstantial" view of the Eucharist (rather than the "transubstantiation" of Wilberforce) and felt closer to Keble's teaching on the early church rather than Newman's understanding of the doctrine of the church. Dibble, "John Bacchus Dykes."

23. Hutchings, "In Praise of John Bacchus Dykes," 52.

> German pietists poets and the evangelical hymn writers. Just as Schubert could not have been the Schubert we know but for the new German lyric verse of his day, the arrival of the piano in middle-class homes, and the kind of society that was ready for what he provided from the kind of verse in instrument, so Dykes in his smaller way could not have been the Dykes we know but for the coming of the evangelical spirit into parish congregations, the setting up of organ or harmonium in place of the barrel-organ or "quire" of assorted instruments and singers of metrical psalms in the west gallery, and the arrival of surpliced chancel choirs imitated from Leeds Parish Church.[24]

The question of word-painting in Dykes, as much as any composer, needs to be seen with the realistic grasp that while there are undoubtedly very effective allusions to the narrative of the hymn, whether in a particular verse or the large text (parts of which may have been excised in later editions of hymnals), it is essential to remember that this topic is not discussed at any length in any of Dykes's correspondence. Indeed, the Newman anecdote above speaks to the larger measure of the text because clearly what words might be highlighted by a harmonic progression or sequence of harmonies in one stanza do not account for the same harmony appearing in a later stanza where no motion is necessary. Indeed, it could even provide relative confusion to a congregant who is being "taught" the narrative with the aid of the tune. Rather we can consider any well-read person, especially a reader as assiduous as Dykes, to have been keenly aware and broadly influenced by the Romantic movement of poetry as espoused by Browning, Coleridge, Tennyson, and Wordsworth as well as the continental composers such as Chopin, Mendelssohn, Schubert, Schumann, and Weber.[25] This noted, there are critical points that sustain analysis, not least from a starting point that Dykes was primarily concerned with setting texts. In his article on *Melita*, Little observes that the plagal opening is common to Dykes, as are subdominant moves generally, and that this tendency has particular bearing for Dykes:

> While the perfect cadence defines the tonic, the plagal cadence rather confirms and extends it: it is in fact an expression of reassurance and of rest . . . in the tune *St. Cuthbert*, to words relating to the Holy Spirit as Comforter, where we find the "comfort" of

24. Hutchings, "In Praise of John Bacchus Dykes," 55.
25. Harper, "Towards an Undertsanding," vii.

> the plagal progression quite unclouded in the first line, and an actual, if brief, subdominant modulation in the third.[26]

This argument is especially persuasive when viewed with the tune *Melita* where the words "strong to save" are aligned with the shift to the subdominant in the second half of the phrase while accompanied by ascending wave-like motion in the lower parts that in turn directs attention toward higher things. A similar allusion could be argued in the third and fourth lines where the slowly ascending (largely) chromatic bass line (B-C-C#-D-D#-E-F#-G-A-B) is bolstered by the richness of the pervading harmony, thus instilling a sense of confidence and resolve that is then taken on by the soprano part (E-F-F#-G-A). The final line of *Melita*, with its relatively simple progressions, provides comparative solace. Throughout the hymn the parts are especially close and this too brings the nature of both congregational worship and domestic music-making to mind. The overall emotional impact of the hymn becomes unavoidable and, through its musical language, the text is easily translatable even on a first encounter. This alliance of poetry and music draws on the sentiments of Matthew Arnold in his *Literature and Dogma* of 1873 where he noted that the idea of God was as much a concept of poetry as it was of biblical exegesis and spiritual doctrine (a fact evident in Newman's *Dream of Gerontius*), which was so popular in the mid-nineteenth century and which drew on Keble's earlier notion of the "churching of Romanticsm."[27] In these respects Dykes's works relate well to Stainer's later commentary:

> The true estimate of a hymn-tune cannot be found by principles of abstract criticism, or by an internal evidence that it exhibits and artist's handicraft. There is something indefinable and intangible, which can render a hymn-tune, not only a winning musical melody, but also a most powerful evangeliser.[28]

One of Dykes's most well-known tunes, *Nicaea*, a setting of Heber's powerful text, is set in a musical style that embraces the author's inspiring tone.

> Heber has produced a hymn in which the normal processes of human sin are acknowledged but transcended in worship and praise. It turns hymnody into a kind of mantra, with "Holy, holy, holy"! as a spell, much as Coleridge has used it in *Aids to Reflection*, where he attacked Descartes as one who "instead of a

26. Little, "Melita," 675–78. Here, Little also discusses similar instances of modulations in *Commendatio*, *Sleep, holy babe*, *St. Aelred*, and *Hollingside*.

27. Harper, "Towards an Understanding," 29–30.

28. Stainer, *Hymn Tunes*, iii

> World created and filled with productive forces by the Almighty Fiat, left a lifeless Machine whirled about by the dust of its own Grinding; as if death could come from the living Fountain of Life; Nothingness and Phantom from the Plenitude of Reality! The Absoluteness of Creative Will! Holy! Holy! Holy!"[29]

The tune by Dykes is replete with symbolism, including the didactic (ecclesiastically canonic) nature of the opening two bars, which have a marching quality to them. By emphasizing the major triad in the opening phrase he alludes to the Trinity (one in three and three in one), and with the ascending line here and then in the tenor (bar 2) and alto and tenor (bar 3) creates a sense of rising adoration,[30] heavenly petitioning, and simple human action through embellishment beneath a triumphant and assured outer texture. The final line reinforces this analysis with the four-square setting of "God in Three Persons" with its majestic soprano sweep (E-B-C#-G#) followed by the surety of a IV-V-I cadence. The tune amplifies the confidence manifest in the text and such is the union of text and tune that it is near impossible to imagine an alternate setting. Thus, Dykes not only provides a tune but manages to provide *the* tune.

CONTRIBUTION TO LITURGY AND WORSHIP

Dykes's biographer, Joseph Thomas Fowler wrote:

> Who that has sung his hymn-tunes does not feel that they came to him as inspirations? He rarely wrote a tune unless the words were sent, or suggested to him, and then the tune seemed at once to adapt itself to the words. This is probably the secret of the success of his tunes. They came from his heart and found their way into the hearts of others. It mattered not who applied to him for tunes, whether churchmen or dissenters, high or low, rich or poor, the work was given, ungrudgingly, as work for God.[31]

His contributions to liturgy are of course two-fold; hymns written and published in his own time and those that remain in constant use, as discussed in the following section. His early published hymns appear in the 1850s in *Congregational Church Music* and later for John Grey's *Hymnal*

29. Watson, "Ancient or Modern," 324.
30. Harper, "Towards an Understanding," 180.
31. Fowler, *Life and Letters of John Bacchus Dykes*, 224.

and its appendix, Parish Church Hymnal and the *Congregational Psalmist.*[32] Although he is largely remembered as a member contributor to *Hymns Ancient and Modern* of 1861, he also wrote for *The Congregational Hymn and Tune Book, The Song of Praise, The Hymnal Companion, The Holy Year, Hymns for Infant Children, The Child's Book of Praise, The Anglican Hymn-Book, The People's Hymnal, A Book of Litanies, Prose and Metrical, The Parish Church Hymnal, The Sarum Hymnal, Congregational Church Music, The Wesleyan Tune-Book* and more than a dozen other publications in addition to leaving many tunes in manuscript.[33]

With such a wide array of publications, Dykes's work was known throughout the country and his travels frequently resulted in a new commission or a thought toward setting a new text. Understandingly, some tunes have been more successful than others but it should be noted that of all the hymn-tune composers of the era, Dykes's work was by far the most well-known. As Temperley notes, "The greatest Victorian hymn tunes were those that combined the artistry of the part-song with the inspiring melody of a truly congregational kind,"[34] and it is this legacy that we also see developed with Goss, Harwood, Parry, and Sullivan in terms of examples that have been retained in hymnals to the present day.

NOTABLE HYMNS

Although not a household name to many a congregant, the hymns of Dykes that continue to be published are nonetheless considered well established in the liturgical repertoire. A broader range of his hymns can be found in English hymnals intended for Anglican use but the following tunes appear consistently across denominations: *Beatitudo, Dominus regit me, Gerontius, Hollingside, Lux Vera, Melita, Nicaea, Rievaulx, St. Agnes, St. Cross, Strength and Stay*. Of these tunes, the most familiar to congregations in the late twentieth and early twenty-first centuries are *Dominus regit me, Gerontius, Melita,* and *Nicaea*

BIBLIOGRAPHY

Dibble, Jeremy. "John Bacchus Dykes." *The Canterbury Dictionary of Hymnology*. Canterbury. http://www.hymnology.co.uk/j/john-bacchus-dykes.

32. Dibble, "John Bacchus Dykes."

33. A comprehensive listing according to Fowler can be seen in Fowler, *Life and Letters of John Bacchus Dykes*, 321–31.

34. Temperley, *Music of the English Parish Church*, 309.

Fowler, John Thomas. *The Life and Letters of John Bacchus Dykes, M.A., MUS. DOC., vicar of St. Oswald's, Durham*. London: J. Murray, 1897.

Harper, Joseph Frank. "Towards an Understanding of Tractarian Hymnody: A Critical Appraisal of the Interaction between Theology, Poetry and Music in Anglican Hymnody between 1840 and 1900." PhD Thesis, University of Durham, 2010.

Hutchings, Arthur. "In Praise of John Bacchus Dykes." *Durham University Journal* (March 1950) 26–28.

Hutchings, Arthur, and Nicholas Temperley. "Dykes, John Bacchus." *Grove Music Online; Oxford Music Online*. http://www.oxfordmusiconline.com/grovemusic/view/10.1093/gmo/9781561592630.001.0001/omo-9781561592630-e-0000008454.

Little, Patrick. "Melita: A Hymn-Tune by J. B. Dykes." *The Musical Times* 131 (December 1990) 675–78.

Quinn, Iain. *The Genesis and Development of an English Organ Sonata*. Abingdon: Routledge, 2017.

Rainbow, Bernarr. *The Choral Revival in the Anglican Church, (1839–1872)*. New York: Oxford University Press, 1970.

Rosen, Charles. *Freedom and the Arts*. Cambridge: Harvard University Press, 2012.

Routley, Erik. *The Music of Christian Hymns*. Chicago: G. I. A. Publications, 1981.

Stainer, John. *Hymn Tunes*. London: Novello & Co., 1900.

Temperley, Nicholas. *The Music of the English Parish Church*. Cambridge: Cambridge University Press, 1979.

Unknown. "Lux Benigna." *The Musical Times* 48 (October 1, 1907) 659.

Watson, John Richard. "Ancient or Modern, 'Ancient and Modern': The Victorian Hymns and the Nineteenth Century." *The Yearbook of English Studies* 36.2 (2006) 1–16.

Chapter 5

American Gospel Song Movement

ROBERT J. MORGAN

HISTORICAL BACKGROUND

WHENEVER CHRISTIANS EXPERIENCE SEASONS of widespread revival, it changes the way we sing. The story of both biblical and church history is filled with new genres of music arising from periods of awakenings. As Vernon Whaley and Elmer Towns write in *Worship Through the Ages*, "Through the centuries, there have been periods of great encounter with God. We often call these periods revivals or Great Awakenings. During these periods of awakening, new methods, styles, processes, and techniques of worship emerge."[1]

This was certainly true in America during the nineteenth century, especially during the so-called Layman's Revival between 1875 and 1900, which generated the era of the gospel song. This movement impacted church music for a hundred years and still affects our worship today. It unfolded in stages. During the 1800s, a series of revivals kept Christianity at the forefront of American history. The second great awakening in the first half of the century represented a merger of the camp revivals on the frontier and the campus revivals spreading through the Northeast. This awakening

1. Towns and Whaley, *Worship Through the Ages*, 5.

created a fertile environment for the growth of one of the greatest Christian innovations of the time—the Sunday school.

The American Sunday School Union was founded in the United States in 1824. In 1830, Francis Scott Key, the organization's president, challenged his colleagues to aggressively establish Sunday schools between Pittsburgh and Denver. Within a few years, over 61,000 Sunday schools were planted. The growth in Sunday school attendance in America rose from less than 100,000 children in 1824 to more than 3,250,000 in 1875.[2]

All these children needed songs to sing, which gave rise to the era of the "Sunday school song," simple, easy-to-sing hymns and choruses written especially with children in mind—songs such as "Jesus Loves Me," which has been called the unofficial theme for the Sunday school movement.[3] One historian wrote, "From the 1840s there developed a new body of song particularly adapted to the American Sunday school—one that spoke in reassuring terms about God's love and a home in heaven."[4]

William Bradbury, a Christian composer and children's music educator, deserves the lion's share of credit for this innovation in hymnody. William J. Reynolds wrote, "First designed solely for children, these songs were simple in character, popular in design, and intended for immediate appeal."[5]

The Sunday school song quickly spread to wider congregational use. It was a natural evolution. As Sunday school children grew up, they wanted to take their Sunday school habits with them. By 1870, many Sunday schools were catering to adults as well as children and entire churches lifted their voices to sing these simpler and more sentimental songs.

In the preface of an 1871 collection of Sunday school songs, the editors explained: "The hymns in this work are not all projected on the plane of childhood. That quiet revolution, by which our Sunday schools for children are passing up to the higher level of Bible schools for all ages, has not been overlooked. Keeping that strictly in view, we have inserted hymns about Heaven, which veteran saints can sing, hymns of Activity for the strong and buoyant, hymns of new Experience for the Christian child; as well as hymns of Invitation for the unconverted, and hymns of Confession for the penitent."[6]

2. Towns and Whaley, *Worship Through the Ages*, 163–64.
3. Blumhofer, *Her Heart Can See*, 182.
4. Clark, *Music and Theology*, 104.
5. Reynolds, *Companion*, 19.
6. Reynolds, *Companion*, 19.

Edwin Wilber Rice, in his 1917 history of the Sunday school movement in America, wrote:

> The American Sunday School Union not only aimed to provide a juvenile literature, but it sought to displace the rollicking and ribald songs by cleaner and purer lyrics set to attractive music. It was a common proverb then, "The devil has all the popular songs." Practically there were no moral songs of hymns of note for children in 1800 or 1810, except the small collection of Watts's *Divine and Moral Songs,* Roland Hill's *Divine Hymns in Easy Language*, and Jane and Ann Taylor's *Original Hymns for Sunday Schools*. There were collections of hymns for children a century earlier, but those of any importance issued from 1700 to 1800 could be counted on the fingers of a person's hand.[7]

Bradbury and his fellow composers such as Lowell Mason changed that by publishing and popularizing a galaxy of Sunday school songs for Christians of all ages. In many churches, these songs supplemented—but did not replace—Watts, Wesley, Newton, Cowper, and the classic hymns of the 1700s.

Rice goes on to point out how these Sunday school songs paved the way for the next powerful wave of emerging church music—the gospel song: "The charming melodies of Lowell Mason and the rhythmic songs of Thomas Hastings, and other musical writers, were composed for the young, and issued by the Union as worthy forerunners of the gospel songs that now fill our land."[8]

The uncomplicated tunes and lyrics of Sunday school songs seeped into church worship and set the stage of an even greater shift in American church music, one that accompanied what is often called the Layman's Revival. This revival arose in part from a New York City prayer meeting planned by Jeremiah Lamphier for noon on Wednesday, September 23, 1857. The location on Fulton Street was in the financial district, which was in the grip of the 1857 Financial Panic. The Fulton Street meetings spread across the East and gripped a nation that was tottering on the edge of the Civil War.

When the war came, it disrupted the revival but it didn't stop it. Indeed, the Civil War was accompanied by continued revivals in both the Northern and the Southern armies.[9] During the war, a brilliant but largely uneducated

7. Rice, *Sunday School Movement*, 147.

8. Rice, *Sunday School Movement*, 150.

9. For further study, see "Untold Story of Christianity." Also Lacy, *Revivals in the Midst of the Years,* chapter 5; and Miller, *They Prayed to the Same God.*

entrepreneur from Chicago named Dwight Lyman Moody became an unofficial chaplain in the Union Army. Making repeated visits to the battlefront, he preached the gospel and cared for the spiritual needs of the soldiers. After the war, Moody continued preaching, and great power accompanied his ministry. Moody was never ordained; he was a layman, but, after all, this period is known as the Layman's Revival, and it's fitting that the man who would become its chief standard-bearer was a layman.

In June 1870, Moody was invited to speak at a convention in Indianapolis. During one service, an employee of the Internal Revenue Service, Ira Sankey, led the singing. Afterward the two men met, and, as Sankey later recalled, Moody began pelting him with questions: "Where are you from? Are you married? What is your business?"

> Upon telling him that I lived in Pennsylvania, was married, had two children, and was in the government employ, he said abruptly, "You will have to give that up."
>
> I was amazed, at a loss to understand why the man told me that I would have to give up what I considered a good position. "What for?" I exclaimed.
>
> "To come to Chicago and help me in my work," was the answer.
>
> When I told him that I could not leave my business, he retorted, "You must; I have been looking for you for the last eight years."[10]

Moody persuaded Sankey to join him as a musical evangelist in his campaigns, and the Moody-Sankey team embarked on a series of remarkable evangelistic endeavors in Great Britain and America. Sankey traveled with a small portable organ (a harmonium made by Mason & Hamlin), and during the meetings he searched out songs that felt warm, simple, evangelistic, and emotional. He called them, "our sweet church songs . . . sung from the heart."[11]

Large choirs were a standard feature of the Moody-Sankey meetings. Sankey insisted on keeping and singing the older hymns, but felt his new sweet church songs should be sung alongside the great English and German hymns. "Old family hymns and tunes should be used," he wrote, "with now and then a Sunday-school song."[12] Indeed, the Sankey hymnbooks are full of these older hymns. But he believed his evangelistic efforts with Moody needed lighter, warmer songs that were easily taught and learned and that

10. Sankey, *My Life and the Story*, 21.
11. Goodspeed, *Full History of the Wonderful Career*, 380.
12. Goodspeed, *Full History of the Wonderful Career*, 381.

touched the sentiment, hit a strong emotional note, and conveyed the gospel. Sankey viewed himself just as truly an evangelist as Moody, and the two men were on the platform near each other, ready at a moment's notice to shift the message from one to the other.

On one rainy night, for example, Moody wound up a sermon in Brooklyn by urging his listeners to engage in the Lord's work with all their hearts. His voice reached the rafters as he told the story of a British woman who, aided by her husband, led 150 people to Christ. "That's the way we do it," Moody thundered. "God help you to lay yourselves out. Go ye all into the vineyard! Don't wait for the harvest, for—hark!"

> At this exclamation, a thrill of indescribable anticipation seemed to pass through the breathless assembly, and then, after a pause, during which only the patter of raindrops on the roof could be heard, the speaker concluded with: "Hark! The voice of Jesus crying, who will go and work today?"
>
> The tones of Mr. Moody's voice had hardly ceased before the same words were repeated by Mr. Sankey's musical voice in a beautiful hymn:
>
> Hark! The voice of Jesus crying,
> Who will go and work today?
> Fields are white and harvest waiting,
> Who will bear the sheaves away?[13]

Many souls made spontaneous, life-changing decisions to follow Christ while listening to a Sankey solo. Rev. E. J. Goodspeed wrote a contemporaneous account of the Moody-Sankey meetings in Great Britain and America, saying:

> As a vocalist, Mr. Sankey has not many equals. Possessed of a voice of great volume and richness, he expressed with exquisite skill and pathos the Gospel message, in words very simple, but replete with love and tenderness, and always with marked effect upon his audience. It is, however, altogether a mistake to suppose that the blessings which attends Mr. Sankey's efforts is attributable only or chiefly to his fine voice and artistic expression. . . . Like his colleague, he likewise has a message to lost men from God the Father; and the Spirit of God in him finds a willing and effective instrument in his gift of song. . . . "It was a few evenings ago," said a youth in the Young Men's Meeting in Roby Chapel, "when Mr. Sankey was singing in the Free Trade Hall 'Jesus of Nazareth Passeth By,' that I was made to feel the

13. Goodspeed, *Full History of the Wonderful Career*, 271–72.

> need of my Savior; and when he came to those words, 'Too late, too late,' I said to myself it must not be too late for me, and I took him to my heart there and then."[14]

Another observer wrote, "The admiration of Mr. Sankey's music is enthusiastic. When he sings a solo a death-like silence reigns, or, as the *Irish Times* describes it, 'It seems that he only is present in the vast building.' When he ceases there is a rustling like the leaves of a forest when stirred by the wind."[15]

Yet another wrote, "We have seen many stirred and melted by his singing before a word had been spoken. Indeed, his singing is just a powerful, distinct, and heart-toned way of speaking, that seems often to reach the heart by short cut."[16]

J. F. Findley Jr., in his biography of Moody, wrote of the impact the Moody-Sankey team had abroad.

> In Scotland . . . Sankey commanded attention simply because solo singing and the use of the harmonium had been all but unheard of. In England, there was a notable tradition of hymnody and congregational singing connected with the evangelical movement, but this tradition had been declining at the time the two Americans came overseas. Consciously or unconsciously, Sankey did something to revive the tradition. Participants in the revival meetings noted that the singing evangelist often did not really sing his songs but instead "spoke" them in a tuneful way. He put primary emphasis on precise enunciation, to make clear the words and their meaning. He made music the servant of the lyric rather than the reverse. . . . The melodies Sankey used were simple, yet when he performed them they often produced a noticeable emotional effect, since he was careful to utilize modulations in tempo and volume both in his voice and in the musical accompaniment.[17]

The stories of those who were converted to Christ mid-song are striking. One "intelligent young man" later testified that he had come to the Moody-Sankey Liverpool meeting in 1875 to scoff and make fun of the proceedings. He sat laughing to himself until

14. Goodspeed, *Full History of the Wonderful Career*, 54–55.
15. Goodspeed, *Full History of the Wonderful Career*, 54–55.
16. Goodspeed, *Full History of the Wonderful Career*, 107.
17. Findley, *Dwight L. Moody*, 176–77.

> that beautiful hymn, "Safe in the Arms of Jesus," was sung. A sudden thrill passed through my whole frame, and then like a dart ran through my very heart. My feelings were awful, but I listened to the next verse, and felt there is a Savior. Who is He? Where is He? Instantly I realized the truth, Jesus is the Savior. I threw myself into His loving arms, and here I am now, rejoicing in Him.[18]

As Sankey collected songs from his collaborators, he taught them to the great crowds attending the meetings. One account explained the process like this:

> Mr. Sankey also sang the verses to the 18th hymn, "Rescue the Perishing," but the audience did not respond as enthusiastically as usual in the chorus. After the services, Mr. Sankey said that this hymn was new, at least he had not had it very long, and that a large portion of the audience was unacquainted with the tune. He was confident they would sing it with the usual force after hearing it a few more times.[19]

These gospel songs spread abroad because of the huge crowds and choirs that attended Moody's rallies. When the duo came to Philadelphia, organizers built an auditorium seating twelve thousand people, including a choir loft for five hundred. Mr. Sankey led the choir and drilled them on the songs he was introducing, and in this way spread his music to churches all across the city.[20]

Early in their campaigns, Sankey collected a scrapbook of songs that seemed suited to mass evangelistic meetings. "I was continually beset with requests for the loan of my 'musical scrap-book,'" he said, "in which alone could be found the songs that were then being sung as solos at our meetings."[21]

While Moody and Sankey were in London, publisher R. C. Morgan offered to publish a collection of the songs used in the Moody-Sankey meetings. "So," Sankey recalled, "I cut from my scrap-book twenty-three pieces, rolled them up, and wrote on them the words 'Sacred Songs and Solos, sung by Ira D. Sankey at the meetings of Mr. Moody of Chicago.'"[22] This was the beginning of one of the most successful publishing ventures in the history of hymnody. With each new edition, Sankey added more hymns. The books

18. Goodspeed, *Full History of the Wonderful Career*, 173.
19. Goodspeed, *Full History of the Wonderful Career*, 256.
20. Goodspeed, *Full History of the Wonderful Career*, 261.
21. Sankey, *My Life and the Story*, 46.
22. Sankey, *My Life and the Story*, 54.

spread far and wide, both in English and in translated editions. During Sankey's lifetime, an estimated 75 million copies were sold, "netting him a profit of $500,000, all of which he gave away to charitable enterprises."[23] Martin Clark wrote, "With the publication and spread of *Sacred Songs and Solos*, the transition from Sunday school songs to revival hymns became a fait accompli and a new model of religious song became available."[24]

At first, these new songs and songbooks were called "Sankey's." People would rush into bookstores and ask for a dozen Sankey's. "Let's sing a Sankey" was the cry. In 1875, Philip Bliss published his own collection of revival hymns, and he called them "gospel songs," and, in so doing, provided a title to this genre of Christian music. Later, updated collections of Sankey hymns were published under the title, *Gospel Hymns and Sacred Songs*.

In this way, the era of the gospel song began. While Sankey composed a few of the melodies for some of the songs he popularized, the Moody-Sankey movement produced a galaxy of lyricists and composers who fueled the era of the gospel song, such as:

- Fanny J. Crosby (1820–1915)—Crosby was of the most remarkable characters in nineteenth-century American Christian history. Indeed, apart from Moody and Sankey, she was the best-known Christian in the United States. Blinded in childhood, Crosby composed lyrics based on a rich storehouse of memorized Scripture and provided the words for thousands of gospel songs.
- Major Daniel Webster Whittle (1840–1901)—After the Civil War, Whittle became an executive of the Elgin Clock Company until Moody recruited him as a Bible teacher, evangelist, and song lyricist.
- Elisha A. Hoffman (1839–1929)—Hoffman was a Presbyterian minister who composed the lyrics of more than two thousand hymns and edited over fifty songbooks.
- Eliza E. Hewitt (1851–1920)—A native of Pennsylvania, Hewitt began her career as a schoolteacher but became disabled and, as an invalid, began writing the lyrics of hymns. She became one of Sankey's favorite lyricists.
- William Bradbury (1816–68)—As we stated earlier, Bradbury was a children's music educator who helped develop and popularize Sunday school songs. He passed away before Moody and Sankey joined forces,

23. Sankey, *Sacred Songs and Solos*, 78.

24. Clark, *Music and Theology*, 106.

but his hymn compositions were widely used by Sankey in meetings across Europe and America.

- Robert Lowry (1826–99)—Lowry was a pastor and educator, best remembered for his musical compositions and editorial work in compiling collections of gospel songs as an editor at Biglow & Main Publishing Company, the largest publisher of gospel music during the Moody-Sankey era.
- William H. Doane (1832–1915)—Doane was an inventor and manufacturer with more than seventy patents to his name. He presided over his business empire from his estate, Sunny Side, in Cincinnati. A dedicated Christian, Doane also wrote hymn tunes and became a longtime collaborator with Fanny Crosby.
- Philip Bliss (1838–76)—From humble origins, Bliss grew up wanting to be a musician, and by sheer determination and giftedness became one of the most revered young musicians of the gospel song era, and, as stated earlier, coined the phrase "gospel song." He and his wife perished in the Ashtabula River Railroad Disaster on December 29, 1876, while traveling to Chicago to join Moody and Sankey for services on New Year's Eve.
- Charles H. Gabriel (1856–1932)—Originally from Iowa, Gabriel was a self-taught musician who wrote the words and composed the tunes to thousands of gospel songs.
- George F. Root (1820–95)—Though he wrote the lyrics to a handful of gospel songs, Root was an accomplished musician who was better known for his gospel tunes.

THEOLOGICAL PERSPECTIVES AND NOTABLE HYMNS

Because the gospel songs of the Sankey era were born in the midst of soul-winning rallies, they are simple, evangelistic, and gospel-centered; and because they evolved from Sunday school songs they were easy to learn, easy to sing, and could be quickly learned at mass meetings.

The golden age of German and English hymns (c. 1520–1820) provided the church with majestic and reverent hymns focused on the worship of God. But many of these new gospel songs were written for non-Christians. They were evangelistic in nature, and Sankey felt he was singing the gospel, even as Moody preached it. Whaley and Towns wrote, "The genre was termed 'Gospel Music' because its message centered on core ideas of the salvation message—sin, grace, redemption, and the experience of conversion."[25] According to William Reynolds, the distinguishing characteristics of the American gospel hymn are: (1) emotional rather than intellectual emphasis; (2) simple phrases repeated over and over; (3) evangelistic emphasis; (4) simple tunes based on popular melody—camp or marching songs and parlor piano music; (5) an easy to learn refrain; (6) words and melodies that can be memorized easily; and (7) a melodic line supported by simple harmonic structure with infrequent changes of chords.[26]

One of Sankey's most effecting songs, "Jesus of Nazareth Passeth By," with words written by a New Jersey schoolteacher, Emma Campbell, was a ballad envisioning the scenes of Jesus passing by certain people or towns in gospel times. The final verse warned the listener, "If you still His call refuse / And all His wondrous love abuse, / Soon will He sadly from you turn / Your bitter prayer for pardon spurn, / 'Too late! Too late!' will be the cry, / Jesus of Nazareth has passed by." In his memoirs, Sankey wrote, "At one of our early meetings in Edinburgh an old gentleman, more than seventy years of age, threw himself down on his knees and, sobbing like a child, said, "I was utterly careless about my soul until last night, but I have been so unhappy since I could not sleep. I seemed to hear ringing in my ears, 'Jesus of Nazareth Passeth By,' and I feel that if I am not saved now, I never shall be."[27]

Another of Sankey's most beloved hymns, "The Ninety and Nine," tells the story of a shepherd searching for a lost sheep that was "Away in the mountains wild and bare, / Away from the tender shepherd's care."

> But all thro' the mountains, thunder-rive,
> And up from the rocky steep,
> There arose a glad cry to the gate of heaven,
> "Rejoice! I have found my sheep!"
> And the Angels echoed around the throne,
> "Rejoice! For the Lord brings back His own."[28]

Sankey explained his theology of worship during a convention of church music held in junction with Moody's New York City campaign in 1876:

25. Towns and Whaley, *Worship Through the Ages*, 189.

26. Towns and Whaley, *Worship Through the Ages*, 189.

27. Sankey, *My Life and the Story*, 204–5.

28. Words by Elizabeth C. Celphane; music by Ira Sankey, published in *Sacred Songs and Solos*, 1874.

> There are hymns which teach and preach the Gospel, and these are not hymns of praise. I believe there is another power of singing which many have not discovered yet, that of preaching the Gospel. There is no praise in the hymn, "Jesus of Nazareth Passeth By," yet it has been blessed to hundreds of souls. It is not praising God at all. When it comes to praising God I will join in the general singing as heartily as any one else. If I want to preach to you in song I would ask you to listen.[29]

It may not be surprising, then, that an entire category of "invitation hymns" arose to urge listeners to give their lives to Christ. These include,

- "Just as I Am" (1836) by Charlotte Elliott
- "Have Thine Own Way, Lord" (1907) by Adelaide A. Pollard
- "I Surrender All" (1896) by Judson W. Van DeVenter
- "Softly and Tenderly, Jesus is Calling" (1880) by Will L. Thompson
- "Jesus, I Come" (1887) by William T. Sleeper
- "Pass Me Not, O Gentle Savior" (1868) by Fanny Crosby
- "Take My Life and Let It Be" (1874) by Frances R. Havergal
- "Whiter Than Snow" (1872) by James L. Nicholson
- "Almost Persuaded" (1871) by Philip P. Bliss
- "Are You Coming Home Tonight" (1883) by an anonymous author

Other themes focused around the blood of Christ and its saving power. In almost every campaign, D. L. Moody preached a sermon about the power of the blood of Jesus, and this became a dominant note in gospel song hymnody. In one of his spellbinding sermons in New York, Moody said, "Why do you like that hymn, 'Just as I am, without one plea, save that Thy blood was shed for me'? Why is it that that hymn is so popular? Why does the Church of God like it and sing it? Why do we sing it so often? Because it has got the precious blood in it."[30] Other gospel songs focused on this theological theme of Christ's blood include:

- "Are You Washed in the Blood?" (1878) by Elisha A. Hoffman
- "Nothing But the Blood" (1876) by Robert Lowry
- "There Is Power in the Blood" (1899) by Lewis E. Jones
- "Saved by the Blood" (1902) by S. J. Henderson

29. Goodspeed, *Full History of the Wonderful Career*, 583.
30. Goodspeed, *Full History of the Wonderful Career*, 497.

- "When I See the Blood" (1892) by John G. Fotte and Elisha A. Hoffman
- "Precious Blood" (1881) by MacLeod Wylie

In a similar vein, the themes of the cross and redemption pervaded the era of the gospel song, based on the conviction that the cross was the very heart of the gospel message. In an age that saw the abolition of slavery in the United States, there was an unspoken bond between current events and redemptive grace. The cross redeems from sin, liberates us, and sets us free:

- "Near the Cross" (1869) by Fanny Crosby
- "Hallelujah for the Cross" (1875) by Horatius Bonar
- "Beneath the Cross of Jesus" (1868) by Elizabeth C. Clephane
- "Redeemed, How I Love to Proclaim It" (1882) by Fanny Crosby
- "Since I Have Been Redeemed" (1884) by Edwin O. Excell
- "I Will Sing of My Redeemer" (1876) by Philip P. Bliss

Many of the gospel songs were designed to motivate believers to spread the gospel and tell the story of Jesus across the street and across the seas. The great era of modern missions had captured the imagination of the American church, and reports told of gospel advancement in Asia, Africa, the South Pacific, and other exotic locations that most people had never before contemplated. At the same time, evangelists like Moody emphasized the role of aggressive soul-winning. Many of the songs of this era helped stir the evangelistic zeal of the crowds who sang them.

- "Stand Up, Stand Up for Jesus" (1858) by George Duffield Jr.
- "Rescue the Perishing" (1869) by Fanny Crosby
- "Tell Me the Old, Old Story" (1867) by Katherine Hankey
- "I Love to Tell the Story" (1866) by Katherine Hankey
- "Tell Me the Story of Jesus" (1880) by Fanny Crosby
- "We've a Story to Tell to the Nations" (1896) by Henry Ernest Nichol
- "I Will Sing the Wondrous Story" (1886) by Francis H. Rowley
- "The Story that Never Grows Old" (1898) by John H. Yates
- "Throw Out the Life Line" (1888) by Edwin S. Ufford
- "Dare to Be a Daniel" (1873) by Philip P. Bliss
- "I'll Go Where You Want Me to Go, Dear Lord" (1892) By Mary Brown and Charles E. Prior

- "Let the Lower Lights Be Burning" (1871) by Philip P. Bliss
- "Lord, Speak to Me that I May Speak" (1872) by Frances Havergal

In keeping with the emotional and comforting nature of the gospel songs, many of them were written to afford Christians the comforts and consolations of faith, which served to enhance the believer's testimony to the world. The years following the Civil War were marked by severe economic cycles and financial collapses, presidential assassinations, and the difficult course of national reconstruction. Modern medical technology was in its infancy, and one of the most magnetic attractions of Christianity involved the comfort found in the presence of God and the promises of Scripture. These understandably became themes that filled the churches with songs.

- "Blessed Assurance" (1873) by Fanny Crosby
- "A Shelter in the Time of Storm" (1880) by Vernon J. Charlesworth
- "He Leadeth Me" (1862) by Joseph H. Gilmore
- "I Need Thee Every Hour" (1871) by Annie S. Hawks
- "It Is Well with My Soul" (1873) by Horatio G. Spafford
- "Safe in the Arms of Jesus" (1868) by Fanny Crosby
- "The Sweet By and By" (1868) by Sanford F. Bennett
- "A Child of the King" (1877) by Harriet E. Buell

One Moody-Sankey defender said, "Theological critics might have said there was nothing in it; but only eternity will reveal how much there came out of it."[31] One historian wrote,

> Sankey's songs were nothing like the old psalm tunes preferred by English Nonconformists or the Scottish Covenanters, nor even the more recent Victorian tunes popularized in *Hymns Ancient and Modern*. They were simply not like anything familiar to worshipers of an Anglican or Nonconformist stripe. They were from another world—the world of the American Sunday school..[32]

Moody and Sankey finally gave out from the strain of their work, but their influence lasted and they established the tone of American church music for the next hundred years. Sankey's voice lost much of its power from the exhaustion of singing to thousands of people without amplification. Yet

31. Goodspeed, *Full History of the Wonderful Career*, 141.
32. Clark, *Music and Theology*, 103.

before his death in 1908, he was able to record a handful of solos on brown wax cylinders and by listening to them we can still hear the resonance and power of his voice.

CONTRIBUTION TO LITURGY AND WORSHIP

After Moody and Sankey passed from the scene, the gospel song era continued into the twentieth century in the same atmosphere of mass evangelism. Billy Sunday and his music director, Homer Rodeheaver, kept the era of gospel song fresh and alive, along with a host of other traveling evangelists, such as George Bennard, who wrote "The Old Rugged Cross" while trudging from church to church, holding evangelistic campaigns.

In the middle of the twentieth century, another famous duo—Billy Graham and Cliff Barrows—burst on the evangelical scene, employing mass choirs in huge stadiums and utilizing recordings, radio, and television to spread the gospel through song and the spoken word. But rather than create a new genre of Christian music, Barrows and his colleague, soloist George Beverly Shea, borrowed heavily from the gospel song era and gave gospel songs a new lease on life.

Even the mid-century songs and choruses of John W. Peterson as well as Bill and Gloria Gather share many characteristics with the gospel songs of the Moody-Sankey era. Indeed, right up until the late 1960s and early 1970s, when another revival, the Jesus movement, created the age of praise and worship music, gospel songs were heard in evangelical churches around the world, intermingled with great hymns of earlier eras. Evangelicals followed Sankey's pattern of adding new songs without forsaking the old.

In the small church in which I grew up, for example, I recall how the song leader would open the service with a majestic eighteenth-century English hymn such as "All Hail the Power of Jesus' Name" before having us turn in our hymnal to Elisha Hoffman's "Leaning on the Everlasting Arms." We often sang Wesley and Crosby side by side. The unspoken philosophy that guided our song leader's selections reflected the words of Jesus in Matt 13:52 (NIV), "Therefore every teacher of the law who has become a disciple in the kingdom of heaven is like the owner of a house who brings out of his storeroom new treasures as well as old."

Until recently, most American worshipers grew up singing a rich tapestry of hymns and gospel songs over the course of a lifetime, memorizing their words and internalizing their message. Believers sang the songs their parents and grandparents had loved, along with newer selections from contemporary musicians. We should bear in mind the risks of tolerating a disposable attitude about our psalms, hymns, and spiritual songs, especially when our worship trends are driven by an industry that, in some cases, no longer values legacy. Every generation should indeed write its own music and express its own praise. But how tragic to forget the richness of Christian worship through the ages! Like Ira Sankey, may the church sing the new songs without forgetting the old. And let the words of Fanny Crosby ever be sung:

This is my story, this is my song,
Praising my Savior all the day long.

BIBLIOGRAPHY

Blumhofer, Edith L. *Her Heart Can See: The Life and Hymns of Fanny J. Crosby.* Grand Rapids, MI: Eerdmans, 2005.

Martin, Clarke. *Music and Theology in Nineteenth-Century Britain.* Burlington, VT: Ashgate, 2012.

Findley, J. F., Jr. *Dwight L. Moody.* Grand Rapids, MI: Baker, 1973.

Goodspeed, E. J. *A Full History of the Wonderful Career of Moody and Sankey in Great Britain and America.* St. Louis, MO: N. D. Thompson & Company, 1877.

Lacy, Benjamin Rice, Jr. *Revivals in the Midst of the Years.* Richmond, VA: John Knox, 1943.

Miller, Robert J. *Both Prayed to the Same God: Religion and Faith in the American Civil War.* Lanham, MD: Lexington, 2007.

Reynolds, William J. *Companion to the Baptist Hymnal.* Nashville: B&H, 1976.

Rice, Edwin Wilber. *The Sunday School Movement and the American Sunday School Union.* Philadelphia: American Sunday-School Union, 1917.

Sankey, Ira D. *My Life and the Story of the Gospel Hymns.* Philadelphia: P. W. Zeigler Company, 1907.

———. *Sacred Songs and Solos: Twelve Hundred Hymns.* London: Marshall, Morgan and Scott, 1976.

Sankey, Ira D., James McGranahan, and George C. Stebbins. *Gospel Hymns Nos. 1 to 6 Complete.* New York: Biglow Company, 1894.

Sunday School Times and Practical Educator. Vol. 22 (October 1908).

Towns, Elmer, and Vernon Whaley. *Worship Through the Ages.* Nashville: B&H, 2012.

"The Untold Story of Christianity and the Civil War." *Christian History Magazine* 33 (1992).

Wilhot, Mel R. "Sing a Sankey: The Rise of Gospel Hymnody in Great Britain." In *Music and Theology in Nineteenth-Century Britain*, edited by Martin Clarke, 97–116. London: Routledge, 2012.

Chapter 6

Frances R. Havergal

Hymns of Personal Devotion

Vernon M. Whaley

HISTORICAL BACKGROUND

Francis Havergal was born on December 14, 1836, at Astley, Worcester, England. She was an exceptionally bright, intellectually astute and well-mannered child. The youngest of six children, she read by the age of four and wrote prose at seven. Havergal was fluent in Latin, French, German, Italian, Welsh, New Testament Greek, and Old Testament Hebrew.[1] She had a prolific memory and memorized entire books of the Bible, including Psalms, Isaiah, the Minor Prophets, and much of the New Testament. As an adult, Francis demonstrated exceptional musical skill, becoming a much sought-after vocal soloist, professional pianist, and composer:

> Her voice was so pleasing and well-trained that she was sought after as a concert soloist, and her piano playing was brilliant. She possessed a marvelous musical memory, and could play through Handel and much of Beethoven and Mendelssohn without notes. She particularly delighted in Handel.[2]

1. Duffield, *English Hymn*, 189.
2. Havergal, *Memorials of Frances Ridley Havergal*, 26.

Francis R. Havergal never married, but instead devoted her life to communicating the gospel to students, writing hymns, and documenting her biblical teaching in books and pamphlets sold by major British and American publishers.[3] Samuel Willoughby Duffield, author of the landmark book *English Hymns* (1894), recounted Havergal's life:

> Her Christianity became her predominant characteristic, and her piety was as attractive as it was profound. . . . The scholarly instinct was strong within her, and her Bible—noted and underlined—was one of the best of proofs that she applied herself earnestly to the noblest themes. She was also finely musical—a performer, vocalist and composer, whom Heller was glad to approve—and the *Songs of Grace and Glory* furnish good proof of this. In poetry she was intensely religious, intensely subjective, and intensely sensitive to all beautiful or inspiring things. Many of her verses (like the "Moonlight Sonata," of which, by the way, she was an almost unrivaled interpreter) are really autobiographic. . . . Her little books of hymns and verses are treasured now all over England and America. Perhaps the keynote of them is her own expression: "Thy will be done is not a sigh, but only a song!"[4]

Rev. James Davidson expands on these observations in John Julian's *Dictionary of Hymnology* (1907):

> She does not occupy, and did not claim for herself, a prominent place as a poet, but by her distinct individuality she carved out a niche which she alone could fill. Simply and sweetly she sang the love of God, and His way of salvation. To this end, and for this object, her whole life and all her powers were consecrated. She lives and speaks in every line of her poetry. Her poems are permeated with the fragrance of her passionate love of Jesus.[5]

Havergal left Worcester, England, in 1860 and secured residence in Leamington, Caswall Bay, Swansea, Scotland and North Wales. She died on June 3, 1879, at the young age of forty-two. Carved on her tombstone by her own request was the text from 1 John 1:7, "The blood of Jesus Christ his Son cleanseth us from all sin."

Four influences shaped Havergal's life, culture, education, theology, understanding of doctrine, and hymn writing: Anglican home life, the

3. Havergal, *Memorials of Frances Ridley Havergal,* 26.

4. Duffield, *English Hymns*, 189–90.

5. Julian, *Dictionary of Hymnology,* 1:496.

Sunday school movement, the holiness movement, and her own deep, personal commitment to Jesus Christ.

Anglican Roots

First, Francis was nurtured and discipled in a devoted Anglican home. Her mother and father, William and Jane Havergal, were deeply pious, committed to formal education, cultural refinement, and spirituality. Francis Havergal's father, Reverend William Henry Havergal, was an Anglican pastor, musician, and composer of over one hundred hymns. Although Anglican in practice, having served one parish for more than twenty-three years, her father was deeply opposed to the teaching of rationalism and liberal theology espoused by many Anglican urban parishes of England. Robert J. Morgan clarifies William Havergal's contribution to English hymnody:

> For nearly 20 years, [Reverend Havergal] devoted his talents to the improvement of church music in England which in the 1840s was at a very low ebb. In his book, *Old Church Psalmody* (1844), he revived the use of the solid tune of early English composers and did much to improve the quality of singing. The American composer Lowell Mason, who visited his church in 1852, reported that the music [in William's parish] was far in advance of anything he heard elsewhere in England.[6]

Havergal's mother, Jane, died when Francis was only eleven. Her mother's death-bed instructions to Francis were to "pray to God to prepare you for all that He is preparing for you." This death-bed statement by her mother became Havergal's personal mission and a catalyst for her ministry all of her adult life.[7]

In August of 1850, young Francis Havergal enrolled in Mrs. Teed's School, a boarding school for young women, whose influence forever changed her life. In 1851, while at Mrs. Teed's School, she formally confessed Christ as Savior: "I committed my soul to the Saviour, and earth and heaven seemed brighter from that moment."[8]

Education opportunities as a young teenager in Dusseldorf, Germany, and Switzerland provided opportunity to study under the tutelage of the most prestigious educators of the day. While in Dusseldorf, Havergal joined

6. Morgan, "Consecrated, Lord, to Thee."
7. Goodwin, "Biographical Sketch of F. R. H."
8. Julian, *Dictionary of Hymnology*, 1:496.

in a class of 110 German-speaking students. She established deep, life-long friendships and graduated with the highest grade point average of the class.

It was in Dusseldorf where she visited an art gallery and saw Sternberg's "Ecce Homo," a striking portrayal of Christ wearing his crown of thorns before Pilate and the Jewish mob.[9] Beneath the painting were the words, "This have I done for Thee; what hast thou done for me?" Profoundly moved by this painting, Havergal was inspired to pen one of her most well-known gospel hymns, "I Gave My Life for Thee."[10]

Sunday School Movement

America and much of Great Britain experienced a great awakening of international proportions during much of Francis Havergal's childhood and early adult years. At first, evangelistic efforts of the Sunday school movement had a major impact on the American and British cultures. Publisher and printer Robert Raikes, a devoted member of the Church of England, established the first Sunday schools in Gloucester, England, during the early 1780s.[11] By 1785, William Fox had organized an official society to promote the Sunday school, which helped with the funding and creation of additional Sunday schools throughout Great Britain.[12]

With the music and worship innovations, resulting from the Sunday school movement in Great Britain and America, came a large number of Sunday school songs. Exceedingly popular with children, the primary purposes of these songs were for use in Sunday school meetings, personal or private devotions, and individual family gatherings. Ideally, the lyric and melody of the Sunday school song emphasized three phases of religious thinking: 1) the joys of heaven; 2) the love of Christ for the person singing; and 3) satisfaction gained in living the victorious Christian life. Much of Francis Havergal's early writings were devoted to and for children, and for use in the Sunday school classroom. Her devotional writings were regularly sought after and published by companies whose focus was the conversion and discipleship of children and young adolescents.

9. Julian, *Dictionary of Hymnology*, 1:496.

10. Clark, *Stories of Fadeless Hymns*, 85.

11. Willis and Barnes, "Robert Raikes," 314.

12. Willis and Barnes, "Robert Raikes," 315.

The Holiness Movement

A third and perhaps more important influence on the life of Francis Havergal was The Laymen's Prayer Awakening, sometimes known as The Layman's Prayer Revival, of 1858. The revival first began in Ireland, Scotland, Wales, and England around 1857. Pheobe Palmer was considered a key founder and "mother of the modern holiness movement."[13]

Palmer's influence was broadly impacted in the life of Havergal and hundreds of other British believers. So much so that by the end of 1859, more than one million unchurched Americans and British converted to Christ. During this era church membership rolls grew, and believers commit themselves to holy living, spiritual accountability, practicing Christian graces, and the advancement of world missions. Scores of organizations, conferences, student and adult Bible camps, and missionary agencies can trace their beginnings to this worldwide prayer movement. For example, the YMCA, the Salvation Army, the China Inland Mission, the Christian Brethren, and the Christian and Missionary Alliance were just a few of the many ministries and denominations born early in this awakening. The strong missionary emphasis of the awakening influenced C. T. Studd and his work in Africa and Hudson Taylor's work in China. The Keswick Movement for the Deepening of the Spiritual Life grew out of the revival in 1875 and in 1881, a local revival in the United States in Maine gave birth to the first Christian Endeavour Society.[14]

Personal Devotion

Lastly, Havergal's commitment to Christ was intentional, personal, and resolute. Testimony of a July 17, 1853, confirmation in her own words reads:

> On reaching our seat very near the rails, I sunk on my knees, and for the first time today the thought of "whose I am" burst upon me, and I prayed, "my God, oh, my own Father, Thou blessed Jesus my own Saviour, Thou Holy Spirit my own Comforter," and I stopped. . . . The words quickly came from my very heart; "Lord, I cannot without Thee, but oh, with Thy almighty help—I do." . . . I was the fourth or fifth on whom the bishop laid his hands. . . . When ["the chief minister"] the words "Defend, O Lord, this Thy child with Thy heavenly grace that she may continue Thine forever, and daily increase in Thy Holy Spirit

13. Galli and Olsen, *131 Christians Everyone Should Know.*

14. Towns and Porter, *Ten Greatest Revivals Ever,* 122.

> more and more until she come unto Thy everlasting kingdom" were solemnly pronounced, if ever my heart followed a prayer it did then, if ever it thrilled with earnest longing not unmixed with joy, it did at the words "Thine forever." . . . But, we returned to our seats, and for some time I wept, why I hardly know, it was not grief, nor anxiety, nor exactly joy.[15]

Havergal gave testimony that she never wrote a hymn, melody, or poem without asking for God's guidance: "I believe my King suggests a thought, and whispers to me a musical line or two, and then I look up and thank Him delightedly and go on with it. That is how my hymns come."[16]

Francis Ridley Havergal was one of the most important contributors to hymnody during the mid-nineteenth century. She wrote lyrics that were theologically profound, deeply personal in application, and devotional in purpose. During this era, she was one of a very few number of women writing hymns and gospel songs with an intentional and robust evangelical theology. During the decades surrounding and encompassing the 1840s and 1870s, "mainline" denominational leadership in England struggled with the notion of integrating popular worship innovations into their liturgies or Sunday worship routines. This disconnect created a void in expressive worship experiences by many congregants. Often congregants chose to find places for meaningful worship experiences in and through venues other than the Church of England or the Catholic parish—mostly outside the church building; which included home prayer meetings, personal or private Bible study and prayer, children's Sunday school classes, and special Bible study gatherings. In her early years, Havergal was not considered a serious hymn writer or composer by the intellectual elite. Often ignored and overlooked, critics deemed her song lyrics and music too sentimental, and for all practical purposes unsuited for the grander presentations of worship in the Anglican Church traditions. But, it was this very personal and devotional character of her songs that endeared so many "grass-rootes" worshipers to Havergal's music. In response to the popular appeal of her songs and poems, Havergal continued to write hymns, songs, poems, and devotional readings specifically targeted to the needs of people outside of the traditionally established, liturgical church. In time, her songs were accepted and often used as models of well-written prose by a broad range of Christian organizations, hymnologists, scholars, and denominations, including the Anglicans.

15. Havergal, *Memorials of Frances Ridley Havergal,* 53–55.

16. Lusher, *Songs and Hymns.*

THEOLOGICAL PERSPECTIVES

Much of the theology in Francis Havergal's hymns reflects the "deeper life" sentiments of the holiness movement and of the Laymen's Prayer Revival in particular. She strategically used her hymn writing as opportunity to proclaim, promote, explain, and expound upon the biblical doctrines of holiness. Her song-lyrics are deeply personal, devotional in intent, saturated with Scripture, theologically robust, victorious in experience, and sensitive to evangelical concerns of her context. According to James Davidson:

> Her religious views and theological bias are distinctly set forth in her poems, and may be described as mildly Calvinistic, without the severe dogmatic tenet of reprobation. The burden of her writings is a free and full salvation, through the Redeemer's merits, for every sinner who will receive it, and her life was devoted to the proclamation of this truth by personal labours, literary efforts, and earnest interest in Foreign Missions.[17]

Samuel Willoughby Duffield wrote in his *English Hymns* of Havergal's commitment to evangelical songs and hymns. "She was an evangelical rather than a High Church worker," he writes, [her lyric places emphasis on] "surrender of the will to Christ, instantaneous conversion, the life of prayer, and altruistic work."[18]

Havergal's theological interest, insight, and prowess are demonstrated by her ability to write hymns that define the full scope of Christian living. She follows the practice of Watts and the Wesley brothers by using hymns as facilitators for proclaiming biblical doctrine.[19] What follows are examples of theological teachings demonstrated in select Francis R. Havergal hymns:

Based on Ps 90:12, "Another Year is Dawning" is a prayer for the "new year," "So teach us to number our days, that we may gain a heart of wisdom."[20] Stanza one places emphasis on the sovereignty of God, his provisions and the presence of the Holy Spirit:

> 1 Another year is dawning:
> Dear Father, let it be,
> In working or in waiting,

17. Julian, *Dictionary of Hymnology*, 1:496.

18. Duffield, *English Hymns*, 189–90.

19. Julian, *Dictionary of Hymnology*, 1:496.

20. This landmark hymn, celebrating the new year, was written by Francis R. Havergal in 1874 for Caswell Publishing. Havergal was careful to ensure her emphasis on God's providential guidance for the new year was adhered to by the editors and publishers

Another year with Thee;
Another year of progress,
Another year of praise,
Another year of proving
Thy presence all the days.

Stanza two draws the singer's attention to yet another doctrine important to the Christian community, the mercies, faithfulness, and grace of God:

2 Another year of mercies,
Of faithfulness and grace;
Another year of gladness
In the shining of Thy face;
Another year of leaning
Upon Thy loving breast;
Another year of trusting,
Of quiet, happy rest.

Stanza three places emphasis upon the doctrines of service, discipleship, and total surrender to God in all that is done:

3 Another year of service,
Of witness for Thy love;
Another year of training
For holier work above,
Another year is dawning;
Dear Father, let it be,
On earth or else in heaven,
Another year for Thee.

"Golden Harps Are Sounding" is one of a very few hymns written for the Christian Church about the ascension of Christ and the unique ministry he has to believers while in heaven. Originally written for inclusion in the *Day Spring Magazine* and *Day of Days* in May 1872 as an "Ascension Hymn for Children," stanza one expounds upon the doctrine of Jesus' ascension in Acts 1:8 and exalted ministry at the right hand of the Father in Acts 5:30–31 and Heb 1:

Golden harps are sounding, angel voices ring,
Pearly gates are opened, opened for the King:
Christ, the King of glory, Jesus, King of love,
Is gone up in triumph to his throne above.

Refrain:
All His work is ended, joyfully we sing:

Jesus hath ascended: Glory to our King!

Stanza two articulates the doctrine of Christ as the Lamb of God as recorded in Rev 4 and 5:

He who came to save us, he who bled and died,
Now is crowed with glory at His Father's side.
Nevermore to suffer, nevermore to die,
Jesus, King of glory, is gone up on high.

Stanza three deals with the doctrine of Jesus as our intercessor and high priest as articulated in the Book of Hebrews. Additional attention is given to the doctrines regarding heaven and promised by Jesus: "I go to prepare a place for you" (John 14:3):

Praying for his children in that blessed place,
Calling them to glory, sending them his grace;
His bright home preparing, faithful ones for you:
Jesus ever liveth, ever loveth too.[21]

According to John Julian, author of *The Dictionary of Hymnology*, this "Ascension Hymn for Children" attained great popularity in the United States during the later part of the nineteenth and early part of the twentieth centuries. Frances Havergal wrote both text and tune (HERMAS) in 1871.[22]

"I Gave My Life For Thee" was written on January 10, 1858, in Dusseldorf, Germany, after looking at a painting of Jesus wearing a crown of thorns. Under the painting was the phrase: "I did this for thee, what hast thou done for me?" Ms. Havergal was so moved by the statement that she wrote the lyric to "I Gave My Life for Thee" in first person, as if Christ was making the case for his disciples to give back to him their lives in service. Stanzas one, three, four, and five below appear in most hymnals. Havergal, however, wrote six stanzas, each dealing with an aspect of God's gift of salvation and the Christian disciple's commitment to lifetime service. The hymn essentially covers the entire scope of the Savior's sacrifice, providing salvation for the entire world. Doctrines dealt with include those of salvation, incarnation, forgiveness, heaven, hell, God's love, and Christian service. What follows are the original six stanzas with scriptural support as provided by the hymnwriter herself:[23]

1 I gave My life for thee,	Gal 2:20
My precious blood I shed,	1 Pet 1:19

21. *Trinity Hymnal*, 310.
22. Julian, *Dictionary of Hymnology*, 1:441.
23. Goodwin, "Biographical Sketch of F. R. H."

That thou might'st ransomed be,	Eph 1:7
And quickened from the dead;	Eph 2:1
I gave, I gave My life for thee,	Titus 2:14
What hast thou giv'n for Me?	John 21:15–17
2 I spent long years for thee	1 Tim 1:15
in weariness and woe,	Isa 53:3
That one eternity	John 17:24
Of joy thou mightiest know	John 16:22
I spent long years for thee;	John 1:10, 11
Hast thou spent one for me?	1 Pet 4:2
3 My Father's house of light,	John 17:5
My glory circled throne,	Rev 4:3
I left for earthly night,	Phil 2:7
For wanderings sad and lone;	Matt 8:20
I left, I left it all for thee,	2 Cor 8:9
Hast thou left aught for Me?	Luke 10:29
4 I suffered much for thee,	Isa 53:5
More than thy tongue can tell,	Matt 26:39
Of bitt'rest agony,	Luke 22:44
To rescue thee from hell;	Rom 5:9
I've borne, I've borne it all for thee,	1 Pet 2:21–24
What hast thou borne for Me?	Rom 8:17,18
5 And I have brought to thee,	John 4:10, 14
Down from My home above,	John 3:13
Salvation full and free,	Rev 21:6
My pardon and My love;	Acts 5:31
I bring, I bring rich gifts to thee,	Ps 68:18
What hast thou brought to Me?	Rom 12:1
6 Oh, let thy life be given,	Rom 6:13
Thy years for me be spent	2 Cor 5:15
World fetters all be riven,	Phil 3:8
And joy with suffering blent,	1 Pet 4:13–16
I gave, I gave Myself for thee,	Eph 5:2
Give thou thyself to me.	Prov 23:26[24]

At first, the intellectually elite and those practicing a liturgical approach to worship leveled significant criticism toward the emphasis of the lyric, deeming it inappropriate for the author to write the lyric, "I gave my life for thee," in the first person. A recasting of the hymn was published for the Society for Promoting Christian Knowledge in *Church Hymns*

24. Goodwin, "Biographical Sketch of F. R. H."

(1871) so that the lyric begins, "Thy life was given for me." The recast never gained popularity in Great Britain or the United States. Even so, it was adopted by the Moravian, Presbyterian, Anglican, Catholic, and Episcopal denominations.[25]

Recasted Lyric:

1 Thy life was given for me!
Thy blood, O Lord, was shed
That I might ransomed be,
And quickened from the dead.
Thy life was given for me:
What have I given for Thee?
Thy life was given for me:
What have I given for Thee?

2 Long years were spent for me
In weariness and woe,
That through eternity
Long years were spent for me:
Have I spent one for Thee?
Thy glory I might know.
Long years were spent for me:
Have I spent one for Thee?[26]

Original Lyric

1 I gave My life for thee,
My precious blood I shed,
That thou might'st ransomed be,
And quickened from the dead;
I gave, I gave My life for thee,
What hast thou giv'n for Me?
I gave, I gave My life for thee,
What hast thou giv'n for Me?

2 I spent long years for thee
in weariness and woe,
That one eternity
Of joy thou mightiest
I spent long years for thee;
Hast thou spent one for me?
I spent long years for thee;
Hast thou spent one for me?

"Like a River Glorious" is a treatise on the benefits of "trusting in the *peace* of God." Using a series of metaphors to communicate the benefits of resting in God's everlasting peace, the author lays a solid foundation for understanding the "Joy of trusting God with all one's life." Ps 37:1–8, 23–26; Ps 46:1–4; Isa 66:12–14a; Col 3:15; and Phil 4:7 support the theology that the "Peace of God" is afforded those committed to trusting in God.

Stanza one promises a growing, perfect, deeper, and victorious relationship with God through his peace:

1 Like a river glorious
Is God's perfect peace,
Over all victorious,
In its bright increase;
Perfect, yet it floweth
Fuller every day;
Perfect, yet it groweth

25. Julian, *Dictionary of Hymnology*, 1:556.

26. *Hymnal*, 1889.

Deeper all the way.

Refrain:
Stayed upon Jehovah,
Hearts are fully blest—
Finding, as He promised,
Perfect peace and rest.

Stanza two promises strength for the day, protection, and a settled spirit through God's perfect peace:

2 Hidden in the hollow
Of His blessed hand,
Never foe can follow,
Never traitor stand;
Not a surge of worry,
Not a shade of care,
Not a blast of hurry—
Touch the Spirit there. [Refrain]

Stanza three designates "God's Peace" as the source of all joy, trial, and comfort:

3 Every joy or trial
Falleth from above,
Traced upon our dial
By the Sun of Love;
We may trust Him fully
All for us to do;
They who trust Him wholly
Find Him wholly true. [Refrain][27]

Frances Havergal is perhaps best known as author of the hymn "Take My Life and Let it Be." Written on February 4, 1874, as a *hymn of self-consecration to Christ*, it has been called a "catalog hymn" in that the writer lists different aspects of her life and offers them to Jesus Christ for use in Christian service. To some, this hymn of Christian commitment is on the level of "Just As I Am" or "I Surrender All." The lyric embodies the scriptural principles of Isa 6:8, Phil 1:20–21; Rom 12:1–2; Mark 10:17–22; and Luke 21:2–3. Each stanza articulates Havergal's personal commitment to give back to God:

27. Additional Scripture documenting the "Peace of God": Ps 17:8; 27:5; 32:7; 37:24; 46:4; 143:9; Isa 26:3; 38:18; 40:12; 48:18; 49:16; 66:17; John 14:27; 1 Cor 1:9; Phil 4:7; Heb 13:20; 1 Pet 1:6.

In stanza one, she offers God her life and days:

1 Take my life and let it be
consecrated, Lord, to thee.
Take my moments and my days;
let them flow in endless praise,
let them flow in endless praise.

In stanza two, she offers God her hands and feet:

2 Take my hands and let them move
at the impulse of thy love.
Take my feet and let them be
swift and beautiful for thee,
swift and beautiful for thee.

In stanza three, she offers God her voice and lips (speech):

3 Take my voice and let me sing
always, only, for my King.
Take my lips and let them be
filled with messages from thee,
filled with messages from thee.

In stanza four, she offers God her silver, gold, and intellect:

4 Take my silver and my gold;
not a mite would I withhold.
Take my intellect and use
every power as thou shalt choose,
every power as thou shalt choose.

In stanza five, she offers God her will and heart:

5 Take my will and make it thine;
it shall be no longer mine.
Take my heart it is thine own;
it shall be thy royal throne,
it shall be thy royal throne.

In stanza six, she offers God her love and herself (her whole being):

6 Take my love; my Lord, I pour
at thy feet its treasure store.
Take myself, and I will be
ever, only, all for thee,
ever, only, all for thee.

"Who is on the Lord's Side?" was written in 1877 and reflects the truth of Exod 32:26 ("Whoever *is* on the Lord's side—*come* to me!"), Josh 24:15 (choose for yourselves this day whom you will serve. . . . But as for me and my house, we will serve the Lord."), and Matt 12:30 (He who is not with Me is against Me, and he who does not gather with Me scatters abroad). The lyric is a call to action and a documentation of a variety of Christian doctrines, including:

A call for commitment to Christ in stanza one:

> 1 Who is on the Lord's side?
> Who will serve the King?
> Who will be His helpers,
> Other lives to bring?
> Who will leave the world's side?
> Who will face the foe?
> Who for Him will go?
> By Thy call of mercy,
> By Thy grace Divine;
> We are on the Lord's side,
> Savior, we are Thine.

A sovereign call for discipleship to Christ in stanza two:

> 2 Not for weight of glory,
> Not for crown and palm,
> Enter we the army,
> Raise the warrior psalm;
> But for love that claimeth
> Lives for whom He died;
> He whom Jesus nameth
> Must be on His side.
> By Thy love constraining,
> By Thy grace Divine,
> We are on the Lord's side,
> Savior, we are Thine.

Gods plan for atonement, Holy Spirit filling and redemption in stanza three:

> 3 Jesus, Thou hast bought us,
> Not with gold or gem,
> But with Thine own life-blood,
> For Thy diadem:
> With Thy blessing filling
> Each who comes to Thee,

Thou hast made us willing,
Thou hast made us free.
By Thy grand redemption,
By Thy grace Divine,
We are on the Lord's side,
Savior, we are Thine.

Victory through Christ and Christian warfare:

4 Fierce may be the conflict,
Strong may be the foe,
But the King's own army
None can overthrow:
Round His standard ranging,
Victory is secure;
For His truth unchanging
Makes the triumph sure.
Joyfully enlisting,
By Thy grace Divine,
We are on the Lord's side,
Savior, we are Thine.

A commitment to providential selection for service, grace, and divinity of Christ in stanza five:

5 Chosen to be soldiers
In an alien land,
Chosen, called and faithful,
For our Captain's band;
In the service royal
Let us not grow cold,
Let us be right loyal,
Noble, true and bold:
Master, Thou wilt keep us,
By Thy grace Divine,
Always on the Lord's side,
Savior, Always Thine.

Interestingly, stanza five is not included in most hymnals and the hymn is sung by every major denomination in America.

CONTRIBUTION TO LITURGY AND WORSHIP

Most, if not all, of Havergal's hymns focus on dedication, offering, commitment, ordination or commissioning, profession of faith, holiness, victorious Christian living, or anniversary of a church or congregation. Six observations summarize Havergal's contributions to hymnody and worship: 1) her lyrics are optimistic, deeply personal, and devotional; 2) her hymns are decisively theological in content; 3) her emphasis consistently includes hymns on holiness, surrender, and victorious living; 4) her hymns reflect a spirit of serving Christ, trusting Christ in all things, and acknowledging the faithfulness of Christ to "the church"; 5) her lyric expounds upon and explains a spirit of seeking and finding; and 6) her lyric, especially those written in the last decade of her life, give strong emphasis to personal commitment, surrender to the working of the Holy Spirit in one's life, and world missions.

NOTABLE HYMNS

According to hymnologist John Julian, Francis Havergal's hymns have been translated into scores of other languages, including: French, German, Swedish, and Russian, as well as other European, African, and Asian languages.[28] Nearly one hundred hymns and seven books written by Francis Havergal have been published. Several were published after her death in 1879 by family and/or music publishers desiring to honor her contribution to hymnody.[29] The popular hymnal *Songs of Grace and Glory* (1873) incorporated 1,100 hymns with music. Fifty-five of these were authored by Havergal, and twenty more are attributed to her father, Reverend W. H. Havergal. John Julian also included fifty-five Havergal hymns in his *Dictionary of Hymnology.*

Her songs were used extensively in Moody/Sankey campaigns and immediately enjoyed popularity at the Kewsick Conference in Kewsick, England. Of the many songs used in the Moody-Sankey meetings,[30] she is best

28. Julian, *Dictionary of Hymnology,* 2:11–14.

29 According to Julian's *Dictionary of Hymnology*, Havergal's more than one hundred hymns were originally published in leaflets and later gathered into seven collections: *Ministry of Song* (1869), *Twelve Sacred Songs for Little Singers* (1870), *Under the Surface* (1874), *Loyal Responses* (1878), *Life Mosaic* (1879), *Life Chords* (1880), and *Life Echoes* (1883), as well as in one large volume, *Poetical Works* (1884).

30. The following are the most familiar of the more than one hundred hymns and songs by Frances Havergal: "All Thy Days Thy Strength Shall Be," "Another Year is Dawning," "God Will Take Care of You," "Golden Harps Are Sounding," "The Half Has Never Been Told," "I Am Trusting Thee, Lord Jesus," "I Bring My Sins to Thee," "I Could Not Do Without Thee," "I Gave My Life For Thee," "Is It for Me?," "Jesus, Blessed Savior," "Jesus, Master, Whose I Am," "Like a River Glorious," "Lord, Speak to Me," "Master,

remembered for "Take My Life and Let It Be," "Lord Speak to Me," "Like a River Glorious," "I Gave My Life for Thee," "Another Year is Dawning," and "Who Is On the Lord's Side?"[31]

Havergal's hymns are included in hymnals representing every major denomination and Christian movement from 1860 through 2010. There is evidence that her songs are sung by a broad spectrum of the Christian community. For example, "Another Year is Dawning" is included in at least 149 hymnals. Her ascension hymn, "Golden Harps Are Sounding," is included in no less than 224 hymnals, followed by "I Am Trusting Thee, Lord Jesus," which is published in 261 hymn books. Her hymn documenting the promised peace of God, "Like a River Glorious," is included in at least 121 hymnals, and "Lord, Speak to Me" is in 368 songbooks and hymnals. "True-hearted, Whole-hearted" is included 233 hymn books, "Who is on the Lord's Side?" is in 367 hymnals, and "Precious Blood of Jesus" is in sixty-six books. By far, the two hymns for which she is best known are "I Gave My Life For Thee" and her consecration hymn "Take My Life and Let it Be"; the former is included in 427 hymnals while the later is included in at least 987 hymn books.

BIBLIOGRAPHY

Clark, Thornburn. *Stories of Fadeless Hymns*. Nashville: Broadman, 1949.

Duffield, Samuel Willoughby. *English Hymns: Their Authors and History*. London: Funk and Wagnals Company, 1894.

Galli, Mark, and Ted Olsen, eds. *131 Christians Everyone Should Know*. Nashville: Broadman & Holman, 2000.

Goodwin, Sherry. "A Biographical Sketch of F. R. H." Havergal Trust. http://www.havergaltrust.com/about-f-r-h/2/.

Havergal, Maria V. G. *Memorials of Frances Ridley Havergal*. New York: E. P. Dutton & Company, 1892.

Speak! Thy Servant Heareth," "O Master at Thy Feet," "O Savior, Precious Savior," "Sit Down Beneath His Shadow," "Standing at the Portal," "Precious, Precious Blood of Jesus," "Take My Life and Let it Be," "Tell it Out Among the Heathen," "Thou Art Coming, O My Savior," "True-hearted, Whole-hearted," "Welcome, Happy Morning" (Music only), and "Who Is on the Lord's Side?"

31. Francis Havergal hymns are included in scores of denominational and non-denominational song books. What follows is a list of select denominational and non-denominational books: *Celebrating Grace: Hymnal for Baptist Worship* (2010) includes three hymns; *Baptist Hymnal* (2008) includes five hymns; *The Celebration Hymnal: Songs and Hymns for Worship* (1997) includes seven hymns; *The Rejoice Hymnal: For the Church at Worship* (1995) includes eight hymns.

The Hymnal: Revised and Enlarged as Adopted by the General Convention of the Protestant Episcopal Church in the United States of America in 1892. James Pott & Co, 1889.

Julian, John, ed. *A Dictionary of Hymnology: Setting Forth the Origin and History of Christian Hymns of All Ages and Nations*. Vols. 1–2. New York: Dover, 1907.

Lusher, Paul. *Songs and Hymns: Frances Havergal*. Grand Haven, MI: Center for Church Music.

Morgan, Robert J. "Consecrated, Lord, to Thee: The Life of Frances Ridley Havergal." Nashville: Unpublished Article, 1984.

Towns, Elmer, and Douglas Porter. *The Ten Greatest Revivals Ever: From Pentecost to the Present*. Ventura, CA: Vine Books, 2000.

Trinity Hymnal. Rev. ed. Suwanee, GA: Great Commission, 1990.

Whaley, Vernon M., ed. *The Rejoice Hymnal: For the Church at Worship*. Nashville: NAFWB, 1995

Willis, Roderick C., and L. Philip Barnes. "Robert Raikes: Author of the Sunday School Movement." In *A Legacy of Religious Educators*, edited by Elmer L. Towns and Benjamin K. Forrest, 305–21. Lynchburg, VA: Liberty University Press, 2016.

Part 8

Twentieth Century

Chapter 7

Standard and Emerging Idioms in Britain and the United States

E. Byron Anderson

HISTORICAL BACKGROUND

What has often been called the hymn explosion, or "new English renaissance," of the late 1960s[1] has shaped a generation and more of denominational hymnals and given birth to the production of many single-author collections in Britain and the United States. There was no one thing that led to this renaissance of hymn-writing. Rather, it was sourced by a confluence of several concerns. One set of concerns included a changing worldview, including a growing unease with the comfort, security, and confidence that seemed to characterize the post-war period of the 1950s in the United States and Britain after the destruction and losses experienced during World War 2; the "shrinking of the world" through the rise of mass communications; the ability to see the world in all its beauty from space, and the growing awareness of our destruction of that beauty;[2] and the "expansion" of our

1. Music, *Christian Hymnody*, 3.

2. As Janet Wootton writes, "By the end of the decade, the world had seen itself from the depths of space, and the fragility of the planet was becoming evident." (Wootton, *This Is Our* Song, 171.)

worldview as countries attained their independence and celebrated their own traditions, languages, and arts.

A second set of concerns reflected changes within the church itself: the completion of contemporary English translations of the Bible, especially the American Revised Standard Version (completed in 1971) and the British New English Bible (completed in 1970) and, parallel to these translations, concerns about archaic and exclusive language in the churches' prayers and songs; the ecumenical liturgical renewal and reform after the Second Vatican Council, which led to renewed attention to the church year and the adoption of common lectionaries; a changing understanding of the church as part of a global community; and the awareness that the emergence of and attention to new theological and social concerns required expression in the churches' song. As Paul Westermeyer has noted, it was not so much that the new theological and social themes were completely absent from earlier hymnals published in the United States and Britain in the 1950s and early 1960s. Rather, these themes, especially those related to social justice and service, had not received the attention now required in a changing social landscape and "did not have the proportions or attractions of gospel hymnody."[3] These earlier hymnals, "like the products of every culture, reflected the period's blind spots."[4] They were, musically and theologically, "traditional." Missing from the church's song were hymns that expressed "contemporary doubts (and, at its best, their resolutions), contemporary hesitations (and, at its best, penitence), and contemporary observation (and, at its best, concreteness)."[5]

Numerous accounts of the English hymn-writing explosion focus on the influence of a series of consultations and informal meetings "held at the ecumenical Scottish Churches House in Dunblane, Scotland, between 1961 and 1969" and which "sought to meet current needs with contemporary hymnody that maintained theological integrity."[6] Alan Luff describes the consultations as bringing together "an ecumenical cross section of clergy, ministers, and musicians 'to take a radical look at Church music'" of the day. They came with the expectation "that new hymns not only needed to be written but could be written."[7] As Luff claims, "The new language of Scripture and liturgy, and our changed beliefs and attitudes about God, the

3. Westermeyer, "Current Theological Trends," 43.

4. Westermeyer, *With Tongues of Fire*, 20.

5. Routley, *Panorama*, 470.

6. Music, *Christian Hymnody*, 3. See especially Fraser, "Beginnings at Dunblane"; Luff, "Twentieth-Century Hymn Explosion"; and Routley's account in *Panorama*, 398.

7. Luff, "Twentieth-Century Hymn Explosion," 11.

church, and the world" required new forms of expression in song,[8] hymns that, for Brian Wren, were "in touch with our time, and in tune with God's timing" while also being "designed for the present time, using metaphors, slogans, and allusions current at the time of writing."[9]

Although the specific products of the Dunblane consultations, including hymns by Erik Routley, Brian Wren, and Fred Pratt Green, were not taken up in British hymnal revisions of the early 1970s. Luff suggests that the influence of these consultations came through "the ferment [they] tried to arouse" and the collaborative spirit and support provided for thinking about congregational song and the need for new texts and tunes.[10] From Routley's perspective, publication of this work in hymnal supplements rather than denominational hymnals made possible "wider exploration and experimentation without the repertoire or economic commitments required of a hymnal revision."[11]

Five prominent hymn-writers whose work emerged from this English renaissance are Erik Routley (1917–82), Fred Pratt Green (1903–2000), Fred Kaan (1929–2009), Timothy Dudley-Smith (b. 1926), and Brian Wren (b. 1936).

Erik Routley served primarily as a "scholar, critic, and encourager" of others.[12] He served in ministry in the Congregational Church from 1943–74, then moved to the United States to become professor of church music at Westminster Choir College. While a hymn-writer, Routley is known more for his writing about hymns. His two volumes *A Panorama of Christian Hymnody* (1979), surveying the history of hymn texts, and *The Music of Christian Hymns* (1981), surveying the history of hymn tunes, provide a comprehensive overview of the history of congregational song. He explored the theological implications of music in worship in his early book *The Church and Music* (1950) and *Church Music and the Christian Faith* (1978).[13] He served as editor of *The Bulletin of the Hymn Society of Great Britain and Ireland* from 1948–74, of the Dunblane collections, and of several hymnals including *Congregational Praise* (1951), *Cantate Domino* (World Council of Churches, 1974), and *Rejoice in the Lord* (Reformed Church in America, 1985). He consistently described hymns as "a kind of song . . . for unmusical people to sing . . . a kind of poetry . . . as unliterary people can utter

8. Luff, "Twentieth-Century Hymn Explosion," 20.

9. Wren, *Praying Twice*, 281.

10. Luff, "Twentieth-Century Hymn Explosion," 15.

11. Routley, *Panorama*, 397.

12. Routley, *Panorama*, 471.

13. See Westermeyer, *Tongues of Fire*, 110.

together."[14] Although his hymn texts, tunes, and other compositions are not as well-known as his other work, he wrote thirty-four hymn texts and ninety-eight hymn tunes. One of his first and best-known texts, "All who love and serve your city," demonstrates his skill with verse and his ability to shape a hymn with homiletic intent. His tune "Sharpthorne," composed to Albert Bayley's "What does the Lord require," demonstrates his ability to shape a tune readily sung by even "unmusical people."

Fred Pratt Green served as a British Methodist pastor and superintendent from 1924–69. Although he had written poetry and plays throughout his life, most of his hymn writing occurred after his retirement, with many hymns written at the specific request of individuals, congregations, or hymnal editors. As with others inspired by the work at Dunblane, he understood his responsibility as a hymn-writer to address the "insights and needs of the time" in the language of the day.[15] He believed, as he stated in an interview with Paul Westermeyer, that hymns should "inspire a congregation to worship; instruct a congregation in Christian truth and practice; and help unite Christians of various denominations."[16] To this end, his concern as a hymn-writer focused on "the practical application and expression of our faith than with theological controversy."[17]

Fred Kaan, though born in The Netherlands, was ordained and served in the United Reformed Church in Britain as a pastor from 1955–68, followed by appointments to international positions with the World Alliance of Reformed Churches from 1968–78, and as moderator in the United Reformed Church from 1978–85.[18] Kaan became a hymn-writer in the 1960s to better serve his congregations, frustrated by what he described as the "remote symbolism, antiquated terminology, and socially unacceptable nature of what was on offer in hymnody."[19] Kaan suggests that the work of the contemporary hymn-writer is that of a "preacher-poet" who, "as a member of, and debtor to, the 'beloved community,' lives under a life-long obligation to try and articulate afresh—both in the realm of spirituality and of activism—what the contemporary Christian experience is all about, to sing the faith (inviting others to sing along with him/her), to rejoice in Christian

14. Routley, *Christian Hymns Observed*, 1.
15. Westermeyer, *Tongues of Fire*, 88.
16. Westermeyer, *Tongues of Fire*, 87.
17. Westermeyer, *Tongues of Fire*, 86.
18. Westermeyer, *Tongues of Fire*, 93.
19. Westermeyer, *Tongues of Fire*, 101.

doctrine, and constantly to translate and implement what he/she hears and sees, tastes, touches, and smells."[20]

Brian Wren also served as a pastor in the United Reformed Church early in his career, followed by positions with the Churches Committee on World Development and Third World First. After 1983, he became a free-lance hymn-writer and workshop leader in Britain and the United States. He moved permanently to the United States in 1991 and served as professor of worship at Columbia Theological Seminary from 2000–2007. Wren's first hymns were published in *Dunblane Praises* (1964). In two major books, *What Language Shall I Borrow—God-Talk in Worship* (1989) and *Praying Twice: The Music and Words of Congregational Song* (2000), Wren explored the power and problems of liturgical language, both spoken and sung. His hymns demonstrate an ability to bring together the personal and communal, offering a realistic view of daily life with its joys and its sorrows and of Christ's presence throughout the whole of human life.[21] Perhaps more so than other writers of this period, Wren continued to revise his earlier work as his ideas evolved and changed. In some cases, hymns were repeatedly revised ("Christ is alive! Let Christians sing," written in 1968, was revised in 1978, 1989, and 1993) and others withdrawn.[22] Wren's hymns have received wide publication in hymnals of the past generation.

Timothy Dudley-Smith is the only Anglican among this group of hymn-writers. He was ordained a priest in 1951, served as Archdeacon of Norwich (1973–81), Bishop of Thetford (1981–91), and retired in 1992.[23] Dudley-Smith locates himself toward the conservative end of the evangelical tradition in the Church of England, claiming "a high view of the authority of Scripture, and that from the inwardness of true religion and the search for personal holiness there comes Christian social concern for love and justice towards my neighbor."[24] He believed that hymns should "relate to the objective truths of the faith with our subjective response."[25] Dudley-Smith was part of "Jubilate Hymns," a group of evangelical Anglican hymn-writers that included Christopher Idle (b. 1938) and Michael Perry (1942–96).[26] Their publications included *Youth Praise* (1966), *Psalm Praise* (1973), and *Hymns for Today's Church* (1982).

20. Kaan, *Hymn Texts*, xv.
21. Routley, *Panorama*, 471.
22. Routley, *Panorama*, 470.
23. "Timothy Dudley-Smith," http://www.timothydudley-smith.com.
24. Westermeyer, *Tongues of Fire*, 46.
25. Westermeyer, *Tongues of Fire*, 47.
26. Music, *Christian Hymnody*, 4.

The above narrative may suggest that only men were involved in the British hymn renaissance; more, the repertoire of new hymns published in denominational hymnals of the past forty years seems to confirm this. However, as Janet Wootton notes, women writers "were finding publication . . . in resources arising from women's worship groups or consciously inclusive communities."[27] While writers such as Wren and Kaan were increasingly sensitive to women's experiences and narratives as well as to concerns for inclusive imagery of and language about humanity and God, Wootton notes that "a new and different kind of language, imagery and theology was emerging . . . a true inclusivity . . . [but] it took a further generation, and the emergence of second-wave feminism before the human experience of women was accepted as valid material for worship and hymnody."[28] Among this group of women writers are Janet Wootton (b. 1952), with hymns such as "Dear Mother God, your wings are warm around us" and "With Miriam we will dance"; June Boyce-Tillman (b. 1943) and her increasingly familiar text "We shall go out with hope of resurrection"; Elizabeth Cosnett (b. 1936) with "Can we by searching find out God"; and Marjorie Dobson (b. 1940), who considers "Birth brings a promise of new life awaking" one of her best hymns.

The hymn-writing renaissance in England influenced a similar, though slightly later and more widespread, development in the United States. It was more widespread, Routley notes, because production of new hymnals in the United States preceded those in Britain.[29] British influence on US hymn-writers also built on what Russell Schulz-Widmar describes as a shared common language, agreement about the "most fundamental Christian concerns and aspirations," and agreement about "how to realize those concerns and aspirations in words and music."[30] US hymn-writers who came to prominence during the 1980s and 1990s and have produced a significant body of imaginative Christian hymnody include Carl P. Daw Jr. (b. 1944), Ruth Duck (b. 1947), Jane Parker Huber (1926–2008), Thomas H. Troeger (b. 1945), and Jaroslav Vajda (1919–2008), among others. They, like those in the British hymn-writing renaissance, have sought to express themselves "in contemporary English" and to address contemporary social and religious concerns, often from the perspectives of late twentieth-century theological movements such as liberation, feminist, and ecological theology. And, like their British colleagues, they have also often engaged a renewed

27. Wootton, *This Is Our song*, x.

28. Wootton, *This Is Our song*, 194.

29. Routley, *Panorama*, 535.

30. Schulz-Widmar, "Hymn Renaissance," 191.

emphasis on the church year and the common lectionary (especially evident in the hymns of Daw and Troeger).[31] As Paul Westermeyer says of all the hymn-writers he profiles in *With Tongues of Fire*, their work reflects "a deep commitment to the world they live in, to its problems and needs, and to its people."[32]

With a PhD in English Literature, *Carl Daw*, an Episcopal priest, served as a consultant to the *Hymnal 1982* committee for the Episcopal Church in the United States and then as secretary and chair of the Standing Committee on Church Music of the Episcopal Church. He was executive director of the Hymn Society in the United States and Canada from 1996 to 2009. It was through the process of "working with the theology and language of hymns" for the *Hymnal 1982* that he began to write hymns himself.[33] His background in literature and theology provides him with "a keen awareness of biblical, historical, liturgical, and literary precedents,"[34] enabling him to develop "skillful paraphrases of biblical and liturgical texts"[35] as well as commentary on the shape of liturgy itself.

Ruth Duck has been one of the most prolific of contemporary hymn-writers in the United States, and certainly the most well-published woman hymn-writer of this generation. An ordained pastor in the United Church of Christ, she served on the liturgical studies faculty of Garrett-Evangelical Theological Seminary from 1989–2016. Duck notes that "advocacy for justice for women in the Church was the impetus for [her] first hymn-writing."[36] Her hymn texts often come from her own search to provide honest expression of her experiences and to connect those experiences with sensory images. Throughout her work has been a concern for inclusive language in worship, attention to the skillful shaping of the language of prayer as well as song, and a desire to develop and use "a variety of gender-connected images" for God.[37]

Jane Parker Huber was a Presbyterian laywoman who served on the committee for *The Presbyterian Hymnal* (1990). Throughout her life and work, she emphasized peacemaking, justice, inclusiveness, and the

31. Music, *Christian Hymnody*, 4.

32. Westermeyer, *Tongues of Fire*, 183.

33. Westermeyer, *Tongues of Fire*, 29.

34. Routley, *Panorama*, 540.

35. Routley, *Panorama*, 540.

36. Duck, in Wootton, *This Is Our Song*, 263.

37. Routley, *Panorama*, 541. In addition to Duck's hymns, see her book *Finding Words for Worship*.

"mutuality of men and women in ministry."[38] The fact that she consciously wrote her texts to fit tunes familiar to American Presbyterian congregations has helped fifty of her hymns find publication in recent hymnals.

Thomas Troeger served as a Presbyterian pastor from 1970–1977, followed by appointments as a teacher of preaching and parish ministry at Colgate Rochester Divinity School, Iliff School of Theology, and Yale University Divinity School. Troeger often takes a homiletic approach to his hymn-writing, combining insights from biblical scholarship with an "ability to maintain and manipulate an image or metaphor across multiple stanzas."[39] Throughout his writing he has sought to help interpret "what it means to be Christian in a global community" and to interpret the Christian faith "to a culture that is not easily able to grasp its meaning."[40] As a musician, Troeger especially understands the ability of music to interpret a text. This is perhaps most evident in the two collections he developed with Carol Doran—*New Hymns for the Lectionary* (1986) and *New Hymns for the Life of the Church* (1992).

A final representative of this group is *Jaroslav Vajda*. A Lutheran pastor, editor, and hymn-writer, Vajda sought to write as a "confessional Lutheran." "The hymn," he claimed, is "an honest confession of faith . . . a public response to God's 'mighty acts' and grace. It grows out of contemporary circumstances and takes on contemporary yet reverent language."[41] Scott Hyslop notes that his work was "primarily intended for liturgical proclamation—by the person in the pew—and contains many of the didactic qualities of Luther's writing."[42] Vajda's hymns are distinctive for their creative musical forms and their "unusual and irregular poetic meters."[43] Vajda is also known for his translations of Slavic hymns.

THEOLOGICAL PERSPECTIVES

As noted above, hymn-writing during this British and American renaissance has been shaped by the need for contemporary and inclusive language in worship, prayer, and song; changing sociocultural concerns and a changing worldview that emerged from a reshaped world order after the experiences

38. Routley, *Panorama*, 538.
39. Routley, *Panorama*, 539.
40. Westermeyer, *Tongues of Fire*, 132.
41. Westermeyer, *Tongues of Fire*, 148.
42. Hyslop, "Now the Joyful Celebration," 29.
43. Hyslop, "Now the Joyful Celebration," 29.

of Auschwitz and Hiroshima, Vietnam and South Africa;[44] new theological concerns, such as care for the environment and changing understandings of various social/cultural practices; and a desire to be both "prophetic and pastoral"[45] in ways that both reflect the faith of the church and enable it to find new ways to express that faith.[46]

Contemporary and Inclusive Language. Brian Wren notes in *What Language Shall I Borrow* the growing cultural awareness that "though language does not determine how we think, it shapes and slants thinking and behavior."[47] This awareness led to the desire by some to "demythologize" theological and liturgical language, with a stress on speaking "more directly in the concrete terms of the here and now, rather than in the imagery of the postponed hereafter."[48] At the same time, this awareness challenged the social and linguistic patriarchal norms of modern Western culture, calling for experiments in naming and praising God that, in Brian Wren's words, are "less idolatrous [in their patriarchy], more freeing, and more true to the Triune God and the direction of love in the Anointed One, Jesus" that are, at the same time, faithful to the biblical witness.[49] Wren's hymn "Bring Many Names" provides one example. In the few words of the second stanza—"strong mother God, working night and day, planning all the wonders of creation, setting each equation, genius at play"—Wren reverses social images of women as the "weaker sex" and emphasizes the intellectual giftedness of women, all the while drawing on the image of Wisdom in Proverbs. With the next stanza—"warm, father God, hugging every child, feeling all the strains of human living, caring and forgiving till we're reconciled"[50]—he reverses images of men as strong and emotionally detached. In Ruth Duck's hymn "Womb of life" the invitation to new birth found in John 3 prompts an image of God as "womb of life and source of being." She follows this with "Word in flesh, our brother Jesus," "Brooding Spirit . . . partner . . . friend" before juxtaposing "Mother, Brother, Holy Partner" with "Father, Spirit, Only Son."[51]

Changing Worldview. The unsettled days of the 1960s, as well as the years since, tempered the optimism of the early twentieth-century social

44. Westermeyer, "Current Theological Trends," 44.
45. Schulz-Widmar, "Hymn Renaissance,"196.
46. Kaan, quoted in Schulz-Widmar, "Hymn Renaissance," 222.
47. Wren, *What Language*, 3.
48. Leaver, "British Hymnody," 561.
49. Wren, *What Language*, 2.
50. Wren, *Piece Together Praise*, 173.
51. Duck, *Dancing in the Universe*, 17.

gospel movement and called for congregational song that is more honest about the world and its peoples, their suffering as well as their joy, our differences and our unity, songs that "embodied a social consciousness about justice."[52] This change in worldview calls for new words and new songs that better express concerns for suffering and justice and that give voice to the worldwide character of the church and the Christian community, rather than seeing the world simply as an object of missionary activity. Fred Kaan's hymn "For the healing of the nations" was an early example of these concerns and remains prominent in many hymnals:

For the healing of the nations,
Lord, pray with one accord;
for a just and equal sharing
of the things that earth affords.
To a life of love in action
help us rise and pledge our word.[53]

Thomas Troeger's hymn "God made from one blood" echoes these concerns, concluding with the petition that God

widen that wisdom and grace to include
the races and viewpoints our families exclude
till peace in each home bears and nurtures the bud
of peace shared by all you have made from one blood.[54]

The world and human bodies. Two seemingly disparate concerns that find their way into the hymns and songs of this period are concern for the environment and our human existence as bodies. What links them are an awareness that all of creation—the world and human bodies—are gifts of God. Dan Damon and Eileen Johnson, in considering the theme of creation in recent hymnody, contrast what they call "happy earth hymns" (such as "All things bright and beautiful"), which reflect an idyllic and pastoral view of the world that encounters neither problem nor threat to its existence, with "hymns that show the earth in peril, vulnerable, and abused."[55] Brian Wren's early hymn "Thank you God, for water, soil and air," inspired in part by NASA photographs of the earth from space, helps address this challenge, moving between thanksgiving for what God has done and is doing

52. Westermeyer, "Current Theological Trends," 44.
53. Kaan, *Hymn Texts*, 34.
54. Troeger, *Borrowed Light*, 172.
55. Damon and Johnson, "Cry for Justice," 9.

in creation and confession for what we have done and are doing through "reckless plundering and waste" and "greed and carelessness."[56]

It is not a stretch to consider the same themes—the contrast between the gift of creation and human abuse of it—as we consider the gift of human bodies. Ruth Duck notes how bodies are both "fragile and strong" as she celebrates the gift of diverse human bodies as a gift of creation:

> Sacred the body God has created,
> temple of Spirit, that dwells deep inside.
> Cherish each person; nurture creation.
> Treat flesh as holy, that love may abide.[57]

Pastoral and prophetic. Perhaps above all, these hymn-writers have sought to be pastoral and prophetic, offering both comfort and challenge to the church. This should not be surprising as many of them began their hymnic work as pastors in congregations. Part of their pastoral response has been to help the church voice its lament as well as its praise. For example, Ruth Duck asks, "God, how can we forgive when bonds of love are torn? How can we rise and start anew, our trust reborn?" Her lament is anchored in a confidence in God's grace and the forgiveness we have received through that grace. She ends with a familiar petition: "As you, O God, forgive our sin, may we forgive."[58] Another part of their pastoral response was to offer a prophetic word, especially to an over-confident and inner-focused church, as we find in Pratt Green's "When the church of Jesus":

> When the church of Jesus shuts its outer door,
> lest the roar of traffic drown the voice of prayer,
> may our hymns, Lord, make us ten times more aware
> that the world we banish is our Christian care.[59]

CONTRIBUTION TO LITURGY AND WORSHIP

As noted above, one of the significant factors that influenced the renaissance in hymn-writing during this period were the liturgical reforms that emerged from the Second Vatican Council in 1965.

56. See "Thank You, God, for Water, Soil and Air," at https://www.hopepublishing.com/find-hymns-hw/hw2607.aspx.

57. Duck, *Circles of Care*, 39.

58. Duck, *Circles of Care*, 40.

59. Pratt Green, *Hymns and Ballads*, 2.

Lectionary and church year. Two reforms in particular had consequences for hymnody: the development and subsequent revision of a common lectionary for Sundays, and renewed attention to the church year. Work with the lectionary made evident a need for more biblical hymnody and, as Robin Leaver notes, brought to awareness biblical texts "for which there was no adequate hymnody."[60] Several hymn-writers, such as Timothy Dudley-Smith and Carl Daw, developed hymns that provide faithful paraphrases of Scripture, often drawing on key words or phrases introduced in newer Bible translations, as Dudley-Smith does when he takes Luke 1:46 in the New English Bible, "Tell out my soul, the greatness of the Lord," as the starting point for his paraphrase of Mary's song. Others, like Daw and Thomas Troeger, have used this renewed connection between Scripture and hymnody for homiletical and liturgical purposes.[61] Daw's hymn "Wild and lone the prophet's voice" sets the common lectionary gospel readings for the second and third Sundays of Advent, which recount the preaching of John the Baptist. Daw represents John's preaching in the second stanza: "Bear the fruit repentance sows: lives of justice, truth, and love. Trust no other claim than those; set your heart on things above."[62] Troeger's hymn on the Transfiguration, "Swiftly pass the clouds of glory," paraphrases the gospel narrative in two stanzas, concluding with a petition that is also homiletic in tone: "Lord, transfigure our perception with the purest light that shines and recast our life's intentions to the shape of your designs."[63]

Song and/as ritual action. Another liturgical reform that emerged during this period was a fuller understanding of the potential for congregation song and hymnody to interpret, accompany, and enrich the ritual and sacramental actions of the liturgy. For example, Fred Kaan's hymn "Now let us from this table rise" points to what the congregation has received at the Lord's Table—renewal of body, mind, and soul, restoration to wholeness—even as it points the congregation to its work of renewal and restoration in and with the world: "the work that Christ began to do we humbly pledge ourselves to share."[64] Similarly, Brian Wren's "I come with joy" describes who we are as individuals, as a community, and as a community transformed by the breaking and sharing of bread at the Lord's Table, culminating with our being sent out "with joy, to give the world the love that makes us one."[65]

60. Leaver, "British Hymnody," 590; and Leaver, "Liturgical Music," 303.

61. Routley, *Panorama*, 540.

62. Daw, *Year of Grace*, 19.

63. Troeger, *Borrowed Light*, 4.

64. Kaan, *Hymn Texts*, 90.

65. Wren, *Piece Together Praise*, 91.

Both hymns seem to have a homiletic function. In contrast, Jaroslav Vajda's hymn "Now the silence" sets out a liturgical theology by describing our and God's actions as they occur through the celebration of the eucharist—our empty hands, our kneeling and pleading, our hearing, the Spirit's visitation, the Son's epiphany, the Father's blessing.[66]

This hymnological renaissance has also helped the church discover some of the ways in which hymns and songs enrich worship. These hymn-writers have provided a renewed sense of the importance of the congregation's voice, with its particular tonal colors, pitches, and rhythms, and provided a means for the congregation's active participation in the "work of worship." They have provided new ways and words with which to create and express unity, joy, and beauty. And, as we see in many of the hymns discussed above, they have given us texts, in some cases melodies, with which to shape an experience of worship as a "whole" rather than as isolated parts sandwiched between an opening and closing hymn. Perhaps, above all, they have given the church a renewed reason to sing.

NOTABLE HYMNS

Carl Daw

As we gather at your table
Like the murmur of the dove's song
O day of peace, that dimly shines

Ruth Duck

Sacred the body God has created
Wash, O God, our sons and daughters
Womb of life and source of being

Timothy Dudley-Smith

Not for tongues of heaven's angels (1 Cor 13)
Tell out my soul (Luke 1)

66. Vajda, *Now the Joyful Celebration*, 37.

Jane Parker Huber

Called as partners in Christ's service
God, you spin the whirling planets
On Pentecost they gathered

Fred Kaan

For the healing of the nations
Help us accept each other
We meet you, O Christ

Fred Pratt Green

For the fruits of his creation
God is here, as we your people
When in our music God is glorified
When the church of Jesus

Erik Routley

All who love and serve your city

Thomas Troeger

God made from one blood all the families of earth
Silence, frenzied, unclean spirit
Wind who makes all winds that blow

Jaroslav Vajda

God of the sparrow
Now the silence, now the peace

Brian Wren

Bring many names
Christ is alive, let Christians sing
I come with joy to meet my Lord

Thank you, God, for water, soil, and air

BIBLIOGRAPHY

Damon, Dan, and Eileen M. Johnson. "A Cry for Justice in Hymnody." *The Hymn* 61 (Autumn 2010) 8–16.

Daw, Carl. *A Year of Grace: Hymns for the Church Year.* Carol Stream, IL: Hope, 1990.

Duck, Ruth. *Circles of Care.* Cleveland: Pilgrim, 1998.

———. *Dancing in the Universe.* Chicago: GIA, 1992.

———. *Finding Words for Worship.* Louisville, KY: Westminster John Knox, 1995.

Fraser, Ian. "Beginnings at Dunblane." In *Duty and Delight: Routley Remembered,* edited by Robin Leaver and James Litton, 171–90. Carol Stream, IL: Hope, 1985.

Hyslop, Scott. "Now the Joyful Celebration: The Hymnody of Jaroslav J. Vajda." *The Hymn Society of Great Britain and Ireland Bulletin* 14 (April 1994) 28–37.

Kaan, Fred. *The Hymn Texts of Fred Kaan.* Carol Stream, IL: Hope, 1985.

Leaver, Robin. "British Hymnody since 1950." In *The Hymnal 1982 Companion,* edited by Raymond Glover, 555–99. New York: Church Hymnal, 1990.

———. "Liturgical Music as Corporate Song 1: Hymnody in Reformation Churches." In *Liturgy and Music: Lifetime Learning,* edited by Joyce Ann Zimmerman and Robin Leaver, 281–307. Collegeville, MN: Liturgical, 1998.

Luff, Alan. "The Twentieth-Century Hymn Explosion: Where the Fuse was Lit." *The Hymn* 58 (Autumn 2007) 11–21.

———. "The Hymn Explosion after 25 years." *The Hymn* 46 (April 1995) 6–15.

Music, David W. *Christian Hymnody in Twentieth-Century Britain and America: An Annotated Bibliography.* Westport, CT: Greenwood, 2001.

Pratt Green, Fred. *The Hymns and Ballads of Fred Pratt Green.* Carol Stream, IL: Hope, 1992.

Routley, Erik. *Christian Hymns Observed.* Princeton, NJ: Prestige, 1982.

———. *A Panorama of Christian Hymnody.* Expanded and edited by Paul Richardson. Chicago: GIA, 2005.

Schulz-Widmar, Russell. "The Hymn Renaissance in the United States." In *Duty and Delight: Routley Remembered,* edited by Robin Leaver and James Litton, 191–216. Carol Stream, IL: Hope Publishing, 1985.

———. "Hymnody in the United States Since 1950." In *The Hymnal 1982 Companion,* edited by Raymond Glover, 600–630. New York: Church Hymnal, 1990.

Troeger, Thomas H. *Borrowed Light.* New York: Oxford University Press, 1994.

Vajda, Jaroslav J. "The Making of a Hymn." *Reformed Liturgy and Music* 30 (1996) 183–88.

———. *Now the Joyful Celebration.* St. Louis: MorningStar, 1987.

Westermeyer, Paul. "Current Theological Trends Affecting Congregational Song." In *We'll Sing and Shout Hosanna: Essays on Church Music in Honor of William J. Reynolds,* edited by David W. Music, 39–58. Fort Worth, TX: Southwestern Baptist Theological Seminary, 1998.

———. "Twentieth-Century American Hymnody and Church Music." In *New Dimensions in American Religious History,* edited by Jay P. Dolan and James P. Wind, 175–207. Grand Rapids: Eerdmans, 1993.

———. *With Tongues of Fire: Profiles in 20th-Century Hymn Writing*. St. Louis: Concordia, 1995.

Wootton, Janet, ed. *This Is Our Song: Women's Hymn-Writing*. London: Epworth, 2010.

Wren, Brian. *Piece Together Praise*. Carol Stream, IL: Hope Publishing, 1996.

———. *Praying Twice: The Music and Words of Congregational Song*. Louisville: Westminster John Knox, 2000.

———. *What Language Shall I Borrow*. London: SCM, 1989.

Chapter 8

Standard Idioms in Canada, New Zealand, and Australia

David Bjorlin

HISTORICAL BACKGROUND

The story of twentieth-century hymnody in Canada, New Zealand, and Australia is marked by diversity. Each country has its own rich heritage of music that stretches far beyond the European settlers and rightly begins with the indigenous people that originally inhabited these lands. The First Nations (Canada), Aboriginal (Australia), and Maori (New Zealand) communities all possessed their own rich traditions of sacred songs, dances, and chants that were too often suppressed by the immigrant settlers that came in later centuries. Further, each immigrant community brought with it a diversity of song largely dependent upon their own ethnic and denominational heritage. Yet because this chapter focuses on the twentieth century, this section will focus on the history of hymnody that began at the turn of the last century in each country.

In Canada, the beginning of the twentieth century marked the first stages of a truly Canadian hymnody. Each denominational tradition struggled with how they were to live out their particular ethnic (most often English) and denominational identities in a new land. Anglicans continued to rely heavily on *Hymns Ancient and Modern* and questioned what would make the song of Canadian Anglicanism unique. Canadian Presbyterians knew that psalmody would always be foundational to their worship but had to discern what other hymns could be used in public worship. The United Church of Canada—newly formed in 1925 by the merger of Canadian Methodist, Congregationalist, and seventy percent of Presbyterian churches—now faced the daunting challenge of creating musical resources that would unite different traditions into a single body. Roman Catholics of French origin, like Roman Catholics around the world, would have to decide what the ground-shaking decisions of Vatican II meant for inculturating French-Canadian song into the liturgy.[1] Because a general overview excludes the possibility of examining each of these traditions in depth, the historical section will examine four particular Canadian hymnals from different traditions and eras—the 1897 and 1918 Presbyterian *Book of Praise*, the 1971 Anglican and UCC *The Hymn Book of the Anglican Church*, and the 1996 UCC *Voices United*—to illumine common challenges for Canadian hymnody over different eras.

As would be expected, the psalter dominated the liturgical song of the Presbyterian Church of Canada in the nineteenth century. Only in 1880 would a hymnal be produced with non-psalter material, in this case 350 hymns and doxologies (words only).[2] In 1885, this hymnal was bound together with an exact reproduction of the psalter and paraphrases of the Free Church of Scotland, which included all 150 metric psalms and sixty-seven paraphrases (along with a few hymns and prose psalms). This move demonstrated both the Canadian Presbyterians' continued reliance on the tradition of psalter singing and the worship resources of their country of origin. Yet, under the leadership of Alexander MacMillan, Canadian Presbyterians expanded their hymnic repertoire with two successive hymnals entitled *Book of Praise* (1897 and 1918). The first edition reduced the number of psalms from 150 to 122 and increased the number of hymns from 350 to 621. The second also sought a more ecumenical reach that moved beyond the bounds of specifically Presbyterian hymnody and embraced hymns from other traditions. This specific story of Canadian Presbyterians tells a much larger story of Canadian hymnody; as denominations came to a new country and comingled in a new land, they began the process of breaking away from their home countries, borrowing from one another's traditions,

1. Because of space constraints, the remainder of this section on Canadian hymnody will focus on Protestant traditions. For a history of Roman Catholic liturgical music, see Blais-Jol, "Liturgical Music in French Canada."

2. All information cited about the Presbyterian hymnal comes from Anderson, "Presbyterian Hymnody, Canadian."

and creating their own Canadian resources, albeit resources that still relied almost exclusively on non-Canadian songs.

If the early Presbyterian hymnals demonstrated Canadian denominations beginning to establish themselves in a new nation, the 1971 *Hymn Book of the Anglican Church of Canada and the United Church of Canada* showed the then-recent flourishing of Canadian text and tune writing. As the title suggests, the 1971 *Hymn Book* was a joint effort of the Anglican Church and the UCC. Hoping to be the first step in a merger of the two bodies, the merger never materialized, and the hymnal proved to be a compromise that pleased neither constituency.[3] However, the hymnal did prove a major showcase for homegrown texts and tunes. Due both to the growing cost of copyright and a desire to cultivate a Canadian hymnic identity, new hymn tunes were commissioned from several Canadian composers.[4] According to Stanley Osborne's companion to the hymnal, thirty Canadian composers contributed fifty-three tunes (not counting harmonizations, descants, etc.).[5] These included tunes composed by Henry Hugh Bancroft, Barrie Cabena, Walter MacNutt, Stanley Osborne, and Healy Willan, among many others. Further, forty-five Canadian text writers contributed forty-five hymn texts and twelve translations. Notable among them were T. Herbert O'Driscoll's "God, Who Has Caused to Be Written" and "From the Slave Pens of the Delta"; Frieda Major's "No Crowded Eastern Street"; R. B. Y. Scott's "O World of God;" and Walter Farquharson's "God Who Gives to Life Its Goodness," sung at the dedication service for *The Hymn Book*. Thus, the history of *The Hymn Book* tells of Canadian national identity being formed and reinforced by hymn texts and tunes written from the Canadian context for Canadian congregations.

Finally, the UCC's 1996 *Voices United* simultaneously demonstrated the continued commitment to a growing Canadian hymnic tradition and to better representing the global nature of the church. Fifty-five Canadians contributed texts and translations to the hymnal.[6] Perhaps most notable among them was United Church of Canada minister Sylvia Dunstan who, before her untimely death, published two collections from which *Voices United* chose thirteen texts, including "All Who Hunger, Gather Gladly," "Go to the World," and "You, Lord, Are Both Lamb and Shepherd." Other prominent Canadian authors included Rob Johns, Margaret Clarkson, and Linnea Good (who also wrote tunes). At the same time as *Voices United* deepened

3. Hull, "Anglican Hymnody, Canadian."
4. Leask, "United Church of Canada Hymnals."
5. Osborne, *If Such a Holy Song*, xiv.
6. Leask, "United Church of Canada Hymnals."

the tradition of Canadian hymnwriting, it also broadened the scope of congregational song by including songs from the First Nations people of Canada as well as Christian communities from the global East and South. A few traditional hymns were translated into the indigenous languages of several First Nation communities, including Ojibway, Mohawk, and Cree. *Voices United* also included the song "O Great Spirit," a melody based on a song of the Nuxalk First Nation written by Nuxalk Doreen Clellamin.[7] The collection also contained songs in many different languages—French, Korean, Japanese, German, Chinese, Spanish, Zulu, and Yoruba—originating in several different countries—Japan, Korea, China, Argentina, Puerto Rico, South Africa, and Cameroon (to name just a selection). The international ecumenical communities of Taizé and Iona were also both represented within its pages.

Due to the similarities in context (mainly English colonies within existing indigenous communities), the story of hymnody in both twentieth-century Australia and New Zealand followed a similar pattern to Canada: 1) early loyalty to the songs of the home country/denomination; 2) a conscious development of one's own national/regional identity by emphasizing homegrown congregational song; and 3) an expanding global and ecumenical consciousness. In Australia, the hymnody of churches at the turn of the twentieth century was dominated by the songs and songbooks of their English progenitors (e.g., Presbyterians sang from the Scottish *Church Hymnary*) with a smattering of songs from the revivalist movement.[8] One of the first major collections to gather burgeoning Australian hymnwriting was the Australian supplement to the Canadian-Anglican *Book of Common Praise* (1947). The supplement included over twenty-five texts and tunes originating in Australia, including three texts by English-born Charles Venn Pilcher.

Following close on its heels, Roman-Catholic poet James McAuley teamed up with musician Richard Connolly to produce original hymn texts and tunes. Beginning with their 1959 *We Offer This Mass* and blossoming in successive editions of *The Living Parish Hymn Book* (beginning in 1964), Connolly and McAuley produced several staples of Australian congregational song, including "Where There is Charity and Love" (JEREMY), "Sing a New Song" (COSMIC PRAISE), and "O Jesus Crucified" (FORBES STREET). As Dianne Gome noted, their work took seriously the directives of the Second Vatican Council's *Sacrosanctum Concilium*, which

7. Donaldson, "Toward a Musical Praxis of Justice," 24.

8. All information cited in this section comes from Gome, "Australian Hymnody" and "Australian Hymnbooks."

"encourage[ed] vernacular language, congregational participation and musical inculturation in the Roman Catholic Liturgy."[9] Along with Jesuit Christopher Willcock, Connolly and McAuley were well represented in the *Catholic Worship Book* (1985) and *Gather Australia* (1995).

The turning point in modern Australian hymnody came with the publishing of the 1977 *Australian Hymn Book* (published internationally as *With One Voice*). Representing Anglican, Methodist, Congregational, Presbyterian, and Roman Catholic Churches (with an optional Catholic Supplement), *Australian Hymn Book* became the foundation and benchmark of Australian hymnody in the modern era selling over one million copies (in a nation of twenty million people!). While still heavily reliant on the hymnic traditions of Great Britain, it included eleven texts from James McAuley, (all set to tunes by Richard Connolly, who also had four of his own texts included), four texts by Granton Hay, and single texts by Wesley Milgate, John Wheeler, and June Wright. Besides Connolly, Australian composers Lawrence Bartlett, Alfred Floyd, and Herbert Davis also had tunes represented in the hymnal.

Like *Voices United*, the second iteration of the *Australian Hymn Book*, *Together in Song* (1999), both broadened its ecumenical reach and deepened the roots of Australian-born song. Ecumenically, both Australian Lutherans and Churches of Christ joined their mainline and Roman Catholic counterparts in the creation of *Together in Song*, expanding the hymnal's corpus to include the Lutheran chorale tradition. Further, while the global perspective is less pronounced, *Together in Song* included songs from Africa, South America, and Asia as well as the Iona and Taizé communities. Like Canadian hymnals, *Together in Song* still underrepresented indigenous song, only including three songs from the Aboriginal or Torres Strait Islands communities.

The hymnal also showcased the continued growth of Australian songwriting. Seventy-five Australian composers and writers are represented in *Together in Song* from a variety of denominational traditions. Two of the most prominent were Lutheran songwriter Robin Mann, whose folk-inspired songs and tunes included "Little Children, Come to Me" and "Feed Us Now, Bread of Life"; and Anglican priest Elizabeth Smith whose texts, most often written with well-known tunes in mind, included "Where Wide Sky Rolls Down" (HANOVER) and "Love Will Be Our Lenten Calling" (PICARDY). Besides the Australian composers already mentioned, Robert Boughen (BENNELONG, BRAMWELL, AND URQUHART), Eric Gross (DRUMMOYNE), and Horace Finnis (BELAIR) all contributed tunes to the

9. Gome, "Australian Hymnody."

collection. Foreshadowing the growing prominence that the praise songs of the Sydney-based charismatic church Hillsong would have on global contemporary Christian music, *Together in Song* included Darlene Zschech's iconic "Shout to the Lord" as well as four songs by one of Hillsong's chief songwriters Geoff Bullock.

Like Australia and Canada before it, New Zealand churches outside of the indigenous Maori communities relied heavily on the hymnic traditions and resources of their country of origin. The story of a truly national hymnic heritage largely began in 1965 with the founding of Contemporary Hymns (New Zealand) by Anglican deacon Sylvia Jenkins, whose mission was to collect, evaluate, and disseminate new hymns written by New Zelanders.[10] The group morphed twice in the next decade and a half, first becoming the committee that produced the New Zealand supplement to the *Australian Hymn Book* and then forming the New Zealand Hymn Book Trust in 1978. Like its Australian counterparts, the trust was purposefully ecumenical including Anglican, Associated Church of Christ, Baptist, Methodist, and Presbyterian churches. Over the next four decades, the trust produced several collections and audio recordings showcasing New Zealand writers and composers including *Alleluia Aotearoa* (1993), *Carol Our Christmas* (1996), *He Came Singing Peace* (2002), and *Hope Is Our Song* (2009). The hymns promoted by the New Zealand Hymn Book Trust tend toward a progressive theology that places high value on social justice and inclusive language. Through the Trust, the work of Colin Gibson ("He Came Singing Love"/TENDERNESS), Margaret (Marnie) Barrell ("We Do Not Hope to Ease Our Minds"), William (Bill) Wallace ("Why Has God Forsaken Me"), and Christopher Norton (HOW LONG, O LORD) was exposed to a national and international audience. Yet it has been the work of Presbyterian hymnwriter Shirley Erena Murray that has proven to be the most influential of New Zealand hymnwriting. Taking up hymnwriting in the 1970s, her texts focused on theological themes that were often overlooked in classical hymnody, including peace, creation care, interreligious dialogue, and the social and linguistic contexts of New Zealand/Maori culture. Often teaming up with Colin Gibson, texts like "Touch the Earth Lightly," "Community of Christ," "Loving Spirit, Loving Spirit," and "God of Freedom, God of Justice" have been published in five individual collections (Hope Publishing) and over one hundred hymnals worldwide.

Like Australia, New Zealand also witnessed a homegrown contemporary praise music movement bolstered by Dale and David Garratt's Scripture

10. All information cited in this section comes from Gibson, "New Zealand Hymnody" and "New Zealand Hymnbooks."

in Song publishing group and the charismatic Anglican St. Paul's Outreach Trust. The two most popular songs that arose from New Zealand's evangelical/charismatic songwriting community to international prominence were Richard Gillard's "Brother, Sister, Let Me Serve You" (often revised to "Will You Let Me Be Your Servant?") and Les Garrett's "This Is the Day."

THEOLOGICAL PERSPECTIVES

Any attempt to speak of consistent theological perspectives shared between thousands of hymns written over one hundred years and across denominational and international boundaries is bound to be limited. So, while the general theological perspectives of these countries' hymnody will be touched on, it seems better to speak of common features—some theological, others not—shared by the most internationally popular of Canadian, Australian, and New Zealand hymnody.

Theologically, many of the well-known hymns from the three countries tend toward a progressive-to-centrist theological viewpoint. As already mentioned, one of the chief characteristics of the hymns of the New Zealand Hymn Book Trust is its liberal theological outlook with a strong emphasis on social justice, inclusivity, environmental care, and even the coexistence of science and faith. The last of these is demonstrated in Colin Gibson's "For the Blast of Creation," which sings a song of praise to God for the creation of the cosmos at the Big Bang:

> For the blast of Creation,
> flinging far into space
> on the winds of the cosmos
> all the gifts of your grace,
> we bring awe, we bring wonder
> (though darkly we see),
> and we praise you who gave us
> our freedom to be.

Australian hymnody tends to be more theologically moderate than its counterparts to the West, often more concerned with particular theological issues rather than expressing a progressive theological worldview. Writing around the time of the new liturgical freedom of the Second Vatican Council, the hymn texts of James McAuley were often focused on making Roman Catholic doctrine understandable and meaningful to congregations who could now sing and pray in the vernacular. Lutheran songwriter Robin Mann often employs a folk idiom to express anger and lament to God with a prophetic edge.[11] This is clearly demonstrated in the second stanza of his "Sorrowing Song":

> Children are crying, hungry for food,
> Sick from diseases—God are you good?
> People are homeless, lost and alone—
> God are you hiding? Where have you gone?

Finally, Elizabeth Smith's texts are influenced most strongly by her feminism, which shapes her gender-inclusive hymn texts on the Trinity, Mary, and the Holy Spirit.[12] For example, in the first stanza of "Now Wisdom's Feast Continues," she uses the feminine imagery of Wisdom/Sophia to write of the Holy Spirit's continued work in the world:

> Now Wisdom's feast continues,
> her well-aged wine still flows,
> the bread of heaven fills us,
> and love of learning grows.
> When faithful people listen,
> when hopeful people pray,
> when loving people flourish,
> they show us wisdom's way.

What all three of these Australian writers share is a desire to communicate faith in clear and simple terms that all Australians might find a place in their song.

Canadian hymnwriters also tend to express a moderate-to-progressive theological imagination in their texts, though with notable exception. Issues of social justice and inclusion are central themes in texts like Gordon Light's "Draw the Circle Wide" or William Whitla's "Let Streams of Living Justice Flow." Chosen as the theme hymn for the 1975 World Council of Churches Assembly in Nairobi, Walter Farquharson and Ronald Klusmeier's "Walls That Divide" is perhaps paradigmatic of this inclusive message:

> Though ancient walls may still stand proud
> and racial strife be fact,
> though bound'ries may be lines of hate,
> proclaim God's saving act!
> Walls that divide are broken down;
> Christ is our unity!

---

11. Hawn, "Congregational Singing from Down Under: An Interview with Australian Robin Mann," 14.

12. Hawn, "Congregational Singing from Down Under: The Hymns of Elizabeth Joyce Smith, Melbourne, Australia," 16.

Chains that enslave are thrown aside;
Christ is our liberty!

While emerging from the same theological milieu as the aforementioned writers, Sylvia Dunstan's texts were often focused on liturgical acts like communion (e.g., "All Who Hunger, Gather Gladly") or baptism (e.g., "Crashing Waters at Creation") as well as the saving work of Christ to "counter what she saw as an erosion of the significance of Jesus Christ in modern liberal Protestantism."[13] In texts like "Christ Is King" and "You, Lord, Are Both Lamb and Shepherd" she explored the paradoxes of the humanity and divinity of Christ, with the latter ending in a stanza of pure adoration:

Worthy is our earthly Jesus!
Worthy is our cosmic Christ!
Worthy your defeat and victory.
Worthy still your peace and strife.
You, the everlasting instant;
You who are our death and life.

The theological outlier in Canadian hymnwriting was Margaret Clarkson, whose texts like "We Come, O Christ, to Thee" and "So Send I You" expressed an evangelical theology of humanity's sinfulness, Christ's atoning death, and the Christian's call to evangelism. For example, she combined all three of these themes in the final stanza of "So Send I You":

So send I you to hearts made hard by hatred,
to eyes made blind because they will not see,
to spend, tho' it be blood, to spend and spare not—
so send I you to taste of Calvary.

Beyond the varied theological viewpoint of its writers, the hymnody of Canada, Australia, and New Zealand shares several common features. First, in all three countries hymnody has tended to be an ecumenical enterprise. Part of this ecumenism seems to be run in the DNA of many Canadian and Australian churches, as demonstrated by the formation of both the United Church of Canada and the Uniting Church in Australia from the union of various denominations. The hymnody collected by these denominations necessitated an ecumenical approach if their hymnals were to serve the multiple histories and theological traditions of their congregations. Moreover, the relatively smaller sizes of denominations spread across large geographical expanses made ecumenism in hymnody a practical matter, especially in Australia and New Zealand. As mentioned earlier, the *Australian*

13. Barthel, "Sylvia Dunstan."

Hymn Book and its predecessor *Together in Song* were produced through the combined efforts of many denominations. Likewise, the New Zealand Hymn Book Trust represented a wide range of denominational perspectives and traditions. While ecumenism is a standard feature of most hymnody, it is even more pronounced in the hymnic heritage of twentieth-century Canada, Australia, and New Zealand.

The second common feature shared between these countries is the role the unique geography of each region has played in forming the themes of hymn texts. In Western Canada, the vast stretches of prairie inspired Walter Farquharson's stewardship hymn "For Beauty of Prairies, for Grandeur of Trees" as well as Frieda Major's Christmas text "No Crowded Eastern Street":

> No crowded eastern street,
> no sound of passing feet;
> far to the left and far to right,
> the prairie snows spread far and white;
> yet still to us is born tonight
> the child, the King of glory.

The wide expanses of the Australian geography and the particularity of its flora and fauna also inspired Elizabeth Smith's "Where Wide Sky Rolls Down," whose first stanza sings,

> Where wide sky rolls down and touches red sand,
> where sun turns to gold the grass of the land,
> let spinifex,[14] mulga[15] and waterhole tell
> their joy in the One who made everything well.

In later stanzas, Smith mentions rain forests, reefs, oceans, tropical birds, red gum trees, tree-ferns, bushland, and other prominent parts of Australia's geographic diversity.

Similarly, the first two stanzas of Shirley Erena Murray's "Where Mountains Rise to Open Skies" show both the geographical influence of New Zealand as well as the cultural inspiration of the Maori people:

> Where mountains rise to open skies
> your name, O God, is echoed far,
> from island beach to kauri's[16] reach,
> in water's light, in lake and star.

14. Spinifex is a common grass that grows in the coastal regions of Australia (and other countries).

15. Mulga is a small tree that grows in the Australian outback.

16. Kauri are the large trees long considered sacred by the Maori people that grow in the far north of New Zealand.

Your people's heart, your people's part
Be in our caring for this land,
For faith to flower, for aroha[17]
To let each other's mana[18] stand.

Yet, perhaps the geographical particularity of Australia and New Zealand are witnessed nowhere more clearly than in their Christmas hymns and carols. While relying heavily on the songs of their immigrant forebears, Christmas texts that sung of "snow on snow on snow" falling "in the bleak midwinter" made little sense in the Southern Hemisphere where Christmas is celebrated in the heat of summer. Some of the first attempts toward hymnic inculturation came in R. F. Inwood's aptly titled *The Christian Year Beneath the Southern Cross* (1906), but perhaps the earliest successful songs were written by John Wheeler and William Garnet James in their series of Christmas carols inspired by the Australian summer. In their "The North Wind Is Tossing the Leaves," instead of snow and cold, the north wind brought leaves and dust to celebrate the Savior's birth:

The north wind is tossing the leaves,
the red dust is over the town,
the sparrows are under the eaves,
And the grass in the paddock is brown;
As we lift up our voices and sing,
To the Christ-Child the heavenly King.

Similarly, in their "Carol of the Birds," they described how the many native birds—brolgas, woodlarks, bell-birds, friar birds, currowongs, and lorikeets—sang their summer song in "orana" (the aboriginal word for welcome) to Christmas:

Out on the plains the brolgas are dancing,
lifting their feet like warhorses prancing.
Up to the sun the woodlarks go winging,
faint in the dawn light echoes their singing:
Orana! Orana! Orana! To Christmas Day.

The most popular recent example of a Southern Hemisphere Christmas text is Shirley Erena Murray's 1992 "Carol Our Christmas" (Upside-Down Christmas), who compares the stereotypical Northern Hemisphere Christmas with the reality of Christmas "Down Under":

Carol our Christmas, an upside-down Christmas:

17. Maori for "all-embracing love."
18. Maori for "dignity, prestige."

snow is not falling and trees are not bare.
Carol the summer, and welcome the Christ Child,
warm in our sunshine and sweetness of air.

Sing of the gold and green and the sparkle,
water and river and lure of the beach.
Sing in the happiness of open spaces,
sing a nativity summer can reach!

As Murray later noted, part of the reason she began writing hymns was the lack of songs that fit the geography and culture of New Zealand: "There was no imagery which evoked our particular environment, no landscape of those to accommodate the Southern Hemisphere seasons . . . no connection with the Maori culture of our society, nothing to sing to articulate our hopes and visions."[19] Thus, Canadian, Australian, and New Zealand hymnwriters have given words that Christians in their particular geographical and cultural contexts can sing truthfully about the God who meets them in the vast prairies, the dusty bush, and the lush coast.

As noted at the beginning of the chapter, the history of sacred song in each country rightly begins with the indigenous people who predate European settlers by millennia. While the history of First Nations, Aboriginal, and Maori musical traditions goes beyond the purpose of this paper, another common question that each country's churches presently grapple with is how best to incorporate the song of Christian indigenous people into the broader hymnody of the church. Such attempts face two important and difficult issues. First, the long and brutal history of suppressing indigenous culture and song made any attempts at inculturating Christianity into the sacred expressions of indigenous people next to impossible for most of the nineteenth and twentieth centuries. Thus, while over one-third of published hymnody in Canada as of 1992 was published in the languages of the First Nations people, the vast majority were translated Western hymns set to traditional Western tunes.[20] This is still the most common practice in the most recent major denominational hymnals.

The second reason for the apparent paucity of indigenous song in modern hymnody is the concern over cultural appropriation. Many native songs and chants are connected to sacred rites of indigenous groups and meant only for those within the community. Speaking from the context of New Zealand and Australia, Colin Gibson explained, "[T]he treasured sacred music of pre-colonial times has been jealously guarded against appropriation by western imperial culture. Maori or Aboriginal languages

19. Murray, "Blessed Assurance," 11.

20. Polman, "Introduction," in McKellar, *Hymn Texts*, 4–5.

texts may be sung to western-style melodies and harmonies, never to modernized versions of ancient chants."[21] While aboriginal hymns and texts are still largely absent in Australia's hymnody, New Zealand's commitment to biculturalism (both Maori and English are official languages) has led to a growing corpus of Maori hymns. The most popular, *tama ngakau marie* (and Murray's paraphrase "Son of God, Whose Heart Is Peace"), has found prominence in recent national and international hymnals, and several other texts by Maori writers are found in the New Zealand Hymn Trust's collections including Taria Kingstone's "*Aue te tu aroa*," "*No te aroa maata noou*," and "*Te Atua mou a Betela*"; Mona Riini's "*E te Iwi*"; and Hirini Melbourne's "*Purea nei e te hau*."

New Zealand writers like Murray also have attempted to honor New Zealand's biculturalism by creating songs inspired by Maori concepts or using Maori words. Besides the previously quoted "Where Mountains Rise to Open Skies," Murray employed the Maori word for fernleaf, *koru*, as an image for the unfurling life of the baptized child:

> Bless her by water, Spirit and sign
> Bring her to share the bread and the wine,
> Draw her, like frond of koru unfurled,
> Open to love and life in your world.

Similarly, her text "When All Else Was Gone" was both inspired by the famous passage from 1 Cor 13 ("And now faith, hope, and love abide, these three; and the greatest of these is love") as well as the Maori greeting song—"*E toru nga mea*"—that served as a gloss on the biblical passage: "There are three things, three very important things which the Bible tells us. There is Faith, and Hope, but the most important thing is Love."[22] Perhaps because New Zealand has made the most effort on the national level to preserve and protect indigenous culture, their hymnody also has the strongest indigenous presence.

Looking toward the future of congregational song in the three countries, one of the key questions to be answered is how the increased immigrant presence, especially from China and South Asian countries, will continue to shape the song of the nations' churches. Obviously, many of these new Canadians, Australians, and New Zealanders join churches within their ethnic communities that will continue to sing their tradition's sacred songs in their new homes, thus making their songs a part of their new nation's identity. Yet, it also offers opportunity for a cross-fertilization of songs as different

21. Gibson, "Finding a Voice Down-Under," 70.

22. Murray, *Touch the Earth Lightly*, 158.

communities share their unique gifts with one another. For instance, while still a citizen of Singapore, Canadian resident Swee-Hong Lim has written many tunes that deftly combine Eastern and Western musical traditions for a new hybrid sound. Only time will tell what new songs may be written and sung from new patterns of immigration.

CONTRIBUTION TO LITURGY AND WORSHIP

As is to be expected, the largest liturgical influence of Canadian, Australian, and New Zealand hymnody is felt in the worship contexts of their specific countries of origin, particular in mainline denominations that played a major role in the creation of these hymnals. Yet, congregational songs from each country have also contributed to the worship of the international community as well. In New Zealand, the hymn texts of Shirley Erena Murray have been published in over one hundred hymnals and translated into nine languages around the world.[23] Her texts are particularly popular in progressive communities that seek inclusive language and texts relating to social justice and environmental care. Through her texts, the tunes of Colin Gibson have also gained an international audience, appearing in over forty hymnals.[24] In Canada, the hymns of Walter Farquharson and Ronald Klusmeier (both individually and in collaboration) have crossed national borders, yet it is perhaps the work of Sylvia Dunstan that is best known to the international community. While only living to 38, fifty-seven of her hymn texts have been published in many English-language hymnals.[25] Australian hymnody is perhaps the least well known outside of the nation, although a few texts by Elizabeth Smith and Robin Mann are found in non-Australian resources. Instead, Australia's main exporter of congregational song is Hillsong, whose songs geared for contemporary evangelical and charismatic worship settings have become a mainstay to millions of Christians across the globe. Based on the self-reporting of CCLI, the copyrighting company that licenses most popular Christian contemporary music, nineteen of the top one hundred songs reported in 2017 were published by Hillsong.

23. Gibson, "Shirley Erena Murray."

24. Gibson and Watson, "Colin Gibson."

25. Barthel, "Sylvia Dunstan."

NOTABLE WORKS

Notable hymnic texts and tunes from the twentieth and twenty-first centuries include:

Canada

- Margaret Clarkson: "So Send I You" and "We Come, O Christ, to You"
- Andrew Donaldson: "Although I Speak with Angels' Tongue"
- Sylvia Dunstan: "Come to Me, O Weary Trav'ler," "Crashing Waters at Creation," "Go to the World," "You, Lord, Are Both Lamb and Shepherd," and "You Walk along the Shoreline"
- Walter Farquharson: "For Beauty of Meadows," "God Who Gives to Life Its Goodness," and "Would You Bless Our Homes and Families"
- Ronald Klusmeier: "Praise to the Lord, All of You" (RICHARDSON-BURTON)
- Swee-Hong Lim (residing in Canada): *chu leung*, *singapura*, and *soon ti*
- Civilia Martin: "His Eye Is On the Sparrow"
- Frieda Major: "No Crowded Eastern Streets"
- T. Herbert O'Driscoll: "From the Slave Pens of the Delta" and "God, Who Has Caused to Be Written"
- William Whitla: "Let Streams of Living Justice Flow"

Australia

- Richard Connolly: CATHERINE, COSMIC PRAISE, JEREMY, and LOVE IS THE FULFILLING
- James McAuley: "O Jesus Crucified," "In Faith and Hope and Love," "Sing a New Song, Sing a New Song," and "Where There is Charity and Love"
- Robin Mann: "Feed Us Now, Bread of Life" and "Little Children, Come to Me" (KRISTIN)
- Rueben Morgan: "Hosanna" and "Mighty to Save"
- Charles Venn Pilcher: "Here, Lord, We Take the Broken Bread," "How Glorious Is God's Greatness!" (translator), and "I Know That My Redeemer Lives" (translator)
- Elizabeth Smith: "God Gives Us a Future" and "Love Will Be Our Lenten Calling"

- John Wheeler: "The North Wind Is Tossing the Leaves"
- Darlene Zschech: "Shout to the Lord" and "The Potter's Hand"

New Zealand

- Margaret "Marnie" Barrell: "Come to the Celebration" and "We Do Not Hope to Ease Our Minds"
- Les Garrett: "This Is the Day"
- Richard Gilliard: "Brother, Sister Let Me Serve You" / "Will You Let Me Be Your Servant"
- Colin Gibson: "He Came Singing Love" (SINGING LOVE), REVERSI, TALAVERA TERRACE, TENDERNESS, and WROSLYN ROAD
- Jocelyn Marshall: "As Jesus Walked the Emmaus Road"
- Christopher Norton: "How Long, O Lord"
- Shirley Erena Murray: "Come and Find a Quiet Center," "Community of Christ," "For Everyone Borne," "Give Thanks for Life," "God of Freedom, God of Justice," "Loving Spirit, Loving Spirit," "Star-Child, Earth-Child," and "Touch the Earth Lightly"
- William (Bill) Wallace: "Why Has God Forsaken Me?"

BIBLIOGRAPHY

Anderson, Donald. "Presbyterian Hymnody, Canadian." *The Canterbury Dictionary of Hymnology.* Canterbury. https://hymnology.hymnsam.co.uk/p/presbyterian-hymnody,-canadian.

Barthel, Alan. "Sylvia Dunstan." *The Canterbury Dictionary of Hymnology.* Canterbury. https://hymnology.hymnsam.co.uk/s/sylvia-dunstan.

Blais-Jol, Josette. "Liturgical Music in French Canada." *The Canterbury Dictionary of Hymnology.* Canterbury. https://hymnology.hymnsam.co.uk/l/liturgical-music-in-french-canada.

Donaldson, Hilary Seraph. "Toward a Musical Praxis of Justice: A Survey of Global and Indigenous Canadian Song in the Hymnals of the Anglican, Presbyterian, and United Churches of Canada through Their History." *The Hymn* 63.2 (Spring 2012) 18–26.

Gibson, Colin. "Finding a Voice Down-Under." *The Hymn Society of Great Britain and Ireland Bulletin* 19.3 (2009) 59–74.

———. "New Zealand Hymnbooks." *The Canterbury Dictionary of Hymnology.* Canterbury. https://hymnology.hymnsam.co.uk/n/new-zealand-hymnbooks.

———. "New Zealand Hymnody." *The Canterbury Dictionary of Hymnology.* Canterbury. https://hymnology.hymnsam.co.uk/n/new-zealand-hymnody.

———. "Shirley Erena Murray." *The Canterbury Dictionary of Hymnology*. Canterbury. https://hymnology.hymnsam.co.uk/s/shirley-erena-murray.

Gibson, Colin, and J. R. Watson. "Colin Gibson." *The Canterbury Dictionary of Hymnology*. Canterbury. https://hymnology.hymnsam.co.uk/c/colin-gibson.

Gome, Dianne. "Australian Hymnbooks." *The Canterbury Dictionary of Hymnology*. Canterbury. https://hymnology.hymnsam.co.uk/a/australian-hymnbooks.

———. "Australian Hymnody." *The Canterbury Dictionary of Hymnology*. Canterbury. https://hymnology.hymnsam.co.uk/a/australian-hymnody.

Hawn, C. Michael. "Congregational Singing from Down Under: An Interview with Australian Robin Mann." *The Hymn* 56.4 (Autumn 2005) 8, 10–11.

———. "Congregational Singing from Down Under: The Hymns of Elizabeth Joyce Smith, Melbourne, Australia." *The Hymn* 56.4 (Autumn 2005) 9, 16.

Hull, Kenneth. "Anglican Hymnody, Canadian." *The Canterbury Dictionary of Hymnology*. Canterbury. https://hymnology.hymnsam.co.uk/a/anglican-hymnody,-canadian.

Kimbrough, S. T., Jr. "Native American/First Nations Peoples of North America: Their Christian Hymns." *The Canterbury Dictionary of Hymnology*. Canterbury. https://hymnology.hymnsam.co.uk/n/native-american-first-nations-peoples-of-north-america-their-christian-hymns.

Leask, Margaret. "United Church of Canada Hymnals." *The Canterbury Dictionary of Hymnology*. Canterbury. https://hymnology.hymnsam.co.uk/u/united-church-of-canada-hymnals.

Milgate, Wesley, and D'Arcy Wood. *A Companion to Together in Song: Australian Hymnbook II*. Sydney: Australian Hymn Book, 2006.

McKellar, Hugh D. *Hymn Texts in the Aboriginal Languages of Canada*. Forth Worth: Hymn Society of the United States and Canada, 1992.

Murray, Shirley Erena. "Blessed Assurance: Beyond Fanny Crosby." *The Hymn* 60.4 (Autumn 2009) 10–15.

———. *Touch the Earth Lightly*. Carol Stream, IL: Hope, 2008.

Osborne, Stanley L. *If Such a Holy Song*. Whitby, ON: Institute of Church Music, 1976.

Osborne, Stanley L., and John Beckwith. "Hymns and Hymn Tunes." *The Canadian Encyclopedia*. http://www.thecanadianencyclopedia.ca/en/article/hymns-and-hymn-tunes-emc/.

Chapter 9

African American Sacred Music and Black Hymnody

Stephen Michael Newby,
Jocelyn Russell Wallace,
and Vernon M. Whaley

HISTORICAL BACKGROUND

The history of African American hymnody is the history of the body of African American sacred Christian music that began with Negro Spirituals, then developed over the past two hundred years into collections of hymns and modern African American gospel music. The thread throughout this sacred music is strong faith in God and a tenacious devotion to Christianity endurant within the African American church. The tapestry woven by the music is a variety of songs developed, expressed, and shared communally. Community is an important construct for the Black church in America. As a community, the Black church weeps together, empathizes together, celebrates together, and worships together. Life experiences are expressed in terms of culture, theology, and song, and it is "this song" that is sung—together.

The rich hymnological story of the African American church is exhaustive.[1] One will find that the musical articulation of Christian faith in Black churches is paramount, and yet, quite distinct within the various Christian denominations. Although the majority of African American Christians identify themselves as Baptists, Methodists, or members of the Church of God in Christ, Methodist, Baptist, Holiness, Pentecostal, Episcopal, and Presbyterian denominations have all shaped and fashioned the music of worship within the African American experience. As Charles Adams has observed,

> Music in Black worship is splendidly various as it runs the gamut from classical hymns and anthems to the sophisticated arranged spirituals to the raw, unadulterated [folk] spirituals, to the Black metered hymn to the jazzy, improvised gospels. All of these types of music are known, rendered, and appreciated in Black churches. There is no other church where such a wide variety of music is integrated, rendered, and sustained within a unified experience of worship.[2]

Singers of traditional Black "gospel" hymnody have most closely followed the African concept of using a *griot* as a soloist, preacher, and/or song leader. *Griot,* a French word, is commonly used to describe the ceremonial role that an African has in stimulating audience participation through spoken and/or sung dialogue or drama.[3]

According to historians Benjamin Elijah Mays and Joseph William Nicholson, during the days of enslavement, "the transference of the musical concepts, embodied in the spiritual into the modern Black Religious context"[4] proved a musical genius, which planted a seed that would influence the future of African American sacred song. Each generation of hymnists and composers stewards this musical treasury, by challenging participants with notions of reconciliation to God, by expressing a theology of salvation and by propelling the Black community toward holistic means of proclaiming holiness, love, justice, and righteousness (c.f., Jer 9:24). African American sacred music continues to articulate musical expressions within the canon of Negro spirituals, "Black hymnody," traditional hymns, concert music, jazz, and gospel.

1. See Abbington, *Readings in African American Church Music*, 2001.

2. Adams, "Some Aspects of Black Worship," in Abbington, *Readings in African American Church Music*, 299.

3. Southern, *Music of Black Americans,* 9–10.

4. Burnim and Maultsby, *African American Music,* 51.

Through the years and across many generations, three influences emerge as primary source material for African American hymnody: *African-American Preaching Traditions*, *Black Hymnody*, and *Leading African American Denominations*.

African Preaching Traditions

In the early eighteenth century, Black clergy inaugurated musical trends, organized their worship liturgies, explained biblical principles, and preached the gospel from their cultural perspective and their understanding of ecclesiastical practice. The practice of using *griot* fused with a strong biblical narrative led the preacher to develop a style of delivery that strongly accentuated congregational inter-action through vocal inflection, repetition, rhythmic-stress pacing, chanted prayers, and call-and-response.

Over the decades, preaching in the Black church community evolved into a complex and at times paradoxical practice. Preaching is central and integral to the worship experience.[5] The preacher played and continues to play various roles including theologian, proclaimer of truth, and master teacher as well as chief worship leader. In the African American culture, every activity in the worship service is fixed on the purposes of the sermon. Good preaching and singing are inseparable and essential for a thriving ministry in the Black church. C. Eric Lincoln and Lawrence H. Mamiya expound on this idea saying, "In some of the more traditional churches, even the sermon (and often the prayers of the ministers or deacon) are still 'sung' in a kind of ritualistic cadence peculiar to the Black church."[6]

Preaching in the African American tradition is not only focused on content but the means and methods for communicating such content.[7] The spontaneous preaching style impacts the way the message is heard. Thus, the preaching itself becomes "dialogical"—an interaction, "call-and-response" between the congregation and the preacher. In the words of Ruthlyn Bradshaw:

> The use of repetition, prevalent in black preaching, is not a time-filler, rather it is a technique used to ensure assimilation

5. Bradshaw, "Preaching in the Black Church," in Abbington, *Readings in African American Church Music*, 2:269.

6. Lincoln and Mamiya, "The Performed Word: Music and the Black Church," in Abbington, *Readings in African American Church Music*, 39–40.

7. See Smith, *Doctrine That Dances*.

> and to elicit response. Indeed repetition is used to generate an atmosphere for congregants to experience the word.[8]

Spur-of-the-moment creation of spirituals by the preacher during the sermon was common and grew out of the preacher's repeatedly sung narrative and the congregation responded accordingly.[9]

Black Hymnody

Wendell P. Whalum suggests that "Black hymnody, categorically speaking, must include all serious music that is sacred to the Black experience."[10] This includes the *early folk songs, folk spiritual, concert spiritual,* and *Gospel song.*

Early Folk Songs

The African American folk song includes the early "pre-spirituals" sung and embraced by the Black community before 1700 and through the early 1800s. In the church, Blacks sang the songs of Wesley, Watts, Newton, and other dissenters from the mid-eighteenth century.[11] The folk songs are more personal in character and include "chants for deliverance," musical expressions of hope, and religious melodies that the African American sang in the cotton and tobacco farmlands of the South. These songs were sung to invented meters and creative harmonies. Usually "lined out" by a leader and sung by the congregation, they were more often slow, mournful, and plaintive. Their beauty is seen and felt in the unsophisticated and primitive nature of the songs themselves coupled with lyrics often based on eighteenth-century English hymnists.[12]

8. Bradshaw, "Preaching in the Black Church," in Abbington, *Readings in African American Church Music*, 270–271.

9. Lincoln and Mamiya, "The Performed Word: Music and the Black Church," in Abbington, *Readings in African American Church Music*, 41.

10. Whalum, "Black Hymnody," in Abbington, *Readings in African American Church Music*, 168.

11. The European influence on African American sacred music is debated fiercely by scholars. There is support that refutes and argues vehemently that the spirituals were devoid of any European influence. In his Oxford University Press monograph, Albert J. Raboteau explains, "The specific debate over African vs. European origins for the Negro spirituals has used up even more ink and paper than the discussion over Africanisms in American culture generally." Raboteau, *Slave Religion*, 352.

12. Adams, "Some Aspects of Black Worship," in Abbington, *Readings in African American Church Music*, 308–9.

Folk Spirituals

Beginning around 1740, folk spirituals were used as communal compositions to be sung by the congregation. The spiritual reflected the experience of the slave and free-man. Having roots in eighteenth-century Black culture, when the need for expression in a common language was strongest, music communicated hope, love, approval, belief, death, and freedom. These early spirituals evolved from the unlettered Negro worshiper of the 1840s and conceived as linear unaccompanied vocal music. The congregation sang these songs without the use of instruments or predetermined harmony.[13] According to Leo H. Davis, the folk spiritual is characterized by "handclapping, foot-stomping, call-and-response, demonstrative behavior, and heterophonic singing. The folk spiritual was usually performed in autonomous environments such as the praise houses and 'invisible church.'"[14]

Concert Spirituals

The concert spiritual is sometimes called "the arranged spiritual." George White, treasurer of Fisk University, popularized the spiritual with the Fisk Jubilee Singers in October 1871. White organized a group of twelve singers from the student body to travel as a fund-raising group for the university presenting "arranged spirituals" in the context of a concert stage. John Work explains:

> Mr. White's intent on a style of singing the spiritual which eliminated every element that detracted from the pure emotion of the song. Harmony was diatonic and limited very largely to the primary triads and the dominant seventh. Dialect was not stressed but was used only where it was vital to the spirit of the song. Finish, precision, and sincerity were demanded by this leader. While the program featured the spirituals, variety was given it by the use of numbers of classical standard. Mr. White strove for an art presentation, not a caricature of atmosphere.[15]

Concert spirituals were successful in introducing to the mainline church and European choral community songs like "Walk Together, Children," "Roll, Jordan Roll," "My Soul's Been Anchored in the Lord," and

13. Work, "The Negro Spiritual," in Abbington, *Readings in African American Church Music*, 19.

14. Davis, "The Spiritual Arrangement since 1999 and Its Use in Contemporary Worship," in Abbington, *Readings in African American Church Music*, 2:120.

15. Work, *American Negro Songs*, 15.

"Going Home in the Chariot in the Morning." In 1873, Fisk University published a "first-time ever" collection of spirituals.

This historical tour by The Fisk Jubilee Singers, extending from 1871–78, captured the attention of the United States and European musical and social elite. So much so, the group was invited to sing before the King of England and Antonin Dvorák included elements of "Swing Low, Sweet Chariot" in his *New World Symphony.*

While George White introduced the concert spiritual to the academic and musical elite, two composers brought the spiritual to the concert stage as a newly established "classical" performance genré. First, twenty-four-year-old African English composer Samuel Coleridge-Taylor (1875–1912) heard spirituals for the first time in 1899 at a Fisk Jubilee concert in London. Fascinated by the creativity of the concert spiritual, he set out to create a collection drawn from the melodic character of the spiritual for pianists to perform on the concert stage. He completed and published a collection of piano arrangements, *Twenty-four Negro Melodies*, in 1905, which performed successfully as part of his concert tour in the United States. Coleridge-Taylor explained the purposes of the songs:

> However beautiful the actual melodies are in themselves, there can be no doubt that much of their value is lost on account of their extreme brevity and unsuitability for the ordinary amateur. What Brahms has done for the Hungarian folk music, Dvorak for the Bohemian, and Grieg for the Norwegian, I have tried to do for these Negro melodies.

The second composer to help establish a tradition for use of "the concert spiritual" is Harry Thacker Burleigh (1866–1949). Burleigh was the first to arrange spirituals for solo voice with piano accompaniment in the style of the German art song. Burleigh's genius lies in his discernment and determination to capture and document in musical scores, the spiritual essence of Black sacred song.

> The spiritual was no longer a folk song in library archives, or the plaintive melody sung to guitar or piano accompaniment. . . . In its arranged form it became music which was alive and an active addition to the American choral repertory, enjoying fast-growing appreciation.[16]

Pre-Gospel Music Period (1900–1930)—The great migration of Blacks from rural to urban contexts during the years surrounding World Wars I

16. Work, "The Negro Spiritual," in Abbington, *Readings in African American Church Music*, 24–25

and II helped spread the appreciation, use, and acceptance of gospel music.[17] Charles Albert Tindley was the first arranger/composer to incorporate melodic and rhythmic principles of gospel singing from the Black "folk church." His protegé, Thomas Dorsey, embellished Tindley's approach and infused blues-based melodies, harmonies, ragtime, and boogie-woogie piano style.[18] As other music forms such as blues and jazz developed during the Nadir and Haarlem Renaissance, many Black church musicians joined Dorsey by crossing over from having sung and played traditional spirituals to singing and playing sacred songs set to music in the style of barrel house, blues, jazz, and rag time.[19]

Traditional Gospel Music Period (1930–69)—Also known as the Golden Age of Gospel, African-American gospel music was disseminated primarily through radio and an efficient oral tradition. With the exception of the National Baptist Convention's hymnal, printed product was limited to one and two-page sheet music that contained melody lines, texts, and primary chords, mostly used for improvisational purposes. Most African-American gospel songwriters did not have their music copyrighted or transcribed to print. Many more did not bother to copyright their songs. Unless songs were preserved on a recording or transcribed to paper through aural dictation, African American gospel, which was tied so securely to oral traditions, was easy prey for publishers who disregarded business ethics for personal gain and financial profit.

In the 1940s and 1950s radio brought new marketing potential to African-American gospel singers. Groups hosted radio programs, advertised music, sold records, and traveled nationwide. The Soul Stirrers with R. H. Harris was one of the most important African-American gospel quartet groups during the decades after World War II. It was one of the first traveling quartets exclusively committed to performing gospel music.

Various events marked a shift away from strictly church performance toward general acceptance of African-American gospel music. The "crossover" between Afro-American and white musical styles, especially in the gospel quartet medium, and the exposure provided by radio and television helped African-American songwriters present their music to a broader market without being taken advantage of or being misunderstood. In turn,

17. Burnim, "Conflict and Controversy in Black Religious Music," in Abbington, *Readings in African American Church Music*, 491.

18. Maultsby, "The Use and Performance of Hymnody, Spirituals, and Gospels in the Black Church" in Abbington, *Readings in African American Church Music*, 77–98.

19. Lewens, *Too Close to Heaven*.

white quartets were able to find unique, fresh, creative new sounds and songs for their own newly established commercial audiences.[20]

Contemporary Gospel Music Period (1969—present)—Sometimes called the Modern Gospel Era, this period of gospel music development is dominated by Pentecostal artists of the Church of God in Christ (COGIC), including André Crouch, Tremaine Hawkins, Walter Hawkins, Sandra Crouch, and the Clark Sisters. Clergy such as Rev. James Cleveland, Rev. Al Green, and evangelist Shirley Caesar "literally preached their compositions into the hearts of their concert hall congregations."[21] These leaders saw their mission to spread "gospel music" to mainstream America as "a calling." Walter Hawkins and André Crouch, in particular, branded an innovation for blending the stylings of pop culture, Jesus movement, and multi-ethnic congregations into their compositions. Gospel music historian Robert Darden describes this timeless canon of musical literature from the west as "religion with rhythm."[22]

Influence of Leading African Denominations

The African Methodist Episcopal Church (AME), the African Methodist Episcopal Zion Church (AMEZ), and the Christian Methodist Episcopal Church (CME) have all contributed heavily to the hymnody of the African American Church. All three groups produced hymnals and provided creative opportunities for talented hymnists to make contributions to their bodies of psalms, hymns, and spiritual songs. Liturgies adhere to a much less conservative theology in the Black Methodist congregations where worship is more formal in its presentation style. Richard Allen is perhaps one of the most important historical and musical personalities in the African Methodist Episcopal Church. It was in 1787, in response to acts of discrimination in the St. George's Methodist Episcopal Church at Philadelphia, that Richard Allen led Blacks to establish the Bethel African Methodist Episcopal Church. Allen became the pastor and established a form of worship based on the cultural preference of his African American congregation. In 1801, Allen published the first hymnal exclusively to and for Black worshipers. This hymnal was modified from that required by the (White) Methodist Episcopal by:

20. Whaley, "Trends in Gospel Music."

21. Lincoln and Mamiya, "The Performed Word: Music and the Black Church," in Abbington, *Readings in African American Church Music*, 55.

22. Darden, *People Get Ready*, 1.

> Replac[ing] complex words and phrases with simpler ones so that the songs "would have more meaning for the illiterate worshipers" in his congregation. He added repetitive refrain lines and choruses to the orthodox hymns. This new text, easily memorized by members who could not read, was sung after each verse. By making these textual changes, Allen insured the complete participation of all church members in the worship.[23]

In addition to Methodist influences, baptistic denominations such as the National Baptist Convention, USA, the National Baptist Convention of America, and Progressive National Baptist Convention, as well as holiness denominations such as the United Holy Church of America (founded in 1886), Fire Baptized Holiness Church of God in the Americas (founded in 1889), Church of Christ Holiness, USA (founded sometime between 1894 and 1896), Church of God in Christ (founded sometime between 1895 and 1897 in Memphis, Tennessee), and Pentecostal Assemblies of the World (1914–1924) have all contributed to the historical development of hymnody in the African American Church.

THEOLOGICAL PERSPECTIVES

This chapter provides a short essay on the very vast topic of the development of African American Christian sacred music and can therefore only be regarded as a survey. At least three distinctive chapters could have been written on spirituals, the development of hymnals, and on the development of Black gospel music. What does unify all three periods and genres is the theological focus of the music. Covenant theology and an African American theology of suffering cannot be excluded when characterizing the theology of the African American church expressed through song. The Bible, more than any other source, provides the textual material for the religious music in the African American church. The biblical accounts of Moses, Jeremiah, Elijah, Ezekiel, Daniel, Jesus, Christ, John [the Apostle], Matthew, Mark, Luke, and others, are interpreted with different insight when viewed with eighteenth and nineteenth-century human bondage as the primary life experience.

Early AME hymnals were influenced heavily by "Wesleyan" theology. Even so, Wyatt Tee Walker believed that Black religious tradition served as a commentary of what was happening in and to the Black community. Much of their sacred music, and the theology it represents, was a response to the Black experience and social community. Walker believed that Black

23. Maultsby, "Use and Performance of Hymnody," 85–86.

hymnody revealed the answers of Christian inquiry such as the nature of Christ, humanity, justice, judgment, and salvation.[24] He explains, "Afro-centric Christian theology proceeds from a different center than does traditional Eurocentric theology. . . . The theology of African American Christians is more experiential than reflective. Ours is a learned and lived theology."[25]

John and James Weldon Johnson's hymn "Lift Every Voice and Sing" is an example of the Afro-centric theological/sociological practice Walker is advocating. Considered the African American National Anthem, the text comes from a poem rendered in 1900, then set to music in 1905. Verse two speaks to this idea of the power of solidarity as broken people become unified in song, spirit, and body. From out of this brokenness, music is born. The rhythm representing the will to live, the melody exemplifying an unborn hope and the text reflecting the spirit of their ancestor's striving for liberation:

> Stony the road we trod,
> Bitter the chastening rod,
> Felt in the days when hope unborn had died;
> Yet with a steady beat,
> Have not our weary feet,
> Come to the place for which our fathers died?
> We have come over a way that with tears has been watered.
> We have come,
> Treading our path through the blood of the slaughtered,
> Out from the gloomy past,
> Till now we stand at last,
> Where the white gleam of our bright star is cast.[26]

Although the theological content of the gospel songs and spirituals was rooted in biblical truth and included major themes of Christian doctrine,[27] some argue that Black gospel music was tainted by a few secular spots, theologically. One reason for this belief is because there was a secret double message in many of the spirituals from which gospel music attained its roots, associating emancipation from slavery with spiritual freedom. This theme of an exodus paradigm can be heard in the lyrics of many of the spirituals. The close relationship between faith in God and emancipation

24. Walker, *Somebody's Calling My Name,* 128.

25. Abbington,"If It Had Not Been for the Lord on My Side," in Abbington, *Readings in African American Church Music,* 2:134.

26. James Weldon Johnson, "Lift Every Voice and Sing" (1900).

27. Adams, "Some Aspects of Black Worship," in Abbington, *Readings in African American Church Music,* 304.

from oppressors expressed by this paradigm is a primary theme of Black liberation theologian, James H. Cone, seen in this reference to the liberating relationship between captive Israel as a type of the African American church. As Israel was liberated from Egypt across the Red Sea, so Blacks would also be set free. It is this theological certainty that characterizes Black worship, enabling Blacks to sing with assurance:

> Oh, Mary, don't you weep, don't you moan.
> Oh, Mary, don't you weep, don't you moan.
> Pharaoh's army got drownded,
> Oh, Mary, don't you weep.

African American gospel music's rocky theological start may also be attributed to mixed acceptance of gospel song into the mainstream of the Black Methodist and Baptist churches during the first half of the twentieth century. Many Methodist and Baptist congregations refused to allow the gospel songs to be part of their worship routine. This was in part due to the heavy influence of secular music styles[28] as well as to the "mixed theology" characteristic of the genre itself. James Abbington suggests that "gospel songwriters compose their songs based upon their personal theology and experience, or without consideration of broader theological implications rather than with any official theological canon in mind."[29]

Other scholars find that a godly focus and christocentricity were dominant and consistent themes in African American Christian sacred music. Louis-Charles Harvey, after researching hundreds of gospel song lyrics concluded, "In black gospel music, Jesus Christ is regarded as the answer to the question of the meaning of black existence. The most fundamental statement made about Jesus Christ is that he is Everything. He is everything because he is *Friend, Protector*, and *Liberator*. It is in fulfilling these roles and functions in the lives of black people that he is regarded as the answer to the question of black life."[30] William B. McClain also supports the idea of the music's consistent godly focus in his pragmatic theological assessment of the gospel song:

> The Gospel song expresses theology. Not the theology of the academy or the university, not formalistic theology or the theology of the seminary, but a theology of experience—the theology of a God who sends the sunshine and the rain, the theology of

28. Lewens, *Too Close to Heaven*.

29. Abbington, "If It Had Not Been for the Lord on My Side," in Abbington, *Readings in African American Church Music*, 2:132.

30. Harvey, "Black Gospel Music," 27.

> a God who is very much alive and active and who has not forsaken those who are poor and oppressed and unemployed. It is a theology of imagination—it grew out of the fire shut up in the bones, of words painted on the canvas of the mind. Fear is turned into hope in the sanctuary and storefronts, and bursts forth in songs of celebration. It is a theology of grace that allows the faithful to see the sunshine of His face—even through their tears. . . . It's a theology of survival that allows a people to celebrate the ability to continue the journey.[31]

CONTRIBUTION TO LITURGY AND WORSHIP

The communal character of African American liturgy and worship is culturally contextualized and theologically expressed, through a cohort of Black epistemologies and personal expressions. These characteristics signify humanity's worship of the Triune God. These liturgies and worship stylings are hermeneutical tasks, shaping her community. Liturgical elements are entrenched with theological heft. The worship encourages personal expression. Within the liturgy and worship, one will easily observe doctrines of Jesus Christ (Christology), Holy Spirit (pneumatology), redemption (soteriology), the church (ecclesiology) and the future (eschatology), with notions and nuances of Christian love, hope, faith and joy, encouraging us to seek a personal relationship with Jesus Christ as Savior and Lord, as well as justice and the pursuit of Christ's Kingdom coming to earth.

Contributions by the African Methodist-Episcopal Church (AME)

AME contributions are numerous and a significant representation of Black culture. The AME published hymnals in 1801, 1818, 1837, 1876, 1892, 1898, 1941, 1954, and 1984. The African American Methodist Episcopal Zion (AMEZ) denomination published hymns in 1839, 1858, 1872, 1892, 1909, 1957,[32] and 1996.[33] And the Christian Methodist Episcopal Church published hymnals in 1891, 1904, 1950, 1987, and 2000. These hymnals were heavily Wesleyan in content and represent the cultural contexts and denominational nuances of the period. Most notable are Richard Allen's

31. Abbington, "If It Had Not Been for the Lord on My Side," in Abbington, *Readings in African American Church Music,* 2:133.

32. Spencer, *Black Hymnody,* 26.

33. Abbington. "If It Had Not Been for the Lord on My Side," in Abbington, *Readings in African American Church Music,* 2:137.

A Collection of Spiritual Songs and Hymns, Selected from Various Authors (1801) and *The African Methodist Episcopal Hymn and Tune Book* (1898). The former represents the first hymnal ever published for or by African American worshipers. The 1898 work is the first African American hymnal to be published with music notation. Heretofore, all hymnals for the Black community were available as "text only" publications.[34] Two individuals published hymnals for the Methodist Episcopal Community but independent of the official AME organization itself: Marshall W. Taylor, a Black preacher/musician published *A Collection of Revival Hymns and Plantation Melodies* in 1883 for the predominantly White Methodist Episcopal Church. The book included "religious folk songs shaped out of the American slave experience" and a significant number of songs from the camp meetings. Charles A. Tindley published *Soul Echoes* in 1908 and *New Songs of Paradise* in 1909. These are significant in that they were intended for singing Sunday school prayer meetings, Epworth League meetings, and social gatherings.

Contributions by the National Baptist Convention

Baptist contributions are limited in scope when compared to the vast output of songs and hymns of the AME, AMEZ, or CME. From 1897 to 1901, the National Baptist Publishing Board produced seven songbooks for use in Sunday school, prayer meeting, student gatherings, and teaching of music theory.[35] *The National Baptist Hymnal*, the earliest *official* hymnal representing the National Baptist Convention, was published in 1903. While organized by Black hymnist, businessman, and publisher R. H. Boyd, the book is modeled after *The Baptist Hymnal* (1886), a publication of the predominantly White Southern Baptist Convention. Other hymn books were published in 1905, 1916, 1918, 1921, 1924, 1927, 1961, 1976,[36] 1977,[37]

34. Spencer, *Black Hymnody*, 4–24.

35. Spencer, *Black Hymnody*, 78–79. National Baptist Publishing Board product produced from 1897–1901 include *Gospel Voices* (1897), *Choice Songs* (1897), *National Tidings of Joy* (1898), *Harp of Zion* (1900) [also called the "Black Young People's Union (B.Y.P.U) Hymnal"], *Pearls of Paradise*, and *Celestial Showers No. 2.* (1901).

36. The Progressive Baptist Convention was established in 1961.

37. "The New National Baptist Hymnal is the premier Black church hymnal published during the post-Civil Rights era and one which reflects the social awareness of Afro-Christianity awakened in the late sixties and early seventies" [Spencer, *Black Hymnody*, 92]. The hymnal includes gospel hymns by Black composers Doris Akers, Lucie Campbell, E. C. Deas, Thomas A. Dorsey, Theodore Frye, C. P. Jones, Magnolia Lewis-Butts, Roberta Martin, Kenneth Morris, C. A. Tidley, Andrae Crouch, and Margaret P. Douroux.

1979,[38] and 1982. It is notable that the 1976 endeavor, *The Progressive Baptist Hymnal,* represents the newly established Progressive National Baptist Convention. In reality, the book is a "special edition" of the *Broadman Hymnal* (1940), which was originally edited by B. B. McKinney for the Southern Baptist Convention.[39]

Contributions by the Church of God in Christ

Contributions by the Church of God in Christ are deeply cemented in the improvisational character of the oral traditions so much part of the denomination. While there were a number of songbooks published for and by the Church of God in Christ, the first official denominational hymnal is the 1982 publication *Yes, Lord!* Published during the denomination's diamond jubilee year, the book title, "Yes, Lord!" is derived from a praise chant composed by Bishop Charles H. Mason, founder of the church in 1896. The chant was used as a "call to worship" before every service by Bishop Mason.[40] The book is a collection of 506 songs that defines for the denomination their Protestant doctrines and theology of worship and adoration; comfort; assurance; God's grace, mercy, and forgiveness; refuge; heaven and everlasting life; the Holy Spirit; Christ's birth; life and ministry of Christ; the crucifixion; Christ's resurrection; the second coming of Jesus; commitment and devotion; aspiration; peace and guidance; renewal and revival; testimony, witness, and evangelism; missions; and patriotic and world peace. Jon Michael Spencer suggests:

> The "Yes, Lord! Hymnal is symbolic of, if not hard evidence of, the evolution of the [Church of God in Christ] from a separatist institution consisting largely of storefront churches housing the "least of them" into an increasingly integrationist institution comprised of numerous grand edifices housing a multiplying middle-class membership.[41]

38. This 1979 publication by the National Baptist Convention USA, *Free Spirit* (1979) included gospel songs by Andrae Crouch, Edwin Hawkins (O Happy Day), and popular songs such as "Climb Every Mountain" and "Michael, Row Your Boat Ashore." Spencer, *Black Hymnody*, 94.

39. Spencer, *Black Hymnody*, 95.

40. Costen, "Published Hymnals in the African American Tradition," in Abbington, *Readings in African American Church Music,* 162–63.

41. Spencer, *Black Hymnody*, 149.

Contributions from the Spirituals

Spirituals also prove to be a significant and influential repository of songs for worship in mainline and evangelical churches worldwide. Examples of such spirituals with wide use are: "Ride On, King Jesus," "Set Down Servant," "I Got a Robe," "Elijah Rock," "Every Time I Feel the Spirit," "I Want Jesus to Walk with Me," "Ride the Chariot," "Give Me Jesus," "Go Down Moses," "Great Day," and "The Battle of Jericho."

Contributions from Social Hymns

Social hymns also represent a significant part of the contribution Black hymnist have made to Protestant worship and Christian liturgy. There is a body of "social gospel hymns" that address the issues surrounding "the collective life," sins of society, perfect brotherhood, freedom, and various other social concerns. While examples of this genre of hymnody are many, two valuable examples are John Oxenham's hymn "In Christ There is No East or West"[42] and William Ballantine's "God Save America."[43]

NOTABLE HYMNS

Beginning around 1910, a clear delineation for Black hymnody began to emerge. Charles Tindley, Charles Harrison Mason, James Weldon Johnson, John Johnson, Thomas A. Dorsey, and Cleavant Derricks gave birth to a new hymnody infused with a blues codification. Many of these songs were "framed with blues chord progressions." Most were included in early hymnals published by and for African American Baptist and AME congregations. The hymns represent highly skilled and trained composers and musicians and are included in *The Gospel Pearls* (1921) and *The Baptist Standard Hymnal* (1924), published by the Sunday School Publishing Board of the National Baptist Convention, USA; and *The African Methodist Episcopal Hymnal* (1954), published by the AME Sunday School Union.[44] By the mid-twentieth century, these well-crafted hymns by African American

42. Lincoln and Mamiya, "The Performed Word: Music and the Black Church," in Abbington, *Readings in African American Church Music*, 50–51.

43. Lincoln and Mamiya, "The Performed Word: Music and the Black Church," in Abbington, *Readings in African American Church Music*, 50–51.

44. Adams, "Some Aspects of Black Worship," in Abbington, *Readings in African American Church Music*, 302–3.

hymnists were found in a number of hymnals published by predominately White denominations. These hymns include, but are not limited to:

- "Life is Like a Mountain Railroad" by M. E. Abby (1891)
- "Lift Every Voice and Sing" by James and John Johnson (1900)
- "I'm a Soldier in the Army of the Lord" by Charles Harrison Mason (1904)
- "The Storm Is Passing Over" by Charles A. Tindley (1905)
- "We'll Understand it Better By and By" by Charles A. Tindley (1905)
- "Nothing Between" by Charles A. Tindley (1905)
- "Take Your Burden to the Lord and Leave it There" by Charles A. Tindley (1906)
- "Hold to God's Unchanging Hand" by Jennie Wilson and F. L. Eiland (1905)
- "We'll Soon Be Done With Troubles and Trials" by Cleavant Derricks (1934)
- "Just A Little Talk With Jesus" by Cleavant Derricks (1937)
- "Precious Lord Take My Hand" by Thomas A. Dorsey (1938)
- "Just A Closer Walk with Thee" by Kenneth Morris (1940)
- "He'll Understand and Say 'Well Done'" by Lucie E. Campbell (c1950)
- "Sweet, Sweet Spirit" by Doris Akers (1973)
- "We've Come This Far By Faith" by Albert A. Goodson (1963)
- "The Blood Will Never Lose Its Power" by Andrae Crouch (1966)
- "O Happy Day" by Edwin Hawkins (1968)
- "Total Praise" by Richard Smallwood (1996)

One may not often see many hymnals used during African American church services today because the members usually know the hymns and songs by heart, having learned them through the oral tradition. Another reason for the infrequent use of hymnals is that contemporary African American church musicians change the meter and style of traditional European hymns used in modern worship services, so the hymns are reinterpreted and sung using a gospel beat, tone, and cadences.

The late Wendell P. Whalum provides a welcome summary of Black hymnody's valuable contribution to liturgy and worship saying,

> The music from the Black church is a music that takes as its license the right to pick and choose that which serves its needs, and if it cannot be found, it may be created. The fact that it begins as outright creation makes creativity part and parcel of all Black music. . . . The offerings are honest and they are intended to serve the human needs of the people, individual and group. As an honest music that, without doubt, has had many positive effects on those who use it, it should have been, at least at the level of the music of the oral tradition, accepted into the larger body of church music of the Christian world.[45]

BIBLIOGRAPHY

Abbington, James, ed. *Readings in African American Church Music and Worship.* Chicago: GIA Publications, 2001.

———. *Readings in African American Church Music and Worship.* Vol. 2. Chicago: GIA Publications, 2014.

Banfield, William C. *Cultural Codes: Makings of a Black Music Philosophy.* Lanham, MD: Scarecrow, 2010.

Boyer, Horace Clarence. *How Sweet the Sound: The Golden Age of Gospel.* Washington, DC: Elliott and Clark, 1995.

———. *Lectures on Afro-American Church Music at the University of Massachusetts at Amherst.* Amherst, MA: Horace Clarence Boyer, 1979.

Bradshaw, Paul, Cheslyn Jones, Geoffrey Wainwright, and Edward Yarnold, eds. *The Study of Liturgy.* Rev. ed. New York: Oxford University Press, 2010.

Burnim, Mellonee V., and Portia K. Maultsby. *African American Music: An Introduction.* New York: Routledge, 2006.

Darden, Robert. *People Get Ready: A New History of Black Gospel Music.* New York: Continuum, 2006.

Floyd, Samuel A., Jr. *The Power of Black Music: Interpreting its History from Africa to the United States.* New York: Oxford University Press, 1995.

Harvey, Louis-Charles. "Black Gospel Music and Black Theology." *The Journal of Religious Thought* 43.2 (Fall 1986/Winter 1987) 19–37.

Kirk-Duggan, Cheryl A. "The Matrix of African American Sacred Music in the 21st Century." *The Journal of Traditions and Beliefs* 1.3 (2014) 7–20.

Lewens, Alan. *Too Close to Heaven: The Story of Gospel Music.* USA/UK, 1996.

Lovell, John. *Black Song: The Forge and the Flame.* New York: Paragon House, 1986.

Maultsby, Portia K. "The Use and Performance of Hymnody, Spirituals, and Gospels in the Black Church." *Western Journal of Black Studies* 7.3 (Fall 1983) 161–71.

Raboteau, Albert J. *Slave Religion: The "Invisible Institution" in the Antebellum South.* New York: Oxford University Press, 2004.

Ramsey, Guthrie P., Jr. *Race Music: Black Cultures from Bebop to Hip-Hop.* Berkeley: University of California Press, 2003.

45. Whalum, "Black Hymnody," in Abbington, *Readings in African American Church Music*, 182–83.

Reagon, Bernice Johnson. *We'll Understand it Better By and By: Pioneering African American Gospel Composers.* Washington, DC: Smithsonian Institution Press, 1992.

Saliers, Don. *Music and Theology*, Nashville: Abingdon, 2007.

Smith, Catherine Parsons. *William Grant Still.* Chicago: University of Illinois Press, 2008.

Smith, Robert, Jr. *Doctrine that Dances: Bringing Doctrinal Preaching and Teaching to Life.* Nashville: B&H, 2008.

Southern, Eileen. *The Music of Black Americans: A History.* 2nd ed. New York: W. W. Norton, 1983.

Spencer, Jon Michael. *Black Hymnody: A Hymnological History of the African-American Church.* Knoxville: University of Tennessee Press. 1992.

Walker, Wyatt Tee. *Somebody's Calling My Name: Black Sacred Music and Social Change.* Valley Forge, PA: Judson, 1979.

Webber, Robert. *Worship Is a Verb: Eight Principles for Transforming Worship.* Peabody, MA: Hendrickson, 1992.

Wilson Consten, Melva. *African American Christian Worship.* Nashville: Abingdon, 2007.

Whaley, Vernon M. "Trends in Gospel Music (1940–1960)." PhD diss., University of Oklahoma, 1992.

Work, John W. *American Negro Songs and Spirituals: A Comprehensive Collection of 230 Folk Songs, Religious and Secular.* Whitefish, MT: Kessinger, 2007.

Wright, Josephine, and Samuel Floyd. *New Perspectives on Music: Essays in Honor of Eileen Southern.* Warren, MI: Harmonie Park, 1992.

Chapter 10

Southern Gospel Music

James R. Goff, Jr.

HISTORICAL BACKGROUND

The genre of religious music known as southern gospel emerged from a combination of practices and technological improvements steeped in nineteenth century American culture and industrial development. As a term, it was practically unknown until late in the decade of the 1970s when it gradually came to be associated distinctly with three and four-part harmony, primarily white, gospel singing. Industry award ceremonies held by the Gospel Music Association, founded in 1964, as well as the developing diversity of gospel music itself prompted the categorization. As a result, music historian Don Cusic could accurately note in 1990 that southern gospel was "in reality, more national than southern, although it remains strongest in the south where it developed."[1]

In earlier decades, the music had simply been dubbed quartet singing or thrown without categorization into the amorphous category of *gospel music*, made popular in the late nineteenth century expansion of gospel songs and lyrics associated with both rural and urban evangelical revivalism. Not explicitly discernable were subtle distinctions related to American

1. Cusic, *Sound of Light*, 95.

race relations—since various forms of the new music were popular in both black and white communities. In the decade of the 1950s, however, as gospel singing found increased avenues for commercial marketing, *Billboard* solved this problem by consistently using the term *sacred* to refer to primarily white gospel singing and *spiritual* to refer to primarily black gospel singing. While useful in designating the racial character of specific performing groups, in both cases the terms allowed no explicit distinction as to whether or not the singing was group or solo. Readers were left to infer that and other important stylistic differences by recognition of specific names and prior knowledge or association.[2]

In many respects, modern gospel singing of all shapes and sizes developed primarily from innovations intended to elicit participation, and was not envisioned as commercial musical entertainment. Long before the emergence of a genre of music identifiable as southern gospel, a number of innovative teaching techniques involving uniquely shaped notes to represent the numerical relationship between notes on a musical scale had been advocated by music teachers. A New England system of shape notes flourished in some circles in the late eighteenth century in the midst of what was known as the better music movement—an attempt to improve what many considered the terrible state of church music singing in the American colonies.[3]

In the early nineteenth century in a young, developing nation, a similar system of teaching involved four distinctly shaped notes (Fa, Sol, La, and Mi). The Fasola-system, as it came to be called, ultimately revolved around the popular *Sacred Harp* songbook, published first in 1844. The four notes chosen were the most often used notes and entire songs could be constructed and performed by learning the relationship between these four foundational sounds. When a song ventured into a more complicated construction adding the three additional notes (Do, Re, and Ti), composers took the same symbols, with one symbol representing two different notes or sounds. Therein lay the origins of what by mid-century became a seething debate between four-noters and seven-noters, aggressive proponents of public music education through teaching the public to sing by observing the shape of specific notes. One of the earliest examples in the growing seven-note camp was William "Singing Billy" Walker's 1866 *Christian Harmony*

2. For an example of how the magazine handled the distinction between white and black gospel artists, see Rolontz, "Sacred Songs Close Kin," 42, 62, as well as the RCA Victor advertisements on pp. 50–51 of the same *Billboard* publication.

3. On the evolution of shape notes and the singing school culture that promoted them, see Goff, *Close Harmony*, 35–54. The earliest comprehensive investigation of the role of shape notes in southern musical development was Jackson, *White Spirituals*.

songbook—a deviation away from the popular *Sacred Harp* system with an expansion to seven different shapes, reflecting the growing diversity in the music. Walker's conversion was instructive, given his 1835 publication of *Southern Harmony*, a four-note songbook collection appearing a decade earlier than the arrival of *The Sacred Harp*. The controversy that emerged over expanding the notation ultimately sealed the fundamental difference in what came to be known simply as Sacred Harp singers versus their related but different seven-note singing cousins. Sacred Harp singers to the present day sing only out of the *Sacred Harp* book—cementing them to a remarkable degree in time. By the 1980s, scholars became fascinated with Sacred Harp, in its own right an interesting retention of rural American music.[4] However, far more important—commercially and culturally—were the efforts of the seven-note music publishers, toward which scholars often showed a remarkable ignorance and indifference, perhaps precisely because it *was* so commercially viable and influential. It was Walker himself who, in his defense of the three new shapes added to create the seven-note system, argued with logic that was difficult to deny: "Would any parents having seven children, ever think of calling them by only four names?"[5] Hidden in those words of wisdom lay the pragmatism of the seven-noters and their influence on the future of gospel music would be significant, especially in the South.[6]

Despite the commercial success of shape-note publishers, rural singing societies, and shape-note singing schools, the musical establishment looked with disfavor on the innovative little shapes—refusing to allow shape notes an entry into the musical curriculum of public schools and denouncing them with a degree of high-brow snobbishness whenever possible.[7] "Dunce notes," they retorted, insisting that real musicians learn the traditional scale of notes on lines and spaces. The beauty of shape notes, however, was that they offered everything that traditional music had offered, the unusual shape of the notes causing no major hardship for the person playing or in fact singing music on the traditional scale. But for the singer trained in shape notes, they offered a unique ability to learn a song quickly by associating and actually singing the "shapes" first. And in the end shape notes survived

4. On the tradition of Sacred Harp, see Dyen, "New Directions in Sacred Harp," 73–79; Cobb, *Sacred Harp*; and Marini, *Sacred Song in America*, 68–99.

5. Brobston, *Daddy Sang Lead*, 39.

6. On the significance of gospel music and the American South, see Malone, *Sing Me Back Home*, 46–54 and 165–96. On Walker's contributions to the world of shape-note music, see Jackson, *White Spirituals*, 55–69.

7. On the importance of singing societies and singing conventions in rural southern life, see Brobston, *Daddy Sang Lead*, 75–112.

best in the rural South, where generations of southerners ignored the advice of those formally trained and insisted on using any reasonable method that taught music effectively. Across the South, especially through the prominence and success of the Ruebush-Kieffer Music Publishing Company of Singer's Glen, Virginia, shape notes increased the musical knowledge and ability of singers both inside and outside church walls.[8]

Southern gospel quartets began formally, at least professionally, in 1910 when Tennessee shape-note music publisher James D. Vaughan sponsored a quartet to travel to Dickson, Tennessee, for a special appearance at a Cumberland Presbyterian camp meeting. For much of the previous decade, Vaughan had transitioned himself from a prominent public school educator into a successful shape-note gospel music publisher—essentially turning his passion for music into a new career. What marked the significance of the 1910 camp meeting arrangement was the fact that Vaughan not only funded the trip but also agreed to pay the quartet members from the proceeds if they would take and sell his latest songbooks. When the quartet recorded greater than expected success, a continuing business deal emerged. Over the next thirty years, Vaughan would sponsor quartets both as salaried employees and also as sharers in the profits of songbook sales. Most of the early successful southern gospel quartets, including the Speer Family, the Blackwood Brothers, and the Stamps Quartet, spent some time as songbook peddlers. The natural development of gospel music quartets thus followed the story of twentieth-century technology. Songbook salesmen progressed to live radio performers; radio gave them a chance to advertise the songbooks and also their area concerts where they might charge a nickel or dime for concert admittance. In particular, their background in shape notes proved fortuitous in juggling the demands of their new schedules. In his later years, the venerable James Blackwood, whose Blackwood Brothers Quartet dated to the mid-1930s in rural Mississippi, recounted how, as a young teenager rolling out of bed long before daylight to do the early farm radio show, he would wait until the last possible moment to throw his clothes on and dash down to the radio station where the group performed live in Shreveport, Louisiana. When the red light came on, however, the boys were animated, ready to sing gospel music. Part of their enthusiasm was their love for singing and performing, but the young men also recognized quite openly that it provided a way out of the drudgery of Depression-era farm work. It was a unique opportunity made possible largely by their acquired proficiency in

8. On the importance of the Ruebush-Kieffer company and its accompanying Virginia Normal Music School (later the Shenandoah Normal Music School), founded in 1874, see Goff, *Close Harmony*, 42–54; Cusic, *Sound of Light*, 94–95; and Harrison, *Then Sings My Soul*, 50–79.

shape notes. When phone callers requested an unknown song, the quartet members would simply grab one of the shape-note hymnals they carried with them and, as long as the requested song appeared in the book, they could sing it live on the radio—having never actually practiced it. The boys, well versed in shape notes, could perform it, in James's words, "the first time, dead on."[9]

In addition to a host of groups who operated under the name Stamps-Baxter or Vaughan, among the most prominent early performing quartets in the 1920s and '30s were the Frank Stamps Quartet, the Speer Family, the LeFevres, the Chuck Wagon Gang, and the Rangers Quartet. Joining these groups with a level of increased prominence during the decade of the 1940s were the Blackwood Brothers, the Homeland Harmony Quartet, the Harmoneers, the Oak Ridge Quartet, and the Statesmen. Also joining southern gospel circles and breaking the boundaries of segregation, at least on stage, were the members of the popular Golden Gate Quartet, the most prominent of the many black quartets to achieve a significant following among white audiences before 1955.[10] Joining these groups and holding a position of prominence during the decade of the 1950s were the Blue Ridge Quartet, the Rebels Quartet, the Jordanaires, the Segos, and the Weatherford Quartet.

Live radio eventually gave way to radio transcription disc recordings so that a quartet could record a series of shows for later airplay—lending them greater freedom for concert travel. Increased concerting combined with the recording of commercial vinyl 78s added yet another cog in the growing wheel of income opportunities. Ultimately, television also gave increased exposure and thus greater opportunity to build a fan base for a quartet's products and performances. In each case, technology gave some groups an edge over their competition. The heyday of the gospel quartets came in the 1950s when some quartets rivaled their secular contemporaries for national airplay and notoriety. The *Arthur Godfrey Talent Scouts* television program, the earliest forerunner of what by the early decades of the twenty-first century became the *American Idol* and *America's Got Talent* phenomenon, featured at least two major gospel quartet winners alongside an array of secular performers—all of whom received valuable publicity and recording opportunities for winning the competition. Both the Blackwood Brothers and the Statesmen Quartet won the competition and secured exclusive RCA recording contracts in the early years of the 1950s.[11]

9. Blackwood, personal interview.

10. On the influence of the Golden Gate and other black quartets in early southern gospel circles, see Goff, *Close Harmony*, 210–11.

11. On the heyday of the gospel quartet popularity, see Goff, *Close Harmony*, 201–17; and Terrell, *Music Men*, 109–49. For a look at the notoriety as well as the pitfalls of

The southern gospel tradition, like other genres of gospel music, evolved and changed. The music thrived in particular in the rural and suburban South and Midwest because the backgrounds of the singers resonated with the experiences of the audience. The developing industry was less tied to the denominational church than it perhaps appeared to the casual observer. Not until the church growth movement of the 1970s did a significant percentage of the concerts take place in a church setting. Rather, the local fairgrounds, high school auditoriums, and municipal arenas were more the fare for successful quartets. But the church was nonetheless important, not only because the message it carried provided the contextual core for the songs but also because—entertainment-laden though it was—the quartet industry drew from shared experiences in the rural and small town church community.

By the late decades of the twentieth century, the groups most associated with southern gospel's continued success were ironically much closer to the tradition of the evangelical church than they had been in the banner years of the mid-1960s when the success of syndicated television programs like *Gospel Singing Jubilee*, begun in 1964, and a handful of lesser-known compilations of gospel singing talent appeared in practically all major markets nationwide. Television launched a number of new quartets quickly to a position of prominence during this period, most notably the Florida Boys, the Rambos, the Happy Goodmans, the Dixie Echoes, the Cathedrals, the Couriers, the Hinsons, the Downings, the Thrasher Brothers, the Imperials, and the Inspirations.[12]

Several factors accounted for the closer church connection in the late decades of the twentieth century, but the most important was undoubtedly the emergence of the megachurch, a venue that provided both a large enough space and the required sophisticated equipment to make major concert appearances possible and desirable. Characterized by a joyous presentation and a tight harmonic structure, southern gospel quartets provided a sound that could captivate an audience—mixing entertainment and worship almost seamlessly in a typical concert appearance. Fans came to listen for the high "first tenor" paralleled by the rumble of the "low bass." Carrying the middle parts were the lead and baritone singers—oftentimes the most versatile singers in the group, fully capable of switching parts when a solo or a unique song structure demanded it.

gospel music fame during this period, see Cheatham, *Bad Boy of Gospel Music*.

12. On the importance of television, see Goff, *Close Harmony*, 221–32, 244–53; Terrell, *Music Men*, 259–65; and Cusic, *Sound of* Light, 154–55.

The southern gospel quartet tradition most often featured four voices, typically but not always male, backed up by a talented pianist. But the tradition always featured and promoted other sounds, both vocal and instrumental. Mixed groups with male and female voices were popular as early as the 1920s with the success of the Speer Family and the LeFevres. Those groups, and many others, also introduced new instrumentation—specifically stringed instruments. By the 1940s, the Lewis Family of Lincolnton, Georgia, added a consistent bluegrass sound to the genre and, while never dominating the industry, it remained as part of the overall genre with many concert festivals including at least one such group in the mix. With the popularity of bluegrass in the late 1940s and then again with the Folk Revival of the 1960s, roots music blossomed. Always present within the amalgam of a bluegrass or folk event was at least some gospel music—featuring a variety of stringed instruments alongside the unique, often high-pitched harmony sound that some in the secular industry dubbed the "high lonesome."[13]

THEOLOGICAL PERSPECTIVES

By its very nature, and consistent with its roots, the music that incorporated what became southern gospel comprised a rather loose theological framework. Partly because the music emerged in a late-nineteenth and early-twentieth century rural American culture that took for granted basic evangelical Christian principles, the writers of early gospel songs constructed their works of art with a broad brush, confident that basic biblical allusions and orthodoxy would suffice.[14] Practically speaking, they also understood—intuitively if not explicitly—that the economic enterprise into which they ventured required the support of large numbers of American Christians and that any theological hair-splitting could be disastrous for the future of their proposed lyrical contributions. Songs drew heavily on the popularity of sounds and styles that had proven prevalent in the secular marketplace as well as in the participatory world of southern singing societies and singing schools. Likewise, most writers steered a safe course with a biblical foundation consistent with most evangelical churches and denominations. As a result, songs alluded to basic themes of salvation, prayer, happiness, and fellowship in Jesus, and ultimate redemption in heaven and the

13. On the presence of bluegrass-inspired gospel, see Goff, *Close Harmony*, 204, 276, and Marini, *Sacred Song in America*, 304–11.

14. On the importance of the late-nineteenth century evangelical revival movement to the expansion and popularity of gospel songs, see Stowe, *How Sweet the Sound*, 91–116.

second coming. References to healing were frequent but rarely emphasized so as to identify the specific theology of the faith healing evangelists. Matters of sanctification and "Christian perfection" were referenced only vaguely since evangelicals espoused a number of different permutations of holiness theology. Likewise, the Holy Spirit could be referenced but rarely with an orientation to the specifics of evidential tongues that might identify the writer as a member of a Pentecostal denomination. Often, songs were simply watered-down, non-theological attempts at praise or faith statements. Popular gospel songsmith Albert E. Brumley's rare but candid comments on songwriting in a January 1971 interview said nothing about the theology of a song, perhaps taking it for granted that a songwriter's theological DNA would come through. His pragmatic approach seemed more devoted to the structural components that made a song memorable and thus enduring.

> A song has got to say something all the way through. If you get weak in one line and strong in another one, why it doesn't seem to do it. It's got to portray a story and have a melody that will carry the message.[15]

In this regard, southern gospel songwriters were quite at home with a developing evangelical ecumenical movement rooted in the success of major evangelists like Billy Graham. They wrote about salvation, grace, healing power, and the second coming easily with little need to over-emphasize or invite objection.

CONTRIBUTION TO LITURGY AND WORSHIP

One of the primary contributions of the late-twentieth-century contemporary praise band was a resurgence of participatory singing rather than performance-based presentation. Teams of singers and musicians led in worship and thus encouraged all worshipers to sing along with them. Ironically, the popularity of praise and worship in church services, though bemoaned by stalwart traditionalists of the hymnbook and gospel song past, meant that events by the early years of the twenty-first century had, in that sense at least, come full circle. Praise and worship teams by their very nature de-emphasized the professionalism and entertainment aspects of the music to return once more to congregations of people participating by singing and presumably singing better—exactly what the shape-note entrepreneurs of the colonial better music movement had envisioned. Though a valid observation, critics often hastened to opine that people sang "better"

15. *History of Southern Gospel*, vol. 1.

and participated more only because the music was so frequently simpler with less emphasis on harmony. Beginning with the contemporary music of the late 1960s, there was also an unmistakable youth movement crossing over into a gospel direction quite different from that of the traditional quartet. Nonetheless, early contemporary gospel music as it emerged in the late 1960s and early 1970s included a number of groups that had been linked to the quartet world that, with the growing diversity of the music, would soon come to be designated "southern gospel." Most notably, the Imperials, a group formed in late 1963 by Jake Hess, the renowned lead singer of the famous Statesmen Quartet, became a genuine crossover group, moving from the traditional sound to the new, youth-oriented contemporary Christian music. Other groups like the Hinsons, the Rambos, the Downings, and the Speer Family also used an array of young talent to begin offering a sound catering increasingly toward the contemporary market. In addition, ministry-oriented groups like the Couriers from Harrisburg, Pennsylvania, converted their music in the 1970s more toward a church and youth worship style geared toward evangelism. Rooted in the Jesus Rock coffee house and youth revival emphases of events like Explo '72, sometimes dubbed the "Christian Woodstock," the new music borrowed freely from the rock 'n' roll rhythms but the lyrics carried a strong Christian message—oftentimes one that was strikingly more biblical than the older gospel music traditions.[16]

Despite the criticisms of older gospel music fans who rebelled against both the sound and the look of much of the new contemporary gospel, the new gospel music won in the economic market place—setting new records for gospel music sales and changing the face of Christian music as a result. In time, church worship began to reflect these fundamental changes in gospel music performance. As churches grew and adopted a more open and frequently a more charismatic style of worship, the music reflected the change. Praise and worship music, championed in the late 1960s and early '70s by the likes of the Bill Gaither Trio, the Lanny Wolfe Trio, and Andre Crouch and the Disciples, and then in the 1980s and '90s by Amy Grant and Michael W. Smith, came to hold a prominent place within the new urban and suburban worship centers—now housed in newer non-traditional settings like shopping centers and in worship complexes that provided a more functional ministry application from that usually possible in an old-style church facility. The praise band was the natural outgrowth of these dramatic changes within the gospel music world.[17]

16. On the importance of the emergence of the Christian contemporary genre, see Cusic, *Sound of Light*, 126–29, 158–63, and 184–99.

17. Bill and Gloria Gaither's role in helping shape southern gospel as a contributing and appreciable part of a much larger world of gospel music has been particularly

NOTABLE HYMNS/SONGS

A handful of songs made popular first in southern gospel circles had by the early years of the twenty-first century made their way into collections of church hymnals and praise and worship compendiums. Among those most recognized were Bill Gaither's "Because He Lives" and "He Touched Me," Albert Brumley's perennially popular "I'll Fly Away," E. M. Bartlett's "Victory in Jesus," Doris Akers's "Sweet, Sweet Spirit," Lanny Wolfe's "Surely the Presence," and Dottie Rambo's "He Looked Beyond My Fault and Saw My Need." Also notable in this regard was the Stuart K. Hine version of the nineteenth century hymn "How Great Thou Art"—possibly the most recognized song connected with the genre due to Elvis Presley's popular rendition pulled almost entirely from his personal affinity for southern gospel quartet harmony.

For many rural Americans, particularly those associated with a wide variety of Holiness, Pentecostal, and Baptist organizations, the hymnal exposure to southern gospel songs was even more pervasive. By the middle decades of the twentieth century, the Nashville-based John T. Benson Publishing Company included a significant number of songs with specific southern gospel connections in their hymnals—most notably those made popular by shape-note publishers like Anthony J. Showalter, Eugene M. Bartlett, James D. Vaughan, and the prominent team of Virgil O. Stamps and Jesse R. Baxter. Standard hymn collections like Benson's 1957 edition of *All-American Church Hymnal* and 1968 edition of *The American Service Hymnal* featured selections made popular in those early shape-note circles, among them Bartlett's "Victory in Jesus" (1939), Showalter's "Leaning on the Everlasting Arms" (words with Elisha A. Hoffman, 1887), Vaughan employee Adger M. Pace's "That Glad Reunion Day" (1940), James D. Vaughan's arrangement of William Hunter's "I Feel Like Traveling On" (1838, arr. 1930s), J. R. Baxter's popular arrangement of the classic "Farther Along" (W. B. Stephens, 1937), and the Albert E. Brumley arrangement of "This World Is Not My Home" (1937). Also enjoying a strong connection within the quartet world were several songs by Assemblies of God minister Ira Stanphill, most notably "Mansion Over the Hilltop" (1949) and "I Know Who Holds Tomorrow" (1950).[18]

---

important as their success with the *Homecoming* video series has demonstrated. See Harper, *Gaithers and Southern Gospel Homecoming*, 19–60.

18. All of these selections except "That Glad Reunion Day" appeared in 1957's *All-American Church Hymnal* and all except "I Feel Like Traveling On" appeared in 1968's *American Service Hymnal*. Stanphill's most enduring quartet number was perhaps "Suppertime" (1950), though that particular song rarely appeared in church worship

Even more important was the 1951 publication by Tennessee Music and Printing of Cleveland, Tennessee, of *The Church Hymnal*, known popularly by those in the pews as "The Red-Back Hymnal." Published in shape notes and stocked with a wide variety of up tempo songs from the rural convention singing tradition, the book probably more than any other single publication kept what was in effect southern gospel roots music before the church-going South. On the fiftieth anniversary of the hymnal's original publication, the editors pointedly recognized the degree to which the core of southern gospel's denominational church audience had been responsible for the hymnal's long run of success:

> Through succeeding years of effective use, this hymnal has achieved significance in Evangelical and Pentecostal churches as a repository of the best of gospel hymnody and convention songs.[19]

In addition, the long-running hymnal and its producers understood clearly the debt owed to a stalwart tradition of "singing conventions, singing schools, revival meetings and camp meetings" using printed collections of shape-note gospel songs. The preface to the commemorative edition gave explicit credit as well to the professional singing groups that made this style of church song popular.

> This type music had an impact on the rural culture when the all-male gospel quartets began to sing it in their radio and concert ministries. Gospel quartets had a huge impact on the printing and recording of gospel music, later producing well-known groups like the Blackwood Brothers Quartet, Statesmen, LeFevres, Homeland Harmony Quartet, and ultimately the Stamps, Chuck Wagon Gang, Speers, Cathedrals, Imperials and many more.[20]

A number of additional songs made popular by southern gospel became well known by the later years of the twentieth century though more from radio and recordings exposure rather than a presence in hymnals. Some of the most prominent of these songs were: "I Bowed on my Knees and Cried 'Holy'" (Nettie Dudley Washington, 1923), "Give the World a Smile" (Otis Deaton and M. L. Yandell, 1924), "Jesus is Coming Soon" (R. E. Winsett, 1942), "What a Savior" (Marvin Dalton, 1948), "This Ole House" (Stuart Hamblen, 1954), "Without Him" (Mylon LeFevre, 1962), "The

hymnals.

19. *Church Hymnal*, foreword.

20. *Church Hymnal*, preface.

Lighthouse" (Ronny Hinson, 1970), "Build My Mansion" (Dottie Rambo, 1970), "Sweet Beulah Land" (Squire Parsons, 1973), "Statue of Liberty" (Neil Enloe, 1974), and "Midnight Cry" (Chuck and Greg Day, 1986).[21]

BIBLIOGRAPHY

All-American Church Hymnal. Nashville: John T. Benson Publishing, 1957.

The American Service Hymnal. Nashville: John T. Benson, 1968.

Blackwood, James. Personal interviews. Anderson, IN, April 3, 1996, and Springdale, AR, August 3, 1996.

Brobston, Stanley Heard. *Daddy Sang Lead: The History and Performance Practice of White Southern Gospel Music.* New York: Vantage, 2006.

Cheatham, Russ. *Bad Boy of Gospel Music: The Calvin Newton Story.* Jackson: University Press of Mississippi, 2003.

Church Hymnal. Fiftieth Anniversary, 1951–2001, Commemorative Edition. Cleveland, TN: Tennessee Printing and Music Company, 1951, 2001. "Foreword" by Delton L. Alford.

Cobb, Buell E., Jr. *The Sacred Harp: A Tradition and Its Music.* Athens: University of Georgia Press, 1978, reprint eds., 1989 and 2004.

Cusic, Don. *The Sound of Light: A History of Gospel Music.* Bowling Green, OH: Bowling Green State University Popular Press, 1990.

Dyen, Doris J. "New Directions in Sacred Harp Singing." In *Folk Music and Modern Sound*, edited byWilliam Ferris and Mary L. Hart, 73–79. Jackson: University Press of Mississippi, 1982.

Goff, James R., Jr. *Close Harmony: A History of Southern Gospel.* Chapel Hill: The University of North Carolina Press, 2002.

Harper, Ryan P. *The Gaithers and the Southern Gospel Homecoming in the Twenty-First Century.* Jackson: University Press of Mississippi, 2017.

Harrison, Douglas. *Then Sings My Soul: The Culture of Southern Gospel Music.* Urbana: University of Illinois Press, 2012.

The History of Southern Gospel Music. Video Documentary, Cat. #GCG-10001. Valley Village, CA: Greystone Communications Group, 1997.

Jackson, George Pullen. *White Spirituals in the Southern Uplands.* Chapel Hill: The University of North Carolina Press, 1933.

Malone, Bill C. *Sing Me Back Home: Southern Roots and Country Music.* Norman: University of Oklahoma Press, 2017.

———. *Southern Music, American Music.* Lexington: The University Press of Kentucky, 1979.

Marini, Stephen A. *Sacred Song in America.* Urbana: University of Illinois Press, 2003.

Rolontz, Bob. "Sacred Songs Close Kin to C&W Music." *Billboard* 65 (December 5, 1953) 42, 62.

Southern Gospel's Top 20 Songs of the Century. 2 vols. Franklin, TN: New Haven Records, 2000, 2003.

Stowe, David W. *How Sweet the Sound: Music in the Spiritual Lives of Americans.* Cambridge: Harvard University Press, 2004.

21. *Southern Gospel's Top 20 Songs*, vols. 1 and 2.

Terrell, Bob. *The Music Men: The Story of Professional Gospel Quartet Singing*. Asheville, NC: Bob Terrell, 1990.

Chapter 11

Roman Catholic Liturgical Renewal Movement

Michael S. Driscoll

HISTORICAL BACKGROUND

On January 25, 1959, the feast of the Conversion of St. Paul, Pope John XXIII announced the creation of the Second Vatican Council, an assembly of Roman Catholic religious leaders meant to settle doctrinal issues. This announcement shocked the world and set into motion an event that would dramatically change not only the Catholic Church but many other churches as well. There had not been an ecumenical council in nearly one hundred years. Vatican II, the twenty-first ecumenical council in the history of the Catholic church, officially began on October 11, 1962, and met in four sessions over the next four years. After the announcement of the council, preparations began that took more than two years. Ten specialized commissions were named to work on various themes from the liturgy to Christian unity. The preparatory commissions consisted primarily of members of the Roman Curia who produced 987 drafts (*schemata*) to be discussed and voted upon by between 2,100 and 2,300 bishops in attendance assisted by their experts (*periti*). Seventeen Orthodox churches and Protestant denominations were also present as non-voting observers.

Logically the first discussion should have been on the nature of the church (*de ecclesia*). After all, this was the unfinished agenda of the First Vatican Council that met in 1869–70 that had been interrupted by the Franco-Prussian War. However, at Vatican II an unusual thing happened when the draft that was pesented for discussion was rejected, having been eclipsed by intervening biblical and patristic studies, which called into question the prevailing model of the church as a hierarchy. Thus, discussion on this topic was tabled and the draft document on the liturgy was substituted. Therefore, in 1963 the *Constitution on the Divine Liturgy* (*Sacrosanctum Concilium*) was promulgated by Pope Paul VI, the successor of John XXII who had died once the council was underway. The *Constitution on the Divine Liturgy* authorized the reform of all the liturgical practices of the church beginning with the Mass, the Eucharistic Liturgy. The changes were dramatic and quite visible, including the widespread use of the vernacular languages instead of Latin, the disuse of ornate clerical and liturgical vesture, the addition of several Eucharistic prayers that could be used alongside the Roman Canon, the revision and abbreviation of the liturgical calendar, and the permission to celebrate the Mass facing the people (*versus populum*), just to mention a few. This constitution also authorized the renewal of sacred music dedicating the entire chapter six to this end. But it would be fallacious to think that the liturgical changes brought about by Vatican II simply fell from the sky. Preparations had already begun well in advance in the form of the liturgical movement.

The liturgical movement (hereafter LM) began in the nineteenth century in continental Europe and England. The origins were ostensibly academic where the liturgy became a focus of scholarly study. Beginning in the Roman Catholic Church, it moved gradually into other Christian churches. For example, in England the Oxford movement was one such manifestation of the LM. One of great fruits of the LM was its influence on the ecumenical movement, which attempted to reverse the divisions that began in the sixteenth century Reformation. The LM was multifaceted and can be summarized by five goals. First, it was an attempt to rediscover the worship practices of the Middle Ages, which in the nineteenth century was held to be the ideal form of worship and expression of faith. Second, it developed as scholarship to scientifically study and analyze the history of worship. Third, it broadened into an examination of the historical nature of worship as an organic human activity. Fourth, it attempted to renew worship in order that it could be more expressive for worshipers and as an instrument of teaching and mission. Fifth, it has been a movement attempting to bring about reconciliation among the churches on both sides of the Protestant Reformation.

In the Roman Catholic Church the first signs of interest in liturgical scholarship arose in 1832, when the French Benedictine abbey of Saint Pierre at Solesmes was founded anew by Dom Prosper Guéranger, who was instrumental in the scientific study of Gregorian chant from the earliest manuscript sources. The monks of Solesmes, well-versed in paleography and codicology, were pioneers in restoring the liturgy in its medieval form. They were particularly interested in recovering Gregorian chant and the liturgical forms of the Middle Ages. Among the great liturgical scholars were Fernand Cabrol and Pierre Batiffol. But one can say that they were more liturgiologists (liturgical scholars) than liturgists (those interested in actual liturgical practice). Contributing also to the LM was the patristic movement. Jacques Paul Migne published editions of various early theological texts in two massive compilations: *Patrologia Latina* and *Patrologia Graeca*. Most importantly for liturgical studies was the discovery of two church orders; first the *Didaché*, one of the earliest manuals of Christian morals and practice, was found in 1875 in a library in Constantinople, and second, the *Apostolic Tradition*, falsely attributed to the third-century Roman bishop Hippolytus, was published in 1900. Both of these documents contained precious liturgical materials that contributed greatly to the liturgical reforms of Vatican II.

Prior to the Second Vatican Council other reforms were already underway. Pope Pius X, elected in 1903, encouraged such reforms. In the same year of his election, he issued a *motu proprio* (a papal legal document meaning from the pope's own initiative) on church music entitled *Tra le Sollecitudini*, inviting the faithful to participate actively in the liturgy, which he saw as a source for the renewal of Christian spirituality. He called for more frequent communion of the faithful, the young in particular. Thus, he lowered the age for children to receive their First Holy Communion to about five or six years old. Subsequently, he was concerned with the revision of the breviary. Pius provided the necessary spark impetus for the LM to continue and grow in the Catholic Church.

Church historians, while acknowledging the importance of Guéranger and Solesmes in the nineteenth century, tend to date the official beginning of the LM in the Catholic Church to the year 1909 in Mechelen, Belgium, at the *Congrès National des Oeuvres Catholiques*. Liturgy was to be the means of instructing the people in Christian faith and life; the Mass would be translated into the vernacular to promote active participation of the faithful. One of the leading participants in the conference, Dom Lambert Beauduin of Louvain, argued that worship was the common action of the people of God and not solely performed by the priest. Many of the movement's principles were based in Beauduin's book, *La Pieté de l'Eglise.*[1] Pastoral considerations were now entering into serious consideration. The LM was now marked by a three-fold focus: liturgical scholarship, pastoral theology, and liturgical renewal.

Elsewhere in Europe, similar growth of the LM was experienced. In Germany Abbot Ildefons Herwegen of Maria Laach convened a liturgical conference in Holy Week of 1914 destined for laypeople. He henceforth promoted research that resulted in multiple publications for clergy and laypeople alike. From this same monastery emerged Odo Casel, one of the foremost German liturgical scholars. His focus was on the Greco-Roman Mystery religions and possible influences this may have had on early Christian worship. He was particularly interested in how worship in all its forms, Christian and non-Christian, spring from our common humanity. In his *Ecclesia Orans* (*The Praying Church*, 1918), Casel studied and interpreted the pagan mysteries of ancient Greece and Rome, discussing similarities and differences between them and the Christian mysteries. His conclusions were studied in various places, notably at Klosterneuburg in Austria, where the Augustinian canon Pius Parsch applied the principles in his church of St. Gertrude, which he took over in 1919. With laymen he worked out the relevance of the Bible to liturgy. Similar experiments were to take place in Leipzig during the Second World War.

In France, the *Dictionnaire d'archéologie chrétienne et de liturgie* (DACL) was published, but most practical experiments in liturgy were initiated after contact with the German and Austrian movements. Most changes occurred after the Second World War. In 1943, the *Centre National de Pastorale Liturgique* was founded and the magazine *La Maison-Dieu* began publication.

The idea of liturgy as an inclusive activity, subversive of individualism, while exciting to some, also raised anxieties in Rome. In 1947 Pope Pius XII issued the encyclical *Mediator Dei*, which warned of false innovations, radical changes, and Protestant influences in the liturgical movement. At the same time, he encouraged the "authentic" liturgical movement, which promoted active participation of the congregation in chant and gestures.

In the United States of America, the LM would take root in various places at different times due to the efforts of individuals. In the 1930s the LM implanted itself onto American soil through the efforts of Dom Virgil Michel OSB of St. John's Abbey in Collegeville, Minnesota. He founded the review *Orate Fratres* (now *Worship*) in 1926 and gradually formed the conference of Benedictines for the promotion of the liturgy. Several themes

1. See English translation, *Liturgy the Life of the Church,* Virgil Michel, tr.

surface in the first issue of *Orate Fratres*: the promotion of liturgical participation, the fostering of the liturgical apostolate, and perhaps most importantly the treatment of the mystical body of Christ as the theological cornerstone of the liturgical movement. As St. John's Abbot Deutsch wrote: "[T]he Liturgical Movement has for its purpose to put the liturgy into our lives; that the centre and very heart of the liturgy is the holy Mass; that, therefore, the main purpose of the Liturgical Movement is to put the holy Mass into the very centre of our lives and to make it and what it stands for, the vitalizing and directing principle of our lives."[2] In the wake of *Mediator Dei* Michael Matthis CSC in 1948 founded a summer program at the University of Notre Dame for the study of the liturgy. Many European liturgical scholars graced the campus each summer, imparting their learning. The program in liturgical studies would become the first graduate program in theology at Notre Dame continuing to this day and helping in the implementation of the *Constitution of the Liturgy* in the years following Vatican II. Mathis tells us that he had undergone his liturgical conversion in 1936 when he was presented with the first volume of Pius Pasch's *The Church's Year of Grace*. Elsewhere in the United States, other individuals who are too numerous to mention were busy working for the good of the LM.

THEOLOGICAL PERSPECTIVES

Music arguably has always been at the heart of the LM. Its importance was signaled by Pius X in his instruction *Tra le Sollecitudini* (TLS) of 1903. This document, issued *ex motu proprio,* had the force of law as a canonical code concerning sacred music. It was the first papal document ever addressed to the universal church that dealt entirely with music. The pope seemed more concerned, however, with the topic of religious music in general and not its particular use in the liturgy. The term sacred music appears a dozen times, while the term liturgical music only three times. Nevertheless, this document was the beginning of many documents issued in the twentieth century dealing with sacred music. Twenty-five years later Pius XI in 1928 would issue his *Divini Cultus Sanctitatem,* affirming the precepts put forward in TLS.

Prior to the Second Vatican Council there were three more Roman documents that had a bearing tangentially or directly upon music: *Mediator Dei* (an encyclical issued by Pius XII in 1947 on the liturgy in general), *Musicae Sacrae Disciplina* (another encyclical issued by Pius XII in 1955 dealing specifically with music), and *Instructio de Musica Sacra et Sacra Liturgia*

2. *Orate Fratres*, 391.

(an instruction issued by the Sacred Congregation of Rites in 1958). Each in its own way would lay the foundations for Vatican II. Prior to Vatican II the Latin Tridentine Mass remained the standard eucharistic liturgy in the Roman Catholic Church. In 1963, the Council adopted, by an overwhelming majority, the *Constitution on Sacred Liturgy*, "*Sacrosanctum Concilium.*" For the first time the vernacular liturgy was permitted, even if to a minor extent in relation to those practiced afterward by national churches. Accompanying this was the encouragement for liturgies to express local culture (subject to approval by the Holy See). The close connection between more intelligible participation in the Eucharistic celebration and carrying one's faith "into the marketplace" exhibited commitment to social justice in one's life. The recovery of the Liturgy of the Hours (also called the *Divine Office*), the daily prayer of the church, was just as startling. As liturgical prayer is the prayer of the church, the Constitution states that "*in choir*" (common) office prayer is always preferable to individual recitation.

The mandate for the liturgical reforms of Vatican II can be found in the second chapter of *Constitution on the Liturgy* (*Sacrosanctum Concilium*), which set out the fundamental principles regarding liturgical reform and strategies on how to achieve this. Article 14 lies at the very heart calling for *full participation* of all the baptized as the cornerstone of the liturgical reforms and has been called the "refrain" of the *Constitution on the Liturgy* appearing sixteen times throughout the document (see CSL 12, 14, 19, 26, 27, 30, 41, 50, 55, 113, 114, 121, 124). The sentence "this full and active participation by all the people is the aim to be considered before all else" has caused much ink to flow in recent decades as authors have debated the meaning of the classic Latin expression *actuosa participatio.*[3]

Music plays a major part in the active participation of the faithful in the liturgy. Chapter six of the *Constitution on the Liturgy* in its entirety is consecrated to sacred music. In earlier liturgical documents the term could

3. The theme of active participation had been a constant within the liturgical movement from the beginning of the twentieth century. Pius X called for it in his *motu proprio "Tra le sollecitudini"* (1903): "The faithful assemble to draw that spirit from its primary and indispensable source, that is, from active participation in the sacred mysteries and in the public and solemn prayer of the Church" (par. 5). Later in 1928 in the apostolic constitution, *Divini cultus*, Pius XI wrote that the restoration of Gregorian chant for the use of the people would provide the means whereby they "may participate in divine worship more actively." However, emphasis was also laid upon an appreciation of the beauty of the liturgy that is capable of stirring the heart of the worshiper, who thereby enters into the realm of the sacred mysteries. Pius XII in his encyclicals *Mystici Corporis* (1943) and *Mediator Dei* (1947) also used the term, but insisted that true participation was not merely external. *De musica sacra* (1958) distinguished between the various levels of participation, indicating thereby that the possibility of profound interior participation was linked to high standards of execution.

have two distinct meanings—one broader, the other more specific. "Sacred music" was sometimes employed as an umbrella term that encompassed multiple categories of music, including Gregorian chant, polyphony, vernacular hymnody, instrumental music, and even music inspired by sacred themes performed in concert. The term was also used more narrowly to refer to music used in the celebration of liturgy. The term is used both ways in this chapter, though most articles focus on the church's tradition of liturgical singing.

Prior to Vatican II, in an attempt to foster active participation at the Eucharist, a distinction was made between High and Low Mass. At the High Mass, due to the technical nature of the music, choirs would normally sing the Ordinary parts (*Kyrie, Gloria, Credo, Sanctus*, and *Agnus Dei* and *Ite missa est*) and the Proper parts (Introit, Gradual, Alleluia or Tract, Sequence, Offertory, and Communion). Hymns, by distinction, found their proper place in the Liturgy of the Hours (or the Office) and were not a part of the High Mass. In the Low Mass, however, popular hymns either in Latin or the vernacular were sung at four strategic moments: opening (or processional), offertory, communion, and closing (or recessional). This became known as the four-hymn sandwich. The hymnody was generally of a devotional nature as evidenced by hymnals of the early twentieth century.

Immediately after the Second Vatican Council there was genuine excitement about the liturgical reform in most circles. However, the changes met some resistance elsewhere. From the musical side of the liturgical reforms, the church seemed to be caught flat-footed in the demand to use vernacular languages in the liturgy. Since the topic is so vast and varied from country to country, let us focus our attention on developments in North America. Initially there was a tendency to use music from anywhere—hootenanny, show tunes, popular music from the radio, folk music, just to mention a few. New hymnals like *Peoples Mass Book* (1964) and the FEL *Hymnal for Young Christians* (1970) supplemented or replaced earlier hymnals like the *Kyriale* (1940) and the *Pius X Hymnal* (1956). A second tendency was to use Protestant hymns, recognizing the longstanding use of vernacular language in worship. Another tendency was to import and translate music from Europe. Certainly, the psalms of Joseph Gelineau, SJ, using the sprung text method of delivery, enjoyed great success in many languages outside the original French. Another French liturgist and composer Lucien Deiss, CSSp, contributed greatly in his musical compositions and writings on the subject of liturgy and liturgical music. To a lesser extent, Dutch composers Bernard Huijbers and Huub Oosterhuis brought to the American scene music that had been used experimentally in Holland prior to Vatican II. One difficulty presented itself in adapting from one language with its unique accentual patterns and structures to another. Nevertheless, these initiatives sensitized American liturgical composers to use biblical texts and lyrics that reflected theological renewal. When the St. Louis Jesuits emerged on the liturgical scene in the 1970s, their music was an instant success due to its straightforwardness, clarity, and widespread use of biblical texts. The group consisting of Bob Dufford, John Foley, Tim Manion, Roc O'Connor, and Dan Schutte, were all Jesuit scholastics at St. Louis University, but not all have remained in the Jesuit Order. Originally they used acoustic guitars and contemporary-style melodies and rhythms to set biblical and other religious texts to music sung in English in response to the liturgical reforms of the Second Vatican Council. The first collection of fifty-eight songs, some dating back as early as 1964, was called *Neither Silver nor Gold*. Their second recording, *Earthen Vessels,* sold over one million albums, and resulted in hymnals such as *Glory and Praise*. Although the list of songs is too numerous for this publication, representative titles will serve as examples of their use of Sacred Scripture. Among Foley's compositions are *One Bread, One Body* (1978, based on 1 Cor 10:16, 17; 12:4; Gal 3:38; and *The Didache* 9), *Come to the Water* (1978, based on Isa 55:1, 2; Matt 11:28–30), *The Cry of the Poor* (1978, Ps 34), and *For You Are My God* (1970, Ps 16). Probably Dufford's best known composition is "Be Not Afraid (1975), which is based upon Isa 43:2–3 and Luke 6:22ff. Schutte composed over 150 hymns; his "*Here I Am, Lord*" (1981) is based on Isa 6:8 and 1 Sam 3. Criticized at times for its contemporary musical style and because people were asked to sing in the voice of God, the net result is that many people came to know the Bible, particularly the psalms, through music.

In the years following the council, several musical publishing houses emerged in the United States, of which only three major ones survived: The Gregorian Institute of America (GIA),[4] World Library Publications (a division of J. S. Paluch),[5] and Oregon Catholic Press (OCP).[6] Additonally, the Liturgical Press at Collegeville, Minnesota, has published a variety of

4. GIA publishes two principle hymnals that contain psalms and canticles, and service music, and are intended to complement each other: *Worship* contains classical hymnody, and *Gather* features contemporary "folk" hymnody. *Lead Me, Guide Me; Ritual Song; Oramos Cantando / We Pray in Song.*

5. World Library of Sacred Music: *People's Mass Book 2003* (original edition 1966; revised and updated in 2003); *We Celebrate*; *One in Faith;* and ¡Celebremos / Let Us Celebrate!

6. Oregon Catholic Press, in hardbound, three principle publications: *Journeysongs* (primarily English language, with some bilingual English-Spanish songs)*; One Faith, Una Voz* (songs in both English and Spanish)*; Flor y Canto* (Spanish language songs); in paperback edition *Breaking Bread* (revised and published annually on a subscription basis).

hymnals.[7] The United States bishops came down on the American principle of free enterprise allowing the companies to sort themselves out, whereas the Canadian bishops forged ahead with a national hymnal, *The Catholic Book of Worship*, currently in its third edition. Among the American hymnals there are a variety in English, Spanish, and mixed language editions. Additionally, an African American hymnal entitled *African American Heritage Hymnal* (GIA) collected spirituals and other songs in the African American tradition. The difficulty lies in the fact that by nature this tradition is very improvisational, thus the hymnal only succeeds in giving a snapshot of how the music was sung at a particular moment in time.

In an attempt to ensure quality, there was a clear movement away from central authority of the sacred congregations in Rome that governed Latin usage to more local governance that could address vernacular usage. Episcopal conferences began to produce directives about liturgical music. In the United States, for example, two directives appeared about liturgical music a decade apart: *Music in Catholic Worship* (1972, and revised edition in 1983) and *Liturgical Music Today* (1982). These documents were a set of recommendations to help pastors and musicians implement the liturgical renewal mandated by Vatican II in the *Constitution on the Liturgy*. It is notable that the instructions speak about songs rather than hymns. The choice of the word song is an indication that many of the compositions since the council were not in the classical hymn structure and that the word song could include all the sung parts of the liturgy, including the ordinary parts. Nevertheless, music publishers continued to use the language of hymnals, with some notable exceptions. Liturgical Press at St. John's in Collegeville, for example, chose to entitle their music book *Sacred Song*.

In the years following the council a distinction was emerging between singing "at" Mass and singing "the" Mass. The goal was to move beyond the four-hymn sandwich and for congregations and choirs to sing the liturgy, particularly the acclamations and songs of the liturgy. The great contribution of *Music in Catholic Worship* (MCW) was the principle of the three-fold judgment in selecting music for worship: musical, liturgical, and pastoral. The musical aspect of the judgment requires that music be artistically sound but cautions not to confuse style with quality. The section on liturgical judgment briefly deals with the hierarchy of musical choices within the Eucharistic liturgy. Participation of all the faithful in some capacity was stressed while various musical ministers, such as cantor, choir, and organist, were delineated and affirmed. The third part, the pastoral judgment, poses the

7. Liturgical Press, in hardbound: *The Collegeville Hymnal*; *By Flowing Waters* (chants for the liturgy, composed by Paul Ford); and in softbound *Sacred Song*.

important challenge in every age: "Does music in the celebrations enable these people to express their faith, in this place, in this culture" (MCW, 39). The difficulty, however, in framing the question in terms of three separate judgments is that it creates the potential for real tensions and raises a question regarding hierarchical order. Who exercises these judgments? Does this presume a separate musical director from the liturgist? Are they one in the same? Does any one of these judgments trump the other two? Does the pastor exercise the pastoral judgment as a kind of veto right? After thirty years of sorting out this tension, the US bishops published a new document entitled *Sing to the Lord: Music in Divine Worship* (2006) as a revision of *Music in Catholic Worship*. Much of what had been already written was restated, but the question of the three-fold judgment was clarified. Rather than thinking of three separate judgments, it was now seen as one single judgement with three aspects. An outgrowth of these documents was the notion of pastoral musician. *Sing to the Lord* (par. 51) addressed the need for a full formation of the church musician: "Preparation for music ministry should include appropriate human formation, spiritual formation, intellectual formation, and pastoral formation."[8] The new document is comfortable adding the language of hymn to the singing of the acclamations, chants, and songs of the Liturgy (STL 21). An entire section is dedicated to hymns, stressing that their original placement was in the Liturgy of the Hours. But then it goes on to say, "Church legislation today permits as an option the use of vernacular hymns at the Entrance, Preparation of the Gifts, Communion, and Recessional. Because these popular hymns are fulfilling a properly liturgical role, it is especially important that they be appropriate to the liturgical action,"[9] seemingly to support the four-hymn sandwich that had been hotly contested in the period immediately following the council.

CONTRIBUTION TO LITURGY AND WORSHIP

The nineteenth century saw the rise of the Cecilian movement for church music reform in Germany as a reaction to the liberalization of the Enlightenment. In the twentieth century, this movement gave way to new associations that would take up the liturgical and musical reforms of Vatican II. On the European scene *Universa Laus* (literally "Universal Praise" in Latin), an international study group for liturgical singing and instrumental music, was formally constituted at Lugano, Switzerland, in April 1966. Based on a group of European liturgists and musicologists that had first started

8. United States Conference of Catholic Bishops, *Sing to the Lord*, par. 51.
9. United States Conference of Catholic Bishops, *Sing to the Lord*, par. 115, d.

meeting in 1962 (though some of its members had been working together for a decade before that), the initial object was to support the work of those charged with presenting and then implementing the liturgical reforms of the Second Vatican Council; some of its members were in fact *periti* at the council. The first trio of presidents were Joseph Gelineau (France), Erhard Quack (Germany), and Luigi Agustoni (Italian-speaking Switzerland). Other distinguished names present at the first formal meeting of the association included Helmut Hucke, Bernard Huijbers, David Julien, and René Reboud. In time this study group of scholars produced two documents of note: *Music in Christian Celebration* (1980) and *Music in Christian Liturgies* (2002). These documents provide a precision in terminology, including the introduction of the foundational term "Christian ritual music." This phrase was seen as a more precise way of describing the relationship between liturgy and music than the more nebulous terms "sacred," "religious," "church music," or "liturgical music." *Universa Laus* maintained that the primary form of ritual music is singing and that singing by the people gathered together is highest in importance.

On the American scene, the National Association of Pastoral Musicians (NPM) was founded in 1976 by Virgil Funk, a priest of the Diocese of Richmond, Virginia. The first convention was held in March 1978 in Scranton, Pennsylvania, and the theme was "Musical Liturgy is Normative." The meeting attracted around eight hundred participants from around the United States, far exceeding the expectation of the organizers. It was at this convention that the Saint Louis Jesuits were introduced onto the national stage along with many popular and learned liturgists. The next year the national convention took place in Chicago, Illinois, and the theme was "Prayer, Performance, Participation." Once again the numbers of attendance surprised and delighted the organization. Clearly there was something about NPM that spoke to clergy and musicians alike. The convention consisted of plenary sessions, music showcases sponsored by the major music publishers, and smaller workshops and breakout sessions. The crowning event was the large convention Eucharist that served as both a celebration and a model of good liturgy. At Scranton, the Eucharist took place in the Catholic cathedral, but in Chicago it was necessary to have it in the convention ballroom due to the overwhelming size. In 1980, it was decided to have regional meetings in order to accommodate the growing number of interested persons and to cover a broader swath of the country. The following year in 1981, the national convention took place in Detroit, Michigan, the theme being "Claim Your Art." The participants numbered around 8,500 again surpassing all expectations. The gatherings served as a place for disseminating knowledge about music and the liturgy and for introducing and distributing new music, including hymnals. The conventions have continued on to the present day, for a time alternating between national and regional meetings, but moving back to the yearly national conventions in the 2000s. In addition to the conventions, the association publishes a bi-monthly magazine with joint subscriptions; both the musicians and the clergy receive the magazine, ensuring that both groups are moving in the same direction liturgically, musically, theologically, and pastorally. The articles vary from the very arcane to the practical. Clearly hymnody lies within the purview of the authors and composers involved in the association.

NOTABLE HYMNS

Among the thousands of songs that have been composed for the liturgy since Vatican II, it is impossible to single out only a few as totally representative of the liturgical movement. Rather, it is more feasible to speak about the various genres of songs that have emerged.

In the genre of biblical texts, certainly the psalms hold pride of place. Many sprung-text versions in the Gelineau-style are used due to their ease of singing and clarity in expression, giving the biblical text priority over the melody. There are additionally through-composed versions of psalms that set the text according to its content and affect. Psalms of lament and penance sound mournful and full of remorse, while psalms of assent are joyful, recalling early pilgrims ascending to Jerusalem. There are also paraphrased versions of the psalms that take poetic license with the text. Then there are songs that set the Old Testament texts, making them accessible to people. This was an important development in introducing many Catholics to texts that had heretofore remained unknown to them. The New Testament is also fertile ground for sung texts. John 6 ("I Am the Bread of Life") or Matt 6 ("Come to Me") are but two songs that set Jesus' words.

Another genre is ritual music, which is devised to accompany the liturgical action. These songs could accompany the entrance or communion processions with music appropriate to the action. Songs of gathering set the stage for the liturgy, while Eucharistic hymns accompany the reception of communion. There are also songs that focus more specifically on the connection between Eucharist and social justice. These songs surprise and challenge those who sing them to work to build the kingdom of God and to live their faith.

Why is music important to the worship and testimony of the church? The answers are more easily felt than articulated, personal as well as doctrinal. The *Constitution on the Liturgy* says that sacred music "adds delight to prayer, fosters unity of minds, and confers great solemnity upon the sacred rites."[10] Music is pedagogical: a means of memorization, making Scripture stick. Music is universal: it enables missionary work, and allows for cultural cross-fertilization. Perhaps most importantly (and most difficult to talk concretely about) music, like God, is ineffable, emotional, and referential to the transcendent.

BIBLIOGRAPHY

Colombari, Bari, and Michael Prendergast, eds. *The Song of the Assembly: Pastoral Music in Practice.* Portland, OR: Pastoral Press, 2007.

Foley, Edward. *A Lyrical Vision: The Music Documents of the US Bishops.* Collegeville, MN: Liturgical, 2009.

Joncas, Jan Michael. *From Sacred Song to Ritual Music: Twentieth-Century Understandings of Roman Catholic Worship Music.* Collegeville, MN: Liturgical, 1997.

Pecklers, Keith. *The Unread Vision: The Liturgical Movement in the United States of America, 1926–1955.* Collegeville, MN: Liturgical, 1998.

Ruff, Anthony. *Sacred Music and Liturgical Reform: Treasures and Transformations.* Chicago: Hillenbrand, 2007.

United States Conference of Catholic Bishops. *Sing to the Lord: Music in Divine Worship.* Washington, DC: USCCB, 2008.

10. *Constitution on the Liturgy*, #112.

Chapter 12

Congregational Song from Ecumenical Movements

Karen B. Westerfield Tucker

HISTORICAL BACKGROUND

During the years 1895–1910, international movements developed that contributed to the designation of the twentieth century as the "ecumenical century." When young people representing various national and regional student Christian movements (SCM) gathered at Wadstena, Sweden, in August 1895, they took the decision to unite for mission globally as the World's Student Christian Federation (WSCF). The missional interests of the SCMs and the WSCF was one contributing factor, fifteen years later in June 1910, in the assembling of delegates from certain Protestant denominations and missionary societies (principally from North America and Northern Europe) in Edinburgh, Scotland, under the banner "The Evangelization of the World in This Generation." In the decades following the Edinburgh Missionary Conference, related groups and movements formed—e.g., the International Missionary Council, the Life and Work Movement (international relations, social ministries), and the Faith and Order Movement (doctrine, worship and sacraments, church order)—all of which would point back to the 1910 meeting as the beginning of the ecumenical movement. Coincidentally, in the year prior to Edinburgh, the Benedictine Lambert Beauduin delivered an address calling for the revitalization of Catholic liturgy and sacred music at the National Congress of Catholic Works held in Malines, Belgium, an event later considered to be the start of the liturgical movement. During the course of the century, the liturgical movement gained the interest and participation of Anglicans, Lutherans, and certain other Protestants, at first individuals and then denominations. In the "ecumenical century," the concerns of the liturgical and ecumenical movements closely intertwined.

Yet it would be an error to assume that ecumenical and liturgical—and musical—exchanges began only in the first decade of the twentieth century. Regarding congregational song, for example, a comparison of hymnbooks and devotional collections shows that Catholics and Protestants held certain vernacular songs in common, even during the sixteenth century.[1] The Anglican John Wesley in the eighteenth century translated selected hymns of Moravian communities and of Lutheran pietism into English for Anglican (extraliturgical) and Methodist (liturgical) use. In the nineteenth century, Catherine Winkworth surpassed Wesley as an English translator of German Lutheran texts, while her compatriot John Mason Neale supplied translations of Greek and Latin hymnic treasures of the Christian East and West. Even so, the twentieth century saw a greater intentional sharing of denominational songs across confessional lines.

The national and international gatherings of Christians in the first decade of the twentieth century included times for worship, daily prayer, and/or devotions with congregational singing. By 1924 the WSCF compiled its own ecumenical and multilingual hymnal under the leadership of Suzanne Bidgrain of the French Reformed Church, whose initials appeared at the foot of the preface. This first edition of *Cantate Domino* contained sixty-four hymns principally in English, German, or French, and each hymn had two translations. The next two editions again include "S.B." with the preface, with the second (1930) expanded to eighty-two hymns and the third (1938) to ninety-five. In the third edition, the majority of texts and tunes have their sources in western Protestant traditions and western musical forms, but non-western sources such as texts and melodies from the Christian East and tunes of non-Christian Asia also have a place. The conclusion of the preface to the third edition indicates the purpose of the book in precatory form: "May God bless this modest symbol of a Christendom united to adore him!"[2] However, the creative inclusion of certain selections in these three editions ultimately proved impractical in that, according to the preface of

1. Bertoglio, *Reforming Music*, 567–624.

2. *Cantate Domino* (1938), 3.

the fourth edition (1951), groups rarely sang these songs. No longer merely an ecumenical anthology, *Cantate Domino* had become a "necessary aid to worship in ecumenical gatherings." The fourth edition contained 119 hymns more representative of global Christianity and in multiple languages, though each hymn had German, French, and English versions.[3] This was the last edition explicitly identified as the World's Student Christian Federation Hymnal, for the book's users expanded far beyond that organization and the SCMs that endorsed it.

At the first assembly of the World Council of Churches (WCC) in 1948, participants used *Cantate Domino* for corporate worship. The WCC brought together in one organization various international ecumenical groups, such as the Faith and Order Movement, but also found impetus from the (Orthodox) Patriarchal and Synodical Encyclical of 1920, which spoke to the need of a fellowship of Christian churches comparable to the League of Nations. Although primarily a Protestant organization at the outset, in the 1960s, the membership of Orthodox churches in the WCC increased and Roman Catholics participated more openly after the Second Vatican Council. This increased ecumenism is evident in the contents of the fifth edition of *Cantate Domino* published on behalf of the WCC and identified as an "ecumenical hymn book." By 1968, *Cantate Domino* had become effectively the songbook of the WCC, and the WCC leadership took the decision to entrust the creation of a new edition to the WCC's Faith and Order Commission and to Erik Routley of the United Reformed Church of England and Wales as general editor. A melody-only edition with 199 hymns and other materials came into print in 1974; Oxford University Press, on behalf of the WCC, brought out a full music edition in 1980, with English and one other language supplied for each hymn (because of space limitations). The 1974 and 1980 versions share a foreword by then WCC General Secretary Philip Potter wherein he offered a summary of the importance of ecumenical corporate song:

> "Singing and making music to the Lord" is an act of thanksgiving, acknowledging the mighty acts of grace of the God and Father of our Lord Jesus Christ. It is something we can delight in doing together, a demonstration of our common life in one Body, reconciled and held together by Christ the head through the Holy Spirit. No wonder the modern ecumenical movement should find its most popular expression in Christians singing each other's hymns.[4]

3. *Cantate Domino* (1951).

4. *Cantate Domino* (1974), vii.

Given such a strong statement about congregational singing in ecumenical contexts and the sharing of hymns across confessional lines, it is surprising that the WCC and the work of its Commission on Faith and Order have not included sustained examinations of congregational song as part of their discussions on worship and sacraments/ordinances.

Despite this silence, the worship resources books produced for successive WCC assemblies served and serve as models for confessional borrowing. In addition, the WCC on occasion published thematic song collections. *New Hymns for a New Day* (1966), brought out by the WCC's Youth Department in cooperation with the World Council of Christian Education, supplied forty-four English texts from international sources and utilized melodies from different cultures. Dutch theologian Albert van den Heuvel, in a substantial preface, noted the formative influence of hymns and songs across global confessions by declaring, "Tell me what you sing, and I'll tell you who you are!"[5] This declaration was also his summons for new songs that addressed new theological insights and the concerns faced by churches and communities around the world. He asked, "Where are the hymns which speak about the humanisation of the structures of our society? Where are the hymns that help us express our new insights into the kingship of God? . . . Where are the hymns which express hope, not in heaven, but on earth?"[6] Andrew Donaldson, editor of the WCC's *HOSANNA!: Ecumenical Songs for Justice and Peace* (2016), a collection related to the theme of the 2013 Assembly, answered van den Heuvel's questions fifty years later by including songs and hymns identified with the issues of creation, economic justice, health and healing, gender and sexuality, and unity and mission. Even with specific hymnic resources and the regular appearance of books with songs for use with WCC gatherings, *Cantate Domino* remains a viable resource for the WCC into the twenty-first century, as references to songs within the book appeared in orders of worship prepared by Faith and Order for the Week of Prayer for Christian Unity.

The production of ecumenical songbooks by international organizations influenced ecumenical conversations around congregational song taking place within nations and world regions, though the reverse was also true. Groups with the principal purpose of promoting hymns and congregational song as sacred musical forms had an ecumenical membership, at first almost entirely Protestant and later with Roman Catholic participation. Among such groups are the Hymn Society of America (founded in 1922; from 1991 in the United States and Canada), the Hymn Society of Great

5. *New Hymns for a New Day*, 6.

6. *New Hymns for a New Day*, 6.

Britain and Ireland (1936), and the Internationale Arbeitsgemeinschaft für Hymnologie (1959), whose membership often included persons responsible for their denomination's musical resources. These persons then had material to enrich their own denominational books and contacts to enable possible collaborative work on an ecumenical book as a tangible sign of Christian unity as well as to save production costs. Ecumenical editorial committees within certain nations produced, for example, *The Hymn Book* (1971) for the Anglican Church of Canada and the United Church of Canada, and *Alleluia Aotearoa* (1993) for New Zealand. An Australian committee with Anglican, Churches of Christ, Lutheran, Presbyterian, Roman Catholic, and Uniting Church representatives created *Together in Song* (1999), an update of the previous ecumenically produced *Australian Hymn Book* (1977). Although not intended to replace denominational hymnals, *Common Ground* (1998) was the fruit of song selections considered by representatives from the major Christian traditions in Scotland. Not all collaborative efforts are entirely successful: a project began in 1979 to provide a single musical resource for British Methodist, United Reformed Church, Churches of Christ, and Wesleyan Reform Union congregations. The committee comprised representatives from these churches and persons from the Congregational Federation, the Baptist Union of Great Britain, and the Church of England. One of the surprises of this work was that a denominationally specific hymn (e.g., a Charles Wesley text for the Methodists) that had fallen out of that denomination's hymnals could be in the book(s) and use of another denomination. Although the ecumenical and collaborative work continued for the duration of the process, in the end the book became *Hymns and Psalms* (1983) for the British Methodists, though the subtitle is indicative of the original intention—"A Methodist and Ecumenical Hymn Book."[7]

National or regional councils of churches sometimes published hymn collections for their member churches and others. As part of its work, the Federal Council of the Churches of Christ in America published *Hymns of the Rural Spirit* (1947) for gatherings related to rural life, including festivals, camps, and conferences. The Federal Council's successor, the National Council of the Churches in the United States in America, brought out *Fellowship Hymnal* (1955), with hospital chaplain J. Obert Kempson as the editor, for use in ecumenical institutions such as hospitals, prisons, and juvenile correction facilities. On the other side of the world, leadership from Daniel Thambyrajah Niles and John Milton Kelley enabled the publication of the *East Asia Christian Conference Hymnal* (1963). This book went through multiple printings prior to the issuance of the trial edition of

7. Watson and Trickett, *Companion*, 1–6.

the ecumenical and multilingual *Sound the Bamboo: CCA Hymnal 1990*, a joint project between the Christian Conference of Asia and The Asian Institute for Liturgy and Music. The final edition, *Sound the Bamboo: CCA Hymnal 2000*, contained 315 hymns in forty-four languages of Asian and Pacific peoples.

American and Canadian representatives from a dozen churches (including Roman Catholic) took a completely different approach with the formation of a Consultation on Ecumenical Hymnody that met fourteen times between 1968 and 1976. After determining that a single ecumenical hymnal was not feasible, the group chose instead to seek consensus on a common repertoire of texts and tunes, and so examined twenty-six existing books that yielded 227 texts and tunes.[8] Future denominational hymnals were to mark these selected texts and tunes as ecumenically shared. Although the Consultation did not entirely achieve its goals, the denominational hymnals produced during and shortly after their deliberations show the influence of their work.[9] C. Michael Hawn undertook a similar project by examining forty hymnals produced in the United States and Canada between 1976 and 1996, in which he noted which of the Consultation's selections had survived. Of the fifty-four hymns that appeared in thirty or more of the hymnals, all but three were on the Consultation's list. Appearing in thirty-nine of the forty hymnals were Congregationalist Isaac Watts's "O (Our) God, Our Help In Ages Past" (tune St. Anne) and "Silent Night" (tune Stille Nacht) in English translation of Roman Catholic priest Joseph Mohr's original German.[10]

The creation of collections of ecumenical congregational song also came from dedicated lyricists and composers who were ecumenists at heart and who collaboratively produced and/or collected resources for use at the "growing points" of the church. The Scottish Churches' Music Consultation cultivated the writing of new songs and hymns by an ecumenical group headed by Ian Fraser and Erik Routley, which circulated as *Dunblane Praises* (1965, 1967). The editorial team of *Ecumenical Praise* (1977)—Carlton R. Young, Austin C. Lovelace, Erik Routley, and Alec Wyton—claimed their collection to be "fully *catholic* in its spread of texts, tunes, poets and composers."[11] Carlton Young later joined S. T. Kimbrough in encouraging poetic and compositional output from across the churches and the globe, which came into print through the "Global Praise" series (1996–). In addition, individual poets, through their own published collections and

8. "Hymns and Tunes," 192–209.

9. Hawn, "Consultation on Ecumenical Hymnody," 26–37.

10. Hawn, "Tie that Binds," 32.

11. Young, *Ecumenical Praise*, preface.

commitments to church unity, contributed to the congregational song that transcended denominational boundaries. For example, the songs of European and English-language hymn writers Albert Bayly (Congregational), Fred Pratt Green (Methodist), Frederick Kaan (Reformed), Timothy Dudley-Smith (Anglican), and Brian Wren (Reformed), all leaders in the "hymn explosion" of the 1960s and 1970s, populated numerous denominational hymnals produced at the end of the twentieth century. Writers with similar dedication to Christian unity continue to emerge in the twenty-first century. Most hymnal revision committees and publishers of hymn collections—Protestant and Catholic—now assume that the contents of their books will include literary and musical riches from outside their own ecclesiastical community in part, to use Philip Potter's words, as a "demonstration of our common life in one Body."

Another source of congregational song emerging from the ecumenical movement comes from religious communities intentionally founded to bear witness to unity in Christ. The Iona Community, founded in 1938 by Church of Scotland minister George MacLeod, is an ecumenical community of men and women who live at the restored abbey on Iona, an island off the west coast of Scotland, but also on the nearby island of Mull, in Glasgow, and around the world. Their distinctive song comes principally from the pens of John L. Bell and Graham Maule, who collaborate with others in their Wild Goose Resource Group (the goose is a Celtic symbol of the Holy Spirit) to produce new songs for their community and the wider church. Texts derive from Scripture, liturgical need, and pastoral and global issues, all of which speak with certainty of God's engagement with God's people. Tunes often come from the folk traditions of Britain, Ireland, and other global sources, and there is a preference for unaccompanied singing. The Taizé community in southeastern France likewise prefers a cappella singing in order to increase attentiveness both to the text and to the voice of God. Roger Schütz-Marsauche, a Reformed Christian active in the Swiss SCM, founded the ecumenical men's community in 1940 as place for both prayer and reconciliation. When Taizé became a place of pilgrimage for international visitors, Brother Roger and others determined their French-language songs were no longer adequate for the daily hours of prayer. Multilingual hymns and canticles were one solution; another was the short and simple chants—many in Latin—that were the fruit of the musical collaboration between Brother Robert Giscard and Paris organist and composer Jacques Berthier. These short songs, responses, and acclamations, repeated multiple times, sometimes in canon, sometimes as ostinatos, have become a principal feature of worship in the style of Taizé. Another ecumenical community, not as well known, is the men's and women's Monastery of Bose in the Province of Biella north of Turin, Italy. Founded by Roman Catholic Enzo Bianchi in 1965 on the day the Second Vatican Council ended, the community initially comprised Catholics, Baptists, and Vaudois, and by 1968 had other Protestants, including a pastor. The growing community continues the practice of thrice-daily common prayer enabled by translations and hymn compositions freshly composed by the group. Some churches are adopting Bose's Italian-language congregational songs and chants, but the range of sharing is currently limited.

THEOLOGICAL PERSPECTIVES

In 1941 Episcopal hymn writer Howard Chandler Robbins presented in pamphlet form the results of a study undertaken by the Commission on Worship of the Federal Council of the Churches of Christ in America to examine ecumenical trends in hymnody. Robbins observed that already the ecumenical movement was having an effect upon (Protestant) worship and more particularly upon the selection of hymns included in new denominational hymnals. Whereas in previous generations of hymnals there were few hymns identified as "common property," recent publications showed significant borrowing from the hymnic treasures of other ecclesiastical traditions. Each denomination's contribution to a broader ecumenical hymnody thus played a part in professing "the whole counsel of God." Ecumenical conversation and a mutual engagement in societal concerns also yielded a common selection of new texts that addressed current and emerging issues. Among the trends that Robbins noted were the inclusion of texts attentive to God's creation, the "social implications of the gospel," and international relations and peace (for which he specifically names John Oxenham's "In Christ There is no East or West").[12]

Robbins's observations were not unique to the United States. With the blossoming of the ecumenical movement, the exchange of denominationally particular hymns across confessions—typically within language groups—was on the increase, and translations were becoming available for old and new texts. National and international efforts related to Life and Work and to Faith and Order, and the conferences they held, stimulated the production and sharing of new texts and tunes, the latter in particular reflective of different cultural styles. Widening local interest in church unity and cooperative work for the common good, along with other factors, inspired texts on a range of topics in both regular and irregular meters. Shifts in popular music styles and the recovery or appropriation of folk idioms outside of the church

12. Robbins, *Ecumenical Trends in Hymnody*, 5–10.

influenced, for the sake of ministry and mission, melodies and rhythms utilized for the church's song. After Vatican II, which saw a chapter on "Sacred Music" included in the "Constitution on the Sacred Liturgy" (*Sacrosanctum Concilium*) that advocated for congregational singing, Catholics in many places engaged more actively in the borrowing for Mass of hymns and songs of non-Catholic origin. While Anglicans, Protestants, and Catholics have welcomed song from Orthodox churches such as, for example, Russian chant settings often mediated through WCC resources, the reverse typically is not the case even for singing outside of the Divine Liturgy.

One of the ideals of the ecumenical movement was to return to sources from the early church (a strategy shared with the liturgical movement) and from those prior to the division of the church East and West in the eleventh century. Hymn texts strongly resonant with the biblical text—but attentive to new methods of exegesis and theological interpretation—had the potential to bridge confessional differences. Textual riches already mined from the first millennium—for example, the English translations by John Mason Neale of texts attributed to Prudentius, Fortunatus, Andrew of Crete, and John of Damascus, some of which had already appeared earlier in editions of *Hymns Ancient & Modern*—found wider appropriation. Early church documents newly discovered or rediscovered, such as a Greek manuscript of the *Didache* in 1873, became a source for song: both Episcopalian F. Bland Tucker's 1939 composition "Father, We Thank Thee Who Hast Planted" (included in *Ecumenical Praise* [1977]), and the third stanza of Jesuit John B. Foley's "One Bread, One Body" (1978) draw directly upon *Didache*. Churches that did not have or that had lost a regular observance of corporate daily prayer/liturgy of the hours found in examining early Christian practice and in participating in prayer at ecumenical events a shared spiritual discipline for which common song could be used, such as new translations of the pre-fourth century lamp-lighting hymn *Phos hilaron*.

Ecumenical bilateral and multilateral discussions engaged questions about doctrinal differences relative to understandings of the Trinity and the Persons of the Trinity, the nature and unity of the church, and sacraments/ordinances. The work of these dialogues was likely one impetus for hymn writers in greater number taking up these topics in the twentieth century. Baptism, long neglected as a subject in song, received significantly more attention by both poets and hymnal committees. God's salvific relationship with water became a focus for numerous hymns, including those by Protestants Fred Kaan ("Out of Deep, Unordered Water" [1965]) and Sylvia Dunstan ("Crashing Waters at Creation" [1987]), which spoke not only to baptism but also to the churches' ongoing concerns with matters of creation care. As Catholic and Protestant congregations after Vatican II embraced a practice of baptism at the Easter Vigil, new hymns related to Easter also appeared. Indeed, in the twentieth century, there was a notable swelling of the number of hymns related to feasts and fasts of the Christian year included in hymnals, especially by denominations long suspicious of such "ritualism." This shift may be a product both of fruitful ecumenical conversation and of a greater willingness by some denominations to use ecumenical lectionaries for preaching and worship planning.

The increasing numbers of hymns and songs written by Protestants that speak to the person of Mary, the Mother of the Lord, may help to mediate the discussion on this subject of doctrinal difference between Catholics, Orthodox, and Protestants in formal bilateral and multilateral dialogues. For many Protestants, most hymnic references to Mary are limited to texts related to the Nativity and to Good Friday. As scriptural canticles were (re) discovered in historic forms of daily prayer used at ecumenical events, and as schemes for evening prayer found a place in Protestant worship and devotional books, hymnists produced fresh metrical versions, paraphrases, and literary expansions of Mary's song (Magnificat) in Luke 1:46–55. Some writers (e.g., Fred Kaan, Edith Sinclair Downing, Adam Tice), sensitive to influences from liberation and feminist movements, emphasized Mary's words as a cry for justice and Mary herself as a model for crossing boundaries.

Among the social issues that have brought the churches together for conversation and action are science, technology and its uses, urbanization, social change, poverty, global migration, and other social ills. In every case, hymn writers across the churches have taken to their pens to put these concerns into the language of poetry and prayer. Throughout the twentieth century, a prominent theme for both ecumenists and hymn writers was that of peace—between individuals, cultural groups, churches, societies, and nations. At the beginning of the twenty-first century, the attention of both groups focuses on the related subject of interfaith and interreligious relationships, a topic to which, in the next generation of hymnals, poets and composers from non-Christian faith traditions may contribute.

CONTRIBUTION TO LITURGY AND WORSHIP

Christian congregational songs are professions of faith, enabling the singers to confess with their lips what they believe in their hearts (Rom 10:9). The sharing of song across ecclesiastical boundaries not only expands and enriches an assembly's repertoire beyond that which may express their ecclesiastical particularity. It also affirms that the diversity that makes up the body of Christ is not limited to what exists in a single congregation or ecclesiastical tradition (cf. 1 Cor 12:12–13). Singing a common hymnody embodies through cantillated word and cadenced breath Jesus' prayer that his disciples might all be one (John 17:21), and enables the church, though divided, nonetheless to glorify God with one voice (Rom 15:5–6). Thus, the sharing of song bears witness to an unacknowledged or a hoped for unity, and may provide the impetus to seek actively a greater unity.

Yet even when the hymnbooks of very different Christian communities contain the same hymns or songs, or when at an ecumenical event those gathered sing together a hymn, is it the case that despite ecclesiastical variety all receive a text in the same way? Much would depend, it seems, on what the text addresses. Hymns and songs related to the liturgical year or hymns that paraphrase a biblical narrative may be read more similarly than, for example, a text that addresses a dogmatic topic such as the nature of the church or one of the sacraments. However, viewed positively, the existence of diverse readings may testify to the many parts that make up the one body of Christ, and may challenge the singers to take the opportunity to address together the extent of those theological differences.

The reality of shared congregational song raises the question of the possibility of "ecumenical worship." Some within the ecumenical movement claim that the language of "ecumenical worship" is problematic insofar as it seems to claim a unity that it not truly present. Others ask how an "ecumenical" form might relate to existing confessional worship traditions. Nevertheless, all worship is ecumenical "in the sense that it is adoration of the God who is revealed to everyone in Jesus Christ, and in the sense that it is open to other Christians, stands in relation to them, stands in relation to the whole tradition and aims to create community."[13] Ecumenical groups experienced in worship planning make clear that worship in ecumenical settings should "help the whole worshiping group to feel that the worship service is their own."[14]

NOTABLE HYMNS

The four hymns/songs here mentioned have a special connection to the ecumenical movement. The first edition of *Cantate Domino* contained the French hymn "À toi la gloire, O Ressuscité," written in 1884 by the Swiss hymn writer Edmond Louis Budry and placed into English by R. Birch Hoyle as "Thine is the Glory." The hymn in French, German, and English served as the "anthem" of the WSCF, and it quickly became such for the

13. Heller, "Ecumenical Worship," 243–44.

14. Heller, "Ecumenical Worship," 243–44.

WCC in its early days. The hymn text, set to a tune by George Frederick Händel, is strongly associated with Easter in many churches.

In preparation for the second assembly of the WCC (1954) at Evanston, Illinois, the then Hymn Society of America solicited submissions of hymns on the assembly's theme "Christ, the Hope of the World." The winning text was "Hope of the World" by the Methodist woman and ecumenist Georgia Harkness. The hymn, in German, French, Spanish, and other languages, appears in numerous denominational hymnals worldwide.

Two texts from the Taizé Community, "Laudate Dominum" and "Laudate Omnes Gentes," are standards at ecumenical events because they are simple refrains, repeated multiple times, that invite participation while offering praise to God. Both texts are in Latin, though they appear in multiple translations, and both come from Ps 117. The tunes by Jacques Berthier are different for each text, and are quite effective with four-part (or more) harmonization.

BIBLIOGRAPHY

Bertoglio, Chiara. *Reforming Music: Music and the Religious Reformations of the Sixteenth Century*. Berlin and Boston: Walter de Gruyter, 2017.

Cantate Domino: World's Student Christian Federation Hymnal. Geneva: World's Student Christian Federation, [1938].

Cantate Domino: World's Student Christian Federation Hymnal. Geneva: World's Student Christian Federation, 1951.

Cantate Domino. Kassel, Basel, Tours, London: Bärenreiter, 1974.

Hawn, C. Michael. "The Consultation on Ecumenical Hymnody: An Evaluation of Its Influence in Selected English Language Hymnals Published in the United States and Canada since 1976." *The Hymn* 47.2 (April 1996) 26–37.

———. "The Tie that Binds: A List of Ecumenical Hymns in English Language Hymnals Published in Canada and the United States since 1976." *The Hymn* 48.3 (July 1997) 25–34.

Heller, Dagmar. "Ecumenical Worship—Experiences, Problems, Possibilities: Some Basic Considerations." In *Worship Today: Understanding, Practice, Ecumenical Implications*, edited by Thomas F. Best and Dagmar Heller, 231–46. Geneva: WCC Publications, 2004.

"Hymns and Tunes Recommended for Ecumenical Use." *The Hymn* 28.4 (October 1977) 192–209.

New Hymns for a New Day. Risk 2.3. Geneva: Youth Departments of the World Council of Churches and World Council of Christian Education, 1966.

Robbins, Howard Chandler, ed. *Ecumenical Trends in Hymnody*. New York: Commission on Worship, Federal Council of the Churches of Christ in America, 1941.

Watson, Richard, and Kenneth Trickett, eds. *Companion to Hymns & Psalms*. Peterborough: Methodist, 1988.

Young, Carlton R., ed. *Ecumenical Praise*. Carol Stream, IL: Agape, 1977.

Chapter 13

North American Metrical Psalters

MARTIN TEL

HISTORICAL BACKGROUND

IN HISTORICALLY CALVINIST REGIONS of Europe the metrical singing of psalms endured as a hallmark of the Reformed tradition. Successive waves of immigrants brought their distinctive psalters with them to North America. Almost without exception one can trace a pattern of decline. While the psalter initially provided immigrant groups with a sense of identity and stability, later generations were often eager to assimilate into the American practices of singing hymns and gospel songs. Lacking the cultural and ecclesial undergirding enjoyed in Europe, the metrical psalter tradition was undermined by the North American free marketplace of worship styles and resources.

The English Pilgrims arrived at Plymouth Rock in 1620 bearing a psalter developed by Henry Ainsworth (1612) during the exile in the Netherlands. Later English transplants brought with them the Sternhold & Hopkins psalter (1562), commonly referred to as the "Old Version." American Puritans were scrupulous about the texts of their psalters, wishing for them to conform as closely as possible to their Hebrew source. This led to the publication of the *Bay Psalm Book*, printed in Cambridge, Massachusetts, in 1640. Soon there were many psalters in use. While the Tate & Brady psalter

(1698 edition), commonly referred to as the "New Version," made inroads in Anglican communities, it would be the *Scottish Psalter* (or *The Psalms of David in Metre*) of 1650 that won the hearts of most Presbyterians in North America.[1]

The first crucial challenge to North American exclusive psalmody was brought by the English nonconformist minister Isaac Watts (1674–1748). Depending upon one's viewpoint, his psalter, *The Psalms of David Imitated in the Language of the New Testament, And apply'd to the Christian State and Worship* (1719), either brought about the revival of English psalmody or its demise. Well-known examples from this psalter include "Jesus Shall Reign Where'er the Sun" (Ps 72), "Our God, Our Help in Ages Past" (Ps 90), and "Joy to the World, the Lord Is Come" (Ps 98). Watts's psalter proved to be extremely popular in North America. It did require, however, some adaptations in order to make it usable in the New World. As implied in the title, Watts infused his psalter with both Christian and national imagery. The North American Congregationalists commissioned Timothy Dwight (1752–1817) to edit out Watts's references to Europe and the British nation and to provide new versifications for those psalms that Watts had cast off as being unfit for Christian worship. One of Dwight's entries for Ps 137, "I Love Thy Kingdom, Lord," demonstrates how far afield versifiers were willing to go in paraphrasing and adapting psalms.[2] The complete psalter was published in 1801 and became popularly known as "Dwight's Watts."[3]

Watts's psalms were popular across the spectrum of churches in the United States. They were in fact a staple of many African American communities. Slaves picked u "Dr. Watts's psalms" from their owners. Much of the language of the psalter, along with the Old Testament exodus narratives, resonated with the plight of the slave. The African American communities also adopted the "lining out" style in which a precentor would sing or call out each line of the psalm ahead of the singing congregation. There is much made of the ornaments and slides added to the tunes: the singing was derided as tortured, cacophonous, and wild by those who would "improve" the situation through "psalmody classes" and singing schools.[4]

1. See chapters 4 and 8 of *Hymns and Hymnody*, vol. 2, for more information on these psalters.

2. Framed by four stanzas which establish that the psalmist's "Zion" should be interpreted as the Christian's "Church," Dwight's interior stanzas (3–6) loosely track the psalm. E.g., *If e'er to bless thy sons / my voice, or hands, deny, / these hands let useful skill forsake, / this voice in silence die.* (Stanza 3)

3. See chapter 14 of *Hymns and Hymnody*, vol. 2, for more information on Isaac Watts.

4. For more information, see Sydnor, "Sing a New Song to the Lord: An Historical

African American communities would not have access to these "improvements" and would thereby preserve this style of singing, particularly in the South. Baptist minister and musician William N. Heard recounts his experience in the 1990s when he arrived from Texas to serve as the musician in a church in Brooklyn, New York, a congregation heavily populated by African Americans of the Great Migration:

> The pastor asked me to lead the congregation in a "metered hymn." I began to call out the lines of Watts's "I Love the Lord, He Heard My Cry." There was a paltry response from the congregation. The pastor stopped the singing and exhorted the congregation: "You know this song. Don't pretend you've forgotten it. There's nothing wrong with letting it out once in a while. Let's try it again." With some trepidation I called out again. He was right. They knew the song. Every ornament. Every slide. This time they let it out![5]

Perhaps music historians have given too much credence to eighteenth-century accounts deriding this style of singing. Many of those who disparaged it stood to profit from the establishment of psalmody classes and the sales of new singing books. The sounds preserved in African American communities suggest that psalm singing may have been more intricately tuneful and beautiful than we have imagined.[6]

Particularly for the largest federations of Presbyterian churches, the disputes over "inspired" metrical psalmody versus "imitated" metrical psalmody would lead to factions and schisms. By the end of the century the freer paraphrases of Watts won the day. The admittance of "Christianized psalmody" paved the way for the introduction of hymns, which Watts also provided. In 1788 the *Presbyterian Directory for Worship* was amended to allow for the singing of hymns. Having reunited after a split between "Old Side" (preferring the 1650 *Scottish Psalter*) and "New Side" (preferring the 1698 "New Version" but more and more embracing Watts's psalter), the Presbyterians published *Psalms and Hymns, Adapted to Public Worship* in 1831, the first sanctioned collection of hymns for Calvinists in North

---

Survey of American Presbyterian Hymnals" in Daw, *Glory to God*, xvii–xvii.

5. In an interview with Martin Tel at Princeton Theological Seminary, November 5, 2005. The Rev. William N. Heard is currently the pastor at the historic Kaighn Avenue Baptist Church in Camden, New Jersey, and the director of HEARDSONG Productions, LLC.

6. Ethnomusicologist Alan Lomax made a field recording of a metered psalm led by Rev. R. C. Crenshaw at New Brown's Chapel in Memphis, Tennessee, and included them in the recording collection *Sounds of the South* (1993). Lomax's archives are available online, http://research.culturalequity.org/home-audio.jsp.

America. This set the stage for the "psalter hymnal" format, the binding together of both a psalter and a hymnal. The Presbyterians would soon divide again into "Old School" and "New School." With this schism new editions of psalter hymnals emerged. However, the maintenance of a discrete metrical psalter was abandoned after the Civil War. The Presbyterians, now divided into northern and southern churches, published hymnals. The psalms appeared in new guises including chants and responsive readings. Many of Watts's metrical psalm versifications were included, but were scattered throughout the hymnal. Though some metrical psalms might still be sung, the consciousness of a metrical psalter was lost and would not reappear for mainline Presbyterians until late in the twentieth century, and then only tenuously.[7]

The continental Reformed settlers brought a separate metrical psalter tradition to North America, the Genevan psalter. Originating in French (completed in 1562) under the watchful eye of John Calvin (1509–64), it was quickly translated into Dutch (Pieter Datheen, 1565) and German (Ambrosius Lobwasser, 1573). Lobwasser's versification served as the model for versifications in Czech (Jiří Strejc, 1587) and Hungarian (Albert Szenci Molnár, 1607). As Calvinist settlers arrived from these lands, they brought their psalters with them. Though the Genevan psalter provided a common platform for psalm singing on the continent of Europe, and for a time in the various linguistic enclaves in North America, there would be no usable English translation of the Genevan psalter until the late twentieth century.[8] As waves of continental European Reformed immigrants came to North America with their Genevan psalters, they followed a similar script. Though initially they sang from their respective Genevan psalters in their native languages, when the time came to assimilate into the English-language culture, these denominations gravitated toward preexisting English psalters.[9]

It is important to note that there were smaller groups of more conservative Presbyterians, mostly of Scottish extraction, that never traded in their "inspired" psalms for Watts. It was the United Presbyterian Church in North America (UPCNA) that would spearhead the most substantive contribution to metrical psalmody in North America in the twentieth century. Their work began in the 1880s with a revision of the *Scottish Psalter*, completed,

7. For more on nineteenth-century metrical psalmody in North America, see Benson, *English Hymn*, esp. 177–95.

8. There was one attempt made by the Dutch. See Brumm, "Congregational Song," 104–6.

9. The Canadian Reformed Church's use of the Anglo-Genevan psalter (*Book of Praise*) is an exception to this pattern. See also Brink "English Metrical Psalmody" in Brink and Polman, *Psalter Hymnal Handbook*, 40–54.

with tunes, in 1887. Early in the 1900s representatives of nine North American Presbyterian and Reformed denominations began to work together to produce a complete metrical psalter that would provide both "a faithful rendering into English of the exact thought of each psalm, and of each part of each psalm" in a language that is "current in the best poetical literature; also of verse that is rhythmical in form, poetic in spirit, and easily sung."[10] In other words, there was a commitment to faithful "inspired" psalmody (a la the *Scottish Psalter*), but in winsome, lyrical language (a la Watts). The work culminated in the *New Metrical Version of the Psalms, adopted on September 22nd, 1909, by the Joint Committee of American and Canadian Churches on a Uniform Version of the Psalms in Meter to be Submitted to the Churches Represented in the Committee.*

It was the UPCNA that brought the entire enterprise to its conclusion in *The Psalter*, commonly referred to as "The Psalter 1912." The genius of this new psalter is its matching of tune to text. From the preface of *The Psalter* 1912 we read:

> In the search for tunes the Committee has made an exhaustive study of the best collections of congregational music in America and Great Britain. The tests constantly applied were harmony with the lofty sentiment and spiritual utterance of the Psalms, genuinely musical quality, promise of permanence, and popular adaptation.[11]

The overall sense of this collection is that it springs from American soil. There are melodies adopted from Lowell Mason (1792–1872) and the American singing school tradition, Appalachian folk sources, but also popular gospel songs. By also including traditional hymn tunes, Christians in exclusively psalm-singing communions were able to enjoy melodies that were otherwise the privilege of hymn-singing churches. "The Earth and Its Fullness" (Ps 24) was set to ADESTE FIDELES ("Hark! The Herald Angels Sing"). "With Grateful Heart My Thanks I Bring" (Ps 138) was set to SOLID ROCK ("My Hope Is Built on Nothing Less"). Adding a refrain to "Christ Shall Have Dominion" (Ps 72), allowed for the lyrics to be sung to ST. GERTRUDE ("Onward, Christian Soldiers"). One of the most conspicuous pairings is "I Thought upon the Days of Old" (Ps 77) with the Scottish folk tune AULD LANG SYNE. The secular folk song joins with the psalmist's prayer in calling to mind the passing of the years, both for good and ill.

The Psalter 1912 includes 413 settings of psalms. (Many psalms appear in multiple versifications with longer psalms broken down into smaller

10. *New Metrical Version of the Psalms*, 3.

11. *Psalter*, 4.

segments.) These versifications are set with no less than 436 tunes. (Thirty-three of the texts are set with two tunes.) No tunes are repeated. Following the example of John Calvin, it was the intention that "a fixed association of tune and words [would be] gained thereby."[12] This was in stark contrast to the precedent set by English and Scottish psalters.

One of the denominations that participated in the "Uniform Version" (1909) was the Christian Reformed Church in North America (CRC). The denomination had been worshiping in Dutch and singing psalms to Genevan melodies. The CRC endorsed *The Psalter* 1912 as their official English-language psalter in 1914. The CRC began to publish their own "psalter hymnals" in 1934, always with a complete psalter and always with *The Psalter* 1912 serving as its core. In the most recent hymnal published jointly by the CRC and the Reformed Church in America (RCA), *Lift Up Your Hearts* (2013), there are still forty-two texts carried over from *The Psalter* 1912. Four very small denominations of Dutch extraction, the Netherlands Reformed Congregations, the Heritage Reformed Congregations, the Protestant Reformed Church, and the Free Reformed Church continue to make use of *The Psalter* 1912.

The Psalter 1912 was less influential in Presbyterian denominations, but significant nonetheless. In 1949, representatives of the UPCNA and the RCA began to explore the possibility of preparing a psalter hymnal together. In 1950, the General Assembly of the Presbyterian Church in the United States appointed a committee to approach the group already working and to inquire as to the possibility of joining in the production of the new hymnal. The Associate Reformed Presbyterian Church and the Presbyterian Church in the United States of America also joined in the project, making it a cooperative project of five American denominations of Presbyterian-Reformed heritage. Their work resulted in the publication of *The Hymnbook* in 1955. Though lacking a discrete psalter, the hymnal included fifty-four texts from *The Psalter* 1912. These versifications joined others retained from the *Scottish Psalter* (1650) and psalm paraphrases by Isaac Watts. In the most recent Presbyterian Church (USA) hymnal, *Glory to God* (2013), there remain nineteen selections carried over from *The Psalter* 1912. The *Trinity Hymnal* (1990), which serves the Orthodox Presbyterian Church and Presbyterian Church in America denominations, includes seventy versifications from *The Psalter* 1912, demonstrating its continuing appeal in the more conservative denominations.

There was one clan of Presbyterians that took metrical psalmody in a different direction. The Reformed Presbyterian Church in North America

12. *Psalter*, 4.

(RPCNA), often referred to as the "Covenanters," felt that the *Uniform Version* of 1909 yielded too much theologically in order to be "current in the best poetical literature."[13] This group tacked closer to the aesthetic of "inspired psalmody." Because they never abandoned the principle of unaccompanied singing, their tunes remained more melodically and metrically simple. The RPCNA's most recent psalter is *The Book of Psalms for Worship* (2010).

Mention should also be made of the metrical psalter tradition within the Presbyterian Church in Canada (PCC).[14] This Canadian denomination's metrical psalter practices align more with developments in the Church of Scotland. Unlike the mainline Presbyterians in the United States, the PCC maintained a discrete (though incomplete) metrical psalter in their denominational hymnals. The most recent edition of the PCC's *The Book of Praise* (1997),[15] edited by Donald Anderson and Andrew Donaldson, begins with 108 metrical psalms (some of them repeated). Though *The Psalter* 1912 continues to prove influential (twelve instances), *The Book of Praise* also maintains eighteen metrical psalms from the 1650 *Scottish Psalter* as well as two paraphrases from the Tate & Brady *New Version* of 1698.[16]

If the eighteenth and nineteenth centuries can be typified as one long ebb of metrical psalmody, the twentieth century seemed to be a period of shifting tides. The CRC denomination built on *The Psalter* 1912 by adding their own versifications in subsequent editions. This was most thoroughgoing in the 1987 *Psalter Hymnal*. Under the editorship of Emily Brink, the committee sought to revive the metrical psalter with many fresh versifications. Though their efforts to preserve the psalter hymnal tradition did not produce the desired effect—this would be the last psalter hymnal for the CRC—the newly minted psalm versifications would make a significant

13. See Copeland, "Experience of Singing the Psalms," xi–xvii.

14. While the Reformed denominations of Dutch extraction are binational, mainline Presbyterians in North America are separated denominationally by nation.

15. Not to be confused with the Canadian Reformed Church's *Book of Praise*. (See n. 9.)

16. *The Book of Praise* (1997) includes new psalm versifications from the RCA's *Rejoice in the Lord* (1985), the CRC's 1987 *Psalter Hymnal* and the PC(USA)'s 1990 *Presbyterian Hymnal*. The 1990 publication of *Psalm for Today and Songs from the Psalms* (edited by David Iliff, Michael Perry, and David Peacock) provided the PCC with a rich source of new psalm settings from the United Kingdom. *The Book of Praise* included many metrical psalms from this collection not previously published in North America by UK poets such as Timothy Dudley-Smith, Stephen Horsfall, Mollie Knight, David Mowbray, Michael Perry, James Seddon, and Paul Wigmore. Also significant are settings by Andrew Donaldson, including arrangements of several non-Western instances of psalm versifications.

contribution to future hymnal collections.[17] A smaller conservative offshoot of the CRC, the United Reformed Church has preserved the psalter hymnal format joining with the Orthodox Presbyterian Church in publishing the *Trinity Psalter Hymnal* (2018).

The RCA had followed a trajectory of loss of a psalter consciousness similar to that of the mainline Presbyterian denominations.[18] In the late 1970s a committee was formed to explore options for the production of a new hymnal. Included in the rationale for the project was a desire to recapture the "Calvinist heritage of psalmody as a central element in the praise of God."[19] These endeavors resulted in the publication of *Rejoice in the Lord: A Hymn Companion to the Scriptures* (1985) appearing posthumously under the editorship of Erik Routley.[20] Though the hymnal did not find traction in the denomination, its recovery of a discrete psalter (though incomplete) served as an important model for the PC(USA)'s *Presbyterian Hymnal: Hymns, Psalms, and Spiritual Songs* (1990).[21] For the first time since the 1830s, the largest body of North American Presbyterians would have a section of their hymnal devoted to metrical psalms.

The reappearance of these discrete psalters within denominational hymnals was significant and influential. This is not to say that they were embraced. As the PC(USA) was preparing to publish a new hymnal, research revealed that the psalter was the least utilized section of their 1990 hymnal. Many suggested letting it go. But, while the Presbyterians did abandon a psalter section in their subsequent hymnal, *Glory to God* (2013), they in fact increased the number of metrical psalms. The RCA and CRC denominations' hymnal, *Lift Up Your Hearts* (2013), likewise abandoned a discrete psalter section while increasing the number of metrical psalms.

17. Poets contributing new versifications to the *Psalter Hymnal* 1987 include David Diephouse, Helen Otte, Ada Rouper-Boulogne, Bert Polman, Marie Post, Calvin Seerveld, Henrietta Ten Harmsel, Clarence Walhout, Stanley Wiersma, and Bert Witvoet. The collection also carried over versifications from previous editions by Dewey Westra, William Kuipers, and Henry Zylstra. New versifications from the UK collection *Psalms Praise* (1973) introduced poets James E. Seddon, Michael Saward, and Christopher Idle.

18. See Brumm, "Congregational Song," 101–30.

19. Brumm, "Congregational Song," 127.

20. Poets contributing new versifications to *Rejoice in the Lord* include Erik Routley, Norman Kansfield, and Daniel Meeter. The collection also served to introduce to North America psalm versifiers from the UK, including Michael Saward, Timothy Dudley Smith, and Ian Pitt-Watson as well as contributions from *The Murrayfield Psalms* (1954).

21. Poets contributing new versifications to *The Presbyterian Hymnal* 1990 include Fred Anderson, Arlo Duba, J. Jefferson Cleveland, Joy Patterson, and Christopher Webber.

Several factors have spurred on this resurgence. There is a professed desire for congregational song that more faithfully reflects Scripture. Alongside the "hymn explosion" of the twentieth century, there has also been a burst of new psalm versifications, many by the same poets of modern hymns.[22] In the psalter hymnal projects of previous generations editorial committees relied heavily on their own clan to supply new versifications. Today many of the finest hymn writers turn to ancient sources for inspiration, including the biblical psalms.[23] And, finally, the liturgical renewal movement continues to press for the more regular use of the psalter in worship.

THEOLOGICAL PERSPECTIVES

The reformer John Calvin offers the first theological warrants for metrical psalmody.[24] He maintains that there is nothing better to sing to God than the prayers that God gives us in Scripture. The Psalms provide all that we need, expressing every possible human emotion. We should look no further for liturgical song. Calvin states that these songs should be sung by everyone. Many today fail to appreciate this emancipation of the congregation's voice, particularly women's voices, which had previously been excluded from worship.[25] In order to be sung by all, the psalms should be translated not only into linguistic vernacular, but poetic vernacular as well. By recasting the Hebrew psalm into Western meter and rhyme, the texts could be united with melodies and more easily sung and memorized by the masses. And, for Calvin, the starting point was a liturgical psalter. While fidelity to the original text was important, Calvin measured the success of the psalter by its function within the liturgy and the strength of poetry and melody. This stands in contrast to what we have inherited from the English Puritans for whom lyricism and beauty may be sacrificed for strict fidelity. In

22. For more, see chapters 7 and 6 of *Hymns and Hymnody*, vol. 3.

23. Many modern composers of English metrical psalmody are part of either The Hymn Society in the United States and Canada or The Hymn Society of Great Britain and Ireland. (See chapter 56.) Recent single-author versifications of the entire psalter have been produced by Michael Morgan (1999, rev. 2010), Martin Leckebusch (2006), and Carl Daw (vol. 1, 2018; vols. 2 and 3, forthcoming). Both Christopher L. Webber (1986) and Fred R. Anderson (2016) have produced versifications of lectionary psalms. R. Mark Shipp is editing a complete psalter by modern versifiers produced for unaccompanied harmony singing in the Churches of Christ tradition (v. 1, 2011; v. 2, 2016; v. 3, forthcoming). Many modern versifiers are represented in the collection *Psalms for All Seasons* (2012). (See p. 1107 of that collection for a list of composers of metrical settings since 1960.)

24. See Witvliet, "Spirituality of the Psalter," 203–29.

25. See McKee, "Context, Contours, Contents," 199, n. 70.

fact, for Puritans, beauty might be considered a red flag, a sign of misplaced priorities.[26]

This liturgical and theological divide can perhaps best be explicated by the psalm versifications themselves. Consider corresponding stanzas of Ps 103:

New Revised Standard Version (1989)

> Bless the Lord, O my soul,
> and all that is within me,
> bless his holy name.
> . . . who redeems your life from the Pit,
> who crowns you with steadfast love and mercy . . .

Sternhold & Hopkins (1565) [8.6.8.6]

> My soul, give praise unto the Lord,
> my spirit, do the same;
> And all the secrets of my heart,
> praise ye his holy Name:
> . . .
> That did redeem thy life from death,
> from which thou could'st not flee,
> His mercy and compassion both
> he did extend to thee;

Scottish Psalter (1650) [8.6.8.6]

> O thou my soul, bless God the Lord;
> and all that in me is
> Be stirrd up his holy name
> to magnify and bless.
> . . .
> Who doth redeem thy life, that thou
> to death may'st not go down;
> Who thee with loving-kindness doth
> and tender mercies crown:

Isaac Watts (1719) [8.8.8.8]

> Bless, O my soul, the living God,
> Call home thy thoughts that rove abroad;
> Let all the powers within me join
> In work and worship so divine.
> . . .

26. For more on this tradition, see chapters 4 and 8 of *Hymns and Hymnody*, vol. 2.

'Tis he, my soul, that sent his Son
To die for crimes which thou hast done;
He owns the ransom, and forgives
The hourly follies of our lives.

These versifications set the stage for North American psalmody in the twentieth century. The *Scottish Psalter* (1650) tilts toward fidelity to the Old Testament. Isaac Watts orientated his versifications toward New Testament fulfillment. Those who compiled *The Psalter* 1912 came from the more Puritan stream of the *Scottish Psalter*, but they were seeking a middle course. While for the most part avoiding explicit christological references, *The Psalter* 1912 in effect smoothed out many of the rough patches of the psalter. Its language was more lyrical and often was composed to fit with tunes popular in North America. This concern for text and tune compatibility was novel for English metrical psalmody. One of its versifications of Ps 103 was set to the tune *PILGRIMS*, then associated with Frederick William Faber's hymn, "Hark, Hark My Soul." The refrain of the metrical psalm from *The Psalter* 1912 echoes Faber's hymn refrain: *Angels of Jesus, angels of light, / Singing to welcome the pilgrims of the night!* These rhyme and tune associations assured that the versifications would have immediate traction.

The Psalter 1912 [11.10.11.10 with refrain]

O come, my soul, bless thou the Lord thy Maker,
And all within me, bless His holy Name;
Bless thou the Lord, forget not all His mercies,
His pard'ning grace and saving love proclaim.

Refrain:
Bless Him, ye angels, wondrous in might,
Bless Him, His servants that in His will delight.

In many ways, *The Psalter* 1912 became the standard of North American metrical psalmody to which later metrical psalters would either adapt or react. The psalter hymnals of the CRC for the most part adapted, but the *Psalter Hymnal* 1987 altered course. Rather than breaking longer psalms into shorter "hymn" settings, as had been the English tradition, the 1987 psalter presented each psalm as a single versification, a la the Genevan tradition. This work exposed many "smoothovers" as well as textual omissions in *The Psalter* 1912, particularly in the imprecatory psalms. The committee filled in the gaps of existing versifications and also prepared and commissioned many new versifications.[27]

27. See n. 13.

The impetus for a return to a metrical psalter for the RCA and the PC(USA) was not so much theological as it was liturgical. The "liturgical renewal" movement provided an opportunity to reclaim the metrical psalter. However, the function of the lectionary psalm—bound to the other lection readings—does not necessarily jibe with the "hymn-like" form of metrical psalmody. John Calvin intended for the psalms to be sung as prayers, whether that be praise, penitence, or lament. Erik Routley, editor of *Rejoice in the Lord* (RCA, 1985), wrote to his hymnal committee about the conundrum of trying to present the lectionary psalms metrically:

> Now if we treat psalms as Bible readings from the Old Testament we take the rough with the smooth, and read them on the assumption that the Old Testament finds its fulfillment, its answer, and here and there its contradiction, in Christ. . . . [M]etrical music transforms what we say into an affirmation at once: it petrifies into affirmation what Scripture intends to convey merely as information or as warning. So I think we should confine ourselves to psalms, or sections of them, which express praise, penitence, and observation of life that do not become embarrassing in the mouths of Christians.[28]

While Watts's and, by extension, Routley's theology of metrical psalmody is the functional theology of most modern hymnals, there has been pushback against its supersessionist assumptions. Most recent psalm scholarship, while acknowledging the importance of psalms as prophetic witness to Christ [cf. Luke 24:44], also lifts up the function of the psalms in their original contexts and, by extension, their possible use as models for personal and liturgical prayers today.[29] The theological conversation continues.

CONTRIBUTION TO LITURGY AND WORSHIP

For hundreds of years after the Reformation metrical psalmody provided a core repertoire of congregational song for Protestant Christians, particularly for those in the Calvinist tradition. As has been noted by both its promoters and detractors, metrical psalmody in the liturgy serves to make the words of the psalmist "our own." When the full spectrum of psalmody is rehearsed in the liturgy the people of God are shaped in the language of prayer.[30] The

28. Routley correspondence to the *Rejoice in the Lord* hymnal committee, "On Metrical Psalms," dated September 25, 1980. (Erik Routley Collection, Talbott Library, Westminster Choir College, Princeton, NJ.)

29. See Patrick D. Miller, Walter Brueggemann, and John D. Witvliet.

30. See Peterson, *Answering God.*

singing church has always turned to the psalms as a source and model for hymns of praise and trust. Psalmody also conjures sentiments that we would otherwise—and in contemporary liturgies essentially do—bar from the liturgy. Sometimes a psalm's words of doubt, hurt, anger, or despair can, as Erik Routley suggests, bring discomfort to the worshiper. Contemporary liturgical theologians such as Walter Brueggemann and John D. Witvliet recommend a discerning incorporation of the full range of the liturgical psalter, discomfort notwithstanding, in order to faithfully shape the people of God.

The psalms not only serve as a source, but also as a model or gauge for all of our congregational song. Theologian and hymnwriter Antonio Alonso puts it this way:

> Praying the psalms has, for me, been kind of like holding up a mirror to the repertoire to which I gravitate and to pay attention to what's missing. . . . [If] what makes it into many hymnals is any barometer, if what I quite naturally want to write is any barometer, the church as a whole . . . has tended toward songs that offer words of praise, confidence, or comfort, while smoothing out the rougher edges of our lives in our public worship, revising, ignoring, softening, or tamping down the fullness of that to which our songs to and about God might otherwise give voice.[31]

As stated, the most significant impetus for liturgical psalm-singing in the twentieth century has been the liturgical renewal movement that flowed out of the Second Vatican Council. Though its associated psalmody is primarily responsorial, the movement also gave cause for many to revisit their own metrical psalmody traditions. And, whereas the mode of singing psalms had long served to differentiate Christian communions from one another (chant/metrical, strict/free), there is more and more an understanding of a continuum of liturgical psalmody and hybrid of forms.[32]

NOTABLE HYMN

The versification of Ps 150, which Martin Leckebusch entitles "See Life As a Psalm"—though neither twentieth-century (2006) nor North American (Gloucester, England)—demonstrates well the promise of modern metrical psalmody.

31. Antonio Eduardo Alonso lecture, "Singing the Psalms as an Act of Radical Hospitality," delivered at the annual meeting of The Hymn Society in the United States and Canada, Waterloo, Ontario, July 17, 2017.

32. See *Psalms for All Seasons*, iii–vi.

Stanza 4:

Yield all that you are to worship the Lord—
see life as a psalm, each moment a chord;
let harmonies flourish and melodies soar—
let all that has breath praise the Lord evermore.
Hallelujah![33]

BIBLIOGRAPHY

Benson, Louis F. *The English Hymn: Its Development and Use in Worship.* Philadelphia, PA: The Presbyterian Board of Publication, 1915.

Brink, Emily R., and Bert Polman, eds. *Psalter Hymnal Handbook.* Grand Rapids, MI: CRC, 1998.

Brueggemann, Walter. *The Message of the Psalms: A Theological Commentary.* Minneapolis, MN: Augsburg, 1984.

———. *Praying the Psalms: Engaging Scripture and the Life of the Spirit.* 2nd ed. Eugene, OR: Cascade, 2007.

———. "Psalms: Voicing a Counter-World." *Reformed Worship* 105 (Sept. 2012) 24–29; *RW* 106 (Dec. 2012) 2–9; *RW* 107 (March 2013) 42–48.

Brumm, James Hart. "Congregational Song in the Reformed Church: Praise, Subversion, Appreciation, and Glimmers of Understanding." In *Liturgy among the Thorns,* edited by James Hart Brumm, 101–30. Grand Rapids, MI: Eerdmans, 2007.

Copeland, Robert M. "The Experience of Singing the Psalms." In *The Book of Psalms for Worship,* xi–xvii. Pittsburgh: Crown and Covenant Publications, 2010.

Daw, Carl P., Jr. *Glory to God: A Companion.* Louisville, KY: Westminster John Knox, 2016.

McKee, Elsie. "Context, Contours, Contents: Towards a Description of the Classical Reformed Teaching on Worship." *Princeton Seminary Bulletin* 16.2 (1995) 172–201.

Miller, Patrick D. *Interpreting the Psalms.* Philadelphia, PA: Fortress, 1986.

———. *The Lord of the Psalms.* Louisville, KY: Westminster John Knox, 2013.

The New Metrical Version of the Psalms. Pittsburgh: United Presbyterian Board of Publication, 1909.

Peterson, Eugene H. *Answering God: The Psalms as Tools for Prayer.* New York: Harper and Row, 1989.

Psalms for All Seasons: A Complete Psalter for Worship. Grand Rapids, MI: Faith Alive Christian Resources, 2012.

The Psalter. Pittsburgh: United Presbyterian Board of Publication, 1912.

Witvliet, John D. "The Biblical Psalms in Christian Worship: A Brief Introduction and Guide to Resources." Grand Rapids, MI: Eerdmans, 2007.

———. "The Spirituality of the Psalter in Calvin's Geneva." In *Worship Seeking Understanding: Windows into Christian Practice,* 203–29. Grand Rapids, MI: Baker Academic, 2003.

33. Set in *Psalms for All Seasons* (150A) to the tune *CHU LEUNG* [10.10.11.11 with refrain] by Swee Hong Lim.

Part 9

Twenty-First Century

Chapter 14

Mainline Protestant and Catholic Hymnals

Kendra Buckwalter Smith

HISTORICAL BACKGROUND

Hymnals of the twenty-first century demonstrate the church's response to sociopolitical and ecclesial developments throughout the preceding century. Prior to this period, beginning with the sixteenth-century Reformation, congregational song of Protestant churches was largely dominated by metrical psalmody, which then gave way to the strophic hymnody of the English hymn tradition beginning in the eighteenth century. By the middle of the twentieth century, Protestants used denominational hymnals comprised primarily of eighteenth- and nineteenth-century hymns. Rendered inadequate, these hymns did not address changing conditions and experiences of the twentieth-century world. In the Roman Catholic Church, Gregorian chant was understood as proper. Sacred polyphony developed out of the Gregorian chant tradition and found its height in the late sixteenth century. Catholics had used hymns for private devotion; however, hymns rarely made their way into liturgical ceremonies. Societal and ecclesial changes necessitated additions to the congregational song of the Catholic Church. With new material produced at unprecedented rates, the late twentieth century found itself in season of expansive hymn writing. These new hymns, addressing pressing issues of the day, found an audience through the publication of new hymnals and supplements. Throughout this time, there was a crosspollination of liturgy and song between Catholics and Protestants.

Sociopolitical Developments

Political, social, and economic issues presented themselves in the latter half of the twentieth century that spurred ecumenical changes to congregational song for both Catholics and Protestants. The feminist movement, the civil rights movement, and the anti-war movement all forged ahead full throttle. Additionally, the assassinations of John F. Kennedy and Martin Luther King, Jr., and reactions against outdated social structures influenced the development of hymnals during this time.

Among Protestant denominations in the early twentieth century, reactions against the emphasis on individualism and rationalism as well as personal pietism characteristic of the modern age led to increased interest in ancient liturgical forms as a way of emphasizing the universal nature of the church. Major themes were increased congregational participation, greater importance placed on the sacraments of baptism and the Lord's Supper, and unity both within and across denominations. Protestant hymnody began to address issues that it had not previously addressed. While Protestant hymnody in the first half of the twentieth century focused on praising God and giving thanks for one's salvation, hymns began to substantially emphasize cultural engagement and created space for repentance, lament, and intercession. Many of these themes are evident in *The Worshipbook—Services and Hymns* (1972) of the Presbyterian Church, *The Hymnal of the United Church of Christ* (1974), and the *Lutheran Book of Worship* (1978).

As the Catholic Church turned to the use of the vernacular, issues of language also affected Protestant hymnals. Among both Catholics and Protestants, hymn writers followed new translations of the Bible, incorporating language common to contemporary English. Questions arose as to whether and how to update older texts. Further attention to language grew out of issues of theology and justice. Growing feminist sentiment challenged the use of exclusively male imagery, anti-war movements challenged the use of battle and soldier imagery used for the church, and increased awareness of other cultures challenged the inclusion of patriotic hymns to avoid glorifying the United States at the expense of other nations. Therefore, many hymnal revision committees in the latter half of the century sought to use language that is inclusive with regard to race, gender, national origin, conditions of disability, and age. *The Worshipbook* (1972), *The Presbyterian Hymnal: Hymns, Psalms, and Spiritual Songs* (1990), *Worship—Second Edition* (1975) for the Catholic Church, *The United Methodist Hymnal* (1989), and *The Hymnal 1982* of the Episcopal Church all demonstrate such attention to language. The United Church of Christ then took a radical approach to inclusive language with the *New Century Hymnal* (1995).

Increasing global awareness led to greater diversity of music included in hymnals in the latter half of the twentieth century. In addition to those hymns written in the tradition of the English hymn, hymnals began to include frontier tunes, African American spirituals, gospel hymns, and music from non-European-American origins.

Ecclesial Developments

In the early twentieth century, a liturgical reform movement in Europe took root, which soon after began to impact the church in the United States with the founding of a number of organizations focused on the liturgy of the Catholic Church. Ventures in liturgical and musical resources abounded throughout pre-Vatican II twentieth-century American Catholicism as the church issued experimental revisions of the liturgy and encouraged active participation of the congregation. At the same time, Protestantism saw a number of denominational realignments and mergers along with liturgical efforts toward unity and increased interest in the liturgical heritage of the church.

It is in this context that Pope John XXIII called the Second Vatican Council, which developed in four sessions during the years of 1962–65. The council's Constitution on the Sacred Liturgy, issued on December 4, 1963, would solidify and intensify liturgical reform throughout the Catholic Church with great impact on Protestant denominations. The constitution holds that the church must meet the demands of people in every changing age as a part of salvation history. Thus, the use of the vernacular was introduced into the Latin Mass and a diversity of music was introduced to support the liturgy even as the church's musical tradition was to be preserved. The liturgy was lifted up as a bond of unity in the church as well as a bond of ecumenical unity.[1] Furthermore, great emphasis was placed on the full, conscious, and active participation of the laity in the liturgy.

With the increase in use of the vernacular in the years following Vatican II, the Catholic Church released new rites in rapid succession,

1. Boccardi, *History of American Catholic Hymnals*, 20.

which necessitated work on translations and appropriate musical response. Protestant hymns flooded the Catholic repertoire and church musicians gained artistic freedom, being no longer bound by traditional forms. It became common to set religious lyrics to popular folk songs. The resulting religious folk songs focused on formation of Christian character without much attention to scriptural influence. Yet they provided an accessible way for congregants to participate in the liturgy through song. The impact of migration led to an increasing number of churches with multicultural and multilingual congregations. This, along with increasing global awareness, led to the inclusion of songs with multilingual texts, world music idioms, and African American songs. With the 1970s came a new generation of folk music composers who paid greater attention to Scripture and engaged more sophisticated compositional technique.

In 1971, the first edition of *Worship* was published for the Catholic Church, followed by a second edition in 1975. Around this time, the hymnal revision projects of Protestant denominations demonstrated the impact of Vatican II. The reforms of Vatican II along with the ecumenical movement led many Protestant denominations to reshape their liturgical forms and resources. With the recovery of the Christian year among Protestant churches, hymns were composed to reflect the liturgical seasons. Many Protestant denominational hymnals placed greater emphasis on ecumenism than preceding hymnals, while also recovering a number of historical features of their particular traditions. For example, *The Worshipbook* (1972) placed liturgies and hymns in a single volume, emphasized congregational participation, and recovered elements of Reformed worship, specifically emphasis on responses and service music, the model of early Reformed psalters, and the reunion of the service of word and sacrament.[2] Similarly, *The Hymnal of the United Church of Christ* (1974) emphasized the role of the laity in worship and the reunion of the service of word and sacrament.

The weekly celebration of the Lord's Supper, which had fallen out of practice among Protestants with the sixteenth-century Reformation, began to return as denominations recovered the classical and historical pattern of worship that included both the proclamation of Scripture and the Lord's Supper. Not only was greater emphasis placed on the Lord's Supper, but the nature of that emphasis shifted as well. The celebration of the Supper became for many mainline churches a true celebration as focus shifted away from the memorializing of Jesus' death and toward the joy of Christ's resurrection and ascension. Thus, the section of hymns appropriate for the Lord's

2. Duba, *Presbyterian Worship*, 27.

Supper in denominational hymnals expanded with new songs pointing to Eucharistic themes of joy and hope, grace and welcome.

Denominational mergers inspired many Protestant denominations to recover a sense of identity in their particular tradition by reaching back to liturgical roots. In drawing on common historic roots, denominations also found an agent for unity first with those coming out of similar traditions, then across denominations. *The Hymnal of the United Church of Christ* (1974), *The United Methodist Hymnal* (1989), and the *New Century Hymnal* (1995) were developed following denominational mergers. The *Lutheran Book of Worship* (1978) was the result of collaboration between a number of Lutheran denominations, some of which later merged to form the Evangelical Lutheran Church in America. *The Presbyterian Hymnal: Hymns, Psalms, and Spiritual Songs* (1990) was developed following the reunification of the divided Presbyterian church and demonstrated increased efforts toward ecumenicism.

Both Catholic and Protestant hymnals continued along these trajectories into the turn of the century. *Worship—Third Edition* was published in 1986 with altered texts for inclusive language where possible. Two years later, the first edition of *Gather* (1988) was published, followed by a second edition in 1994. The *Gather* series contained music in popular idioms and was intended as a companion to the more traditional *Worship* series. Subsequently, Catholic hymnals began to trend toward including contemporary and culturally diverse material alongside classical hymns in a single volume. These volumes include two editions of *Gather Comprehensive* (1994 and 2004). *Worship—Fourth Edition* (2011) marked even greater musical diversity.

With the publication of *The Revised Common Lectionary* in 1992, hymn writers began looking primarily to Scripture for hymn texts, basing hymns on the passages set forth in the lectionary cycle. This marked a "shift from the predominantly experiential hymns of the late nineteenth century to a more objective exposition of Scripture."[3] Many Protestants also found renewed interest in singing both metrical and responsorial psalms. Especially in the midst of the great awakenings, increasing attention was paid to the affections of worshipers. Many Presbyterians, Methodists, and the Reformed Church in America began moving away from the strict scriptural song of the psalters of Geneva, England, and Scotland in the eighteenth- and nineteenth-centuries in favor of later compositions engaging practical

3. Brink, "When in Our Music," 45. Examples of hymns reflecting this trend include "A Prophet-Woman Broke a Jar" (Brian Wren, 1991); "A Sower Came from Ancient Hills (Herman G. Stuempfle Jr., 1998); "A Woman and a Coin" (Jaroslav J. Vajda, 1990); and "Silence! Frenzied, Unclean Spirit" (Thomas H. Troeger, 1984).

theology and emotional inspiration, while the Christian Reformed Church (CRC) remained committed solely to metrical psalms in public worship until 1934. The Reformed Presbyterian Church of North America (RPCNA) still holds to this tradition, having published *The Book of Psalms for Worship* (2010). This volume continues the historical and ecclesiastical tradition of previous psalters, yet offers substantially revised renderings of the psalms in updated language.

Entering the Twenty-first Century: Emerging Themes

Changes in the sociopolitical and ecclesial context around the turn of the century greatly impacted hymnal revision projects. Toward the end of the twentieth century, committees had opportunity to make changes to the church's liturgical materials in response to positive developments—greater inclusion and recognition of women's rights, growing diversity in churches, active church outreach, and communication and cooperation across denominational lines. These hymnal revisions were underway in a time when America was at the height of unbridled economic wealth prior to the 1990s recession. The Cold War was coming to an end, the Berlin Wall fell, and stocks rose. American Christians felt empowered to solve the problems they faced.

In many ways, such optimism no longer defines the twenty-first century church as it responds to a post-9/11 context in which a sense of vulnerability and fear leading to racial and religious profiling permeates the general psyche of American society. With increased global conflict and repeated instances of terrorism, attention to language with concern for justice continues with more significant urgency, as does recognition of diversity within the church. Furthermore, as optimism in human progress wanes, the church seeks to point worshipers more substantially toward God's action in the world. Some have done so in part by expanding their hymnals beyond the liturgical year to more broadly include the entire scope of the biblical narrative from creation to recreation.

Increasingly, hymnals include congregational song from diverse sources and styles. Toward the end of the twentieth century, the Catholic Church began expanding hymnals once centered on traditional hymnody to include contemporary and culturally diverse selections. Whereas the *United Methodist Hymnal* (1989) and *The Presbyterian Hymnal* (1990) were eventually accompanied by supplements (*The Faith We Sing*, 2000, and *Sing the Faith*, 2003, respectively) offering more contemporary material, later projects in both denominations aim to include a diversity of sources within a single volume.

Gather—Third Edition

The third edition of *Gather* was published for the Catholic Church in 2011. While "comprehensive" is no longer included in the title, this edition continues to build on the variety and flexibility of the *Gather* series. This collection includes contemporary material published since the publication of *Gather Comprehensive—Second Edition.*

Worship—Fourth Edition

Published in 2011, the fourth edition of *Worship* followed the 2011 implementation of the *Roman Missal, Third Edition.* It is organized according to the liturgical life of the Catholic Church beginning with the Liturgy of the Hours, followed by a section of psalms and canticles, and a section of Rites of the Church. The collection draws upon a greater diversity of material than previous editions and includes bilingual (English and Spanish) texts. It also demonstrates greater attention to hymn texts. Many texts were compared with original versions, restoring original wording or previously omitted verses, and in some cases were edited with attention to theology and poetry.

Evangelical Lutheran Worship

Recognizing increased diversity among its congregations, the Evangelical Lutheran Church in America (ELCA) published *Evangelical Lutheran Worship* in 2006. The collection includes a core of congregational song that is representative and reflects the materials the denomination perceives to be most important to hold in common across the church. It also offers a much larger and ever-growing body of material accessible to congregations in both print and electronic form. The first section of the volume includes material related to the church year, followed by orders of service with integrated liturgical music. The second section consists of psalms for singing, other service music selections, and finally hymns arranged by categories beginning with the church year and continuing with thematic categories and several national songs.

Psalms for All Seasons

The Christian Reformed Church in North America published *Psalms for All Seasons: A Complete Psalter for Worship* in 2012. The collection draws upon a wide variety of approaches and styles including contributions both from the long history of Christian psalmody and more contemporary psalm settings from various traditions and cultures. For each of the 150 psalms, the psalter includes the complete text marked for responsive reading or chanting; a prayer of response; notes about the psalm and potential liturgical uses; and one or more musical settings. The wide range of material encourages engagement with the full emotional scope of the psalms.

Lift Up Your Hearts: Psalms, Hymns, and Spiritual Songs

The Reformed Church in America and the Christian Reformed Church in North America partnered to publish *Lift Up Your Hearts: Psalms, Hymns, and Spiritual Songs* in 2013. The volume includes a wide variety of resources from various cultures, languages, and musical genres. Selections are organized according to two broad sections. First, "The Story of Creation and Redemption" reflects the whole story of God's relationship with God's people beginning with creation and humanity's fall into sin, through to the promise of the new creation. The second section, "Worshiping the Triune God," follows the basic order of worship according to the Reformed tradition. The collection continues the long history of psalm singing common to both denominations by including all 150 psalms integrated thematically throughout the collection.

Glory to God: The Presbyterian Hymnal

The Presbyterian Church (USA) published *Glory to God* in 2013. The collection and its organizational structure points to eschatological consummation as the source of the church's hope and assurance in the midst of anxiety and division prevalent in the twenty-first century church. Selections are organized in three broad sections: "God's Mighty Acts," "The Church at Worship," and "Our Response to God." This comprehensive structure places hymn texts within the context of the grand narrative of God's plan for creation. In addition to highlighting connection to the whole of the biblical narrative, *Glory to God* points to communion with all the faithful by incorporating a wide variety of material from diverse liturgical and cultural contexts. Psalms are included in appropriate categories throughout the hymnal as opposed to appearing in one collected section of psalms as in the 1990 hymnal. The distribution of 141 psalm settings throughout the 2013 hymnal marks a recovery of the Reformed heritage of psalm singing with an emphasis on the connectivity between Scripture and the life of the worshiper within salvation history.

Further Revision Projects

The United Methodist Church

In the fall of 2017, a new Hymnal Revision Committee of the United Methodist Church began work to create a print and digital resource. While a core of material will be included in the print version, General Conference will approve a supplemental collection of music and worship resources that may be customized for different contexts. Using cloud technology, the Standing Hymnal Advisory Committee will periodically update and revise the resource.

The Episcopal Church

The 2015 General Convention of the Episcopal Church approved a resolution to prepare a plan for the revision of the 1979 Book of Common Prayer. Along with this resolution, the convention called for a plan for the revision of *The Hymnal 1982*. Both are to take into account the church's diversity and to consider the use of current technology for distribution and access.

THEOLOGICAL PERSPECTIVES

To be sure, the theological perspectives conveyed through different denominational hymnals vary depending on the convictions of the denomination. Yet there are certain developments in hymnal production in and immediately preceding the twenty-first century that point beyond cultural trends to common deep theological convictions that have played out in hymnal revisions. These are convictions not only about God, but also about the ways in which God's people are to posture themselves in an ever-changing cultural context, the way worshipers are to live as God's people both when they approach God in worship and when they engage daily life in the world. With the turn of the century, trends with regard to hymnal revision include continued attention to the use of language, focus on unity in diversity both within and among denominations and cultures, and a growing shift in focus from the worshiper to God.

Sociopolitical Developments

Attention to the language used for God and humanity in congregational song is rooted in convictions regarding theology and justice—namely that all those created by God are to be acknowledged with equity. The expansion of language used for God beyond the use of male pronouns and those terms that may perpetuate oppressive social structures is rooted in a conviction that God transcends gender and social constructs.[4]

The increasing inclusion of musical idioms from the worldwide church points to growing emphasis on the theological conviction of the unity of the body of Christ and the need to receive and learn from a diversity of gifts and perspectives. The incorporation of different musical and cultural expressions within a single hymnal aims toward unity so that congregations might recognize oneness shared in Christ.

The church has felt deeply the impact of modern/postmodern preoccupation with the individual, the uncertainty and division that permeates the world, and continued decline among mainline Protestant and Catholic churches. In this context, early twenty-first century hymnals redirect attention toward God's redemptive promises. Both through hymn selection and organizational structure, hymnals pay increased attention to the eschatological promise in a way that points the worshiper toward God's action in leading the world to its telos. Twentieth-century hymnals demonstrate a

4. Some hymn texts have been altered to remove masculine pronouns for God, while others have been maintained but are accompanied by hymns that draw on feminine pronouns and broad imagery for God. One example is the hymn "Bring Many Names" by Brian Wren (1986) in which God is referred to as "strong mother," "warm father," "old, aching," "young, growing," and "great, living." Hymnal committees also demonstrate sensitivity to language that might be seen as dangerous or discriminatory, including militaristic language, dark/white contrasts, and certain physical abilities that do not apply to all people. The *New Century Hymnal* provides ample examples. With sensitivity to gender inclusion, "Good Christian Men, Rejoice," is now "Good Christian Friends, Rejoice" (hymn number 129). While scripturally, the use of the word "dark" often represents sin or evil, racial tensions in American society render the association problematic. Thus, drawing on the confessional language of Ps 51 in which the psalmist implores God to "purge me with hyssop, and I shall be clean; wash me, and I shall be whiter than snow" (verse 7, NRSV), the hymn setting reads "purer than snow" (hymn number 657) so as to avoid association with skin color. Sensitivity to those with disabilities led the committee to change "At the cross where I first saw the light" to "where I first found the light" in "Alas! And Did My Savior Bleed" (Isaac Watts, 1707, hymn number 199).

progression from other-worldly engagement rooted in personal experience and hope of salvation, to increased cultural engagement.[5] Early twenty-first century hymnals have begun to link the two, emphasizing cultural engagement with a Kingdom of God grounding and orientation.[6] The confidence in human progress that once characterized much of the church threatens to place more trust in the worshiper than in the promises of God. Yet, trust in the future that God has planned for the world cannot lead to disengagement with the world in which the worshiper is called to live. As Christians look forward to the promises of Christ's coming Kingdom, they are called to participate in those promises in a way that makes them known to the world. The selections found in mainline Protestant and Catholic hymnals of the twenty-first century and the ways in which they are organized shape worshipers into lives that reflect this reality. *Gather Comprehensive—Second Edition* includes the section "Kingdom/Reign of God." *Lift Up Your Hearts* points to the promise of the new creation with the section, "Hope for Things to Come," including subsections "Christ's Second Coming" and "The New Heaven and Earth." *Evangelical Lutheran Worship* includes the section "End Time." In *Glory to God*, the final two subsections of the broad category "God's Mighty Acts" are "Christ's Return and Judgment" and "A New Heaven and a New Earth." The very last subsection of *Glory to God* is "Trusting in the Promises of God," under "Our Response to God." As certain hymns are placed within these categories, the themes they express are interpreted within the context of Christ's ongoing, redemptive work in the world. The eschatological promise includes Christ's judgment. With decreased confidence in human progress has come increased recognition that the world is in need of Christ's judgment. The eschatological categories in each of these hymnals treats Christ's second coming and judgment not as something to inspire fear, but rather hope and assurance in the promise that it is Christ who will right all that is wrong in the world.

5. For example, "All Who Love and Serve Your City" (Erik Routley, 1966), addresses urban issues; "Thank You, Lord, for Water, Soil, and Air" (Brian Wren, 1973), is both a hymn of thanksgiving and confession addressing ecological issues; and "For the Healing of the Nations" (Fred Kaan, 1965), which addresses the ways in which those who experience personal salvation are called, not just to rest in that salvation, but to participate in God's healing work throughout the world.

6. Note, for example, that in *The Presbyterian Hymnal: Hymns, Psalms, and Spiritual Songs* (1990), Erik Routley's hymn "All Who Love and Serve Your City" (1966) was placed in the section "Church: Mission," emphasizing the activity of humanity in the text. However, in *Glory to God: the Presbyterian Hymnal* (2013), the hymn appears in the section "Christ's Return and Judgment," grounding the text's references to human activity in the context of God's activity and the church's eschatological hope.

Ecclesial Developments

The theological convictions of both the ecumenical movement and the liturgical movement impact the theological perspectives conveyed through twenty-first century hymnals. Both significantly point to the importance of identity as and unity in the Body of Christ. For both Catholics and Protestants, the image of the church as the Body of Christ lifts up a particular baptismal consciousness wherein the baptized, as a new creation through water and the Spirit, is called to full and active participation in the church and its worship. The baptized is engrafted into a diverse community bound together by Christ's leadership. God relates to God's people in context. And as this occurs, the diversity of contexts in which God relates to people offers insights for others. God transcends the particular experience of any one person or culture. Hymnal revision trends of the late twentieth and early twenty-first century demonstrate increased value placed on the experience of others alongside thoughtful reflection on that which defines the experience of a particular community. In the midst of division in the church, the move to incorporate different cultural expressions within a single hymnal points to the oneness shared in Christ. Further, this points to the conviction that all God's people have valuable gifts to offer the worldwide church as well as the conviction that God transcends the expression or experience of any one community. Thus, as churches diversify their congregational song, they discover anew and more fully the God they worship.

Both the individual hymns selected for inclusion in a collection and the organizational framework of those selections impacts the theological perspective conveyed by a particular hymnal. The twentieth century saw increased emphasis on the liturgical year as a point of unity across denominations, thus making it a logical framework around which to organize hymnals. However, hymnals of the twenty-first century have pushed the unifying emphasis even further. In the case of *Glory to God* and *Lift Up Your Hearts*, salvation history serves as the organizational framework. Because the liturgical year is based on the life of Christ, it is contained within salvation history. Thus, organization according to salvation history does not exclude the liturgical year, but incorporates it in a more complete expression of the biblical narrative. Increased emphasis on the primacy of God's word, which characterized the twentieth century, is continued here in an engagement of the complete scriptural canon.

CONTRIBUTIONS TO LITURGY AND WORSHIP

Having examined both the sociopolitical and ecclesial dimensions leading to the development of mainline Protestant and Catholic hymnals in the twenty-first century, we may now investigate the joint implications in the context of twenty-first century worship.

As denominations seek to respond to the needs of a church that is diverse both culturally and liturgically, a wider variety of congregational song is included with each new hymnal revision. With the increased breadth of material in hymnals, including a diversity of music from both the historical treasury and the contemporary context, hymnals of the twenty-first century serve to preserve tradition in the midst of innovation. With the revival of forgotten or ignored practices, certain denominations are provided a rootedness in the richness of their traditions. Yet the great attention paid to finding fresh expressions of eternal truths in an ever-changing world has simultaneously increased accessibility to those truths. Furthermore, the various forms of expression included within one volume enable the worshiper to hold in tension diversity and unity in the body of Christ. With the inclusion of gifts from the global church, the consciousness of the worshiper is expanded through interaction with texts and music of cultures beyond one's immediate context and familiarity as a reminder that each worshiper is part of a larger body beyond its own worshiping community. This allows for both increased understanding of different cultures and greater engagement with the God who transcends the experience of any one person or culture. With the expanding repertoire of congregational song, the worshiper finds new points of entry into the story of God, as well as new language and imagery with which to proclaim that story. Thus, hymnals of the twenty-first century provide a sense of continuity with a long line of worshipers through the history of the church as well as continuity with the worldwide church, pushing beyond the apparent dichotomy between traditional and contemporary and beyond differences that would separate cultural expression.

In addition to a broader scope of material, the church is seeking new and varied methods of delivery. With changes in musical preferences, the outpouring of Christian contemporary music, and technological developments, many churches have entered the twenty-first century relying heavily on Christian Copyright Licensing International (CCLI) to acquire lyrics and music for contemporary worship songs. With this resource and others, churches have access to a vast array of musical options, yet with little guidance toward those musical resources that align with their denominational tradition and theology. Hymnals published in the twenty-first century, particularly those with electronic resources, provide worship planners and church musicians with a certain grounding to their musical selections by providing a clear canon of material from which to draw. It further encourages more discernment when drawing on material from outside the canon. This grounding is an important function of hymnals in the twenty-first century. In the context of globalization and the continued individualism of postmodernity, distinctions between theological convictions of denominations become blurred. The overarching claim of personal preference and relativity of truth necessitate some direction and clarity for a people defined by the community of Christ.

Combined sociopolitical and ecclesial developments have begun to bridge the divide between texts that praise God without direct connection to the work of God in the world on the one hand, and those songs that focus on cultural engagement without significant rooting in Scripture on the other. Both the material included in twenty-first century hymnals and the organization of that material encourages worshipers to understand engagement with the world in the context of God's ongoing action. Newer collections of hymns create space not only for praise of God, but also for repentance, lament, and intercession, allowing worshipers to sing the breadth of humanity's response to God and the world. The salvation history framework of hymnals like *Glory to God* of the PC(USA) and *Lift Up Your Hearts* of the CRC and RCA challenges worshipers to shape their worship and experience by a deep understanding of the full scope of the biblical narrative.

In addition to greater musical and cultural diversity of material, hymnals of the twenty-first century include a wider breadth of material from which to draw for various portions of the liturgy such that worshipers discover new (or in some cases, recover old) ways of participating in the liturgy through song.

NOTABLE HYMNS

The scope of this chapter is far too limited to name the many hymnists who have made notable contributions to twenty-first century hymnals. Though, certain hymns stand out in their ecumenical popularity and in their expression of theological convictions that have come to the fore in recent years. What follows is a mere sampling of such hymns.

Marty Haugen (b. 1950) is one of the more prolific and ecumenically popular hymnists across twenty-first century hymnals. His hymn "Gather Us In" (1982) can be found in both Catholic and Protestant hymnals. The text draws on scriptural references and sacramental imagery to form a corporate prayer to God. It points to future hope that is brought into the present in the experience of the diverse and inclusive Body of Christ. "All Are Welcome" (1994) similarly depicts life as the church, the Body of Christ. Both of these hymns demonstrate efforts toward unity and ecumenism, strong reliance on Scripture, a sacramental understanding of the church, and a situating of human action within the context of God's redemptive work in the world.

"Freedom is Coming" is a traditional South African song published in 1984. In its expression of eschatological hope, this song has a present orientation, emphasizing that Jesus is in fact coming and along with him, freedom is coming. The song was written in protest of Apartheid in South Africa. The racial segregation of the mid- to late-twentieth century represents the norms and powers of the present age. Yet the worshiper's assurance in the coming of Christ marks an acknowledgment of and participation in God's Kingdom. The song is associated with Ps 114, which celebrates God's act of freeing Israel from Egypt. The psalmist writes, "tremble, O earth, at the presence of the Lord" (verse 7, NRSV). This presence is known in God's liberation of and provision for Israel, and it is known in the freedom of South Africans. The song's presence in both Catholic and Protestant hymnals provides an example of increased incorporation of music from the global church.

The hymns of Bernadette Farrell (b. 1957) appear in hymnals across denominations. Her 1993 hymn, "Christ, Be Our Light," demonstrates the broad scope of human experience addressed in twenty-first century hymnals. While the verses convey lament, longing, and intercession, the refrain is a prayer of hope and assurance. The text draws together Christ's promise that he is the Light of the world (John 8:12) and his charge to the church to be the light of the world (Matt 5:14). As worshipers sing of present struggles, they are reminded with each refrain that Christ is working his promise of redemption through them.

BIBLIOGRAPHY

Blumhofer, Edith L., and Mark A. Noll, ed. *Singing the Lord's Song in a Strange Land: Hymnody in the History of North American Protestantism*. Tuscaloosa: The University of Alabama Press, 2004.

Boccardi, Donald. *The History of American Catholic Hymnals since Vatican II*. Chicago: GIA Publications, 2001.

The Book of Psalms for Worship. Pittsburgh: Crown and Covenant, 2010.

Brink, Emily R. "When in Our Music God Is Glorified: Classic Contemporary Protestant Hymnody." In *New Songs of Celebration Render: Congregational Song in the Twenty-first Century*, edited by C. Michael Hawn, 39–68. Chicago: GIA Publications, 2013.

Clyde, Arthur G. *The Language of the New Century Hymnal*. Eugene, OR: Wipf & Stock, 1996.

Discipleship Ministries. "Revision Committee Begins Work on New Version of the United Methodist Hymnal." September 21, 2017. https://www.umcdiscipleship.org/resources/revision-committee-begins-work-on-new-version-of-united-methodist-hymnal.

Duba, Arlo D. *Presbyterian Worship in the Twentieth Century: With a Focus on the Book of Common Worship*. Louisville, KY: Westminster John Knox, 2014.

Evangelical Lutheran Worship. Minneapolis, MN: Augsburg Fortress, 2006.

The Faith We Sing. Nashville: Abingdon, 2001.

Gather. Chicago: GIA Publications, 1988.

Gather—Second Edition. Chicago: GIA Publications, 1992.

Gather—Third Edition. Chicago: GIA Publications, 2011.

Gather Comprehensive. Chicago: GIA Publications, 1994.

Gather Comprehensive—Second Edition. Chicago: GIA Publications, 2006.

Glory to God: The Presbyterian Hymnal. Louisville, KY: Westminster John Knox, 2013.

Harmon, Kathleen. "Singing the Paschal Mystery: Roman Catholic Liturgical Music after Vatican II." In *New Songs of Celebration Render: Congregational Song in the Twenty-first Century*, edited by C. Michael Hawn, 3–36. Chicago: GIA Publications, 2013.

The Hymnal 1982. New York: Church Hymnal Corporation, 1985.

The Hymnal of the United Church of Christ. Philadelphia: United Church Press, 1974.

Lift Up Your Hearts: Psalms, Hymns, and Spiritual Songs. Grand Rapids, MI: Faith Alive Christian Resources, 2013.

Lutheran Book of Worship. Minneapolis, MN: Augsburg, 1978.

Mouw, Richard J., and Mark A. Noll, eds. *Wonderful Words of Life: Hymns in American Protestant History and Theology*. Grand Rapids, MI: Eerdmans, 2004.

The New Century Hymnal. Cleveland, OH: Pilgrim, 1995.

Pecklers, Keith F. *The Unread Vision: The Liturgical Movement in the United States of America 1926–1955*. Collegeville, MN: The Liturgical, 1998.

The Presbyterian Hymnal: Hymns, Psalms, and Spiritual Songs. Louisville, KY: Westminster John Knox, 1990.

Psalms for All Seasons: A Complete Psalter for Worship. Grand Rapids, MI: Faith Alive Christian Resources, 2012.

Psalter Hymnal. Grand Rapids, MI: CRC Publications, 1987.

Routley, Erik. *An English-Speaking Hymnal Guide*. Edited by Peter W. Cutts. Chicago: GIA Publications, 2005.

Schilling, S. Paul. *The Faith We Sing*. Philadelphia: Westminster, 1983.

Sing the Faith. Louisville, KY: Geneva, 2003.

The United Methodist Hymnal. Nashville: United Methodist, 1989.

Worship. Chicago: GIA Publications, 1971.

Worship—Second Edition. Chicago: GIA Publications, 1975.

Worship—Third Edition. Chicago: GIA Publications, 1986.

Worship—Fourth Edition. Chicago: GIA Publications, 2011.

The Worshipbook: Services and Hymns. Philadelphia: Westminster, 1970, 1972.

Chapter 15

Hymn Society in the United States and Canada

Carl P. Daw, Jr.

HISTORICAL BACKGROUND

Given that the first substantive book printed in the English colonies of North America in the seventeenth century was a metrical psalter, the so-called *Bay Psalm Book* (1640); it is surprising that there was no organization devoted to the promotion of congregational song in North America until the first quarter of the twentieth century, and that the beginnings of the Hymn Society in the United States and Canada were quite small. On January 19, 1922, five "hymn writers residing in New York City and vicinity"[1] made their way to the Presbyterian Building at 156 Fifth Avenue and gathered in the office of Calvin Weiss Laufer (1874–1938), the musical editor for the Presbyterian Board of Publication. The other four participants were Emily Swan Perkins (1866–1941), a Presbyterian laywoman who was an amateur organist and composer; Caroline Bird Parker (1877–1959), an editor of hymnals for the Century Company; Carl Fowler Price (1881–1948), a Methodist insurance broker who was well regarded as a hymnologist and musician; and Augustus Sherwood Newman (1848–1928), a Methodist

1. Hymn Society, Minutes, January 19, 1922, 2.

businessman with a similarly strong musical avocation. Also notable are the other four persons invited to this meeting who sent regrets: Frank Mason North (1850–1935), Methodist minister, social activist, and hymn writer; William Pierson Merrill (1867–1954), noted Presbyterian pastor and hymn writer; Henry Sloan Coffin (1877–1954), prominent Presbyterian pastor, seminary president, and hymnal editor; and Karl Pomeroy Harrington (1861–1953), Methodist organist and Latin professor.

The organizational history that has developed for almost a century since this small beginning is a fascinating story. Incorporated as the Hymn Society of America in 1938, the Hymn Society grew from what first began as a five-member "club."[2] In 1989, it became the Hymn Society in the United States and Canada. Previous histories, while documented effectively in several detailed accounts,[3] are concerned primarily with the internal changes the Society has undergone. This present survey, however, focuses on the ever-widening effect this organization has had on the larger hymnic landscape.

The same five people who gathered for the initial exploratory meeting reconvened on January 28, 1922, in a meeting room of the same building. The principal item of business was to receive the report of the committee on organization (consisting of Laufer, Perkins, and Price as chair). A notable feature of this document is the comprehensiveness of this fledgling society's stated objectives:

> to cultivate the devout use of better Christian hymns and hymn-tunes; to encourage the writing and publishing of hymns that express the temper of modern Christian life and thought, and also of hymn-tunes of genuine musical merit and best adapted to congregational singing; to secure the union of hymns and tunes that are closely related in emotional content and worshipful significance; to promote the collection of hymnodic data, new and old, encourage research and stimulate full discussion and the special preparation of addresses, articles and reviews upon subjects hymnodic; to the end that there may be improvement and greater inspiration in these hymnodic and musical modes of praise and prayer in the worship of God.[4]

2. Hymn Society, Minutes, January 19, 1922, 2.

3. Reid, *Sing with Spirit and Understanding*; Reid, *Continuing Sing with Spirit and Understanding*; Van Burkalow, "Sixty Years of the Hymn Society"; McKellar, "History of the Hymn Society"; Loftis, "Hymn Society in the United States and Canada."

4. Hymn Society, Minutes, January 28, 1922, 5.

While those objectives have continued to inspire and shape the activity of the Hymn Society, the original assumptions about membership have changed significantly. At first only hymnal editors, authors of hymn texts, and composers of hymn tunes were eligible for membership. Furthermore, each new member had to be nominated by a current member and approved by two-thirds vote of the members present at the time. Yet even from the beginning membership was divided into active and honorary members, the latter being persons who had made significant contributions to hymnody but who often lived outside the New York City area (some as far away as the United Kingdom and China). By 1929, the membership categories expanded to associate membership for interested clergy and church musicians.[5] Through later decades, the categories continued to evolve to meet changing circumstances, so that the current categories are individual or institution (church, school, or library), student or active military, retired, family, and life member.[6]

The five founders' announced intention to encourage the writing and publishing of hymns and hymn tunes became an active endeavor much sooner than they could have anticipated. At the third meeting of the Society on February 20, 1922, one of the people present (as the guest of Carl Price) was Henry Webb Farrington (1880–1931), who had recently won a competition sponsored by Harvard University with a text titled "Our Christ" (first line: "I know not how that Bethlehem's Babe"). Before the fourth meeting a month later, Farrington had written to Price offering to fund a prize for a new tune for his text if the Hymn Society would be willing to undertake a search for one. The Society agreed and appointed five judges to receive and evaluate the musical manuscripts.[7] The search continued for a year, and more than a thousand entries came in from a wide range of people and from as far away as Europe.[8] In the end, the winning tune was Veritas (reflecting the Harvard motto), composed by the well-known blind organist of the Evangelical Lutheran Church of the Epiphany in New York City, John Nicholas Burnham (1871–1949?). A few years later, the excitement over Charles Lindbergh's nonstop flight to Paris that led to the New York parade for him inspired one of Carl Price's enthusiastic friends to offer to fund a search for "a hymn for airmen." The resulting influx of 1,276 text submissions came from all over the United States and several foreign countries. The winner, in fact, was May A. Rowland (1870–1959) of Eastbourne, England,

5. Reid, *Sing with Spirit and Understanding*, 9.

6. www.thehymnsociety.org/membership.

7. Hymn Society, Minutes, March 20, 1922, 12–13.

8. Hymn Society, Minutes, April 19, 1923, 40; May 26, 1923, 43.

whose hymn began "God of the shining hosts that range on high." The distinguished British organist of St. Bartholomew's Church, New York, David McKinley Williams (1887–1978), won a subsequent search for a tune.[9]

In 1929, a search for a new hymn on the theme of peace yielded no text that met the Society's standards. However, a year later in searching for a new missionary hymn, the Society received more than a thousand submissions, from which "Eternal God, Whose Power Upholds" by Henry Hallam Tweedy (1868–1953) of Yale Divinity School was declared the winner. Chosen to set it from among nine hundred entries was the tune Sarah, by the London-based Welsh composer Rhys Thomas (1867–1932).[10]

In 1942, three hymns were deemed prize-worthy. The first, designated as "a hymn of Christian faith in time of stress" was by Thomas Curtis Clark (1877–1953) and began "Thou Father of us all, On thy great name we call." Two hymns "of personal Christian dedication" were also found to be of equal merit: "O Thou, the Way Eternal" by Katharine L. Aller (1880–1964) and "Come Thou, My Light That I May See" by Hugh Thomson Kerr (1871–1950).[11]

While World War II gripped the nation, the Hymn Society undertook a search for hymns that were patriotic, Christian, and "free from the hatreds and fears that seemed to possess the world."[12] Twelve such hymns selected from the submissions eventually formed a publication *Hymns of Christian Patriotism* (1945) as a part of the series of Hymn Society Papers.[13] This publication was the precursor of thirty-three hymn collections the Society published between 1952 and 1982, most of which are discussed below under Theological Perspectives. The best of these texts and tunes were anthologized in 1992 as *Holding in Trust.*[14]

Although the original objectives adopted in 1922 included the intention "to encourage research," nothing specified directions for promulgating this research. While it was standard protocol for speakers at Hymn Society meetings to provide a copy of their papers for the Society's archives, there was no provision for distributing them to the membership. Discussions concerning how to disseminate the research took place at the meetings in the 1927, but it seemed that the projected costs were prohibitive. Then early in

9. Hymn Society, Annual Report 1927–28, 192; Reid, *Sing with Spirit and Understanding*, 55.

10. Reid, *Sing with Spirit and Understanding*, 56.

11. Reid, *Sing with Spirit and Understanding*, 56.

12. Reid, *Sing with Spirit and Understanding*, 56.

13. Hymn Society, *Hymns of Christian Patriotism.*

14. Black et al., *Holding in Trust.*

1930s the noted hymnologist Louis Fitzgerald Benson (1855–1930) offered to initiate a series identified as "Papers of the Hymn Society" by writing the first paper and by paying for the printing of enough copies to send it to all members without charge.[15]

Benson inaugurated the series with an examination of the poetic texts from John Bunyan's *Pilgrim's Progress* that hymnal editors have treated as hymns. Fittingly, the second publication in the series, *The Religious Value of Hymns* by William P. Merrill, found its inspiration in a sermon Merrill preached at the January 1931 memorial service the Hymn Society held for Benson. Thus was launched a succession of occasional publications that continued for fifty more years with thirty-five numbered papers. The range of topics was wide and varied, but the papers usually took the form of brief monographs. Some representative titles: IV. Waldo Selden Pratt, *The Significance of the Old French Psalter* (1933); VII. Henry Wilder Foote, *An Account of the Bay Psalm Book* (1940); IX. Ruth Ellis Messenger, *Christian Hymns of the First Three Centuries* (1942); XII. Luther D. Reed, *Luther and Congregational Song* (1947); XIII. Norman Victor Hope, *Isaac Watts and His Contribution to English Hymnody* (1947); XVIII. J. Vincent Higginson, *Hymnody in the American Indian Missions* (1954); XX. John Henry Johansen, *The Olney Hymns* (1956); XXII. Alfred Burton Haas, *Charles Wesley* (1957); XXXV. Portia K. Maultsby, *Afro-American Religious Music: A Study in Diversity* (1981). There was a subsequent effort to revive the papers with a new monograph series launched by Hugh D. McKellar's *Hymn Texts in the Aboriginal Languages of Canada* (1992), but no further items followed.

Perhaps the shortest but most influential Hymn Society Paper was: VI. Carl F. Price, *What Is a Hymn?* (1937). In this seven-page essay Price examined various ancient and modern definitions before concluding with his own, which has been frequently cited:

> A Christian hymn is a lyric poem, reverently and devotionally conceived, which is designed to be sung and which expresses the worshiper's attitude toward God, or God's purposes in human life. It should be simple and metrical in form, genuinely emotional, poetic and literary in style, spiritual in quality, and in its ideas so direct and so immediately apparent as to unify a congregation while singing it.[16]

The frequency of papers diminished during the 1950s because the Hymn Society had finally realized the long-deferred dream of publishing its own journal.

15. Reid, *Sing with Spirit and Understanding*, 31.

16. Price, *What Is a Hymn?*, 7.

First issued in October 1949 and simply titled *The Hymn*, this quarterly publication continues to provide researchers, poets, composers, church musicians, religious educators, and publishers with a forum for a wide array of hymnological concerns. In particular, *The Hymn* has become one of the few significant periodicals addressing historical and ongoing research on hymns, while also introducing new texts and tunes. Not the least of its virtues comes from the widely ecumenical scope of its readers, so that it offers a means of sharing concerns that transcend denominational (and national) boundaries. *The Hymn* also serves as a valuable vehicle for keeping the wider membership informed about occurrences at the annual conferences, often by printing the plenary addresses and other presentations.

Nothing epitomizes the vitality of the Hymn Society better than the annual conferences. Although the Society always held annual meetings, those events normally focused on organizational business and their attendees mostly came from the environs of New York City. Following the Society's reorganization in the mid-1970s,[17] the emphasis shifted to providing hymn-related plenary addresses, workshops, introductory occasions for new hymnals, and hymn festivals. Such expanded programming necessitated a comparably expanded schedule, and what had been a one-day meeting became a multiday conference. In addition, the venues were no longer limited to New York but took place in a wide range of locations in various parts of the United States and Canada, usually on the campus of a college or university with appropriate facilities for meetings, housing, and dining. This pattern of moving around the continent had the dual advantage of bringing each year's annual conference nearer to members who might not be able to attend an event at greater distance and of offering an opportunity for the Hymn Society to make itself known to people who might not have heard of it. One of the principal strategies for the latter concern was to make the evening hymn festivals (often held in local churches) open to anyone in the area who might wish to attend, and the number of local residents on these occasions often equaled (or even exceeded) the number of conferees present.

Conference workshops (called "sectionals" in Hymn Society lingo) have frequently been devoted to practical matters related to the writing of hymn texts and the composing of hymn tunes or to the accompaniment of hymnsinging. Because the interest in such topics has often exceeded the time that can be committed to them during an annual conference, the Society began to offer (often just before or after the annual conference) a series of three- to five-day hymn writing conferences for both authors and

17. McKellar, "History of the Hymn Society," 12–13.

composers, and these continued from the 1980s into the early 2000s. There were also occasional multi-day events for organists who wished to improve their hymn-playing skills, and in 1998 people who wanted to strengthen their appreciation of hymnic history could attend a freestanding three-day "Crash Course in Hymnody."

THEOLOGICAL PERSPECTIVES

Because it has always been an ecumenical organization, the Hymn Society has generally avoided endorsing theological topics of a confessional or creedal nature. Any given issue of *The Hymn*, for example, may include attention to hymns, hymnals, and hymnists of varying denominational allegiances. Yet there are some significant theological implications inherent in the hymn searches the Society has conducted and the hymn collections it has published.

Reflecting the increasing twentieth century interest in Trinitarian theology,[18] several notable texts have emerged from Hymn Society searches. The 1977 search for "New Psalms for Today," for example, yielded Welsh American Jeffery Rowthorn's (b. 1934) Trinitarian paraphrase of Ps 148 beginning "Creating God, Your Fingers Trace." Similarly, the 1988 search for "New Hymns with a New Vision of the Living God" elicited ninety-seven entries from which the chosen winner was "O Threefold God of Tender Unity" by New Zealander William L. (Bill) Wallace (b. 1933).

One aspect of Trinitarian theology sometimes mistakenly limited to the First Person rather than encompassing the full Godhead is the theme of God as creator, with the consequent attention to humanity's role as stewards of creation. Although the collection published as *Ten New Stewardship Hymns* (1961) lacks a clear indication of its scope in that title, it was always intended to emphasize "God's ownership of the earth and all that it holds, and man's [sic] responsibility to use the earth's resources for the welfare of all God's children."[19] When a related collection came out in the following decade, it provided a fuller and more descriptive title: *Sixteen New Hymns on the Stewardship of the Environment* (1973). The eight hundred entries submitted for this search indicated the nascent and increasing interest in this subject.

From Trinitarian theology, there is but a small step to pneumatology, so it is fitting that the previously mentioned search for "New Hymns with

18. LaCugna, "Current Trends in Trinitarian Theology," 141–47; Thompson, *Modern Trinitarian Perspectives*, 3–19.

19. Reid, *Sing with Spirit and Understanding*, 63.

a New Vision of the Living God" in 1988 identified as an honorable mention New Zealander Shirley Erena Murray's (b. 1931) "Loving Spirit, Loving Spirit," which joined a number of hymns on the Holy Spirit then emerging. Anticipating this interest a decade before was Finnish American Frank von Christierson's (1900–1996) "Eternal Spirit of the Living Christ," which first appeared in the Hymn Society's collection *New Hymns, Songs and Prayers for Church and Home* (1974).

Pneumatology naturally leads to ecclesiology. In dealing with this theological topic, the Hymn Society has reflected its inherently ecumenical nature by doing much to promote ecumenical causes. As part of the preparation for the Second Assembly of the World Council of Churches in Evanston, Illinois, in 1954, the Society invited poets to submit texts on ecumenical themes, and more than five hundred authors submitted their entries. From these submissions, the Hymn Society published *Eleven Ecumenical Hymns* (1954) for use, first at the Assembly and later in the churches. The winning text, *"Hope of the World": A New Ecumenical Hymn* (1954), written by American theologian Georgia Harness (1891–1974), appeared separately with two tunes and in French and German translations. The ongoing ecumenical concerns of the Society are also reflected in its publication of two significant listings of hymns used across denominational boundaries: "Hymns and Tunes Recommended for Ecumenical Use"[20] and C. Michael Hawn's "The Tie that Binds: A List of Ecumenical Hymns in English Language Hymnals in English Language Hymnals Published in Canada and the United States since 1976."[21]

One topic that garnered widespread ecumenical support was "the mission of the church," a phrase that was understood to be synonymous with "the purpose of the Church."[22] The announcement of this search continued:

> Why did Christ found the Church? What is its work? . . . The theme is broader than the time-honored term "missions," both home and foreign, though it includes that also. It covers the purposes of church membership, of evangelism, of worship, of Christian education; and what is meant by "the renewal of the Church."[23]

With such a broad understanding of the topic, it is not surprising the number of texts submitted for this search, though only nine of them found

20. Hymn Society, "Hymns and Tunes," 192–209.

21. Hawn, "Tie that Binds," 25–37.

22. *The Hymn* 19:3 (July 1968) 68.

23. *The Hymn* 19:3 (July 1968) 68.

publication in *Nine New Hymns on the Mission of the Church* (1969). This collection was in addition to the previously issued *Ten New Hymns on the Ministry* (1966).

As may be evident in the discussion of the hymn collections already mentioned, the Hymn Society has often cooperated with other ecumenical organizations by conducting searches for hymns related to that organization's concerns. In 1967, for example, "at the request of, and in conjunction with, the Lord's Day Alliance of the United States," the Hymn Society initiated a call for hymns celebrating scriptural events that occurred on the first day of the week "together with the relevance and importance of the day in the life of the church and world now."[24] The publication of *Twelve New Lord's Day Hymns* (1968) resulted from the evaluation of three hundred and fifty submissions.

Scripture, always an important theological topic for ecumenical consensus, provided a theme for publications in the middle part of the twentieth century. In anticipation of the publication of the Revised Standard Version, the Hymn Society conducted a search for Bible hymns with more than five hundred submissions received. *Ten New Hymns on the Bible* (1952) represented the best of these submissions. The winning text by British-American Sarah E. Taylor (1883–1954) appeared both in this collection and separately as *The Divine Gift: A New Hymn on the Bible* (1952). Somewhat more than a decade later, another collection issued to celebrate the 150th anniversary of the founding of the American Bible Society found publication in *Fifteen New Bible Hymns* (1966).

Given the date of its founding and the prominence of Presbyterians and Methodists among the early members, it is not surprising that many of the hymns stimulated and published by the Hymn Society show a decided commitment to social gospel concerns. Collections evidencing these concerns include: *Five New Hymns on the City* (1954), *Fourteen New Rural Hymns* (1955), *Twelve New World Order Hymns* (1958), *Seven New Social Welfare Hymns* (1961), *The Hymns of Frank Mason North* (1970), and *Nine Hymns for Human Relations Day* (1977).

Following the two World Wars and the numerous other conflicts that characterized the first half of the twentieth century, there was widespread appeal surrounding Jürgen Moltmann's generative 1964 work *Theologie der Hoffnung*, which became available in English as *Theology of Hope: On the Ground and the Implications of a Christian Eschatology*. The Hymn Society participated in this theological trend by making its principal 1970

24. *The Hymn* 18:2 (April 1967) 34.

project the winnowing of more than five hundred entries in a hymn search that yielded *Seven New Hymns of Hope* (1971).

A significant proportion of the Hymn Society's publications fall within the category of practical or pastoral theology. Attention to children, youth, and Christian education characterizes the most prominent cluster of concerns in this area. Such collections include: *Five New Hymns for Youth by Youth* (1955), *Two More New Hymns for Youth by Youth* (1956), *Three More New Hymns for Youth by Youth* (1957), *Four More New Hymns for Youth by Youth* (1958), *Fifteen New Christian Education Hymns* (1959), *One More New Hymn for Youth by Youth* (1959), *Twelve New Hymns for Children* (1965), and *New Hymns for Children* (1982). There has also been significant attention to family and home life: *A New Hymn on the Home by Harry Emerson Fosdick* (1956), *Thirteen New Marriage and Family Life Hymns* (1961), and *New Hymn Songs and Prayers for Church and Home* (1974). It is also worth noting that the Society's awareness of a hymnic gap has often anticipated the attention given to a topic by society, as evidenced by *Ten New Hymns on Aging and the Later Years* (1976).

Practical theology reflected in the attention to Christian education is more than just a focus on youth. A concern for a more comprehensive understanding of spiritual formation motivated the publication of *Amazing Grace: Hymn Texts for Devotional Use* (1994),[25] focuses on the subtopic of spiritual formation. Evidencing the Society's longstanding appreciation of the devotional dimensions of hymn texts, this collection provides a representative grouping of hymns for meditative reading and reflection.

In recent years, societal issues lacking representation in existing hymnody have been the practical and pastoral focus of the Hymn Society's collections. Among these have been the attacks of September 11, 2001, which led to the publication of *Songs of Remembrance* (2002).[25] Some of these hymns were also included in the more comprehensive collection *Hymns in Times of Crisis* (2016). In response to perceived threats to immigrants and refugees, the Society published *Singing Welcome: Hymns and Songs of Hospitality to Refugees and Immigrants* (2017). Reflecting recent technological changes, these last two collections are available by request from the Society's website.[26]

25. *The Hymn* 53:3 (July 2002).

26. Polman et al., *Amazing Grace*.

CONTRIBUTION TO LITURGY AND WORSHIP

The principal contribution of the Hymn Society to liturgy and worship has been to develop a deeper appreciation for the significance of hymns as articulations of faith, as expressions of praise, and as prayers of supplication and thanksgiving. Through its conferences, its research projects, and its publications, especially *The Hymn*, the Society has provided abundant encouragement for those interested in the history, theology, and origins of hymns. The Society has fostered attention to the life and work of authors and composers, to the contexts that gave rise to specific hymns, and to the milieu where each hymn found welcome and use. At the same time, the Society has been mindful of how hymns are used today, how specific hymns and songs might need careful revision for speaking to present-day congregations, and how performance practices can enhance their effectiveness.

To use a biblical metaphor, the Hymn Society has been the leaven that has raised a broadly based awareness and use of hymns with fuller attention to their potential and with the added benefit of lessening denominational insularities. Because its influence has been so widely dispersed through so many musical and liturgical leaders, the incremental increases in appreciation and in attention to appropriate and effective use are almost imperceptible at the individual level, but the cumulative effect has been remarkable.

One tangible means of tracking this enhancement is to consider the publication of hymnals since the founding of the Society. Many of the more recent hymnals contain hymns discovered by Hymn Society searches and later copyrighted by the Society. Often the ecumenical hymn lists the Society has published have directly influenced the selection of hymns in these books, and some of them explicitly identify such hymns in their indexes. Nevertheless, nearly all of them will bear witness to raised expectations about the visual presentation of the hymns and their attendant details. Increasingly, efforts are underway to make the language of hymns comprehensible and inclusive, as well as theologically trustworthy. The most recent books also include interpretive notes to help bridge the gaps in understanding between singers and the song.

A second significant contribution of the Hymn Society with regard to worship has been the fostering of hymn festivals.[27] Such festivals distinguish themselves from a spontaneous or freeform hymn-sing by the careful planning that precedes them. The customary format intersperses previously selected hymns with readings from Scripture or other materials, so arranged as to illustrate and illuminate a unifying theme. Historical, devotional,

27. McAll, *Hymn Festival Movement*, 3–22.

doctrinal, and seasonal themes shape the focus of festivals. Often choirs are involved in order to provide vocal leadership or to add variety by singing selected stanzas, but the principal focus always remains on the singing of the congregation.

Hymn festivals usually occur at times other than the regular worship services of a congregation, and they often represent a liturgical pattern distinct from customary worship patterns, either by being more structured than many Free Church styles or more flexible than some traditional liturgies. They are therefore able to maintain the character of being supplemental to established worship patterns rather than in competition with them. At the same time, the contextualizing dimensions of a hymn festival offer a means of enhancing the regular services of a congregation by providing a deeper appreciation and understanding of festival hymns when they recur in ordinary worship.

Because hymn festivals are not limited to the worship patterns of any denomination, they provide excellent opportunities for ecumenical cooperation. A shared hymn festival is also often a means of allowing several smaller congregations to engage fuller musical resources (such as additional instrumentalists) than each could manage alone. It is especially appropriate that congregations who may already be mutually engaged in social action ventures, but who cannot share in each other's formal worship, find such occasions to sing and pray together. In fact, interfaith cooperation can be an important witness, as when Christians and Jews join for a festival based on the psalms as an expression of solidarity following a series of anti-Semitic incidents in a community.

The Hymn Society's promotion of hymn festivals has taken several forms. A brief history of the hymn festival movement, along with outlines of several model festivals, formed one of the papers of the Hymn Society at midcentury.[28] In addition, the printed and electronic resources made available to Hymn Society members regularly include notices of past and upcoming hymn festivals, and *The Hymn* frequently prints full scripts of stimulating festivals. It is also customary to hold an ecumenical hymn festival in any locale that is trying to launch a Hymn Society chapter. However, as mentioned earlier, the Society's most engaging advocacy of hymn festivals occurs at the annual conference, where four evening festivals and one midday festival bring together conference attendees and people from the community where the conference is located. Nothing commends hymn festivals more effectively than the experience of these events.

28. McAll, *Hymn Festival Movement*, 3–28.

A third significant contribution of the Hymn Society to liturgy and worship has been to foster an increasing awareness of the global resources available to supplement the Western texts and tunes in most hymnals. The annual conference in 1999 with the theme "Think Globally, Sing Locally" was a watershed moment for the Society. Using only non-Western materials led primarily by Asian, African, and Latin American musicians, this event provided a pivotal experience in helping members of the Society move from regarding global song as an occasional possibility to regarding it as an expected part of future conferences. This attitude, in turn, has led to increased use of global resources in the congregations of many Hymn Society members as well as in several hymnals compiled since then.

A fourth and very promising contribution has only recently begun to unfold. Officially launched on October 15–16, 2017, in Dallas, Texas, after several years of preparatory work and the addition of a fulltime staff member, the Center for Congregational Song represents a new expression of the Society's ongoing commitment to provide a range of practical resources to encourage and implement improved congregational involvement in the musical dimensions of worship. These efforts take the form of various online resources brought together at www.congregationalsong.org and occasional workshops and other events around the United States and Canada. The Center's mission statement reflects the Society's commitment to "encourage, promote, and enliven congregational song, because we believe the holy act of singing together shapes faith, heals brokenness, transforms lives, and renews peace."

NOTABLE HYMNS

Listed here are the twelve most widely used hymns among the more than three hundred hymn texts for which the Hymn Society has gained the copyright as the result of searches and published collections.[29] The number in brackets is an estimate of the number of hymnals in which each text has appeared;[31] that figure does not take into account permissions for one-time use, which have become an increasingly important means of gauging how often hymns are actually sung.

"As Men (Those/Saints) of Old Their Firstfruits Brought" by Frank von Christierson [27]

"Creating God, Your Fingers Trace" by Jeffery Rowthorn [22]

29. Susan Gilbert, Hope Publishing Co., email, November 6, 2017.

"Eternal Spirit of the Living Christ" by Frank von Christierson [12]

"Forgive Us, Lord, for Shallow Thankfulness" by William Watkins Reid [5]

"Glorious Is Thy Name, Most Holy" by Ruth Elliott [9]

"God Has Spoken by His Prophets" by George W. Briggs [43]

"God, Whose Giving Knows No Ending" by Robert L. Edwards [25]

"Help Us, O Lord, to Learn" by William Watkins Reid, Jr. [19]

"Hope of the World" by Georgia Harkness [56]

"Loving Spirit, Loving Spirit" by Shirley Erena Murray [18]

"O God of Every Nation" by William Watkins Reid, Jr. [28]

"O God of Light" by Sarah E. Taylor [24]

Among the dozens of tunes for which the Hymn Society holds the copyright, the following two have proved the most popular:

Conrad 10.4.66.66.10.4 by Paul Liljestrand [10]
Who's My Neighbor 11.8.11.88 by Jan Wesson [5]

BIBLIOGRAPHY

Black, George, et al., eds. *Holding in Trust.* Carol Stream, IL: Hope, 1993.

Hawn, C. Michael. "The Tie that Binds: A List of Ecumenical Hymns in English Language Hymnals Published in Canada and the United States since 1976." *The Hymn* 48:3 (July 1997) 25–37.

The Hymn Society. "Hymns and Tunes Recommended for Ecumenical Use." *The Hymn* 28:4 (October 1977) 192–209.

———. *Hymns of Christian Patriotism.* Papers of the Hymn Society XI. New York: The Hymn Society of America, 1945.

———. Minutes, 1922–1931. Hymn Society Archives, Boston University School of Theology.

The Hymn Society (website). www.thehymnsociety.org.

LaCugna, Catherine Mowry. "Current Trends in Trinitarian Theology." *Religious Studies Review* 13:2 (April 1987) 141–47.

Loftis, Deborah Carlton. "Hymn Society in the United States and Canada." In *The Canterbury Dictionary of Hymnology*, edited by J. R. Watson and Emma Hornby. https:// hymnology.hymnsam.co.uk.

McAll, Reginald L. *The Hymn Festival Movement in America.* Papers of the Hymn Society XVI. New York: The Hymn Society of America, 1951.

McKellar, Hugh D. "A History of the Hymn Society in the United States and Canada, 1922–1997." *The Hymn* 48:3 (July 1997) 8–16.

Polman, Bert, et al., eds. *Amazing Grace: Hymn Texts for Devotionals Use.* Louisville, KY: Westminster John Knox, 1994.

Price, Carl F. *What Is a Hymn?* Papers of the Hymn Society VI. New York: The Hymn Society of America, 1937.

Reid, William Watkins. *Continuing Sing with Spirit and Understanding: The Story of the Hymn Society of America, 1962–1972.* New York: The Hymn Society of America, 1972.

———. *Sing With Spirit and Understanding: The Story of the Hymn Society of America.* New York: The Hymn Society of America, 1962.

Thompson, John. *Modern Trinitarian Perspectives.* Oxford: Oxford University Press, 1994.

Van Burkalow, Anastasia. "Sixty Years of the Hymn Society of America, 1922–1982." *The Hymn* 33:1 (January 1982) 12–15.

Chapter 16

Postcolonial Congregational Song

Lim Swee Hong

HISTORICAL BACKGROUND

Postcolonial Congregational Song is a relatively new genre of music that is gaining traction in the field of North American hymnody/Christian congregational song in the twenty-first century. Predominantly speaking, these songs are the musical fruits of Christian communities situated in the Global South, referred to in some contexts as the Two-Thirds World. Interest in this genre may be attributed to the changing geopolitical landscape of the world in the mid-twentieth century as well as the dramatic shift in attitude of the church toward the vernacularization of worship and music in that same era.

Given the complexity of this genre and the sociocultural forces involved in its formation, it is not feasible to provide comprehensive analytics on the subject matter with its global dimension.[1] Thus, the approach chosen for this essay is to present a broad overview of this musical genre, its three strands and their characteristics. Where needed, historical background is provided to clarify the properties of these strands.

1. For example, in comparison to Victorian English hymnody or the German chorale, postcolonial congregational song covers many more ethnicities, faith traditions, and sociocultural influences.

Though generalization is able to offer a landscape view and to spotlight distinctive features, it is important to keep in mind that this strategy has a tendency of marginalizing normative practice to the sidelines and potentially convey exceptional practice as normality. Also, this essay will make use of musical samples from Asia as illustrations. This does not imply exclusivity of the region as being the best representative of postcolonial songs but rather attests to the limitation of the author's knowledge of specific examples from other regions. Notwithstanding the Asian musical samples, the asserted statements remain largely accurate for the Global South.

Postcolonialism: Agenda and Agency

Broadly speaking, postcolonial studies trace its beginning to 1978 with the publication of Edward W. Said's *Orientalism*.[2] According to philosophy professor David Bradnick, Said's book "unmasked Eurocentric assumptions ascribed to Oriental life, thus generating a misrepresentative reality in the Western imagination that was imposed upon Eastern people."[3] Thus, this research engagement holds at its core an optics that arises from the grassroots—the perspective of the local community and its context. This approach is concerned with sociocultural economic legacies, impact of colonization, and the attribution of power in societies particularly in the light of Western hegemony.

Within Christian theology, postcolonial theologians call for new hermeneutical lenses to examine longstanding traditions and practices that bear implicit bias for Western ideals in the 1990s. To some extent, these approaches share similar traits to methodologies in contextual theology or the processes for inculturation as advocated by Roman Catholic scholarship decades earlier, albeit taking a much more critical stance against Western influence.

Michael N. Jagessar and Stephen Burns advocated for a postcolonial investigation of Christian worship in 2011 through the thought provoking work, *Christian Worship: Postcolonial Perspectives*.

Essentially, they called into question traditional Christian assumptions with their embedded Western influences, and sought to employ hermeneutical lenses that acknowledge the ethos and context of "the colonized."[4] Yet, this advocacy is not really new since it bears close resemblance to earlier efforts of adaptation like contextualization or inculturation. Admittedly and

2. Said, *Orientalism*.

3. Bradnick, "Postcolonial Theology," 1.

4. Jagessar and Burns, *Christian Worship*.

again, these were less assertive in addressing issues of power and Western hegemony associated with colonialism.

Historically speaking, efforts toward self-determination were symptomatic of the changes in the geopolitical and sociocultural landscape in the second half of the twentieth century. In the aftermath of the Second World War, the pace of decolonization quickened. According to the Office of the Historian in the United States Department of State, "Between 1945 and 1960, three dozen new states in Asia and Africa achieved autonomy or outright independence from their European colonial rulers."[5] On the African continent these include Libya (1951), Ghana (1957), Guinea (1958), Togo (1960), Côte D'Ivoire (1960), Niger (1960), Nigeria (1960), Sierra Leon (1961), and Algeria (1962). Examples in Asia include Vietnam (1945), Korea (1945), Taiwan (1945), Indonesia (1945), Philippines (1946), India (1947), Burma (1948), Palestine (1948), Ceylon now Sri Lanka (1948), Cambodia (1953), Laos (1953), Malaya (1957), and Singapore (1963).

In turn, decolonization led to the rise of nationalism and growing local identity awareness as can be seen by the dramatic increase of member countries in the United Nations from 51 to 99 (1945—1960).[6] Within the church, this awareness was addressed through various platforms including the formation of inter-church organizations like the World Council of Churches in 1948 that was modeled after the League of Nations (1920–1946), the predecessor of the United Nations (1945-).[7] This growing awareness of cultural distinctiveness eventually manifested itself in liturgical revitalization particularly at the Sixth General Assembly of the World Council of Churches in Vancouver (1983).

In the realm of theological publications, the relationship between Christianity and culture became a key theme. An example with missiological implication was H. Richard Niebuhr's *Christ and Culture* (1951). Within the area of ecclesial pronouncements, the promulgation of *Sacrosanctum Concillium* (Constitution on the Sacred Liturgy) by the Roman Catholic's Second Vatican Council in 1963 and the Statement on Worship and Culture of 1996 produced by the Lutheran World Federation at its meeting in Nairobi, Kenya, demonstrated the same concern particularly for grass roots participation in worship. Equally significant and mentioned earlier was the active and intentional engagement of non-Western liturgical leadership and the showcasing of ethnic liturgical resources at the Sixth General Assembly of the World Council of Churches in Vancouver (1983). This effort

5. Office of the Historian, "Decolonization of Asia and Africa."

6. United Nations, "Growth in United Nations Membership."

7. World Council of Churches, "History."

translated into increased awareness and receptivity of Postcolonial Congregational Songs to the churches in Western Europe and North America.

Consequently, as North American denominations proceeded to renew their hymnals, these songs found their way into the corpus of denominational hymnody that was previously largely Eurocentric in significant numbers. An example of how this occurred was the approach taken by the United Methodist Church. The committee for the official hymnal, upon the union of the Methodist Church and Evangelical United Brethren, constituted part of the official repertoire from supplemental worship resources commissioned earlier, including the Asian American collection, *Hymns from the Four Winds* (1983) curated by I-to Loh.[8] Not surprising, the United Methodist Hymnal became distinctive for its multicultural repertoire at that time.

In the article, "Asian and Asian American Hymns in USA hymnals," the author provided a chart that showed the increased presence of Asian hymns in American hymnals. For example, the *Lutheran Book of Worship* (1987) had only two Asian hymns but its *Evangelical Lutheran Worship* (2006) included ten; *The Presbyterian Hymnal* (1990) featured only four Asian songs in contrast to the thirty-six works found in its *Glory to God* hymnal (2013).[9] The significant proliferation of these songs was aided in no small part by the Global Praise program found in the General Board of Global Ministries (GBGM)—the mission board of the United Methodist Church. This project was established in 1993 under the leadership of S. T. Kimbrough Jr. who facilitated and championed the collection and dissemination of this genre when he served as the Associate General Secretary in Missions and Evangelism on GBGM. His advocacy enabled local North American congregations to have ready access to these "global songs" for corporate worship use.

Within the academic field of musicology, the establishment of comparative musicology, later known as ethnomusicology in the 1970s, strengthened the research momentum for non-Western music making. Within the American Evangelical circle, some ethnomusicologists began to harness their expertise for worship and missional purposes leading to the establishment of the ethnodoxology movement in 1997.[10] By 2010 other ethnomusicologists decidedly formed the Special Interest Group for Sacred/Religious Music within the Society for Ethnomusicology. In 2011 the biennial conference *Christian Congregational Music: Local and Global Perspectives* was organized and launched at Ripon College, Oxford. Consequently,

8. Loh, *Hymns from the Four Winds.*

9. Lim, "Asian and Asian American Hymns."

10. Aniol et al., "Worship from the Nations."

some of the investigations presented at the academic event were published under the Conference's Congregational Music Studies Series. At present, a new collection of ethnomusicological essays entitled *Music as Local and Global Positioning: How Congregational Music-Making Produces the Local in Christian Communities Worldwide* is being prepared for publication.[11]

THEOLOGICAL PERSPECTIVES

It is important to note that much of these efforts were undertaken to showcase congregational music making bearing indigenous nuances. While this effort seems noble—to advocate for nascent development of indigenous congregational song—one could argue that this is not a complete representation of Postcolonial Congregational Song practice but rather only one iteration out of many—and one that is significantly shaped by globalization. Pointedly speaking, it is an expression welcomed and accepted by churches in the West specifically because of its exoticism and accessibility. From the perspective of Latino Episcopalian liturgical scholar Juan M. C. Oliver, this attempt to incorporate global songs into North America seems to be "a project of the colonizing, dominant culture . . . a monocultural Anglo version of multiculturalism that wants to host, invite, and include" or incorporate "the other in otherwise Anglo realities and structures."[12] Clearly, Oliver perceives the effort of global song music making as just another form of colonization.

As I have asserted elsewhere, not all non-Western Postcolonial Congregational Songs can become "global songs." More often than not, the process of change from local to "global" results in the loss of integrity particularly when its *sitz im leben* is ignored.[13] C. Michael Hawn echoes a similar concern about the place of Postcolonial Congregational Song in North America commenting that the label "global music" is problematic given its uncanny association with globalization, which is often associated with "the spread of Western economic approaches and cultural values."[14] In addition, Marissa Glynias Moore, an emerging liturgical scholar, in her essay published in the recent edition of *The Hymn* noted that the practice of postcolonial congregational song by North American congregations is "fraught with

11. Ingalls, Swijghuisen Reigersberg, and Sherinian, *Music as Local and Global Positioning*. Earlier titles in the publication series can be found at https://congregationalmusic.org/content/publications.

12. Oliver, "Just Praise," 267.

13. Lim, "Where Is Our Song Going?"

14. Hawn, "Christian Global Hymnody," 24.

ethical concerns" even if the intention is well meaning.[15] Moore asserts that the paucity of contextual information in geographical context, performance practice, and extramusical narratives of the songs affect efforts of accurate rendition and unintentionally promote cultural appropriation and ethno-tourism. In light of this, it is clear that postcolonial congregational song is a genre that needs to be managed thoughtfully to minimize concerns over ethno-tokenism and cultural appropriation.[16]

CONTRIBUTION TO LITURGY AND WORSHIP AND NOTABLE HYMNS

Postcolonialism: Congregational Song and Its Expressions

Broadly speaking, postcolonial congregational song is defined as the repertoire of peoples that have experienced or are still going through decolonization. It is the musical expression of communities who sing about their faith in relation to their sociocultural context. Without a doubt, these songs form and sustain their Christian identity. Typically speaking, these communities tend not to have a prominent voice in society and are often located on societal margins. Oftentimes, they may also be subjected to discrimination and persecution by the dominant local culture. Postcolonial congregational songs consist of three intertwining strands—the adopted, adapted, and contextual song forms that reflect the broad tenor of these decolonized Christian communities.

Adopted Song Form

Prior to the mid-twentieth century, congregational songs stemming from Western Europe and the United States dominated Christian worship soundscape globally. Not surprising then, hymnals even in colonized missional lands continue to feature Western hymnody translated or paraphrased into local languages while retaining its original Western music. This expression of the missional church, the transplanted-translated or adopted song form is the foundational musical expression of postcolonial Christian worship practices outside Western Europe and North America. An example of this is George Root's "The Lord Is in His Holy Temple" (Figure 16.1). Though the

15. Moore, "Treating the 'Other' as a 'Thou,'" 9.
16. Lim, "What Is the Right Kind of Worship?"

hymn has fallen out of favor in North America, it remains widely sung by Chinese Christian diaspora worldwide.

Figure 16.1: "The Lord Is in His Holy Temple" by George Root. Used with permission.

WORDS: Habukuk 2:20
MUSIC: George F. Root (1820-1895)

IRREGULAR
QUAM DILECTA

Public Domain.

Adopted song's preeminence as a non-Western congregational song type came about through a confluence of influences, particularly the desire for orthopraxis and the concern about syncretism by the missional church. In those times, local cultural nuances were also deemed inadequate by embedded missionaries and unsuitable to convey the gospel. The situation was further hampered by the lack of suitable scholarship to resolve this impasse. As a result, minimal effort was made to develop local congregational songs that reflected their cultural settings. Nevertheless, this song form serves as a tangible means for the nascent local faith community to experience the universality of the church beyond its setting.

To sum up, the adopted song form sees the original Western lyrics replaced by a translation or paraphrase in the vernacular while retaining the original Western music (melody and possibly four-part harmony). On rare occasion, the Western melody might be modified to accommodate the local language. However, more often than not, the syntactical needs of the local language are largely ignored. Even though such works may be a less than effective communication vehicle, they embody a rich missional past and thus remain a valuable musical staple of the churches in the Global South and serve as the heart songs of its people. In recent years, Western contemporary Christian worship songs have superseded Western hymns as the next generation of adopted work, enabling it to remain the dominant strand in postcolonial congregational song. Thus, while this strand is dominant in most non-Western ecclesial settings, I contend that it will not appeal to nor satisfy Euro-Americans given their unvoiced expectations for something "different," particularly among those who strenuously advocate for indigenous expressions. Without a doubt, this is the principal strand of congregational song for the postcolonial communities, a musical testament of a missional heritage that continues to guide and shape the postcolonial church.

Adapted Song Form

Following World War 2, global political landscape underwent significant changes. Western colonial powers rapidly decolonized the majority of their territories giving rise to new sovereign states. Parallel to this development, Christian denominations that were in decolonized lands became autonomous or chose to reorganize themselves as national churches such as the *Church of South India* (established in 1947), and the 三自教会 *Sānzì Jiàohuì* (Three-Self Church) of China (established in 1951). A review of church history in both Latin America and Africa reveal a similar trend.[17] Many of the churches in decolonized lands adopted the stance for self-determination. This was most evident in their efforts in governance, financial support, and propagation but less successful in its worship particularly in Christian rituals and songs. Efforts in new songs tend to make use of existing Western musical templates. Nevertheless, there were nascent efforts to contextualize by way of harnessing local folk songs holistically, particularly tunes with minimal cultural baggage or association. Examples of this approach include setting the Japanese folk tune SAKURA to the Christian text "Praise the Lord" by Nobuaki Hanaoka (1946–2011), and the Indonesian/Malaysian folk song RASA SAYANG to the text "Now Let Us Tell of Your Victory" by retired Malaysian Methodist minister Samuel Liew (1942–) (Figure 16.2).

17. Ewald, "South American Hymnody," and Hawn, "African Hymnody." 17.

Figure 16.2: "Now Let Us Tell of Your Victory" by Samuel Liew. Used with permission.

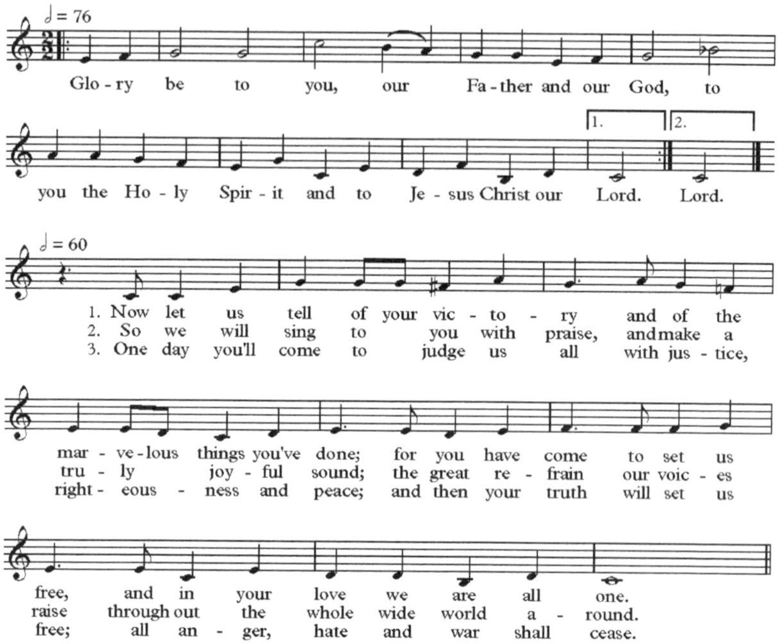

WORDS: Psalm 98:1-2, 4-6 RASA SAYANG
MUSIC: Indonesian/Malaysian folk song adapt. Samuel Liew

This practice of text replacement also known as *contrafacta,* a long tradition in Western music, can also be found in the music making effort of indigenous Canadian/Native American Christian communities. An example of this is the text of Rev. Susan Beaver, "This Your Love, so Fills My Soul" set to the Bluegrass song, "I Am Weary, Let Me Rest" by Peter "Pete" Van Kuykendall (aka Pete Roberts). (Figure 16.3)

Figure 16.3: "This Your Love, so Fills My Soul" by Susan Beaver. Used with permission.

This Your Love, so Fills My Soul[18]
Holy God, our faithful witness
to the tears that take their toll.
How I pray with joy while knowing:
This, your love so fills my soul.

18. Words © 2012, Susan Beaver. All rights reserved18.

Looking on your sweet creation
I see anger, fear and pain.
People lost, so torn and lonely.
How can we bear this again?

Broken lives and broken spirits
shattered on this bleak cold day.
Warm our homes with loving kindness;
by your light we'll see our way.

You give life in ev'ry moment.
It's to you I give my praise.
Even when I cannot feel you,
you are there in all your ways.

Holy God, our faithful witness
to the tears that take their toll.
How I pray with joy while knowing:
This, your love so fills my soul.

Aside from the compositional device of *contrafacta* that dealt with lyrics, the growing awareness of developing local musical expression has given rise to effort to reclaim local musical expressions. However, such efforts tend to rely on Western Christian congregational song as their template. In the initial foray, various indigenous distinctive musical style traits like different scale tunings and vocal stylistic renderings of melodies were abandoned. The stripped down local melodies are then provided with the Western practice of harmonization. The *East Asia Christian Conference* hymnal of 1963 is a classic example of this effort even as it reflects the continued dominance of Western music making in adapted song form.[19]

Retuning is another technique practiced in adapted song form. In this approach, existing Western hymn texts are matched to new local tunes. A recent example of this is Judson W. Van DeVenter's "I Surrender All" set to a tune by young musician Khuan-Ee Cheah (1981–) for her English-speaking congregation at Blessed Christian Fellowship in Penang, Malaysia (Figure 16.4). In this setting, what is readily apparent is the move away from part-writing that is commonly associated with Western strophic hymns while adopting the approach of a single melody with guitar chords.

In Asia and other postcolonial milieux, the approach of writing congregational song featuring a single melody with or without guitar chords has become rather prevalent since local music making is far more improvisatory

19. Niles, *East Asia Christian Conference Hymnal.*

and aural-based, unlike its Western counterpart, notwithstanding the ubiquitous contemporary worship song genre prevailing worldwide.

Figure 16.4: "I Surrender All" by Khuan-Ee Cheah. Used with permission.

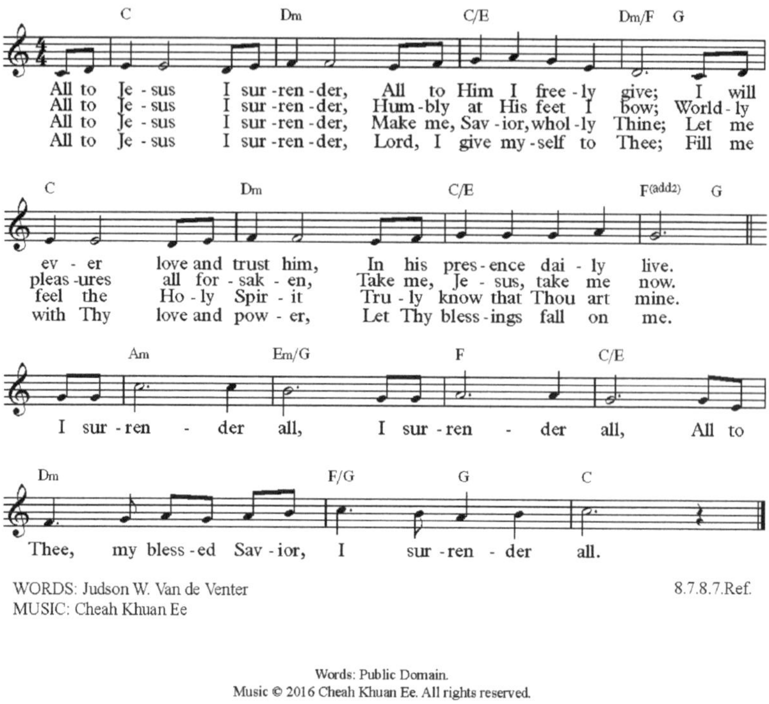

In summing up, the adapted strand juxtaposes local expressions to the Western musical template. This approach offers postcolonial faith communities the means of enshrining their missional heritage while asserting their local sociocultural identity. For many non-Western congregations, this method provides a safe way of negotiating their faith identity among other religious traditions in the society and yet be an avenue for asserting their distinctiveness. This strand is increasingly popular and growing in importance as Christian communities become increasingly aware of the need for their identity to reflect their cultural setting but are not quite prepared to ignore their Western missional heritage. One can readily detect the beginning of hybridity in this musical expression.

Contextual Song Form

The local sociocultural reality plays a key role in shaping music making for this particular strand. In this song form, the hybridization approach purposefully leans toward grassroots idioms where contextual realities shape its expressions. Indeed, the contextual song approach strives to favorably showcase local cultural idioms. For instance, vocal performance is idiomatically notated to reflect local music making practice—glides, melissmas, et. al. However, as Hawn observed,

> Since Asia has three great notational systems, attempts to place Asian traditional song into Western notation brings the dangers of colonializing the song itself. Various cipher notations used by missionaries made the melodies somewhat readable for Westerners, but also stripped them of local stylistic nuance. Western notation (vs. oral transmission) is more efficient, but bears with it inherent colonial tendencies unless accompanied by a recording. At its best, Western notation is only an approximation.[20]

Earlier on, this effort of contextualization saw no qualm in appropriating music from other faith traditions such as Buddhist or Hindu chants and resetting them with Christian texts. However, in recent years the strong rejection by postcolonial Christian communities over the concern of syncretism has given rise to much broader hybrid expressions that addressed this issue. As a result, the arbitrary juxtaposition of local materials is less common. Rather in vogue is the careful craftsmanship in the musical construct. Not surprisingly, there can be several iterations of this strand of music depending on the sociocultural locations and the *in situ* cultural awareness of the creators in their music making. I offer the following as sonic artifacts of the contextual song form. First, "Lord of the Universe," a composition by John Barathi (1960–) from India (Figure 16.5). In this work, one can discern the "South Asian" tenor through the choice of musical tuning and the notated ornamentation matched to the lyrics *Namaskarem*. What is less obvious from the score is that the song lends itself to a performance practice in a culture that embodies an oral (aural) improvisatory tradition that regards notation as guide rather than ultimate gauge of music making.

20. Hawn, email correspondence with the author, October 23, 2017.

Figure 16.5: "Lord of the Universe" by John Barathi. Used with permission.

To that end, contextual song form serves to bridge the distinction between oral and written music tradition. It is far more amenable to different renditions, particularly when melodic embellishment (ornamentation) is of the essence. Another example of this strand would be songs in the Khmer hymnal *Christian Hymn and Worship Book of the Cambodia Christian Methodist Association.*[21] In this collection, the varying efforts of contextualization can be seen in its single melody congregational songs—ranging from the grafting of traditional Khmer folk or court melodies with new texts to newly composed local nuanced works *sans* Western harmonization. Again, one must not be misled by this seemingly simple approach given the oral (aural)-based local musical culture. Indeed, "what you hear may not be notationally rendered" is a distinctive feature of the contextual strand of postcolonial congregational song.[22]

21. Kimbrough and Sam, *Christian Hymn and Worship Book.*

22. Hawn, email correspondence with the author, October 23, 2017.

For most postcolonial Christian communities, the concept of binary opposition that is favored by normative Western philosophies is not helpful. Writing from his perspective in the field of linguistics, Steve Campsall explains, "Binary opposition can be shown to work in ways that maintain and reinforce stereotypical ideas, values and beliefs, what are called a culture's or society's 'worldview' or dominant ideologies."[23] Overall, while most Western scholarly enterprises tend to support this concept that calls for demarcation, non-Western Christian communities in postcolonial settings prefer the synthetic approach, which leans toward holding both Western and local in tension and mutual respect. This stance is akin to the ancient philosophical principle of Yin Yang (阴阳) that shapes the Chinese worldview. In this school of thought, the desired outcome is balance/harmony where coexistence is normative and equilibrium yields wellness. To that end, postcolonial congregational contextual songs vary in their degree of hybridization. An embodiment of this balance is the set of John and Charles Wesley hymns, *Mil Vozes para Celebrar,* curated by Brazilian worship professor Simei Ferreira de Barros Monteiro (1943–) for the Methodist Church in Brazil.[24]

In summary, the contextual form of the postcolonial congregational song is the strand that garners most attention from outsiders because of its distinct soundscape. More often than not, its tenor is the result of the effort on the part of the creators of locating their Christian identity in the local at the expense of established tradition, parameters, and mindset of ecclesial norms. Growth in this genre is painstakingly slow because Global South churches see it as treading onto syncretism even though it is warmly feted by Global North churches through publications and use. Hawn offers an apt observation on this dilemma. He writes,

> I think that the "feting" by the Global North carries with it an expectation that the Global South should really be singing this or that when the Global South has its own ideas about what they should be singing. If the Global North is still superimposing its ideas of what should be sung by the Global South, then this bears the residual effect of colonialization.[25]

Perhaps in time postcolonial Christian communities will readily embrace this strand with greater enthusiasm seeing it as their birthright rather than a veiled attempt of syncretism. In so doing, the communities may come to realize the non-musical significance of this strand in purveying the issue of

23. Campsall, "Binary Opposition."

24. Monteiro, *Mil Vozes para Celebrar*.

25. Hawn, email correspondence with the author, October 23, 2017.

worth and dignity and enabling the meta-narrative of the local to be told and for Christianity to grow its roots into the culture. Yet, such work cannot be forced by external agencies but must have its impetus from within the local milieu. To that end, this strand is nurtured by local awareness and theo-ethical underpinning to sustain its development in a process that cannot be forcibly hastened. Unfortunately, the relative paucity of credible theo-liturgical scholarship in the local milieu, particularly in Asia, coupled with the long-standing exposure to Western Christian culture means that such contextual effort is less known and less appreciated by the *in situ* constituency. Equally disheartening is the low priority given by local ecclesial leadership to actively promote local creative efforts. Indeed, as Hawn observed, "the church context (manifest in many versions) adds a layer of complexity to the discussion."[26]

CONCLUSION

In this essay, I have identified key agencies and agenda in postcolonial congregational song and placed them within a historical context so that its development and status may be made clear. Thereafter, I described the three strands of this musical genre—the adopted, adapted, and contextual forms—spelling out their characteristics in relation to the concerns of the churches in the Global South. In particular, I pointed out that the issue of syncretism is a significant determinant in the manner in which local music making by postcolonial communities evolve.

The majority of these postcolonial congregational songs are therefore likely to retain their missional heritage vis à vis Western musical practice to minimize rejection by its local stake holders. Throughout this essay, I stated that postcolonial congregational song describes a genre of music that originated from settings that are undergoing processes of decolonizing. They are the heart songs of a people in a specific location and setting and are unequivocally shaped by it. Without a doubt, the different strands of adopted, adapted, and contextual are the communal song expressions of that relationship.

Hence, it is important to not see these as stages of development as if one thread might supersede the other. Rather, a postcolonial-centered perspective would have us understand that the various threads coexist as an expression of hybridity in congregational music making. By encompassing these multiple expressions, the identity of the faith community is sustained

26. Hawn, email correspondence with the author, October 23, 2017.

with integrity. It also enables the faith community to locate itself within the spectrum of the universal church with its past, present, and future.

To that end, the unvoiced expectation and demand for exotic soundscape and musical practice by well-meaning Western liturgical music scholars or practitioners need to be attenuated in deference to the effort of the local postcolonial community. Such a stance can minimize the rehashing of colonial mentality that perpetuates the stereotypical naïve understanding of postcolonial congregational song.

BIBLIOGRAPHY

Aniol, Scott, et al. "Worship from the Nations: A Survey and Preliminary Analysis of the Ethnodoxology Movement." *Artistic Theologian: Journal of Ministry and Worship Arts* 3 (2015) 2–21.

Bradnick, David. "Postcolonial Theology." In *The Encyclopedia of Christian Civilization*, edited by George Thomas Kurian. Malden, MA: Blackwell, 2011. DOI:10.1002/9780470670606.wbecc1095.

Campsall, Steven. "Binary Opposition." Web essay. http://www.englishbiz.co.uk/extras/binaryopposition.htm.

Ewald, Werner. "South American Hymnody." *The Canterbury Dictionary of Hymnology*. http://www.hymnology.co.uk/s/south-american-hymnody.

Hawn, C. Michael. "African Hymnody." *The Canterbury Dictionary of Hymnology*. http://www.hymnology.co.uk/a/african-hymnody.

———. "Christian Global Hymnody: An Overview." In *Music and Mission: Toward a Theology and Practice of Global Song*, edited by S. T. Kimbrough, Jr., 23–40. New York: General Board of Global Ministries—GBGMusik, 2006.

———. "Landscapes and Soundscapes: How Place Shapes Christian Congregational Song." In *The Changing World Religion Map: Sacred Places, Identities, Practices and Politics*, edited by Stanley D. Brunn, 2659–79. Dordrecht, Netherlands: Springer, 2015.

Office of the Historian. "Decolonization of Asia and Africa, 1945–1960." Milestones: 1945–1952. United States Department of State. https://history.state.gov/milestones/1945-1952/asia-and-africa.

Ingalls, Monique M., Muriel Swijghuisen Reigersberg, and Zoe C. Sherinian, eds. *Music as Local and Global Positioning: How Congregational Music-Making Produces the Local in Christian Communities Worldwide*. New York: Routledge, 2018.

Jagessar, Michael N., and Stephen Burns. *Christian Worship: Postcolonial Perspectives*. Sheffield: Equinox, 2011.

Kimbrough, S. T., Jr., and Sarin Sam, eds. *Christian Hymn and Worship Book of the Cambodia Christian Methodist Association*. New York: General Board of Global Ministries—The United Methodist Church, 2001.

Lim, Swee Hong. "Asian and Asian American Hymns in USA Hymnals." *The Canterbury Dictionary of Hymnology*. https://hymnology.hymnsam.co.uk/a/asian-and-asian-american-hymns-in-usa-hymnals.

———. "Just Call Me by My Name: Worship Music in Asian Ecumenism." In *The Ecumenical Review*, edited by Stephen G. Brown, 502–15. Geneva: World Council of Churches, 2017. DOI: 10.1111/erev.12317.

———. "What Is the Right Kind of Worship . . . If You Want North American Congregations to Sing Global Songs?" *Global Forum on Arts and Christian Faith* 5:1 (2017) 48–57.

———. "Where Is Our Song Going?" Plenary Address for the Launch of the Center for Congregational Song of the Hymn Society in the United States and Canada, October 16, 2017.

Loh, I-to, ed. *Hymns from the Four Winds*. Nashville: Abingdon, 1983.

McCoy, Andrew M., and John D. Witvliet. "Putting Christian Congregational Song on the Geographer's Map." *The Changing World Religion Map: Sacred Places, Identities, Practices and Politics*, edited by Stanley D. Brunn, 2611–25. Dordrecht, Netherlands: Springer, 2015.

Monteiro, Simei, ed. *Mil Vozes para Celebrar*. E-book. Curitiba, Paraná: Simei Monteiro, 2017. http://charleswesley.com.br/ch/index.php/hinario/.

Moore, Marissa Glynias. "Treating the 'Other' as a 'Thou': Recontextualization and the Search for Origins in Global Song Transmission." *The Hymn* 68:1 (Winter 2017) 9–15.

Niles, Daniel T., ed. *East Asia Christian Conference Hymnal*. Kyoto: East Asia Christian Conference, 1963.

Oliver, Juan M. C. "Just Praise: Prayer Book Revision and Hispanic/Latino Anglicanism." *A Prayer Book for the Twenty-first Century*. New York: Church Publishing, 1996.

Said, Edward W. *Orientalism*. New York: Pantheon, 1978.

United Nations. "Growth in United Nations Membership, 1945–Present." Membership; United Nations. http://www.un.org/en/sections/member-states/growth-united-nations-membership-1945-present/index.html.

Westerfield Tucker, Karen B. "Methodism's 'World Parish': Liturgical and Hymnological Migrations in Three Ecclesiastical Generations." *Liturgy in Migration: From the Upper Room to Cyberspace*. Collegeville, MN: Liturgical, 2012.

World Council of Churches. "History." https://www.oikoumene.org/en/about-us/wcc-history.

Chapter 17

Hymnody of the Global South, Part 1

History, Ontological Perspectives, and Dissemination

C. Michael Hawn

HISTORICAL BACKGROUND

Congregational song has from its beginnings had a global consciousness. In the early years of Christianity, this consciousness was not necessarily tied to the continents of the globe, but to a cosmic awareness that singing was an antiphonal experience between the choirs above the firmament and the echoing multitudes below the firmament. Such a "global" perspective is evident at the moment of the incarnation when the angelic chorus announced this singular event by singing, "May glory be given to God in the highest heaven!," and the mortal chorus is invited to respond, "may peace be given to those he is pleased with on earth!" (Luke 2:14, NIRV). Regretfully, it appears that the chorus of earthly mortals must continue to practice their song, even after two thousand years, since we are unable to sing "peace on earth" in tune. This cosmic antiphonal practice was not articulated in actual sound, but by a platonic ideal of the music of the spheres. Note this "cosmic" dialogue in Latin Christian hymnody as early as the fourth century:

O ye heights of heaven adore him;
angel hosts, his praises sing:
powers, dominions, bow before him
and extol our God and King;
let no tongue on earth keep silent,
every voice in concert ring
evermore and evermore.[1]

The antiphonal chorus is also evident in the Easter hymn by the Greek monk John of Damascus (ca. 655–ca. 745) in the eighth century:

Now let the heavens be joyful!
Let earth the song begin!
Let the round world keep triumph,
and all there is therein![2]

As exploration by sea increased and the presence of colonial powers became prominent around the world, especially during the eighteenth and nineteenth centuries, a cosmic understanding of "global," though not abandoned completely in congregational song,[3] gave way to *terra firma*, a geographical understanding of the continents. The paraphrase of Ps 117 by Isaac Watts (1674–1748) indicated an emerging, though ethnocentric, early eighteenth century global consciousness. The British Empire was taking shape and with it, the expansion of the modern missionary movement.[4]

From all that dwell below the skies,
Let the Creator's praise arise;
Let the Redeemer's name be sung
Through ev'ry land by every tongue.
Eternal are thy mercies, Lord;
eternal truth attends thy word;
thy praise shall sound from shore to shore
till suns shall rise and set no more.[5]

1. "Of the Father's Love Begotten," Marcus Aurelius Clemens Prudentius (ca. 348–ca. 413); trans. John Mason Neale (1854) and Henry Williams Baker (1859).

2. Trans. by John Mason Neale (1862).

3. Note Charles Wesley's Easter hymn, "Christ, the Lord Is Risen Today" (1739):
Christ the Lord is risen today, Alleluia!
Earth and heaven in chorus say, Alleluia!
Raise your joys and triumphs high, Alleluia!
Sing, ye heavens, and earth reply, Alleluia!

4. See specifically, Carey, *Enquiry into the Obligations of Christians*, for a perspective on eighteenth-century missionary views in England.

5. Published in Watts's collection *The Psalms of David* (1719) under the heading, "Praise to God from all Nations."

Though Christian song has been transmitted across language groups and cultures since the apostolic era, the first wave of global song in the modern era[6] was the hymns that accompanied the European and, later, the North American missionaries to the ends of the earth, translated into many languages and accepted broadly by the peoples of the world as global sung expressions of the Christian faith.

By the end of the nineteenth century, John Julian's (1839–1913) *A Dictionary of Hymnology: Setting for the Origin and History of Christian Hymns of All Ages and Nations* (1st ed., 1892) bore witness to the effects of the mission movement in an extensive entry by William Rawson Stevenson (1823–89), editor of the *Baptist Hymnal,*[7] entitled "Foreign Missions." Though the examples of hymnody beyond the Western world cited in Stevenson's article were anecdotal at best, this twenty-page summary (in the smallest type face possible!) is amazing for its day and provides some substance for the ambitious subtitle of Julian's *Dictionary—Christian Hymns of All Ages and Nations.*[8]

Erik Routley (1917–82) provided a mid-twentieth century perspective, just prior to the Second Vatican Council, in his short monograph entitled *Ecumenical Hymnody* (1959). Routley had been asked to address the Council of British Missionary Societies on what was called "Ecumenical and Missionary Hymnody." Routley noted the observation of the Council "that there was some disquiet among those who are especially concerned in the overseas and ecumenical work of the church for the paucity and the indifferent quality of our 'missionary' hymns.'"[9] Although Routley would edit the fifth edition of *Cantate Domino* in 1980 for the World Council of Churches twenty-one years later, he confesses in 1959 that he is "virtually ignorant of the musical traditions which prevail among most of the non-European races among whom Christian missionary work is carried on."[10] His anecdotal evidence being limited to a few hymnal collections that he had acquired from South Africa and China, Routley laments the general quality of European hymns that have found their way into these hymnals.

6. One can make a case for the plainsong of the Roman Catholic Church, the metrical psalms of the Genevan psalter, and the chorales of the German Reformation, for example, as global song from Europe as well, though none traveled as broadly and quickly as did the hymns carried by eighteenth and nineteenth century Protestant missionaries. See Young, "Old and New Global Song and Mission," 9–13.

7. Stevenson, *Baptist Hymnal.*

8. Stevenson, "Missions, Foreign," 739–59.

9. Routley, *Ecumenical Hymnody*, 5.

10. Routley, *Ecumenical Hymnody*, 5.

The focus of Routley's essay moves the conversation from hymns in Christian missions to ecumenical hymnody.

Riding the ecumenical wave of the World Council of Churches formed in 1948, Routley set the stage for a discussion of global congregational song:

> The note which in these present times we wish to sound, if we are not to accept with passive resignation the prevalent tendency to think of missionary work as one thing and the ecumenical movement another, is the conception of missionary work as partnership. If we look far enough ahead we can see . . . that it can hardly be the Lord's will that missionary work should always mean preaching the Gospel to dark-skinned people while ecumenical work should always be study groups to see how far Methodists and Presbyterians can agree about church order.[11]

Routley challenged the church "to attend to the need for a truly ecumenical hymnody which will have little to do . . . with the processes of missionary work, but will provide a vehicle for the praises of a growing world-church."[12] While desiring to free the world-church of hymns specifically focused on a paternalistic sense of Christian missions, he was not aware at this point of hymns that spoke to the ecumenical concerns of the entire church other than those from Europe and North America.

The Second Vatican Council (1962–65) provided an impetus to include voices beyond the Euro-North American sphere in English-language hymnals. At the cusp of the twenty-first century, global song in worship is moving beyond provincial definitions that focus only on ecumenism as inter-confessional dialogue, reclaiming the original meaning of the word from the Greek *οἰκουμένη* (oikoumene), "the whole inhabited earth."

Questions, Terminology, and Definitions

World congregational song challenges conventional assumptions based on Western hymn practice. Philip Bohlman acknowledges that any discussion of world music begs the ontological question, "What is music?"[13] From the perspective of Western hymnology, the study of global congregational song raises an analogous ontological question, "What is a hymn?" Many of the

11. Routley, *Ecumenical Hymnody*, 16. See also, *Cantate Domino*. The melody-only edition (1974) was not edited by Routley. Although listed as the 4th edition, four previous hymnals under the name *Cantate Domino* were published in 1924, 1930, 1938, and 1951.

12. Routley, *Ecumenical Hymnody*, 17.

13. Bohlman, *World Music*, 6.

songs cited in the following chapter may not meet a strict definition of a hymn according to historical Western practice.[14] Global hymnody takes a variety of forms. The following chapter references only a sampling of global hymns that are most accessible to Christians in the Euro-North American world and appear in current hymnals.[15]

The diversity and complexity of ecumenical-global congregational song challenges many Western ontological assumptions about the nature of a hymn and the experience of congregational singing. For example, singing with the world church often encourages us to look beyond the printed page and incorporate improvisatory oral-tradition practices. Songs from the Global South often invite us to join in with our bodies as we sing. Many songs are through-composed rather than structured in a classic Western stanza form. Some songs have relatively few words. Some press us to sing in languages we do not speak. A number are group compositions that come from the experience of a community with no recognizable single composer. In most cases music and text are composed by the same person or community and are inextricably linked. Many are accompanied by instruments that are not often available to Western congregations. At the same time, countless songs from the broader world church sound almost identical to classic Western hymns. When singing global hymns, our ontological assumptions may be challenged.

What is "global hymnody"? "Global hymnody" is often used interchangeably with world, ethnic, international, or multicultural music. "Third-World music" has been used occasionally, but is inaccurate (Japan, for example, is not a "third-world" country) and, more importantly, carries vestiges of colonialism. The term "global hymnody," however, also presents some difficulties. For a while, songs from the "Two-thirds World" were used, but this reference, while recognizing the population of the church beyond the West, still seemed to imply that the "first third" was more important. "Global South" has more recently been adopted in postcolonial conversations to refer to countries with a colonial past. It will be used in this and the following chapter interchangeably with a cautious understanding of "global."

A primary question relates to perspective: What hymnody is global and what hymnody is not? If this chapter were being written on another continent, for example, Africa, Australia, Europe, or South America, the physical location and cultural orientation of the authors would change the

14. By Western historical practice, I am referring to hymns in stanzas, especially from Europe and later the United States, from the Reformation to the mid-twentieth century.

15. For an introductory discussion, see Young, "Ethnic and Minority Hymns," 17–27.

perspective and require a different definition of "global." "Global," though seemingly a universal term, is still subject to a specific social location.

As mentioned earlier, the Western hymns introduced by missionaries during the eighteenth, nineteenth, and first half of the twentieth centuries became the global musical currency of the church universal. Late in the twentieth century, European and North American churches became aware of music produced by Christians from non-Western cultures. Interest in global music today reflects a demographic shift between 1950 and the turn of the twenty-first century. Where once 70 percent of baptized Christians lived in the Northern Hemisphere, now only 30–35 percent of Christians do. The remaining 65–70 percent of Christians lives in the Southern Hemisphere.[16] This second wave of global hymnody from two-thirds of the Christian world, the Global South, is the primary subject of this and the following chapter.

A second difficulty with the term "global hymnody" is the political nature of "globalization." As an economic strategy, globalization is often associated with the spread of Western commercialism and cultural values around the world—especially those from the United States. This connection of globalization—and, by association, the term "global"—with cultural assimilation is unfortunate. For the most part, those who promote the use of global music within Euro-North American worship have the opposite intent; they strive to bring the authentic musical voice of Christians from the far reaches of the globe into Western worship as a reminder that the church, though gathered locally, is a part of the universal body of Christ.

For the purpose of this chapter, global hymnody will signify Christian songs originating beyond Euro-North American cultural contexts. Since the late twentieth century, hymnals produced in the United States, Canada, and some countries in Europe include Christian songs primarily from sub-Saharan Africa, Asia (especially eastern Asia), Latin America (primarily Spanish-speaking countries), Portuguese-speaking countries, and the Caribbean. Christian music from the Middle East, Eastern Europe, the former Soviet Republics, and the Polynesian islands has been less widely disseminated except in ecumenical international collections and worship resources. Christian music created co-cultures in the United States, such as African American and Native American peoples, is beyond the scope of this essay. Musical co-cultures within the United States such as African American and Native American styles are significant, but beyond the scope of this essay. Indeed, the musics from these cultures may rightly be called the "true"

16. See Jenkins, *Next Christendom*, 79–105, for a detailed discussion of the growth of Christianity in the Southern Hemisphere and its influence on the shape of Christianity in the Northern Hemisphere.

music from the United States. Though global hymnody often makes use of instrumental and dance structures, the focus here is upon congregational songs. For the sake of convenience, global "hymnody" and global "song" will be used interchangeably with songs from the Global South in this and the following chapter with the understanding that these songs are also ecumenical hymnody in the broadest sense of that term.

How have these songs come to North American hymnals? The transmission of global song reflects the migrations of our age, the frequency of international confessional and ecumenical gatherings, the relative ease and proliferation of publications, and the desire of many to experience ways of singing and praying beyond their cultural context of origin. This migration often reflects the struggles and crises of particular members of the world church.[17] Ethnomusicologists usually research the music of a specific ethnic group or tribal context in detail. The wide variety of musical styles and the integral relationship of any particular music to its cultural context make it difficult for ethnomusicologists to make universal assertions about the meaning of their area of research in the broader global musical arena. Because of the number, variety and complexity of various world musical systems, ethnomusicologists speak of world *musics*.[18] While music making is a universal phenomenon, music is not a universal language.[19]

The broad survey of selected cultures undertaken in the following chapter runs the risk of superficiality and may give the impression that music from a given continent is monolithic in style. The opposite is true. The musics of Africa, Asia, and Latin America are extremely varied in language, instruments, vocal styles, and rhythmic complexity. The examples that appear in North American hymnals are but brief glimpses of what is happening in the world Christian church. Furthermore, the selection of global materials by North American hymnal committees draws upon, by its nature, the most accessible music from other cultures.[20] Moreover, by the time a given song appears in print in a North American hymnal, the sending culture may have moved on to newer songs. Therefore, a survey of the theology of global song will be, by necessity, limited in scope, and even anecdotal.

17. South African Freedom Song that expressed resistance to apartheid in the last half of the twentieth century is a case in point. Another example includes selected songs composed in the midst of political oppression in Latin America.

18. See Bangert, "Dynamics of Liturgy and World Musics," 183–203.

19. See Blacking, *How Musical Is Man?* 6–7.

20. For a more complete discussion of the criteria for choosing global song for worship, see Hawn, "Praying Globally," 205–29.

Influences of Vatican II

With some few exceptions, congregations beyond European and North American contexts sang primarily Western hymns in translation before the liturgical reforms of the Second Vatican Council (1962–65). While folk tunes from "native" cultures appeared occasionally in Western collections, these tunes were often domesticated by eliminating intervals difficult for Western singers and by adding keyboard harmonizations that were usually incompatible with the original musical style. Even original compositions by non-Western musicians were regularly composed in Western musical styles. Colonial missionaries and their converts often assumed that indigenous cultural forms were technically and aesthetically inadequate or even inherently evil, incapable of conveying sound Christian theology. Admittedly, specific melodies, musical instruments, and rhythmic patterns are often associated with non-Christian cultural practices. In many cultures, however, indigenous musical resources have been wedded with the gospel to produce musical expressions that are both liturgically faithful and culturally relevant.

One primary method of dissemination of global song is through the collections produced for the international assemblies such as those of the Lutheran World Federation and the ecumenical gatherings of the World's Student Christian Federation.[21] These collections foreshadowed to a degree liturgical inculturation—the examination of the reciprocal relationship between worship and culture and the conscious incorporation of cultural elements within liturgy—encouraged by Vatican II.[22] This may be seen in the difference between compilations produced before and after Vatican II. Four hymnals—all editions of *Laudamus* with the exception of the first assembly, which used a small collection entitled *Hymnal for the Assembly*—were used in assemblies of the Lutheran World Federation (LWF) before Vatican II: Lund, 1947 (36 hymns), Hanover, 1952 (71 hymns), Minneapolis, 1957 (74 hymns), and Helsinki, 1963 (108) hymns. English, German, and Spanish were the normative languages for each entry with the exception

21. Additional international venues, especially in Asia, are the gatherings sponsored by the YMCA and YWCA. For example, the Asian Alliance of YMCSs engaged I-to Loh as editor of the song collections *Songs of Our People* (1987) for the 12th YMCA Leader's Conference in Tozanso, Japan, and *Songs of Our People II* (1991) for the 13th Leader's Conference in Bangkok, Thailand. *Worship with Singing/Cultes avec Chants/Adoración y Canto* was produced for those attending the World YWCA Council in Kenya (2007) reflecting carefully and thematically prepared liturgies with a mixture of global song staples and fresh materials.

22. See Chupungco, *Liturgical Inculturation*, 29, for a definition of liturgical inculturation. Alyward Shorter also provides a complementary definition in *Toward a Theology of Inculturation*, 11.

of four Latin hymns. The major cultural expansion in collections during this period was the broader inclusion of Scandinavian hymnody (Norway, Finland, Denmark, Sweden)[23] from three hymns in 1947 to 18 hymns, including hymns in Norwegian, Danish and Swedish languages, in 1963. LWF Assembly collections since the 1970 assembly in Evian have incorporated many more hymns and languages from the two-thirds world.

Cantate Domino was the hymnal of the World's Student Christian Federation from its first edition in 1924 edited by Suzanne Bidgrain (1879–1961) to the fourth edition in 1951 edited by R. C. Mackie. French, German, and English dominate the languages and the countries of origin. One African selection, a hymn from South Africa by the Xhosa prophet Ntsikana (c. 1780–1821), appears in the second (1930) and third (1938) editions. Between five and seven hymns from Asian sources are found in the various editions. Eastern European and Scandinavian hymns (often in the original languages) are in more abundance in these collections. *Cantate Domino* did not demonstrate greater inclusion of hymns from the Global South until it became a hymnal for the World Council of Churches in 1974. The impact of Vatican II was profound on these international and ecumenical hymnals.

Sacrosanctum Concilium (*Constitution on the Sacred Liturgy,* 1963) produced by Vatican II promoted liturgy inculturated in the linguistic patterns, metaphors, dance, and music of individual cultures while sharing a common historical liturgical shape throughout the world. Roman Catholic Mass settings based on specific musical/cultural idioms began to appear in the 1960s. This document acknowledged that the "Church respects and fosters the genius and talents of the various races and peoples" (par. 37). Ecclesiastical control of the incorporation of cultural elements was given in part to knowledgeable persons in specific regions, especially in the areas of the "administration of the sacraments, sacramentals, processions, liturgical language, sacred music, and the arts" as long as these practices were carried out within the norms established by *Sacrosanctum Concilium* (par. 39).[24]

Because of the context of the reforms within Roman Catholic Church, incorporation of local cultural musical styles often took place within the ordinary of the Mass rather than in specific hymns, since congregational

23. Technically, Scandinavia consists of Norway, Sweden, and Denmark. Finland, Iceland, and the Faeroe Islands are often included in the region.

24. The *Ten-year Report of The Milwaukee Symposia for Church Composers* (1992), an ecumenical document with no standing in the Roman Catholic Church, elaborated on the proposals of Vatican II in the section entitled, "Cross-Cultural Music Making." Through this document, liturgical inculturation also caught the attention of many Protestants.

singing was an anomaly in the Mass before Vatican II.[25] While the reforms provided in *Sacrosanctum Concilium* gave great impetus to the liturgical inculturation movement, there were notable exceptions that predate Vatican II, especially in Africa, such as *Missa Luba*, a Congolese Mass, which was the result of encouragement provided by Fr. Guido Haazen (1921–2004), a Franciscan priest from Belgium. Another, *Misa Criolla* by Ariel Ramírez (1921–2010), an Argentine Folk Mass, was composed in 1964 immediately after the initial reforms of Vatican II.

By composing in vernacular styles, these Masses paved the way for reinforcing cultural identity through congregational music. Even though the forms of the Mass are set, composers find ways to contextualize them for their own situations. In performance, the *estribillos* (refrains) are often used to engage the community directly allowing them to move and observe the ritual action while singing. Cantors or choirs often sing the stanzas, freeing the congregation to sing without written music if they choose. While some are not hymns in the classic sense (perhaps more properly they may be called ritual music), these congregational acclamations provide a way for the people to sing as a part of the liturgy. The insertion of words beyond the texts of the ordinary of the Mass blurs the distinction between a hymn and ritual song.

Ecumenical Gatherings: Contributions of the World Council of Churches

The World Council of Churches' (WCC) publications, international assemblies, and church music symposia are important sources for global song. Initial efforts centered on *Cantate Domino* (melody edition, 1974; full-harmony edition, 1980), published by the WCC and edited by Erik Routley (1917–82). This version, containing 202 selections in thirteen languages with participation by Roman Catholics and, for the first time, Orthodox Christians, was a radical departure from the four earlier editions published by the World's Student Christian Federation. Texts appear in the original language and usually in English, French, and German. In spite of the broader global perspective of the fifth edition, the collection retained the feel of a European hymnal and many of the songs were harmonized without regard to the culture of origin. Later, more culturally-focused publications such as *African Songs of Worship* (1986), edited by Taiwanese ethnomusicologist I-to Loh (b. 1936), and *Brazilian Songs of Worship* (1989), edited

25. Historical exceptions do exist. See Ruff, *Sacred Music*, 102–4, for hymns used in the Mass in Germany.

by Brazilian theologian and composer Jaci Maraschin (1929–2009), avoid some of the pitfalls of *Cantate Domino.*[26]

The sixth General Assembly in Vancouver (1983) was a turning point for integrating global song into the shared ecumenical liturgies of the WCC. The diversity of the music from around the world became the primary means for embodying an ecumenical and global faith. Liturgical/musical *animateurs* (animators) from most continents provided leadership for assembly worship. Publications of songs from this assembly and subsequent events in Canberra, Australia (1991), Harare, Zimbabwe (1998), Porto Alegre, Brazil (2006), and Pusan, Korea (2103), have become important sources for disseminating global song throughout the world. In addition to leading global song in a wide variety of venues around the world, WCC *animateurs* were often composers, editors, or translators, greatly enhancing the dissemination of global resources.[27]

Other Disseminators of Global Song

Scotland's Iona Community has also been at the forefront of promoting global song. John Bell (b. 1949), a minister of the Church of Scotland (Reformed), and the members of the Wild Goose Resource Group (WGRG) edited two global collections, *Many and Great: Songs of the World Church* (1990) and *Sent by the Lord* (1991). Subsequent publications by the WGRG usually include global songs among their varied contents, providing a sung complement to the prophetic message of justice and peace for which the community is known. These global efforts complement Bell's musical contextualization on a local level as he often matches Scottish and Irish melodies with texts composed by himself and the WGRG.[28]

Geoff Weaver (b. 1943) is one of the leading musicians in the Anglican Church in the dissemination of Christian global song. He taught in the United Kingdom before working under the auspices of the Church Mission Society (CMS) for eight years in Hong Kong. After serving as director of music at Bradford Cathedral, he was on the staff of the CMS Training College in Selly Oak, Birmingham. For eight years Weaver served as director

26. For more information on Routley's contribution to global song, see Hawn, "Cantate Domino," 12–13.

27. Though there were some attempts to develop more *animateurs* through regional conferences, the WCC was not able to sustain these. One example was a workshop that took place in San José, Costa Rica, March 5–13, 1988. The results of this gathering may be found in Sosa, *Todas Las Voces.*

28. For more information on John Bell, see Hawn, "Wild Goose Sings," 189–223.

of studies/outreach for the Royal School of Church Music. A composer and arranger, his most notable publications in global song include three editions of *World Praise* (1993, 1995, 2000) prepared for congresses of the Baptist World Alliance, edited with David Peacock (b. 1949).[29] In his capacity as music director for the 1998 and 2008 Lambeth Conferences, Weaver has included an unprecedented amount of global song in the liturgy of the international gatherings of the Anglican community.[30]

The focus on culture and worship by the Lutheran World Federation (LWF) and its assemblies has set the stage for incorporating global song into liturgy. *Laudamus*, with six editions from 1952–90, was a collection used in these gatherings. The 1990 supplement was the first to focus on global song. *Agape: Songs of Hope and Reconciliation* (2003), compiled by Maggie Hamilton and Päivi Jussila for the assembly in Winnipeg, is the most diverse to date with 111 entries in forty languages. Over fifty entries are from the Southern Hemisphere. Gerhard Cartford (1923–2016) and Mark P. Bangert (b. 1938), participants in LWF consultations on worship, have been among the foremost proponents of global song for the Lutheran (ELCA) Church in the United States.[31]

The United Methodist Global Praise Project (GPP) has made significant contributions to the dissemination of global song.[32] Begun in 1993 through the General Board of Global Ministries, the GPP was led by S. T. Kimbrough, Jr. (b. 1936), general editor, until 2006 with Carlton R. Young (b. 1926) serving as musical editor. The GPP has brought together leading church musicians and composers from around the world to share songs, plan publications, and design conferences that encourage the singing of global songs by local congregations. *Global Praise I* (1996, rev. 1997), *Global Praise II* (2000), and *Global Praise III* (2004), timed to appear at the quadrennial General Conferences of the United Methodist Church, are collections with a broad diversity of world song. Additional collections focused on the contributions of specific regions of the world.

Mennonite congregations have been exposed to global song through Mennonite World Assemblies' song collections produced for these events, and their primary hymnal, *Hymnal: A Worship Book* (1992), a joint publication for congregations in the Believers Church Tradition. Mary Oyer (b.

29. Discussion with Geoff Weaver, London, England, June 28, 2008. A more recent collection complied by Geoff Weaver is *In Every Corner Sing: Song's of God's World.*

30. The most recent publication is *Lambeth Praise*, edited by Geoff Weaver.

31. The LWF has also contributed a framework for examining the relationship between worship and culture. See the "Nairobi Statement on Worship and Culture."

32. See Kimbrough, "Practical Considerations," 22–29; and Kimbrough, *Music and Mission.*

1923), a primary proponent for global song among Mennonites, studied music extensively in Africa and taught with I-to Loh in Taiwan.[33] A tradition with a strong sense of world missions, Mennonites use global song as a symbol of partnership in mission with Christians around the world.

Recently the International Council of Ethnodoxologists (ICE) has been formed by Evangelicals to promote global Christian music. Founders of ICE include ethnomusicologists Frank Fortunato (b. 1946), Robin Harris (b. 1961), Roberta King (b. 1949), and Paul Neeley (b. 1958). According to Robin Harris, "The ICE network exists to encourage and equip Christ-followers in every culture to express their faith through their own heart music and other arts. ICE facilitates online networking and provides resources for the development of culturally appropriate Christian worship, utilizing insights from ethnomusicology, missiology, worship studies, and the arts."[34]

The following chapter introduces specific theologies that have resulted in songs from the creation of songs from the Global South and the incorporation of them into Western collections.

BIBLIOGRAPHY

Bangert, Mark P. "Dynamics of Liturgy and World Musics: A Methodology for Evaluation." *Worship and Culture in Dialogue*, edited by S. Anita Stauffer, 183–203. Geneva: The Lutheran World Federation, 1994.

Blacking, John. *How Musical Is Man?* Seattle: University of Washington Press, 1973.

Bohlman, Philip V. *World Music: A Very Short Introduction*. New York: Oxford University Press, 2002.

Cantate Domino: An Ecumenical Hymnbook, 4th ed., ed. Erik Routley. London: Bãrenreiter, 1980.

Carey, William. *An Enquiry into the Obligations of Christians to Use Means for the Conversion of the Heathens in which the Religious State of the Different Nations of the World, the Success of Former Undertakings, and the Practicability of Further Undertakings are Considered*. Leicester, England: 1792. www.wmcarey.edu/carey/enquiry/anenquiry.pdf.

Chupungco, Anscar. *Liturgical Inculturation: Sacramental, Religiosity, and Catechesis*. Collegeville, MN: Liturgical, 1992.

Hawn, C. Michael. "Cantate Domino: Erik Routley and Global Song." *The Hymn* 53:4 (October 2002) 12–13.

33. A festschrift with DVD honoring Mary Oyer was recently published: *Nurturing Spirit Through Song: The Life of Mary K. Oyer*, edited by Rebecca Slough and Shirley Sprunger King.

34. Correspondence from Robin Harris, June 13, 2008. See www.worldofworship.org, for more information. Though formed by Evangelicals, Paul Neeley states that "ICE is a network open to anyone who can affirm a basic creed such as the Nicene Creed." Correspondence from Paul Neeley, June 19, 2008.

———. "The Wild Goose Sings: John Bell and the Music of the Iona Community." In *Gather into One: Praying and Singing Globally*, 189–223. Grand Rapids: Eerdmans, 2003.

———. "Praying Globally—Pitfalls and Possibilities of Cross-cultural Liturgical Appropriation." *Christian Worship Worldwide*, edited by Charles E. Farhadian, 205–29. Grand Rapids: Eerdmans, 2007.

Jenkins, Philip. *The Next Christendom: The Coming of Global Christianity*. New York: Oxford University Press, 2002.

Kimbrough, S. T., Jr., ed. *Music and Mission: Toward a Theology and Practice of Global Song*. New York: General Board of Global Ministries, GBGMusik, 2006.

———. "Practical Considerations for Promoting Global Song." *The Hymn* 51:4 (October 2000) 22–29.

"Nairobi Statement on Worship and Culture: Contemporary Challenges and Opportunities." In *Christian Worship: Unity in Cultural Diversity*, edited by S. Anita Stauffer, 25–28. Geneva: Lutheran World Federation, 1996.

Routley, Erik. *Ecumenical Hymnody*. London: Independent, 1959.

Ruff, Anthony. *Sacred Music and Liturgical Reform: Treasures and Transformations*. Chicago: Hillenbrand, 2007.

Shorter, Alyward. *Toward a Theology of Inculturation*. Maryknoll, NY: Orbis, 1988.

Sosa, Pablo D., ed. *Todas Las Voces: Taller de Música y Liturgia en América Latina*. Costa Rica: Ediciones Sebila, 1988.

Stevenson, W. R., ed. *The Baptist Hymnal: A Collections of Hymns and Spiritual Songs*. London: E. Marlborough, 1885.

———. "Missions, Foreign." *Dictionary of Hymnology*, edited by John Julian, 739–59. London: John Murray, 1892.

Young, Carlton R. "Ethnic and Minority Hymns in United States Mainline Protestant Hymnals 1940–1995: Some Qualifying Considerations." *The Hymn* 49:3 (July 1998) 17–27.

———. "Old and New Global Song and Mission." *Music and Mission: Toward a Theology and Practice of Global Song*, edited by S. T. Kimbrough, Jr., 9–13. New York: General Board of Global Ministries, GBGMusik, 2006.

Chapter 18

Hymnody in the Global South, Part 2

Theological Perspectives and Hymns

C. Michael Hawn

THEOLOGICAL PERSPECTIVES

Broadly speaking, theological themes found in the congregational song of the Global South are as diverse as those in Western hymns. One may find songs that consider God's acts in creation, incarnation, atonement, resurrection, pneumatology, soteriology, eschatology, sin, Christology, the Trinity, and ecclesiology, just to name some theological topics covered in a Western systematic theology course or a survey of Christian doctrine. Because of the geographical and cultural contexts in which songs of the Global South appear, however, these songs contain significant variations from Western ways of theology thinking.[1]

Several dangers crop up in any attempt to offer a survey of theological themes found in the hymnody of the Global South. The first is obvious: the

1. It is interesting to note that Zimbabwean state president and Methodist minister Canaan Banana did not approach theology "systematically" because the difficulties faced by the Zimbabwean people did not fit the theological categories he had received during his study in Great Britain. See Banana, *Come and Share*, 187. Thus, even the constructs by which we order our theological discourse are determined in part by our social and cultural orientation.

topic is too broad to do it justice in this forum. While many chapters in this text focus on a specific hymn writer, this chapter and the preceding one have the audacity to attempt a theological summary of the songs of two-thirds of the world's Christians in a limited space. Therefore, this chapter is as an initial reflection on the topic—a conversation starter—rather than an exhaustive compendium of theological concepts. Rather than a summary of lyrical theology found in the congregational songs of the Global South, the following signifies only an initial awareness that Christians beyond the Western world have much to offer.

A second danger is the human tendency to set up a dichotomous framework—us-versus-them—in an analysis of the differences between one's established views and perspectives that come from those beyond our personal or, perhaps in this case, Western theological/philosophical constructs. One cannot rid ourselves of theological bias totally, but we can view the theological contributions of those of the Global South as complementary to our own perspectives. Rather than taking a dichotomous approach, it is encouraged that the reader approach variations on theological themes expressed in the Global South as an opportunity to fill out our praise—a posture of humility and possibility that realizes that no one cultural perspective can fully embrace the One who came as a male for all humanity, at a specific time for all time, and within a particular cultural context for all cultures.

An example of dichotomous thinking across cultures would be to superimpose Hellenistic assumptions of matter on to some expressions of creation found in the Global South. Plato's distrust of the material world as imperfect or inferior to eternal immaterial concepts may cause a Western singer to view some songs on the theme of creation from non-Western cultures as pantheistic or syncretistic. While all lyrics should stand the test of theological scrutiny, some, when encountering songs on the theme of creation expressed by those whose empirical experience with the natural created order is more integral to their lives, may have a tendency to jump to the conclusion that specific songs from the Global South are inherently pantheistic or inappropriately syncretistic. I would suggest that it is easier to spot the perceived syncretistic speck in another's eye rather than the potential syncretistic log in our own.[2] Just as the study of a "foreign" language sheds light on our mother tongue, so does singing the theology of those beyond our culture of origin enhance our understanding of inherited theological opinions.

2. Cf. Matt 7:3.

The final danger is to restrict congregational song to a verbal theological discourse. Without a doubt, theology is a part of the lyrics, but it is also contained in the musical aspects that convey the lyrics, the voices of those who sing those lyrics, and the liturgical structures that offer the framework for experiencing and sharing those lyrics within the gathered body of Christ. A more complete analysis would entail not only an examination of the words that are sung, but also the music, singers, language, culture, and nature of corporate worship.

Varieties of Songs in the Global South

Global congregational singing draws upon a diverse repertoire of songs. As discussed in the previous chapter, it is impossible to define a global hymn in a single, concise manner. Several genres exist and may appear within a single liturgy. Genres include:

1. Western hymns taken directly from European or North American hymnals, sung in a colonial language, and accompanied on organ or piano.
2. Western hymns translated into a vernacular language, often with some melodic and/or rhythmic alterations to accommodate the vernacular language of the receiving culture.
3. Western hymns sung with oral tradition performance techniques such as leader-response and use of percussion.
4. Blending of Western hymns with traditional compositional techniques including improvised harmonies, parallel harmonic progressions, and in some areas multipart improvisatory vocal singing, as well as increased use of percussion and dance, further disguising the Western origins of the hymn.
5. Melodies reflecting the vernacular musical styles of the Global South with texts written by Western missionaries or in collaboration with indigenous musicians.
6. Congregational song compositions by musicians from the Global South in Western or blended musical idioms.
7. Congregational songs composed by indigenous musicians in thoroughly traditional musical styles.[3]

3. James R. Krabill outlines six stages in, "Encounters." His stages are importation, adaptation, alteration, imitation, indigenization, and internationalization. Though Krabill's stages are similar to the seven genres outlined above, my approach, unlike Krabill's, does not suggest progressive stages through which church music must pass,

The examples cited in this chapter will draw primarily from the last two categories of this list. A further caveat should be mentioned. In some cases, the music and musical instruments from specific cultures are not deemed worthy or appropriate for use in Christian worship because of long-standing association with pagan traditions. Westerners, even well-meaning ones who are not aware of these associations, may critique a culture in the Global South for not using "their own" music. This is often the case in northeastern Asia where hymns sound quite Western. In other areas of the world, musicians have developed "hybrid" musical styles for the church that combine compositional structures and indigenous instruments from the local culture with harmonic aspects of colonial cultures. This would be more common in parts of sub-Saharan Africa. In these cases and others, the choice of Western, hybrid, or indigenous music, various instruments, and musical structures to convey the words is a theological statement beyond verbally expressed doctrine.

Selected Theological Reflections

Having set the context for an introduction to selected theological emphases in congregational songs of the Global South, we choose three areas for further development: creation, incarnation/Christology, and the Christian journey. We will draw representative examples primarily from Latin/South America, Asia, and sub-Saharan Africa.

Creation

Western Christian congregational song is replete with hymns on the theme of God's acts as witnessed in creation. From St. Francis of Assisi's (c. 1181–1226) canticle "All Creatures of Our God and King" (thirteenth century) through Isaac Watts's (1674–1748) "I Sing the Almighty Power of God" (1715) and Cecil Frances Alexander's (1818–1895) "All Things Bright and Beautiful" (1848), the focus is on the natural created order. While St. Francis refers to the various elements of nature (fire, earth, air, water) in familial terms (brother, sister, mother), Watts and Alexander paint vivid pictures of the elements of nature employing hypotyposis in which humanity is an onlooker, standing outside the verbal portrait, whose role is to

but seven ways that colonial and African cultures interact in the composition of hymns. Individual composers may focus only on one or two of these genres without moving on to others. Likewise, a composer may enter at any point in the spectrum of practices outlined above.

observe and enjoy what God has done. Later hymns such as Eleanor Farjeon's (1881–1965) "Morning Has Broken" (1931) increase the connection between the natural created order and humanity with empirical language that appeals to a broader range of senses—sight, sound, touch. Rather than an onlooker, Farjeon, drawing upon the sensibilities of Romantic poetry, places humanity in the picture. With later twentieth century writers such as Fred Pratt Green (1903–2000), humanity is not only in the picture, but an active player, even a co-creator with God in the preservation of the planet. "For the Fruit of All Creation" (1970) acknowledges the role of humanity in leaving resources for future generations—"for the plowing, sowing, reaping, / future needs in earth's safekeeping" (stanza 1)—and our responsibility not just to the natural created order, but also to humanity itself—"in our worldwide task of caring / for the hungry and despairing / in the harvest we are sharing" (stanza 2). Other writers such as Brian Wren ("Thank You God for Water, Soil, and Air," 1973), Shirley Erena Murray ("I Am Your Mother," 1996), and Thomas Troeger ("Each Breath Is Borrowed Air," 2002) reflect the full shift from observing the natural created order to ecology, praying for the survival of all creatures.

Mexican American composer Carlos Rosas (b. 1939) composed "Cantemos al Señor" (1976) as a joyful entrance hymn for a setting of the Mass entitled *Rosas del Tepeyac* ("Roses of Tepeyac"). Tepeyac is the hill, now located in Mexico City at the site of the Basilica of Guadalupe, where St. Juan Diego (canonized in 2002 as the patron saint of indigenous peoples) is said to have had his vision of the Virgin Mary, Our Lady of Guadalupe, in December 1531. Part of Juan Diego's vision included blossoms appearing in December, out of season, on a rocky hillside. The incipit of "Cantemos al Señor" ("Let Us Sing to the Lord") is reminiscent of the Psalms (96, 98, 147, 149), but the entire hymn captures the spirit of Ps 19:1, "The heavens are telling the glory of God; and the firmament proclaims God's handiwork" (NRSV). While the hymn may be sung as a general hymn of praise to the God of creation, the historical context of the composition places it within the narrative of a poor indigenous farmer who was privileged to receive a special revelation from God through a vision of the Virgin Mary who spoke to him in his native language and caused a barren hillside to bloom in the cold of December. The music—an animated 6/8 meter—includes a refrain that lifts the hymn from a description of nature in the stanzas to sheer joy—"¡Alleluya! ¡Alleluya! Cantemos al Señor. ¡Alleluya!" While God's creation is to be enjoyed for its grandeur ("grandeza") and beauty ("bellas"), it is also a sign of God's love, faith, and hope ("que exprese nuestro amor, nuestra fe y nuestra esperanza").

"Cantemos al Señor" is reminiscent in spirit to "De Colores," a traditional folksong of Mexico that extols the beauty of nature in exquisite detail. "De Colores" is associated with Roman Catholic Cursillo retreats and has long been an unofficial anthem of the farm worker movement. Undoubtedly, many who sing "Cantemos al Señor" will recall the exuberant spirit of the rich, varied, and vibrant colors expressed in "De Colores."

"Rise to Greet the Sun" (1931) was written by a leading Chinese theologian, Chao Tzu-ch'en (1888–1979). The perspective is that of a farmer who sets out at dawn to till the soil and make a simple living for his family. Composed during a time of political oppression and economic poverty throughout much of China, the writer honors a simple way of life and the basic values of love of God and hard work. In the translation by Chinese missionaries Bliss and Mildred Wiant, prepared for the Chinese union hymnal *Hymns of Universal Praise* (1936), the farmer greets the rising sun like a "warrior-like and strong / comely as a groom," a reference to Ps 19:4–5: "Their line is gone out through all the earth, and their words to the end of the world. In them hath he set a tabernacle for the sun, which is as a bridegroom coming out of his chamber, and rejoiceth as a strong man to run a race" (KJV). In addition to the visual display of the rising sun, the writer has empirically rich references to the sounds and sights of "birds pass[ing] high in flight" and the smells of "fragrant flowers [in] bloom." It is in the beauty of the early morning that the peasant sets to his daily tasks: "I my toil resume."

The second stanza combines the beauty of nature with an upright ethical behavior. Reminiscent of Confucian philosophy, the hymnwriter prays for safety, and faithful and good "conduct, actions calm and mild." In traditional Chinese society, it is important that the roles of the elder and the young person should be in harmony; in light of this, the farmer prays to "venerat[e] age and teach . . . youth." This appropriate service indicates a right conduct that belies the underlying ethical system of Confucian philosophy. In the final stanza, the farmer indicates that, by trusting Jesus, he will be "freed from ill [under] fair blue sk[ies]." God will supply the simple things—a "cotton coat" and "plain food"—thus satisfying "all my countless needs."[4]

This hymn reminds us of the interrelationship between the creator who shapes the seasons and the farmer who works the land, a model of stewardship of rather than dominion over creation. The gifts of creation are received with thankfulness and responsibility. God is actively supporting the farmer and his family, refuting any deistic interpretation that assumed that God was not active in the universe after the initial act of creation. Just

4. See Hymn 677, in Young, *United Methodist Hymnal*.

as God sustains the farmer through the fruits of creation, the farmer honors his neighbors and family. Humility and a simple lifestyle sustain the farmer in both his physical needs and his relationships. All is balanced and in harmony. The pentatonic musical setting, LE P'ING ("peaceful joy") by Hu Te-ai (BC 1900) supports Ciao's text. The natural created order is more than the panoply of beauty created for our enjoyment, but a manifestation of a God who sustains life if we honor the creator and seek balance in our ethical relationships with the land and humanity. Another translation by Francis W. Price, "Golden Breaks the Dawn" (1953), is poetically beautiful, but less precise in communicating the meaning of the original Chinese.

Filipino composer Francisco F. Feliciano (1941–2014) offers yet another theological perspective on creation in this lyrical meditation. "Still, I Search for My God" (1977):

> Still, I search for my God in silence,
> I marvel at the universe, the world it contains,
> its beauty, its harmony!
> Creator of such perfection, who else could it be?[5]

Neither an exuberant celebration of the natural creative order nor an objective "painting" of the panoply of creation viewed from outside, Feliciano calls us to an inner calm. Meditating on creation transforms the singer from within.

One senses the awe of Ps 19:1, "The heavens declare the glory of God; and the firmament shows His handiwork" (NKJV). Living in the crowded streets and frenetic existence of Manila, the poet created an oasis of several acres of tranquility and natural beauty in the city's heart for the study of music and liturgy.[6] The scene depicted could describe many places on earth. For those living in a dense urban environment, however, one must seek peace and mystery intentionally. Feliciano, a Roman Catholic, was inspired by a Buddhist meditation exercise in composing this hymn:

> Imagine that you are standing in front of a calm lake. The lake is still and tranquil, and you can see the reflections of the further shore. You take a tiny pebble, and toss it into the midst of the reflections with respect, as if it were an offering to the ancient gods that live in the depths of the waters. The stone plops into

5. © 1977 Francisco F. Feliciano. All attempts have been made to secure permission to cite a single stanza of this hymn from Samba Likhaan (Manila, Philippines), the church music program that Dr. Feliciano founded and at which he taught until his death in 2014, but no response has been received from the publisher.

6. The space created was the school founded by Feliciano and formed the heart of the Asian Institute of Liturgy and Music or Samba Likhaan.

> the water, and disappears without trace, leaving behind waves of concentric ripples.
>
> Each ripple presents you with a slightly different perspective on the reflections of the other shore. You watch the ripples radiating from the place where the stone vanished, as they widen and fade and eventually disappear altogether. Then once the lake's surface is still once more, the reflections have returned to normal, and you toss in another offering.[7]

The musical setting is almost chant-like with a simple guitar harmony that provides sparse chordal support for the melody. In performance, the singers may choose to hum a sustained pitch throughout while a soloist intones the text. This frees the singers to meditate with eyes closed or on an appropriate image, perhaps a still pond from a Japanese garden. Like other hymns on creation, trees, birds, rivers, and breezes are invoked to set the scene, drawing upon several of the senses (stanza two). The hymn concludes with a quiet joy resulting in a total oneness with the natural order of creation: "When I am moved to worship, peace reigns in my heart" (stanza three).

Many other examples might be cited on the theme of creation from the songs of the Global South. These three, however, demonstrate that place and context matter. Some with traditional Western theology views may be uncomfortable with Confucian and Buddhist overtones in the cited texts, yet these are not examples of careless syncretism, but a careful integration of local cultural influences into a Christian worldview.

Incarnation/Christology

Congregational songs on the incarnation are particularly subject to social and geographical location. Christina Rossetti's (1830–94) "In the Bleak Midwinter" (c. 1872) used winter metaphors common to England to capture the bitter, harsh spiritual landscape encountered by the incarnate God, manifest in Jesus, born in the political oppression faced by Jews in the Roman occupation of Palestine:

> In the bleak midwinter,
> Frosty wind made moan,
> Earth stood hard as iron,
> Water like a stone.

7. This exercise was described to me by the composer in a conversation in Manila, July 1996. The quotation is from Bodhipaksa, "Reflections in Mindfulness."

Snow had fallen, snow on snow,
Snow on snow,
In the bleak midwinter,
Long ago.

Rossetti was not implying, as some have suggested, that it was snowing in Palestine.

The Unitarian minister from Massachusetts, Edmund Sears (1810–76), composed his famous Christmas hymn "It Came Upon the Midnight Clear" in 1849 on the cusp of the Civil War. Interestingly, this is one of the few Christmas hymns to avoid any mention of the birth of Christ, focusing on the canticle of the angels, "peace on earth" (Luke 2:14). Knowing the historical context sheds light on the interpretation of the text:

Yet with the woes of sin and strife
The world has suffered long;
Beneath the angel strain have rolled
Two thousand years of wrong;
And man, at war with man, hears not
The love-song which they bring;
O hush the noise, ye men of strife
And hear the angels sing. [stanza three]

The original stanza four is a not-too-veiled reference to slavery:

And ye, beneath life's crushing load,
Whose forms are bending low,
Who toil along the climbing way
With painful steps and slow,
Look now! for glad and golden hours
Come swiftly on the wing.
O rest beside the weary road,
And hear the angels sing!

New Zealand hymn writer Shirley Erena Murray (b. 1931) offers a view of Christmas from the Southern Hemisphere in "Carol Our Christmas" (1986):

Carol our Christmas, an upside-down Christmas:
snow is not falling and trees are not bare.
Carol the summer, and welcome the Christ child,
warm in our sunshine and sweetness of air.[8]

8. The entire text is available from the publisher at http://www.hopepublishing.com.

In many ways, this hymn is the equivalent from the Southern Hemisphere of Rossetti's "In the Bleak Midwinter" composed in England approximately one hundred years earlier.

Given the nature of the incarnation itself, the Son of God, born in a particular place, time, and culture for all places, times, and cultures, one should not be surprised that the social and geographic locations of Christmas hymns for this season are often more specific than congregational songs on other theological themes.

Tom Colvin (1925–2000) was a Scottish missionary serving Africa, and for a time in Malawi, and wrote "That Boy-Child of Mary" (1969). This hymn makes use of a Malawian tune and a text by Colvin that draws upon a particularly important sub-Saharan birth ritual, the baby naming ceremony. Many African Christians find a connection between the naming of Jesus in the temple (Luke 2:22–38) and the meaning of names given to newborn children in Africa. African names often express the child's place in the family order, aspirations for the child, and, among Christians, may include a biblical name.

An African infant-naming ceremony is a festive family gathering, often eight days after the baby's birth. Following a lavish meal, various family members submit names. The father announces the names and their meanings. At the conclusion of the ceremony, the baby's name is revealed to all gathered and the infant is passed around to everyone. Names in African communities have power.

This hymn is a baby-naming song for the infant Jesus. The stanzas alternate between a question and response. Like a baby-naming ceremony in many African cultures, the stanzas of this hymn tell the meaning of Jesus' name—"God ever with us." A later stanza places Jesus in our family order—"Gift of the Father to human mother makes him our brother." Finally, this newborn child carries the hopes for the whole world because he has come to save us.[9]

"Holy Night, Blessed Night" was written by Sheng Ye Qing and Sheng Ye Jing in 1921. With a text composed by the Revs. Wei-yu Zhu and Jing-ren Wu and a melody by Pastor Qi-gui Shi (b. 1929), who now resides in Shanghai, China, the text of this hymn is so close to the Austrian "Silent Night" (1816) by Joseph Mohr with music by Franz Gruber, that it has been called the "Chinese Silent Night." Indeed, the spirit of the Mohr-Gruber collaboration seems to have captured the imagination of a number of Chinese poets. Pastor Shi composed the pentatonic melody SHENG YE JING in

9. Unlike other hymns from the Global South included in this chapter drawn from categories 6 and 7 on the list at the beginning, this hymn reflects category 5. The entire text is available from Hope Publishing Company at http://www.hopepublishing.com.

1982 in honor of his teacher, Rev. Zhu. The English version, a paraphrase by Taiwanese missionary Kathleen Moody, demonstrates the close affinity with the original Austrian hymn.

> Holy night, Blessed night,
> Stars shine brightly, earth is still:
> Hills and valleys, field and woodlands,
> All surround the small town of Bethlehem.
> In a manger Christ the Lord sleeps.[10]

The theology of the incarnation comes to use through the distinctly Chinese melody. Pastor Shi's intent was to compose a melody that would be in a musical idiom that Chinese Christians would understand and feel, bringing the birth of Christ closer to them.[11]

Many songs from the Latin American context focus on the journeys of the Holy Family (La Sagrada Familia), both on the road to Bethlehem and the flight to Egypt. In cultures where many are refugees seeking freedom from oppression, these particular parts of the nativity narrative are exceptionally powerful. The Puerto Rican carol "Hacia Belén se encamina" (The journey toward Bethlehem) captures the first journey. The Mexican Christmas custom of La Posada (the inn or hostel), where neighborhood groups reenact the Holy Family's search for shelter by visiting different homes in the community, indicates an emphasis on hospitality and care for the traveler. While the textual content may be similar to Western hymns, the singing of these songs in Latin American contexts may evoke a deeper level of poignancy because the singers may have family members who have migrated to other countries, thus identifying strongly with journeys in the Christmas narrative.

The Christian Journey

Hymns on the Christian journey are abundant in Western traditions. Songs that express this journey in the first person singular run deeply in our sung history. For example, see Georg Neumark's (1621–81) "If Thou but

10. This translation was prepared for *Sound the Bamboo* (1990), ed. by I-to Loh, and is used by permission of the United States distributor of this hymnal GIA Publishing, Inc., Chicago, IL 60638. Used by permission. All rights reserved.

11. Conversation with Rev. Qi-gui Shi, October 2013, in Shanghai, China. The complete hymn may be heard in English sung in a Malaysian church by a Chinese Malaysian girl under the direction of church musician and hymnal compiler Mary Gan at https://www.youtube.com/watch?v=BXuJtWTTK6E. Taiwanese hymnologist I-to Loh arranged the melody under the pen name Pen-li Chen.

Suffer God to Guide Thee" (1657) with a translation (1863) by Catherine Winkworth (1827–78). "Guide Me, O Thou Great Jehovah" (1745) by the famous Welsh pastor and hymnwriter William Williams (1717–91) captures the experience of the personal walk beautifully. Over one hundred years later, Joseph Gilmore's (1834–1918) "He Leadeth Me" (1862) and Fanny Crosby's (1820–1915) "Close to Thee" (1874) echo the perspective of many gospel songwriters who write in the first person singular. The refrain often solidifies the personal journey. Such is the case with Crosby: "All along my pilgrim journey, / Savior, let me walk with thee." More recently, Kathleen Thomerson (b. 1934) reinforces the personal walk with Christ in "I Want to Walk as a Child of the Light" (1966) and John Bell (b. 1949). Graham Maule's (b. 1958) "Will You Come and Follow Me" (1987) offers a call to discipleship in the first person singular.

These are balanced with hymns in the first-person plural such as Isaac Watts's "Come We that Love the Lord" (1707), with the refrain by Robert Lowry (1826–1899), "We're Marching to Zion" (1867). Another examples is "Lead On, O King Eternal" (1886) by Ernest Shurtleff (1862–1917), the final stanza stating: "We follow not with fears . . . We journey in its light." Recently, Marty Haugen's (b. 1950) "Gather Us In" (1982) represents the focus on the gathered body of Christ, following the mandates of the Second Vatican Council (1962–65).

Some examples from the Global South may shed further light on Christians who come from cultures that are much more community based and also in situations where ethnic, political, or religious oppression is common. The South African Freedom Song "Siyahamba" is one of the most prominent examples. It is helpful to understand the song's use in its community of origin, especially in the antiapartheid movement of the last century. Songs like "Siyahamba" often originated with groups like Amadodana, a Methodist young men's group. Usually translated as "We are marching in the light of God," these few words contain layers of meaning. "We" is a word of community—the community of those living and the community of the living dead. In African traditional society, those who have died are still with us and their witness may influence the actions of the living. "Marching" is an action that unifies the community as they move physically and spiritually in the same direction. "The Light of God" has meaning on several levels. While a symbol of creation and of Jesus Christ, the light of the world, "light" is also commonly referred to in songs of healing (*ngoma*) throughout Central and Southern Africa. According to Christian anthropologist John Janzen, "Let darkness be replaced with light" is coded language for "seeing clearly."[12] God is the source of clear sight in the midst of the struggle, the font of discernment and truth. As we march, we can see our way ahead. Our path is clear. Where there is light, there is hope. Another example from the same tradition is "Hamba nathi mkululu wethu" ("Come, walk with us, the journey is long"). Though songs of few words, the meaning, like African proverbs, is highly contextual and complex.

"Somos Pueblo que Camina" ("We Are People on a Journey"), from *La Misa Popular Nicaragüense* (1968), is a representative example of an entrance song from one of the Central American Mass settings composed in the wake of the Second Vatican Council. The journey is a difficult one—a path of pain ("la senda del dolor"). It is a path to "la cena del Señor" (the table of the Lord) where all will be nourished including the humble and the poor ("los humildes y los pobres"). This is a journey for those who are thirsty for justice ("sedientos de la justicia") and searching their liberation ("buscan su liberacion"). A similar theme emerges in the hymn by the Spanish priest Cesáreo Gabaráin (1936–1991), "Camina, Pueblo de Dios" ("Walk on, O People of God") composed in 1979. The journey of God's people takes place, leading to a new law ("nueva lay"), a new alliance ("nueva alianza"), and a new creation ("nueva creación) in light of the resurrection of Christ. In the final stanza, the journey of God's people today takes its cue from Israel as a pilgrim people ("Israel peregrino").

CONCLUSION

Many chapters in this volume have presented in varying degrees a somewhat comprehensive theological understanding of a hymnwriter, composer, or movement within the history of Christian song. In contrast, this brief introduction to the songs and issues involved in singing and understanding the theology of Christians from the Global South is, at best, anecdotal.[13] The purpose here is to bring to light the importance of the relationship between song and place—social, ethnic, and geographic locations—or the connection between landscape and soundscape. While our sung faith reflects eternal truths of Christian theology, our perspective in place, time, and culture influences our understanding of eternal truth. No one culture or continent contains a corner on eternal truth. Twenty-first century singers have the

12. Janzen, *Ngoma*, 111–18.

13. See Hawn, *Gather into One*; and Hawn, "The Rise of Ecumenical Global Song" in *New Songs of Celebration Render*, 209–345, for further study. The following chapter by the author explores more specifically the relationship between sound and location: Hawn, "Soundscapes and Landscapes," 2659–79.

opportunity more than any previous generation to fill out their praise and, in doing so, gain a worldwide perspective of how God through Christ is manifest throughout all time and space.

BIBLIOGRAPHY

Banana, Canaan. *Come and Share: An Introduction to Christian Theology*. Harare: Mambo Press, 1991.

Bodhipaksa. "Reflections in Mindfulness." *Windmind Buddhist Meditation*, February 13, 2007. www.wildmind.org/mindfulness/four/reflections.

Hawn, C. Michael. *Gather into One: Singing Praying Globally*. Grand Rapids, MI: Eerdmans, 2003.

_____. *New Songs of Celebration Render: Congregational Song in the Twenty-First Century*. Chicago: GIA Publications, 2013.

_____. "Soundscapes and Landscapes: How Place Shapes Christian Congregational Song." In *The Changing World Religion Map: Sacred Places, Identities, Practices and Politics*, edited by Stanley D. Brunn, 2659–79. New York: Springer Netherlands, 2015. http://link.springer.com/chapter/10.1007/978-94-017-9376-6_139.

Janzen, John M. *Ngoma: Discourses on Healing in Central and Southern Africa*. Berkeley: University of California Press, 1992.

Krabill, James R. "Encounters: What Happens to Music When People Meet." In *Music in the Life of the African Church*, edited by Roberta King, 57–80. Waco: Baylor University Press, 2008.

Young, Carlton R., ed. *The United Methodist Hymnal*. Nashville: United Methodist, 1989.

Chapter 19

Contemporary Praise and Worship Music

GREG SCHEER

HISTORICAL BACKGROUND

FROM ITS HUMBLE BEGINNINGS five decades ago, contemporary praise and worship has come to dominate the landscape of modern worship. Though it is a relatively recent development, its roots reach back to the nineteenth century evangelistic revivals. Pioneers such as William Booth of the Salvation Army and outreach duo Dwight Moody and Ira Sankey used music in distinctly nonliturgical ways; music was the bait to bring in unbelievers and prepare them for an evangelistic sermon. Indeed, this song/sermon pattern became the new liturgy of Evangelical worship for years to come, led by musician/preacher duos: Billy Sunday and Homer Rodeheaver, Billy Graham and George Beverly Shea, Joel Osteen and Israel Houghton.

The nineteenth century revivals also established the pattern of church music closely following the popular music styles of the broader culture. From the Johann Strauss-influenced waltzes of Fanny Crosby to the Billy Joel-style ballads of Michael W. Smith, the Evangelical tradition has always been a student of popular culture—and thus, of youth culture. In the mid-twentieth century, the Evangelicals continued to orient themselves toward youth culture with a new focus on church youth groups and outreach organizations such as Youth for Christ. New music emerged in this context, including youth musicals such as *Tell It Like It Is* (1969) and the songs of Bill Gaither.

As unlikely as it seems, this affinity for youth culture primed Evangelicals to welcome the hippies who were converted to Christ in the late 1960s. These "Jesus People" were steeped in the hippy culture of Haight-Ashbury, but adapted quickly to Evangelicism, including its music. The most notable early example of pairing hippy music with a gospel message was by a group from Calvary Chapel in Costa Mesa called Love Song. Love Song's music impressed pastor Chuck Smith so much that he helped fund the 1971 recording *The Everlastin' Living Jesus Concert*, the first of Maranatha! Music's many recordings.

At first, all of this music was simply "Jesus music," shared at coffee houses, churches, and concerts. Soon, however, two distinct strands emerged: one strand focused on evangelism and outreach. Like William Booth before him, early Christian rocker Larry Norman asked, "Why Should the Devil Have All the Good Music?"[1] Randy Stonehill, Don Francisco, and others who performed concerts and recorded albums that closely followed contemporary secular styles joined him in asking this question. Their goal was to introduce young people to the gospel in a voice that was familiar to them. This strand of Jesus music eventually became "contemporary Christian music" (CCM), with its own record labels and radio stations. Though originally created to spread the gospel to those who otherwise might not hear it, it quickly became an insular industry—a safe musical choice for Christian parents who wanted to let their children listen to pop music without being corrupted by the worldly influences of secular culture.

The other strand of Jesus music was focused inside the walls of the church. Musicians such as Karen Lafferty ("Seek Ye First," 1972) wrote simple Scripture-based choruses that quickly spread through youth groups and churches. This repertoire of "Scripture songs" was eventually gathered into the 1983 collection, Maranatha! Music's *Praise Chorus Book*, which became the "bible" of early praise music. Indeed, the genre centered on Maranatha! Music for a number of years.

It is important to distinguish between these two strands of Jesus music. CCM was the evangelistic, outward focused branch of the family tree, whereas the Scripture choruses that came to be known as "praise and worship" (or P&W, sometimes called "contemporary worship music," or CWM)

1. This was also the title of one of the songs from his seminal 1972 album, *Only Visiting This Planet*. See also Gregory Thornbury, *Why Should the Devil Have All the Good Music?: Larry Norman and the Perils of Christian Rock*, 2018.

were intended for the church.[2] Unfortunately, many scholars have confused the two or have pinned the sins of one on the other while building a case against it.

Though P&W was the runt of the Jesus music litter during these early years, it nonetheless exerted considerable influence on America's worship landscape in the decades to come. It moved from the subculture into the suburbs as Jesus people began to have families and settle down. These baby boomers took their love of heart-felt Scripture songs into local congregations as well as new churches built specially around the ethos of these grown-up Jesus people.

As the genre became more enmeshed with the church establishment, there was a notable turn from the intimate Scripture songs of the previous era toward the extroverted, even triumphalistic tone of the "praise chorus." Praise choruses such as Jack Hayford's "Majesty" (1981) and Rick Founds' "Lord, I Lift Your Name on High" (1989) were louder, faster, and more festive than anything of the previous era. This new musical confidence was supported by a fledgling worship industry that continued to flourish at Maranatha! Music and grew to new levels with the 1987 founding of Integrity Music. Integrity published an incredibly successful series of albums featuring notable worship movements around the world, including Australia's Hillsong, the Brownsville Revival, and Graham Kendrick's March for Jesus. Whereas the Maranatha! style was relaxed folk played on the guitar, Integrity (and its Hosanna! subsidiary) was more Pentecostal, more polished, and generally led by piano and full band. Sometimes this took the form of crossover Black gospel artists like Ron Kenoly; other times it was Madonna-twinged synth pop like Gary Oliver's song "Celebrate Jesus" (1988).

Another important development during this era of growth was the founding of Christian Copyright Licensing International (CCLI) in 1988 by Howard Rachinski. Before the advent of praise choruses, churches had relied on hymnals to aid their singing. Now they needed a way to legally print or project the songs they were using. Rachinski's CCLI created a blanket license agreement between churches and publishers that allowed churches to use the music legally and allowed publishers to collect royalties easily.[3] In short order, CCLI-licensed song projection replaced hymnals in many churches. In a sense, the CCLI catalog became the hymnal of the genre.

CCLI not only solved local churches' music licensing problem, it created a revenue stream for those who wrote the songs. Suddenly, writing

2. For further discussion of CCM, P&W, and their relation to the church and culture, see Howard and Streck, *Apostles of Rock*.

3. This is similar to the blanket licenses BMI and ASCAP provide for music performances.

worship songs was a viable way to earn an income. CCLI became the conduit of a fortuitous marketing model: worshipers who heard a song in church on Sunday were likely to buy a CD or a concert ticket of the artist, which led to more radio time, which caused more churches to sing the song. It is not many genres of music that enjoy the marketing power of a captive audience! As one record executive put it: "the church is our radio station."[4]

Soon the worship industry had matured to the point that *Christianity Today* declared "The Triumph of the Praise Song" on the cover of its July 1999 issue. Contemporary songs accompanied by praise bands were becoming the dominant form of worship in American churches. However, the genre remained bound to its church context; it had yet to become a phenomenon in the broader pop culture landscape.

This changed with Darlene Zschech's 1993 breakout hit, "Shout to the Lord" and Martin Smith's "I Could Sing of Your Love Forever" (1994). Zschech, part of Australia's Hillsong megachurch, did for P&W what Amy Grant had done for CCM a decade earlier: she had the talent and good looks of a bona fide pop star and an album full of crossover hits. Smith's band Delirious? helped normalize worship recordings and concerts independent of church affiliation.

This new era differed from the previous in significant ways: Recordings now focused on performers rather than songs. Previous releases were concerned primarily with introducing new songs to churches; CDs were snapshots of a worship movement or an influential church rather than a particular performer. These new releases always had a "face"—a performer or a group that could be marketed. With this shift toward performer-based projects, the genre moved away from a generic light rock style as worship artists attempted to create their own unique sound. They also moved away from the vocal ensembles of the previous era, instead favoring lead singers with an identifiable vocal style. Further, the recordings began to have higher production values; instead of live concert recordings, they favored the precision and polish of the studio, just like their secular pop counterparts.

Worship concerts and tours became more prevalent during this time. Churches were still the bread and butter of the worship industry, but increasingly, festivals and concerts were viewed as the main event. Megachurches were another part of the industry network. Many megachurches were big enough to host the most popular bands' concerts, and some churches even hired worship celebrities—a sign of prestige akin to court composers of centuries past.

4. Danny McGuffey, chief marketing officer for Integrity Media, as quoted in Price, "Praise & Worship."

One result of these changes is that the life cycle of worship songs on the CCLI top 20 charts began to look more like the secular Top 40 than worship charts of the previous decade. Whereas songs from previous eras—"Seek Ye First," "As the Deer"—remained in the CCLI's Top 20 songs for decades, new songs tended to rise and fall within a few years. These binge and purge cycles are typical of music that is marketed to the point of saturation and then dropped for the next shiny thing.

Other factors served to further increase worship music's market reach during this time. Large gatherings such as Promise Keepers and the March for Jesus introduced the music to millions. Megachurches not only hosted concerts, but churches like Chicago's Willow Creek became the template for thousands of smaller churches; these megachurches grew networks and hosted conferences that introduced new repertoire to eager church leaders. *Worship Leader* magazine, formed in 1992, became the voice of contemporary worship. Beginning in 1997, the magazine was accompanied by *SongDiscovery*, a CD and booklet of new songs.

Serendipitously, as the worship branch of the Christian music tree flourished, it was a time of instability for CCM. As CCM matured, it had begun to test the boundaries of the genre: was CCM music written by Christians or music written about Christ? P&W had no such identity crisis. It was music written to God and about God; the market responded appreciatively to this singular focus.

All of these changes pointed to one thing: P&W was becoming pop music. Though Darlene Zschech and other best-selling artists commanded the spotlight during these years, the Vineyard worship movement and its influential leader John Wimber gained traction behind the scenes. Until this time, contemporary worship had concerned itself primarily with music style. Now that it ruled the pews it began to ask deeper questions about the meaning of worship. The Vineyard's focus on passion and intimacy became the closest thing contemporary worship had to a theology of worship. Wimber explained the movements of worship similarly to the outer courts, inner courts, and holy of holies of the Old Testament: worship began by calling each other to worship, then talking about God and his attributes, finally turning the focus to an intimate, one-on-one encounter with Jesus.

This neo-Pentecostal approach to worship connected with a postmodern generation that placed experience before reason. They were immersed in the commercial success of contemporary worship, but longed for something that felt more authentic. They found it in the Passion Conferences that emerged in the new millennium. By 2000, forty thousand students were packing stadiums to worship with leaders such as David Crowder, Chris Tomlin, and Matt Redman at Passion's OneDay gathering, where songs such as Matt Redman's "The Heart of Worship" (1999) tapped into the millennial desire for intimacy.

What had started as periodic conference/revivals quickly became a template for worship in local churches. Large, concert-like para-church gatherings translated well into the megachurch context, especially as megachurches tried to meet the needs of a new generation that sought the excitement of the "immersive worship experience" (full band, loud sound system, concert lighting) with the ecstatic intimacy of Vineyard-style worship.

Music publisher/record label WorshipTogether became the voice of this new repertoire. Like Maranatha! and Integrity in decades past, WorshipTogether gathered a stable of like-minded songwriters, performers and publisher affiliates: Chris Tomlin, sixsteprecords, Kari Jobe, Hillsong, David Crowder, and Matt Redman.

WorshipTogether songs made huge inroads into the church's repertoire, but none had more impact than Chris Tomlin's. Tomlin has had so many hits—"How Great Is Our God" (2004), "Amazing Grace/My Chains Are Gone" (2006), and "Our God" (2010) are just a few among hundreds—that CNN referred to his as "the most widely sung music on the planet today."[5] Though some deride him as warmed-over U2, Tomlin's knack for guileless, tuneful songs, combined with his "guy next door" demeanor proved to be exactly what America wanted from a worship leader.

Hillsong continued to be popular in a post-Zschech era, targeting themselves toward a variety of markets under the Hillsong United, Hillsong Young and Free, and Hillsong Kids labels. Whereas Chris Tomlin's music style followed in the footsteps of the guitar-driven folk rock like Delirious? and Matt Redman, Hillsong followed their own church's legacy for well-crafted pop anthems, expertly performed. Hillsong—the church—expanded exponentially in the 2000s, planting churches all over the world and providing a church home to thousands, including stars such as Justin Bieber. Hillsong's music certainly played an important role in the expansion of the Hillsong brand. By 2016, Hillsong had even released a movie, *Let Hope Rise*, which documented the church's rise to prominence and Hillsong United's recent tour.

It was during this time that the "bridge" became a prominent feature in many praise songs. In pop music, the bridge serves as a contrast to the verse and chorus, usually occurring two-thirds of the way through the song. Up

5. Marrapodi and Foreman, "Chris Tomlin." Other statistics from the same article estimate that by 2012 Tomlin had sold 4.2 million albums and had 6 million digital downloads. CCLI's Howard Rachinski says, "Our best guess would be in the United States on any given Sunday, 20 to 30 million people would be singing Chris Tomlin's songs."

to this point, it had been excluded from worship songs because it increases the complexity of a song's form. However, because the genre during this era had become a performance music—pop music distributed via recordings—rather than a folk music, it became common.

Though the songs of this era became more performance-oriented and complicated in their musical form, they had never been more harmonically simple or lyrically thin. In the wake of the popularity of these simple, repetitive songs, a resistance grew against what was perceived as the shallow theology of Tomlin, Hillsong, *et al.*

Some churches rejected modern P&W completely, never straying from traditional hymnody. Others attempted to supplement P&W's simple sentiments with the more substantial content of hymns, combining them in "blended" worship services. In the late 1990s, a unique movement sprouted up in the Reformed University Fellowship (an outreach of the Presbyterian Church in America, or PCA), in which historic hymn texts were sung to new tunes. These tunes tended to be in a folk-rock style, accompanied by guitar. From their origins on college campuses, these "retuned hymns" spread to the PCA, other Reformed churches, and the larger Evangelical church.[6] Retuned hymns tended to be sung by those who wanted to separate themselves from mainstream P&W.

Perhaps the most prominent voice among those calling the church to a more theologically robust worship life was Keith Getty. Getty and his cowriters, wife Kristyn and "In Christ Alone" collaborator Stuart Townend, wrote songs in a modern soft-rock in a style that functioned like hymns. These were strophic (multi-verse) songs that developed from one verse to the next, unlike the verbatim repetitions typical of praise songs. Getty's music moved beyond P&W's thematic sweet spot—praise—into areas previously found only in hymnal indices: communion, prayers of illumination, church seasons, etc. The melodies featured memorable tunes (often using pentatonic scales), few syncopations, and simple song forms such as AABA. This endeared Getty's songs—which he dubbed "modern hymns"—to those who had previously resisted contemporary worship songs, and made those who had grown tired of P&W's spiritual bon bons feel like they were getting a substantial meal. To be fair, Getty was not the first or only contemporary songwriter to compose substantial strophic songs; most notably Graham Kendrick (with whom Getty has collaborated) wrote in a similar vein decades earlier.

6. For a more comprehensive treatment of the movement, see Scheer, "Retune My Heart."

If the retuned hymn movement and Keith Getty's somewhat more intellectual approach represented one reaction to the praise pop of the day, another was to delve deeper into the Pentecostal side of P&W. This approach was pioneered by the Kansas City International House of Prayer, beginning in 1999. "IHOP," as it was known, hosted 24/7 "harp and bowl" worship—non-stop spontaneous worship that wove song, prayer, and Scripture together. Even more than Wimber's Vineyard—by whom they were clearly influenced—IHOP focused on extended periods of intimate worship, a meeting of Christ and bride that took on almost sexual overtones. They drew liberally from Song of Songs and spoke freely of "entering the chambers" and "lovin' on Jesus."

Though an underground movement, IHOP influenced the expectations of the next generation's worship leaders. In the 2010s, Bethel Music and its youth affiliate, Jesus Culture, carried the torch for free-flowing, "prophetic" worship. Prophetic worship at IHOP was literally prophetic: spontaneous prophecies sung over a repeated, improvised bed of music. Prophetic worship in the Bethel context tended to begin with pre-composed (rather than improvised) songs that nonetheless left plenty of time and space for spontaneous worship from all the worshipers and prophetic utterances and singing from those who had that gift.

Given this context, it is not surprising that most prophetic[7] worship songs took a shape that would support this worship context. The songs tended to be very simple harmonically, rarely using more than four chords. This allowed the musicians to improvise easily during extended times of speaking, singing, and free prayer. This doesn't make for music interesting to theorists and connoisseurs, but it follows a long tradition of music intended to support spiritual ecstasy, from Sufi whirling dervishes to Shaker dances. Dynamics are the most interesting musical parameter of prophetic worship songs. Unlike praise songs of previous generations that tended to have set forms and little dynamic fluctuation, prophetic songs varied from whispered prayer to full-throated shouts of praise.

The length of songs dramatically increased in this context. Earlier praise songs rarely lasted longer than four minutes, but prophetic worship songs regularly lasted well over ten minutes. A lot of this expansion took place in the song's bridge. "Here I Am to Worship" (Tim Hughes, 2000), one

7. The titles *spontaneous* and *prophetic* tend to be used interchangeably. More precisely, *spontaneous worship* refers to the broader style of free-flowing worship that allows worshipers to voice their own sung or spoken adoration (sometimes called "soaking"); *prophetic worship* describes spontaneous worship in which a leader exercises his or her prophetic gifts; that is, speaking words given to them by God. See Johnson, "Spontaneous vs. Prophetic Worship."

of the earliest praise songs to include a bridge, repeated the line, "I'll never know how much it cost to see my sin upon that cross" a mere four times. In comparison, the studio version of Hillsong United's "Oceans/Where Feet May Fail" (2012) is nine minutes long, a full four minutes of which is devoted to the bridge.

THEOLOGICAL PERSPECTIVES

Contemporary P&W, in all its divergent forms over the course of its five-decade history, shares some common traits: Pentecostalism is in its DNA, it speaks with an Evangelical accent, and it is simultaneously conservative theologically and progressive musically.[8]

The Jesus people traded in the "turn on, tune in, drop out" mentality of the hippy culture for the experience of being "high on Jesus" that Christianity offered. Indeed, many of the Jesus movement's progenitors—Chuck Smith and Lonnie Frisbee, among others—were Pentecostals. Contemporary P&W still reflects these Pentecostal roots today.

Pentecostal worship is known for its exuberance—worshipers raise their hands, shout, and dance in the Spirit—but Pentecostal worship theology goes deeper than mere exuberance. Pentecostals' openness to signs and wonders takes various forms in their worship, most notably glossolalia (speaking or singing in tongues), prophecy, and miracles. Modern Pentecostals often downplay more extreme manifestations of the Spirit, but each generation has had notable exceptions such as the Toronto Airport Blessing in the 1990s and Bethel Church today. This expectation of God's miraculous intervention can be heard in songs such as "Break Every Chain" (Will Reagan, 2009) popularized by Jesus Culture and viewed one hundred million times on YouTube in Tasha Cobb's rendition.

> There is power in the name of Jesus [3x]
> To break every chain, break every chain, break every chain. [2x]
> There's an army rising up. [3x]
> To break every chain, break every chain, break every chain. [2x]
> I hear the chains falling [7x]

Spiritual warfare is another prominent theme in Pentecostal worship. Songs supporting this theology range from general spiritual warfare, such as "The Battle Belongs to the Lord" (Jamie Owens-Collins, 1985) to specific

8. Two other notable ways of summarizing P&W's traits can be found in Scheer, "Shout to the Lord," 175–205; and Lim and Ruth, *Lovin' on Jesus*, 2–3.

calls to battle the devil such as "Enemy's Camp" (Kenny Gatlin, 1987) from the Brownsville revival:

> Well, I went to the enemy's camp
> and I took back what he stole from me. (4x)
> You know he's under my feet. (6x)
> Satan is under my feet.

Most importantly, though, Pentecostals gave P&W its penchant for ecstasy. This "third blessing" (salvation and sanctification being the first two blessings according to Wesley-Holiness adherents) has remained a consistent mark of Pentecostal worship. Whether or not one can prophecy or perform miracles, Pentecostal worshipers expect the Spirit to enable intimate communion with Jesus. This altered state of worship takes many names: "lost in the Spirit," "baptized with fire," "lovin' on Jesus," "soaking," "breaking through," and "entering the chamber." This latter image from Song of Solomon was taken up by Vineyard's John Wimber, whose worship theology suggested that worship move toward climactic intimacy with Jesus.

This goal of intimacy in worship has taken on romantic—even sexual—overtones in some P&W music. There are dozens of songs, for example, about entering the king's chambers.[9] Utilizing Song of Solomon as an allegory for spiritual intimacy is nothing new, but coupling it with a pop music style—a genre known for its sensuality—pushes the message to a whole new level. If one were to hear Vineyard's "Draw Me Close" (Kelly Carpenter, 1994) out of context, it would be difficult to distinguish from a romantic pop song:

> Draw me close to you
> Never let me go
> I lay it all down again
> To hear you say that I'm your friend
>
> You are my desire
> No one else will do
> 'Cause nothing else can take your place
> To feel the warmth of your embrace
>
> You're all I want
> You're all I've ever needed
> You're all I want

9. An image taken from Song of Solomon 1:2–4: "Let him kiss me with the kisses of his mouth! For your love is better than wine, your anointing oils are fragrant, your name is perfume poured out; therefore the maidens love you. Draw me after you, let us make haste. The king has brought me into his chambers."

Help me know you are near

Without context, Darrell Evans's "Your Love Is Extravagant" (1998) sounds downright naughty:

Your Love is extravagant
Your friendship. . . mmm. . . intimate
I find I'm moving to the rhythms of your grace
Your fragrance is intoxicating
In our secret place.

The goal of experiencing intimacy within worship is supported not only by the theological bent of the lyrics, but also by the long stretches of music that characterize both Pentecostal worship and P&W. These "praise sets" allow time and space for worshipers to enter a different emotional state. In many ways, the music provides a blank slate upon which each worshiper individually engages God.

If Pentecostalism gave P&W its style, Evangelicalism gave it its theological foundation. Indeed, it could be argued that P&W is merely an extension of the theological and musical ethos established in the nineteenth century evangelistic revivals. The music of Evangelicalism, then and now, has supported its core tenants: conversionism, activism, biblicism, and crucicentrism.[10]

What does P&W's "Evangelical accent" sound like? It is, first of all, personal. Evangelical worship strives to be heartfelt rather than scripted. It aims to support personal piety rather than corporate creed. This focus on the individual's engagement can lead to "Jesus and me" songs. (As opposed to repertoire that speaks in a corporate voice and is more robustly Trinitarian.) Hymnologists have long derided "In the Garden" (C. Austin Miles, 1913) for its sentimental, individualistic viewpoint, but Evangelical individualism is alive and well in "Above All" (Lenny Leblanc, 1999):

Crucified laid behind a stone.
You lived to die rejected and alone.
Like a rose trampled on the ground,
You took the fall and thought of me
Above all

10. Four hallmarks of evangelical religion according to British historian David Bebbington, as quoted in National Association of Evangelicals, "What Is an Evangelical?": *Conversionism*: the belief that lives need to be transformed through a "born-again" experience and a life-long process of following Jesus. *Activism*: the expression and demonstration of the gospel in missionary and social reform efforts. *Biblicism*: a high regard for and obedience to the Bible as the ultimate authority. *Crucicentrism*: a stress on the sacrifice of Jesus Christ on the cross as making possible the redemption of humanity.

Evangelicals are historically anti-ritual and anti-liturgical. This is, in part, a result of a focus on heartfelt piety in worship. Repeated rituals are too austere to support that goal. Liturgical patterns are not explicitly mandated in Scripture, making them seem the "vain repetitions" of human invention. In the final analysis, ritual and liturgy simply seem too "Catholic." Protestants, and especially Evangelicals, have defined themselves over and against Roman Catholics and other "cultural Christians," and their worship follows suit.[11]

Evangelicals embrace evangelistic outreach as a part of worship, a unique approach first established in the nineteenth century Evangelical revivals. Evangelism is seen in the worship structure itself, in the "altar call" or "ministry time" that closes many services—a time for non-believers to give their lives to Christ. It was also seen in the "seeker services" in the 1990s, in which churches such as Willow Creek in suburban Chicago stripped their churches of crosses, pipe organs, and any other vestiges of religion that might discourage unbelievers from attending.

This evangelistic impulse leads to a final aspect of Evangelical worship in general, and P&W in particular: it is simultaneously conservative theologically and progressive musically. Evangelicals have always been a "back to basics" people, focusing on personal piety and theological orthodoxy. So, while the early Jesus people came from a culture of drugs, free love, and anti-authoritarianism, they were baptized into a fundamentally conservative strain of Christianity that included in its ranks even stricter variants such as Pentecostals, Wesleyan-Holiness movement, and Fundamentalists.

In practice, this took the shape of a repertoire focused heavily on central themes of the Evangelical faith with an eye toward personal holiness. The songs drew liberally from Scripture. Interestingly, early Jesus music was frequently written in King James English ("As the deer panteth for the water," "I Exalt Thee"). True, some songwriters included colloquialisms like "groovy" and "outta sight," but the core repertoire featured texts that were surprisingly conservative. Though modern P&W no longer uses the KJV, it continues to use conservative language, using masculine pronouns for God, gender exclusive terms for humans, and hierarchal language ("Master")—all of which progressive hymn writers no longer employ.

Instructive are the themes that P&W leaves out. There are few songs that address themes hymns have historically addressed, such as the Trinity, the church universal, and providence; or subjects modern hymnists have tackled: social justice issues like poverty, structural ills such as racism and

11. It should be noted that some Evangelicals have been won over to the use of liturgical patterns through the influence of Robert Webber and other Evangelical leaders' embrace of an "Ancient-Future" worship.

corporate greed, or progressive themes like gender equality and LGBTQ inclusion. It's understandable that Evangelical worship music would shy away from themes more typically the domain of mainline or liberal denominations, but they have also avoided significant portions of Scripture: lament is almost entirely lacking, the Old Testament is addressed infrequently, and there is little grappling with the dark and difficult questions of Scripture (Job's suffering, Paul's more thorny exhortations, or even Jesus' difficult teachings).

Consider, for example, the recent flap over "In Christ Alone." The Presbyterian hymnal committee (PCUSA, the liberal branch of the Presbyterian church) requested permission of the authors, Stuart Townend and Keith Getty, to alter the line, "the wrath of God was satisfied." While text alterations are exceedingly common in hymnal editing, this one caused a firestorm of controversy, with the songwriters' fans using it as an occasion to accuse the PCUSA of abandoning orthodoxy.[12] This was less an argument of theology and more an opportunity for Evangelical believers to mark their territory as opposed to—and more faithful than—progressive Christians.

While it is important to Evangelicals to stake their claim as theologically orthodox, their conservatism doesn't extend to their choice of music. In fact, they strive to be as progressive as possible in musical style. This has been true since the early days of Evangelicalism, when music was used by Moody/Sankey et al. as a draw for revival meetings. The trend continues today, with the assumption that church music should be in a culturally relevant music style, creating no barriers between the gospel and unbelieving ears.

Evangelicals don't feel compelled to hand down a shared cultural heritage of the Christian community; instead, music is used for its utility to connect to the secular culture. Therefore, early Jesus music sounded like The Eagles or James Taylor, praise choruses from the 1980s echoed the bright synth pop of Madonna, and Hillsong Young and Free echoes the dancehall rhythms of EDM (electronic dance music). Perhaps P&W exemplifies a favored Evangelical biblical maxim, "In the world, but not of it."

CONTRIBUTION TO LITURGY AND WORSHIP

The impact of P&W cannot be underestimated. Since the 1990s when P&W was declared the victor of the worship wars, it has only grown. The worship industry has largely overtaken CCM. Worship artists are promoted via radio, recordings, concerts, and the local church. Megachurches, which are

12. Scheer, "Orthodoxy in Christ Alone."

overwhelmingly modern in worship style, are home to half of America's Christians.[13] Pentecostalism—the fastest growing branch of Christianity throughout the world[14]—primarily utilizes forms of P&W. Even the African American church has traded much of its traditional Black gospel repertoire for P&W. It seems that P&W can be "all things to all people."

P&W's dominance is only part of its influence. It has significantly altered modern worship's liturgical landscape. First, it caused a blurring of lines between *worship* and *worship concert*. In the past, a worshiper could expect a number of liturgical acts to take place within a given service—communion, intercessory prayer, confession—because there was historic precedent or denominational mandate. Today, modern worshipers' expectations are shaped outside of the liturgical context. The worship concert leads worshipers to expect an extended song set played by a full band and amplified by a sound system and stage lighting in their local congregation. Indeed, worship artists and megachurches are the "cathedrals" of our day, establishing patterns that trickle down to smaller churches which look to them as paradigms of success.

The most fundamental liturgical shift this has caused is the elevation of music, the expansion of the "song service," and the heightened role of the music leader. Where once music served the liturgy, now it *is* the liturgy. The two-part structure of song service and preaching has become the norm in Evangelical churches and has even made great headway into mainline denominations.

Wen Reagan argues that this liturgical shift is the "pentecostalization of American Christianity."[15] As Evangelical churches adopt P&W as their music style, they tacitly take on many of the theological and liturgical assumptions of Pentecostal worship. Modern worship focuses on the worshiper's experience, as opposed to doctrine dissemination, spiritual formation, or establishing a communal identity. Music is the tool that supports this

13. Thumma, "Open the Doors," 1.

14. Pew Research Center, "New Face of Global Christianity."

15. Reagan, "Beautiful Noise," 14: "As evangelicals and eventually mainliners adopted CWM, they came to integrate Pentecostal and charismatic forms, values, and theologies into their worship services. The result was the pentecostalization of American Christianity. The bodily liturgies (the swaying, the raising of hands, the open palms); the intimate, informal lyrics that directly connected the worshiper with God; and the dynamic nature of rock music that was accessible to worshipers, yet commanded and drove the emotional tenor of the sanctuary, all emerged from a Pentecostal sensibility that emphasized the affective nature of worship. As American Christians embraced songs like 'Shout to the Lord,' 'Lord I lift your name on high,' and more recently 'Mighty to Save,' they also assumed a charismatic theology of worship that prioritized experience and emotion over doctrinal dissemination and intellectual assent."

goal. It's no wonder that the music portions of worship have grown in recent years and sometimes dwarf the time allotted to preaching.

Because long stretches of music take up as much as half of a worship service, music has become a more important part of a church's identity. Denominational loyalty has declined in favor of an identity based on music style. As music style and demographic preferences have become part of church marketing, more churches are employing high profile worship leaders who appeal to their target audience. In some cases, it is a worship star like Israel Houghton or David Crowder (Lakewood Church, Houston, and University Baptist, Waco, respectively) serving as the public face of a church's worship ministry. In other cases, churches craft their identity around their music, for example, Hillsong Church in Australia and Bethel Church in Redding, California (and their related music groups and publishing arms).

Many have sounded the alarm, warning that today's church rests on a slippery slope of human emotion rather than the solid foundation of God's word. This may be true, but it is also true that P&W has helped Christians reclaim physical and emotional worship postures that, though biblical, have been ignored for centuries. In a sense, P&W has allowed for the emergence of a historically unique liturgy: a liturgical template in which songs are not the content of worship, but the medium. P&W songs serve as a blank canvas upon which the worshiper and the Spirit paint. Those who criticize the lack of content in P&W repertoire—especially in comparison to content rich hymnody—are perhaps missing the point. Like mood music for love-making, P&W accompanies worship, but doesn't necessarily inform its content. Of course, this too is a theology of worship.

It is instructive to understand these songs in their liturgical context. A compelling example is the YouTube video of Bethel Music leading "King of My Heart."[16] Musically, the song is minimalist: just four chords throughout the seventeen-minute performance. Lyrically, it is a collection of extra-biblical *non sequitors*:

> Let the King of my heart
> Be the wind inside my sails
> The anchor in the waves
> Oh, He is my song
> Let the King of my heart
> Be the fire inside my veins
> The echo of my days

16. This specific rendition of the song by John Mark and Sarah McMillan (2015) currently has over 21 million views on youtube as of the writing of this chapter. The video can be found here: https://www.youtube.com/watch?v=g6_BLuhroHQ.

> Oh he is my song
> You are good, good, oh-ohh (repeat)
> You're never gonna let
> Never gonna let me down (repeat)

Yet, for the song's lack of content, observing the ritual that unfolds as it is sung shows how powerful of a vehicle it can be. The music swells in waves that rise and crash into the near-silence of whispered prayers from around the auditorium. Prophetic worship leader Steffany Gretzinger serves as something of a shaman for the experience, following the mood of the crowd one minute and bringing them to an emotional climax the next as she writhes, hollers, and sings prophetic words in the Spirit.

If Luther were to be dropped in twenty-first century worship, he would hardly recognize it. The seismic shift in liturgical practice goes well beyond physical changes: baptismal fonts and crosses overshadowed by band gear, Bibles replaced by projection systems, and offerings collected with the swipe of a credit card. He would be surprised—and likely dismayed—that the church's robust historic liturgy has been largely replaced by the two-part structure of emotionally driven song set followed by personal-application sermon. He would wonder why congregational singing has narrowed to themes of praise and salvation, leaving out psalmody, liturgical music, and the broader biblical witness. He would worry that the priesthood of all believers has handed over their responsibilities to a narrow band of spotlighted priest-musicians on elevated stages at the front of the church; he would certainly lament the volume of the worship band compared to that of the congregation's voice. He would question why the communal actions of worship—public prayer, creed, communion—had been largely replaced by an impulse toward individual devotion.

Luther's opinion of contemporary P&W is conjecture, of course, but it points out how far the theology and practice of worship has changed in recent years. P&W has gathered the voices of Evangelicalism, Pentecostalism, youth culture, pop music, and mass marketing into one choir; this choir (or worship team, as it were) has become the loudest voice of modern Christian worship.

NOTABLE HYMNS

Scripture Song (1971–77)[17]

- "Seek Ye First" (1972, Karen Lafferty)

17. Song eras drawn from Scheer, "Shout to the Lord."

Praise Chorus (1978–92)

- "Majesty" (1981, Jack Hayford)
- "Shine, Jesus, Shine" (1987, Graham Kendrick)
- "Lord I Lift Your Name on High" (1987, Rick Founds)

Praise & Worship (1993–98)

- "Shout to the Lord" (1993, Darlene Zschech)
- "I Could Sing of Your Love Forever" (1994, Martin Smith)
- "The Heart of Worship" (1997, Matt Redman)

Emerging Worship (1999–2008)

- "Here I Am to Worship" (2000, Tim Hughes)
- "Forever" (2001, Chris Tomlin)
- "In Christ Alone" (2001, Stuart Townend and Keith Getty)
- "Come, Holy Ghost" (2005, Bruce Benedict and Ray Mills)

Prophetic Worship (2009–present)

- "10,000 Reasons/Bless the Lord" (2011, Jonas Myrin and Matt Redman)
- "Holy Spirit/You Are Welcome Here" (2011, Bryan and Katie Torwalt of Jesus Culture)
- "Oceans/Where Feet May Fail" (2012, Houston, Crocker, Ligthelm of Hillsong United)

BIBLIOGRAPHY

Di Sabatino, David. *The Jesus People Movement: An Annotated Bibliography and General Resource*. Seal Beach, CA: Jester Media, 2003.

Eskridge, Larry. *God's Forever Family: The Jesus People Movement in America*. Oxford: Oxford University Press, 2013.

Howard, Jay R., and John M. Streck. *Apostles of Rock: The Splintered World of Contemporary Christian Music*. Lexington: The University Press of Kentucky, 1999.

Johnson, Brian. "Spontaneous vs. Prophetic Worship." Worship U. https://worshipu.com/spontaneous-worship-vs-prophetic-worship/.

Lim, Swee Hong, and Lester Ruth. *Lovin' on Jesus: A Concise History of Contemporary Worship*. Nashville: Abingdon, 2017.

Marrapodi, Eric, and Tom Foreman. "Chris Tomlin, King of the Sing-Along." CNN Blogs, March 9, 2013. http://religion.blogs.cnn.com/2013/03/09/the-most-sung-artist-on-the-planet/.

Pew Research Center. "The New Face of Global Christianity: The Emergence of 'Progressive Pentecostalism.'" April 12, 2006. http://www.pewforum.org/2006/04/12/the-new-face-of-global-christianity-the-emergence-of-progressive-pentecostalism/.

Price, Deborah Evans. "Praise & Worship: Thank Heavens for the Music!" *Billboard* 116 (April 24, 2004) 35–36.

Reagan, Wen. "A Beautiful Noise: A History of Contemporary Worship Music in Modern America." PhD diss., Duke University, 2015. https://dukespace.lib.duke.edu/dspace/bitstream/handle/10161/9836/Reagan_duke_0066D_12773.pdf.

Scheer, Greg. "Orthodoxy in Christ Alone." Reformed Journal Blog, August 6, 2013. https://blog.perspectivesjournal.org/2013/08/06/orthodoxy-and-in-christ-alone/.

———. "Retune My Heart to Sing Thy Grace: How Old Hymn Texts Found a New Home among Evangelicals." *The Hymn* 65.4 (Autumn 2014) 19–27.

———. "Shout to the Lord: Praise & Worship from Jesus People to Gen X." In *New Songs of Celebration Render: Congregational Song in the Twenty-First Century*, edited by C. Michael Hawn, 175–205. Chicago: GIA, 2013.

Thumma, Scott. "Open the Doors and See All the People: Profile of Large Protestant Churches 500–1,799 in Attendance." http://hirr.hartsem.edu/Summary-Report-Large-Churches-500-1,799-in-Attendance.pdf.

Chapter 20

Retuned Hymn Movement

Bruce H. Benedict and Lester Ruth

HISTORICAL BACKGROUND

The retuned hymn movement (RHM) is an expression of church music that began in the 1980s focused around writing new tunes to forgotten hymn texts from the eighteenth and nineteenth centuries. The initial surge came from young adults associated with Reformed University Fellowship (RUF), the college ministry of the Presbyterian Church in America (PCA). The most notable group associated with the catalyzing of this movement was Indelible Grace, a montage of musicians propelled by Rev. Kevin Twit, the RUF pastor at Belmont University in Nashville, Tennessee. Twit was also the former college pastor at Christ Community Church in Franklin, Tennessee, a church filled with Nashville musicians. The impetus for Twit and other RUF pastors' work was an intentional desire to provide a theological and pastoral alternative to the songs of the contemporary praise and worship movement (CPWM).

Brian Murphy, an early student contributor to the movement at both Auburn University's RUF and later at Red Mountain Church in Birmingham, Alabama, captured the sentiment that propelled the early retuners: "I feel like I have more in common with these old hymn writers than I do with

Christians today, because of [the hymn writers'] ability to embrace doubt and struggle with belief."[1]

While there were a few forerunners of this movement providing modern musical settings of old hymn texts—James Ward's jazzy resetting of "Rock of Ages" (Trinity Hymnal, 1990) and Vikki's Cook's retune of the Charlie Bancroft text "Before the Throne of God Above" by People of Destiny International (now known as Sovereign Grace Ministries/Music) in 1997—Indelible Grace Music was the main popularizer of retuned hymnody through its productions and online hymnal.

Five distinct impulses have fueled the RHM: 1) A reaction against the commodification of worship music, 2) a resurgence of historical church practices in broader American evangelicalism, 3) the rise of Neo-Calvinism in the American religious milieu, 4) a musical movement in step with the growing popularity of Americana, and 5) the utilization of new technologies that facilitated creating and sharing music and musical resources from the grassroots.

Reaction Against the Commodification of Worship Music

By the late 1990s contemporary worship music was a big business propelled by the growth of both the megachurch and a music industry that was close to making worship a commodity that sold well. Against that milieu some younger Christians wanted something they perceived as more raw, authentic, and intimate.

Matthew Smith, an early contributor to Indelible Grace at Belmont University, pointed to this impulse in an interview for *ByFaith* magazine. Highlighting the distance between older hymn texts and a commodified sphere of worship, Smith noted, "In a world where everything is over-hyped, slick, and marketable, it's refreshing to see these texts written without any of that baggage." Smith posed a question that linked antiquity with authenticity: "What could be more authentic than a folk song written 250 years ago in a tiny English village for a congregation of 30?"[2]

Kevin Twit likewise remarked on older hymns' same appeal to a younger generation of Christians at the end of the twentieth century, "There is most definitely a hunger and longing among the emerging generations, college students and twenty-somethings, to connect with something real and solid rather than the faddish and ephemeral."[3] Consequently, the

1. Morgan, "Old Hymns."
2. Morgan, "Old Hymns."
3. Twit, "My Grandmother Saved It," 30–31.

RHM has tended to avoid the publishing industry of CPWM by using public domain texts and providing an online hymnal where charts and demos are accessible free of charge. Nonetheless, the movement has not been immune to the draw of commercial success such as when a number of prominent, commercially successful artists released the 2004 album entitled *Passion: Hymns Ancient and Modern*.

A Renewed Interest in the Historic Church

A willingness to draw upon resources from the worship of past Christians has also fueled the RHM. The March 2005 issue of *CCM* magazine, for example, did a feature-length report on the renewed interest in hymns among some well-known contemporary Christian music artists. The article featured Kevin Twit who remarked, "I talk about a sign my mom found at an antique store once: 'My grandmother saved it, my mother threw it away and now I'm buying it back.' I think a lot of younger people are feeling that, saying [the baby boomer generation] handed us Christianity with no connection to tradition."[4] Jars of Clay keyboardist Charlie Lowell, commenting on his group's retuning efforts, added, "The image we kept tossing around while making the record was the idea of roots and wings, digging into what's gone before us and giving flight to these words through new melodies."[5]

As well as being a rich source of raw material, old hymn texts were also familiar to many in the movement. The hymns provided a safe place to test out the theologies and emotions of prior Christians while also yielding guidance for today's Christians interested in exploring worship that looked different than their upbringing, that is, worship more steeped in liturgical forms and sacraments. The broader RHM, therefore, has retuned texts from almost every century of the church to the present.

The Rise of Neo-Calvinism

For much of the RHM, the recent rise of Neo-Calvinism also undergirded an interest in older hymn texts since Neo-Calvinist musicians found these hymns—in contrast to recently written songs—expressed key elements of their theology and piety.[6] Several factors contributed to its rise including the growing prominence of a number of Neo-Calvinist pastors such as Tim

4. Rumburg, "All Things," 32.
5. Rumburg, "All Things," 32
6. Van Biema, "New Calvinism."

Keller, John Piper, Mark Dever, and Mark Driscoll as well as the success of the English Standard Version (ESV) Bible translation and the popularity of conferences and blogs such as the Gospel Coalition and Together for the Gospel.[7] This rise also saw a marked fixation on urban church planting, local artisanship, and entrepreneurial innovation such as hipster coffee shops or record production, and even extended into the African-American community with artists such as Trip Lee, Shai Linne, and spoken word artist Jackie Hill all with high profile associations with leading pastors in this movement.[8] This young generation of Neo-Calvinists heard a gospel that consistently preached a creative God that called his creatures to cultural stewardship and to the cities where culture was shaped.

A Musical Movement in Step with the Resurgence of Americana

In the late 1990s the RHM gained popularity in the wake of the reappropriation of southern folk traditions as well as the perceived authenticity that accompanied them. A critical hallmark of this reappropriation was the soundtrack for the film *O Brother, Where Art Thou* (2000) with its use of period folk music from the early twentieth century, music good enough to win an Academy Award. Not surprisingly, the review of Jars of Clay's 2005 retuned hymn album *Redemption Songs* in *CCM* magazine captured the impulse: "Filled with jangly banjos, fiddles and dulcimers, *Redemption*, thankfully, has more in common with the swampy feel of *O Brother Where Art Thou?* than with the slick and polished "praise team" sound so popular in many of today's larger churches."[9] A broad range of artists from David Crowder to Rend Collective to Mumford & Sons—not to mention early Indelible Grace albums—have reflected this cultural influence in popular music.

The Utilization of New Technologies in Creating and Sharing Music

At the end of the twentieth century the RHM also caught an updraft in the rise of technologies that disrupted the traditional economic systems of the music industry. Utilizing the invention of the mp3 and peer-to-peer

7. Hansen, "Young, Restless, Reformed"; Matt Smethurst, "If John Piper Rapped."
8. McCracken, *Hipster Christianity*, 111–132.
9. Ciani, "How Sweet the Sound!," 49

(P2P) file sharing, along with innovations in home recording software and technologies, the movement sidestepped the traditional record industry to create and share songs through a burgeoning independent music scene. The Grassroots music site was a central resource for indie Christian artists in the 1990s and gave Indelible Grace its first national distribution. Later, CDbaby, the growth of blogging, and other sites such as iTunes and Bandcamp connected artists directly with fans, churches, and worship planners.

If the 1990s saw the first steps of the retuned hymn movement, then the last twenty years have seen its growth into adulthood as interest in the RHM has exploded. From 1996 to 2016 over 150 albums have been released, almost all exclusively from college ministries or local churches.[10] This does not take into consideration a bevy of other hymn-related projects released by more mainstream recording artists like David Crowder, MercyMe, Fernando Ortega, Chris Tomlin, Amy Grant, and Caedmon's Call, or by organizations like the Charles Wesley Society.

The RHM continues to adapt and morph as local contexts change. And while the early RHM was largely white, suburban evangelicals, artists and churches across the racial and socioeconomic divide are now participating. Examples of this increasing diversity include Alabanzaré (retuned hymns translated into Spanish), Urban Doxology (retuned hymns with urban sounds and styles), Liz Vice, the Jackson State University RUF, High Street Hymns, and The Porters Gate Worship Project with its songs on justice and Christian vocation.

THEOLOGICAL PERSPECTIVES

An assessment of the theological perspectives of the retuned hymn movement should take into account both the dominant themes of the hymns that have been retuned and the theological motivations of those who are composing the new tunes.

By and large the hymns utilized by the retuned hymn movement come from historical Evangelical sources to be sung by evangelicals today. In other words, the dominant theological perspectives of retuned hymns highlight themes that resonate in evangelical piety across history. Thus, certain classic characteristics of Evangelicalism can be used to identify the heart of what the hymns are likely to say about God, humanity, salvation, and the world. Not surprisingly, the hymns tend to focus on Jesus Christ and his redeeming work, especially that work accomplished through his atoning death on the cross. Other key historic evangelical themes would be a sense

10. Benedict, "List of Retuned Hymn Projects."

of utter human dependency upon the grace of God, the reliability of that grace for salvation and daily discipleship, and need for and hope of changed lives through that grace. Likewise the hymns will presume the reliability of the biblical witness to God's saving activity for humankind and the necessity for Christians themselves to witness to and offer this salvation of the gospel.

With these characteristics in mind, one can anticipate what most retuned hymns are likely to say. The hymns communicate that God has acted decisively in history through Jesus Christ, especially in the way Christ's sacrificial death has brought about the prospect of salvation for the worshiper.[11] The hymns focus on the person of Jesus Christ, not only in his past redeeming work, but also through Jesus's ongoing work as the mediator of human relationship with the divine.[12] The hymns rejoice in the worshipers' transformation already experienced, hope for continued transformation,[13] and seek continuing divine help to remain faithful in the struggles, sufferings, and trials of Christian discipleship.[14] The hymns speak of the human heart as the regular means of discernment of spiritual things, thus emphasizing right affections as the qualification required for discernment of spiritual things. When this tendency toward affect is present, the hymns reflect not only their roots in Evangelicalism but in Pietism. Even as the hymns rely upon the human heart and affections as primary arenas for engagement with God, many of the hymns confess a depraved human nature and thus rely upon God as the only source of ultimate hope. Finally, some hymns extend an invitation for others to believe, experience salvation, and begin the pilgrimage of faithful Christian discipleship toward God's ultimate consummation of all things.[15]

Notwithstanding Evangelicalism's classic appeal to being biblical and orthodox, it is striking to note what are not likely to be dominant theological themes in the lyrics. The person, work, and role of the Holy Spirit are likely to be secondary themes in this hymnody. Likewise reflection on the nature and work of the church are usually overlooked except as the exhortations

11. An example of an atonement hymn is "There is a Fountain Filled with Blood" (ca. 1771) by William Cowper, retuned by The Welcome Wagon.

12. "He will hold me fast" (1906) by Ada R. Habershon, music by Robert Harkness, arranged by Keith and Kristyn Getty.

13. See "Jesus I am Resting, Resting" (1876) by Jean Sophia Pigott, retuned by Page CXVI.

14. Consider on these themes hymns like "Dear Refuge of My Weary Soul" by Anne Steele (1717–78), retuned by Kevin Twit; "Through the Love of God Our Savior [All Must Be Well]" (1847) by Mary Bowley Peters, retuned by Matthew Smith; and "Jesus, I My Cross Have Taken" (1825) by Henry Francis Lyte, retuned by Bill Moore.

15. An example of a retuned hymn on ultimate things see "Away with our Fears" (1746) by Charles Wesley, retuned by Zac Hicks.

and appeals found in some hymns imply the church as an evangelizing entity. And if a specific retuned hymn holds true to larger patterns of classic Evangelical hymnody, there will be a weak Trinitarian dynamic as the hymn is unlikely to mention all three persons of the Godhead or describe divine saving activity as a cooperative activity of all three. These omissions, of course, are general tendencies. Exceptions do exist like Cardiphonia's collections on the Holy Spirit or on Charles Wesley's hymns on the Trinity.

The manner by which hymns articulate theology—not to mention the number of composers involved—hinders a more precise analysis of their theological specifics. In most instances, especially in the texts that gain the widest popularity, the way in which theology is expressed is somewhat ambiguous, although evocative. As Richard Mouw once put it, song lyrics are "compacted theology."[16] The compacting largely derives from the poetic nature of the lyrics. Limited in the number of words they use, song lyrics as poetry play with rhyme and meter, misdirection, lack of definition, and the stretching of words beyond what one would expect in order to evoke emotion and create experience. They suggest rather than exhaust theological themes, lifting up enough theology to trigger a Christian worshiper's sentiments while also seeking to illicit an experience of the theology while singing these hymns. An example of this could be the singing of Christ's atonement. It is often common for a hymn to highlight a particular theory of the atonement—and perhaps multiple theories within the same text—without detailing the particulars of that suggestion.[17] In these settings, worshipers do not receive a fully orbed discourse on this theological topic; instead, hymns introduce the topic without explaining the nuanced intricacies. Even on key theological points, song texts tend to be suggestive and evocative, not exhaustively clear.

Nonetheless, this propensity away from specificity can be moderated to some degree when the hymn retuners themselves have a strong theological identity. For example, Neo-Calvinism, as noted above, has had an impact on much of the origins of this movement and the hymns to which it is attracted are typically theological in nature. Not surprisingly, the hymns chosen for retuning are historical examples with substantive theological

16. Mouw, "Introduction," xiii–xiv.

17. Consider how the stanza from Charles Wesley's "O For a Thousand Tongues to Sing" (retuned many times) hints at the Christus Victor theory of the atonement: "He breaks the power of canceled sin, / he sets the prisoner free; / his blood can make the vilest clean, / his blood availed for me." Or consider how Red Mountain Music's retuning of Joseph Swain's "How Sweet to Wait Upon the Lord" insinuates a penal substitution theory: "To see, while prostrate at his feet, / Jehovah on the mercy-seat; / And Jesus, at the Lord's right hand, / With his divine atonement stand!"

girth, often including doctrines such as the magnifying God's glory, the all-sufficiency of Christ's atonement, and the utter dependency of humanity upon God's grace.

Moreover, as the movement has grown a tendency toward strategic targeting and curating of certain historic types of hymn texts (e.g., Charles Wesley's *Hymns on the Lord's Supper*, Pentecostal texts, Anne Steele texts, and John Mason Neale hymn texts) has meant that some recent expressions of retuned hymns bear the marks of a more specific theological perspective.[18]

Most retuned hymn texts come from a well-established, popular repertoire. That is especially true, it seems, for those who only occasionally venture into retuning. An examination of the most retuned texts by Charles Wesley, for instance, shows they tend to be standards within both Methodism and the larger church. These standards include hymns reflecting the theological points mentioned above, including "And Can It Be," "Christ the Lord is Risen Today," "Come, Thou Long-Expected Jesus," "Jesus, Lover of My Soul," "Love Divine, All Loves Excelling," and "O For a Thousand Tongues to Sing." More comprehensive retuners like Reformed University Fellowship (Indelible Grace) or the Charles Wesley Society might branch further afield in their search for texts to provide a fuller corpus of songs for worship. The latter society, for example, has searched through the breadth of Wesley texts to provide retuned collections about social justice and caring for the poor.[19]

However, the various ways in which retuners rework older texts provide subtle shifts away from classic Evangelical theology and piety as expressed in older hymn texts. As British scholar Martin Clarke has noted, composing entirely new musical settings for existing texts—thus leaving the texts largely unchanged—is only one way in which hymn texts are retuned.[20] Retuners also repurpose texts in two other ways, both of which provide windows into some evolution in Evangelical theology and piety. One way is to use fragments from older hymns that are embedded in entirely original words and music. Sometimes the appropriation is obvious and direct as with Paul Baloche's and Aaron Shust's "Mighty Fortress." In this case

18. Cardiphonia has focused on unique collections such as Charles Wesley's *Hymns on the Lord's Supper* or a nineteenth century hymnal with over eight hundred hymns to the Holy Spirit for a Pentecost season project. Kevin Twit of Indelible Grace has focused on the texts of Anne Steel because of their language of suffering. Sojourn Music released two records of Isaac Watts hymn texts with a particular focus on his Psalm renderings. Amanda Noel recently released a retuned collection of Fanny Crosby texts. And the Charles Wesley Society has obviously been a perennial supporter for new settings of texts by that songwriter.

19. Kimbrough and Young, *Help Us to Help Each Other*.

20. Clarke, "Sing an Old Song."

the amount of original lyrics and tune makes a direct link with Luther's original. But sometimes the appropriation is more subtle as in "Awake My Soul" by Chris Tomlin, Jesse Reeves, Jason Ingram, and Daniel Carson. This latter hymn has phrases that suggest reference to Thomas Ken's "Awake, My Soul, and With the Sun" and Edwin Hatch's "Breathe on Me, Breath of God" without utilizing anything obvious from either older hymn. The other way retuners repurpose older hymn texts is by adding new choruses and bridges to an existing text and tune, as does Paul Baloche by fusing Charles Wesley's hymn stanzas from "Hark the Herald Angels Sing" with the chorus from Baloche's and Jason Ingram's "King of Heaven."

Regardless of which alternative method for retuning is used, both express the shift in current Evangelical theology and piety away from historic Evangelicalism. As can be seen in contemporary worship songs generally, these alternative methods show modern composers are more reflective about the act of worship itself and more likely to utilize statements of praise, worship, and adoration directly addressed to God (or Jesus) as prayer. It is striking, for example, in how newly appended choruses will directly pray in a way the original lyrics did not, or will intensify the prayer element in the original lyrics.

Beyond the theological themes likely found in retuned hymns, an account of the theological perspective of the retuned hymn movement must include some sense of the theological motivations of many retuners. The time of the movement's emergence in the late 1990s suggests these motivations went beyond the liturgical iconoclasm of baby boomers that had so characterized much of the emergence of contemporary praise and worship. Whereas baby boomer rejection of inherited forms and tradition drove the non-Pentecostal strands of contemporary praise and worship in the 1980s and early 1990s, the key proponents of retuning hymns articulated a desire to find guidance in the past. Kevin Twit, for example, the campus minister behind the rise of Indelible Grace Music, expressed a vision for the use of historic materials, valuing their role in shaping younger Christians. Twit articulated this vision saying,

> We have found that the great hymns of the church have unparalleled power to mold us in our calling. . . . In an age of instant gratification, we need the help of these (past) poets of the church to help us live and think as genuine Christians, and to embrace the vital truths captured in these hymns (from the past).[21]

21. See the liner notes for the CD, *Pilgrim Days* (2001).

Such attitudes reflect a larger reappraisal by evangelicals of the usefulness of closer engagement with church tradition.

CONTRIBUTION TO LITURGY AND WORSHIP

While articles have been written about the RHM, no definitive study exists on the breadth and impact of this phenomenon. Neither does a study exist on the impact the movement might be having more broadly on the composition of contemporary worship songs. Nonetheless, some suggestions about the possible contributions of the movement are possible.

The most obvious contribution is the way the movement has preserved classic hymn texts and introduced them to a new generation of worshipers familiar with band-based worship, using rhythmically driven forms of popular music. The sound of the music itself helps build a bridge to older song texts that might not otherwise find application and appreciation if a worshiper presumed the texts necessitated a maintained connection to earlier tunes and with styles of music not based on current forms of popular music. Thankfully, the retuned hymn movement clearly demonstrates that this assumption is false.

And in the movement truth has rhyme and meter, too. Thus a more subtle contribution is the way in which the movement introduces a countercultural element to worshipers' perceptions about how Christian doctrine and experience should sound in the art form of poetic song lyrics. Linguists have noted a shift since the 1960s toward the colloquial in terms of a cultural presumption about the authenticity and truthfulness of poetry and other forms of linguistic art. Simply put, that which sounds more colloquial tends to be perceived as more authentic and truthful. This presumption can be seen not only in the lyrics of rock and folk music but also in the lyrics of contemporary worship songs. In contrast, by utilizing lyrics that predate the 1960s, the RHM expresses Christian doctrine and experience in older poetic forms that employed a more careful and regular use of rhyme and meter. This more restricted crafting of English runs counter to broader cultural presumptions about what truth sounds like. These older hymn lyrics might be the only place in a worship service where there is still archaic English based on the King James Version Bible, a feature that tends to accentuate the countercultural nature of using older hymn texts.

More generally, retuning hymns provides a source of training and education for modern hymn writers. As current composers study the texts of older hymn writers, they learn how to write their own texts in the strophic forms of the past, using the poetic techniques of older lyricism.

Retuning hymns also provides a lab of experimentation for contemporary composers. Because so much of the material is in the public domain, musicians today can playfully experiment with these texts by combining rap with the hymn texts or adding more contemporary forms of chorus and bridge to older verses, as noted above. Retuning older texts has also allowed modern songwriters to explore liturgical topics generally underrepresented in this era of band-based contemporary praise and worship: baptism, the Lord's Supper, creeds, and texts for the church year.

Retuned hymns might also expand worshipers' expectations about what to experience in a worship song. This expansion arises from the greater verbosity of a typical hymn as compared to a contemporary worship song. The larger number of stanzas and the expanded length of poetic lines allow a hymn to explore thoughts and sentiments more fully than a typical contemporary worship song.

Finally, the retuned hymn movement indicates a maturing of the larger contemporary praise and worship phenomenon. It is no longer unique or exceptional in churches to have band-based worship utilizing rhythm-driven, popular forms of music. As the novelty of this form of worship has dissipated since the late 1990s, we can expect that worshiping congregations are ready to explore acts of worship like hymns that have a more historic pedigree. Not surprisingly, much of the appeal for the retuned hymn movement has come not from baby boomers but from young adults who have never known a worship landscape that did not include contemporary praise and worship. Scholars have noted a growing desire for more classic aspects of Christian worship and even perhaps some churches' disdain for some aspects of contemporary praise and worship.[22] The retuned hymn movement is further evidence of this broader appeal of the past.[23]

The breadth of this shifting attitude toward the past can be seen in the accelerating presence of hymn related materials in Christian Copyright Licensing International's (CCLI) recent lists of top songs. Since the start of the millennium a steady stream of hymnic materials, while not technically retuned hymns, has appeared in CCLI's top twenty-five and top one hundred lists. Examples would include "The Wonderful Cross" (based on Isaac Watts's "When I Survey the Wondrous Cross"), "Amazing Grace (My Chains Are Gone)," "Happy Day," "Cornerstone" (based on Edward Mote's "My Hope is Based"), and "At the Cross" (suggestive of the nineteenth century refrain added to the Watts's text "Alas! And Did My Savior Bleed"). Moreover, retuned hymns have begun to find their way in new hymnals

22. Wuthnow, *After the Baby Boomers*, 223–25.

23. Buschart and Eilers, *Theology as Retrieval*, 139–40.

from denominations such as the Christian Reformed Church, the Reformed Church in America, and Reformed Baptists.

If worshipers are aware of the historic roots for these pieces (which is not a given since contemporary composers and their publishers are not always clear about the connection to historic hymns) then this level of retuning has the potential for teaching these worshipers about the liturgical past and the history of our faith. Given the breadth of use of the most popular contemporary worship songs, any retuned hymns that become popular will implicitly teach worshipers not to fear the past but to see tradition as a source for continuing renewal of the church.

NOTABLE HYMNS

The earliest hymns of the RHM were connected to local RUF college groups and tuned either by the college pastor or one of the students. Early in the movement, new songs circulated primarily through RUF's summer conferences and then through the Indelible Grace online hymnal. Christopher Miner, a student at Vanderbilt University in Nashville, Tennessee, in the early 1990s, tuned some of the movement's most enduring songs in these circles: "On Jordan's Stormy Banks," "God Be Merciful to Me (Psalm 51)," "O Love that Will not Let Me Go," and "From the Depths of Woe (Psalm 130)." Many of the well-known Miner songs are found on Indelible Grace's second album, *Pilgrim Days*, and the first two have found their way into recent hymnals from the Christian Reformed Church. Other notable songs were contributed by Kevin Twit and a large group of writers associated with Indelible Grace such as Matthew Smith and Sandra McCracken. A live CD recorded at Nashville's Ryman Auditorium in 2010, *The Hymn Sing: Live in Nashville*, gathered many of the most popular songs originating with Indelible Grace.

Among early attempts to produce and distribute albums through regular commercial channels were Caedmon's Call's 2001 album entitled *In the Company of Angels*, the Passion Conference's live album named *Passion: Hymns Ancient and Modern*, and the 2005 album from Jars of Clay entitled *Redemption Songs*.

Beyond the college-based or music industry-related attempts at retuning, the RHM has also thrived at a range of local churches scattered across the United States. Some of the more prolific contributors have been Red Mountain Church in Birmingham, Alabama; Park Slope Presbyterian Church in New York City; Sojourn Church in Louisville, Kentucky; Green

Lake Presbyterian Church in Seattle, Washington; and City Church in San Francisco, California.

More recently, another wave of projects has begun to explore other genres of music and liturgical topics. Zac Hicks at Cherry Creek Church in Denver recorded retuned hymns with an arena rock vibe in a 2012 album entitled *The Glad Sound*. Cardiphonia Music produced a series of albums exploring the church year including *Hymns for the Ascension*. And Bifrost Arts Music used the stylings of indie rock to record two albums of retuned hymns: *Come O Spirit* and *Salvation is Created*. High Street Hymns in Richmond, Virginia, incorporated rap into their version of "Come Ye Sinners" on *Love Lives Again*, and indie darling Sufjan Stevens produced The Welcome Wagon's first record, *Welcome to the Welcome Wagon*. Additional groups such as Getty Music, Sovereign Grace Music, Reformed Praise, the Charles Wesley Society, and Page CXVI also have contributed to the overall movement with retuned and modern hymn settings that elevated metric hymnody with popular music forms.

BIBLIOGRAPHY

Benedict, Bruce. "A List of Retuned Hymn Projects." Cardiphonia & The LIturgy Fellowship Community. https://cardiphonia.org/2013/07/29/list-of-retuned-hymn-projects/.

———. "Refurbished Hymns in an Age of Vintage Faith: Millennials and the Retuned Hymn Movement." *Liturgy* 32.1 (January–March 2017) 54–61.

Berry, Kierstin. "The Marks of Indelible Grace." *Grassroots Magazine*, October 27, 2005. http://web.archive.org/web/20051027130032/http://www.grassrootsmusic.com/feature/indelible.

Borger, Joyce, John D. Witvliet, and Martin Tel, eds. *Lift Up Your Hearts: Psalms, Hymns, and Spiritual Songs*. Grand Rapids: Faith Alive Christian Resources, 2013.

Buschart, W. David, and Kent D. Eilers. *Theology as Retrieval: Receiving the Past, Renewing the Church*. Downers Grove, IL: InterVarsity, 2015.

Ciani, Michael. "How Sweet the Sound!" *CCM* (March 2005) 49.

Clarke, Martin V. "Sing an Old Song to the Lord." Unpublished paper, Integrating Theology and Contemporary Worship Conference, The London School of Theology, July 17, 2017.

Hansen, Collin. "Young, Restless, Reformed." *Christianity Today* 50.9 (September 22, 2006). http://www.christianitytoday.com/ct/2006/september/42.32.html.

Kimbrough, S. T., and Carlton R. Young, eds. *Help Us to Help Each Other: Hymns for Life and Ministry with the Poor by Charles Wesley*. The Charles Wesley Society, 2010.

McCracken, Brett. *Hipster Christianity: When Church and Cool Collide*. Grand Rapids: Baker, 2010.

Morgan, Melissa. "Old Hymns for a New Generation." *Byfaith* 17 (October 1, 2007). http://byfaithonline.com/old-hymns-for-a-new-generation.

Mouw, Richard J. "Introduction." In *Wonderful Words of Life: Hymns in American Protestant History & Theology*, edited by Richard J. Mouw and Mark A. Noll, xiii–xiv. Grand Rapids: Eerdmans, 2004.

Rienstra, Ron. "Roots and Wings: Musical Makeovers for Classic Hymns and Hymn Texts." *Reformed Worship* 66 (December 2002). http://www.reformedworship.org/article/december-2002/roots-and-wings-musical-makeovers-classic-hymns-and-hymn-texts.

Rumburg, Gregory. "All Things Bright and Beautiful." *CCM* (March 2005) 26–33.

Scheer, Greg. "Retune My Heart to Sing Thy Grace: How Old Hymn Texts Found a New Home among Evangelicals." *The Hymn* 65.4 (Autumn 2014) 18–26.

Seay, Davin. "The Hymnal: An Endangered Art Form?" *Worship Leader* 22.1 (January–February 2013) 40–43.

Smethurst, Matt. "If John Piper Rapped: Jackie Hill Offers Christian Hedonism in Debut Album." *The Gospel Coalition* (December 11, 2014). https://www.thegospelcoalition.org/article/if-john-piper-rapped/.

Twit, Kevin. "My Grandmother Saved It, My Mother Threw It Away, and Now I'm Buying It Back." *Reformed Worship* 70 (December 2003) 30–31. https://www.reformedworship.org/article/december-2003/my-grandmother-saved-it-my-mother-threw-it-away-and-now-im-buying-it-back.

Van Biema, David. "The New Calvinism." *Time* (March 12, 2009). http://content.time.com/time/specials/packages/article/0,28804,1884779_1884782_1884760,00.html.

Wuthnow, Robert. *After the Baby Boomers: How Twenty- and Thirty-Somethings Are Shaping the Future of American Religion*. Princeton: Princeton University Press, 2007.

Timeline for Volume 3

Mel R. Wilhoit

Note: There are timelines for the appropriate eras also contained in Volumes 2 and 3.

In most surveys of hymnody, a *topical approach* that focuses on one idea at a time (such as psalmody, Reformation hymnody, or African-American hymnody) is the logical way of organizing information, tracing the history of each development from its inception through its maturity, decline, or the present day.

The approach of this Timeline seeks to trace a *chronology of hymnological developments*, often combining or juxtaposing events that normally would not be related under a topical approach (such as the year 1926 with the founding of the Stamps-Baxter Music Company and the beginnings of the American liturgical movement, or the year 1940 with the founding of the monastic Taize community in France, and the publication of Southern Baptist's *Broadman Hymnal*).

However, rather than just produce long lists of hymn writers or hymnal publications, there has been some attempt to group items where they share a common subject or time-period (such as the 1833 Oxford movement, 1850s Sunday school songs, or 1978–99 grouping of "Hymn Renaissance" hymnals).

There has also been an attempt to compile related information, such as subsequent editions of hymnals, under the first date of publication (1549 lists the Church of England's *Book of Common Prayer* and refers to subsequent editions through the present era).

To provide a larger historical context for hymnological developments, dates of a few major historical events have also been provided. Obviously, a timeline purporting to cover the entire history of hymnody must be *selective* rather than *comprehensive*—which means that a great deal of important information has been omitted. Hopefully such omissions will drive the reader to further study.

INTERPRETIVE KEY TO THE TIMELINE

EVENT: Regular type
PERSON: **Bold typeface**
HYMN TEXTS: "In Quotation Marks"
HYMN TUNES: CAPITAL LETTERS
PUBLICATION such as Hymnal/Collection/Book: *Italics*

YEAR

ca 1800 — Beginning Romantic movement in hymnody: focus on Christian year, emotionally sensitive texts, elegant forms

Beginning of camp meeting movement (often called Second Great Awakening); produced folk hymns (WARRENTON coupled with "Come, Thou Fount of every blessing / I am bound for the kingdom" and PROMISED LAND coupled with "On Jordan's stormy banks I stand") and Black spirituals ("Go, tell it on the mountain," "I want Jesus to walk with me," "I've got peace like a river," "Let us break bread together," "Lord, I want to be a Christian," "There is a balm in Gilead," "We are climbing Jacob's ladder," "Were you there when they crucified my Lord")

1800–1880 — British Evangelical Stream of Hymnody: **Thomas Kelly**'s "Look ye saints, the sight is glorious" (1809), "The head that once was crowned with thorns" (1820), **Thomas Moore**'s "Come, ye disconsolate" (1816), **John Bowring**'s "In the cross of Christ I glory" (1825), **Charlotte Elliott**'s "Just as I am" (1834), **Horatius Bonar**'s "I lay my sins on Jesus" (1834), "I heard the voice of Jesus say" (1846), **Henry Francis Lyte**'s "Praise, my soul, the King of heaven" (1834), "Abide with me" (1847), **Dorothy Thrupp**'s "Savior, like a shepherd lead us" (1836), **Sarah Adams**' "Nearer, my God to thee" (1840),

Cecil Alexander's "All things bright and beautiful" (1848), "Once in royal David's city" (1848), "Jesus calls us o'er the tumult" (1852), **Frederick Faber**'s "There's a wideness in God's mercy" (1854), **Anna Waring**'s "In heavenly love abiding" (1850), **John Bode**'s "O Jesus, I have promised" (1866), **Katherine Hankey**'s "I love to tell the story" (1866), **George Croly's** "Spirit of God, descend upon my heart" (1869), **Elizabeth Clephane**'s "Beneath the cross of Jesus" (1868), **Francis Havergal**'s "Lord, speak to me" (1872), "Like a river glorious" (1874), "Take my life and let it be" (1874), **Edwin Hatch**'s "Breathe on me, Breath of God" (1878), **George Mattheson**'s "O love, that will not let me go" (1882)

1800 Beginning of Second Great Awakening among Presbyterians with revivals in Logan County, KY, and beyond; carried on by Methodists, featuring camp-meeting songs

1801 "I love thy (your) kingdom, Lord" Psalm paraphrase by **Timothy Dwight**

Richard Allen's *Collection of Spiritual Songs and Hymns*, first hymnal compiled expressly for use in an African-American congregation

1802 **William Little** and **William Smith**'s Singing-School tunebook, *The Easy Instructor*, that introduces the 4 shape-note system called Faw Sol La

1805 **Jeremiah Ingalls**' *Christian Harmony* containing numerous folk hymns such as anonymous tune I LOVE THEE (then called CHARITY) to folk hymn "I love thee, I love thee" (1801)

1808 Publication of **William Blake**'s "And did those feet in ancient time" becomes unofficial English national hymn when paired with Hubert Parry's tune JERUSALEM (1916)

1812 **William Gardiner**'s *Sacred Melodies* (plus 1815 edition containing tune LYONS by **Joseph Martin Kraus**, traditionally attributed to **Michael Haydn**, and paired with "O worship the King"); collections introduce melodies adapted from classical composers **Haydn, Mozart, Beethoven**

War of 1812 between England and United States results in **Francis Scott Key**'s "O say, can you see" ("The Star Spangled Banner,"1814) set to **John Stafford Smith**'s tune "The

Anacreontic Song"; adopted as official National Anthem by Congress, 1931

1813 **John Wyeth**'s *Repository of Sacred Music, Part Second*, containing many folk tunes

1818 **Joseph Mohr**'s "Silent night" and **Franz Gruber**'s tune, STILLE NACHT

1820 First official approval by Church of England of singing hymns (as opposed to only Psalms) with approval of **James Cotterill**'s *Selection of Psalms and Hymns for Public Worship* (9th ed.)

James Montgomery's "Go to dark Gethsemane"

1822–69 **Lowell Mason** publishes numerous musical collections, including *Boston Handel and Haydn Society Collection of Church Music* (1822), dedicated to choral music, congregational song, children's choirs, and music education; publications include his tunes for HAMBURG (1824 for "When I survey the wondrous cross"), OLIVET (1832 for "My faith looks up to Thee"), ANTIOH (1839 for "Joy to the world"), AZMON (1839 for "O for a thousand tongues to sing"), BETHANY (1856 for "Nearer my God, to Thee")

1825 **James Montgomery**'s "Angels from the realms of glory"

1827 *Hymns Written and Adapted to the Weekly Church Service of the Year* by **Reginald Heber** containing "The Son of God goes forth to war," "Brightest and best of the sons," "Holy, holy, holy, Lord God, Almighty," "O God, that madest earth and sky," "From Greenland's icy mountain"

1830 **Rowland Pritchard's** tune HYFRYDOL, popular with many texts such as Wesley's "Come, thou long-expected Jesus" (1744) or J. Wilbur Chapman's "Jesus, what a friend for sinners" (1910)

1831 **Joshua Leavitt**'s *The Christian Lyre* for use in **Charles Finney**'s revival meetings

The Copyright Act of 1831 included music in its legal protection as a property right; Registry of Copyrights opened (1870) in Library of Congress; effective protection of copyrighted tunes in hymnals forced many publications to rely more heavily on public-domain tunes, especially from England

Samuel Francis Smith's "My country 'tis of thee" ("America") set to tune for "God Save the King (Queen)"

1831–87 Mid-century Denominational Hymnody: **Ray Palmer**'s "My faith looks up to thee" (1830), **Samuel Smith**'s "My country 'tis of thee" (1831), **James Russel Lowell**'s "Once to every man and nation" (1845), **Edmund Sears**' "It came upon a midnight clear" (1849 with **Richard Willis**' tune CAROL, 1850), **Elizabeth Prentice**'s "More love to Thee" (1856), **George Webb**'s "Stand up, stand up for Jesus" (1858), **Julia Ward Howe**'s "Mine eyes have seen the glory" (1861), **Joseph Gilmore**'s "He leadeth me" (1862), **William Featherstone**'s "My Jesus, I love Thee," (1862 to **Adoniram Gordon**'s tune GORDON, 1876), **Mary Ann Thompson**'s "O Zion, haste" (1868), **John Zundel**'s tune BEECHER (1870 for "Love divine, all loves excelling"), **John Greenleaf Whittier**'s "Dear Lord and Father of mankind" (1872), **Mary Lathbury**'s "Break Thou the bread of life" (1877), **Daniel Roberts**'s "God of our fathers, whose almighty hand" (1876, coupled with **George Warren**'s NATIONAL HYMN, 1892), **Washington Gladden**'s "O Master, let me walk with Thee" (1879), **Ernest Shurtleff**'s "Lead on, O King Eternal" (1887)

1832 **Lowell Mason** founds Boston Academy of Music

Lowell Mason and **Thomas Hastings** publish *Spiritual Songs for Social Worship*

Thomas Hastings' tune TOPLADY (for "Rock of Ages, cleft for me")

1833–83 Oxford movement (also called Tractarian movement, after series *Tracts for the Times*) influenced hymnody: **John Henry Newman**'s "Lead, kindly Light" and **Robert Grant**'s "O worship the King" (1833), **Henry Alford**'s "Come, ye thankful people come" (1844), **Frederick Faber**'s "Faith of our fathers, living still" (1849), **Matthew Bridges**' "Crown Him with many crowns" (1851), **William Chatterton Dix**'s "As with gladness men of old" (1858), "What child is this" (1865), **William Whiting**'s "Eternal Father, strong to save" (1860), **Christopher Wordsworth**'s "O day of rest and gladness (1862), **John Monsell**'s "Fight the good fight" (1863), **Sabine Baring-Gould**'s "Onward, Christian soldiers (1864), **William Walsham How**'s "For all the saints" (1864), **Folliott Pierpont**'s "For the beauty of the earth" (1864), **Edward**

Plumptre's "Rejoice, ye pure in heart" (1865), **Samuel Stone**'s "The church's one foundation" (1866), **Walter Chalmers Smith**'s "Immortal, invisible" (1867), **Henry Baker**'s "The King of love my shepherd is" (1868), **Dorothy Gurney**'s "O perfect love" (1883); plus the translation of many Medieval Latin hymns by **John Mason Neal** ("O come, O come, Emmanuel"). Culminates in *Hymns Ancient and Modern* hymnal (1861)

1835 **William Walker**'s shape-note, Singing School tunebook, *Southern Harmony*, is first collection to combine **Newton**'s text "Amazing grace" with pentatonic tune, NEW BRITAIN

1840 **Felix Mendelssohn**'s MENDELSSOHN coupled with "Hark, the herald angels sing"; employs chorales in larger choral and orchestral works (*Reformation Symphony #5*: "A Mighty Fortress")

1844 **B. F. White** and **E. J. King**'s 4-shapenote tunebook, *The Sacred Harp*, containing folk tunes: BEACH SPRING, HOLY MANNA (coupled with "Brethren, we have met to worship"), NEW BRITAIN (coupled with "Amazing grace"), RESTORATION ("I will arise and go to Jesus"), WONDROUS LOVE (coupled with "What wondrous love is this")

1846 **Jesse B. Aikin**'s tunebook, *The Christian Minstrel*, introduces 7-shape notation (do, re, mi, fa, sol, la, ti, do)

William Clayton's "Come, come ye saints" (originally "All Is Well"), the anthem of Mormon pioneers

1850s Sunday school songs include **William Bradbury**'s collections (*Oriola*, 1859; *The Gold en Chain*, 1861) and tunes WOODWORTH (for "Just as I am," 1849), BRADBURY (for "Savior, like a shepherd lead us," 1859), SWEET HOUR or WALFORD (for "Sweet hour of prayer," 1861), CHINA or JESUS LOVES ME (for "Jesus loves me," 1864), SOLID ROCK (for "My hope is built on nothing less," 1863), **Robert Lowry**'s "Shall we gather at the river" and its tune HANSEN PLACE (1864), ALL THE WAY (for Crosby's "All the way my Savior leads me," 1873), **William Doane**'s tunes for **Fanny Crosby**'s songs PASS ME NOT ("Pass me not, O gentle Savior," 1868), NEAR THE CROSS ("Jesus, keep me near the cross," 1869), RESCUE ("Rescue the perish ing," 1869), TO GOD BE THE GLORY ("To God be the glory," 1875), Phoebe Palmer

Knapp's ASSURANCE (for Crosby's "Blessed assurance," 1873)

1851 YMCA (in America) founded in Boston

1852 Scholar **Johannes Zahn**'s *Die Melodien des Deutschen Evangelischen Gesangbuches in vierstimmigem Satze für Orgel und für Chorgesang* (*The Melodies of the German Protestant Church*); plus later monumental works of hymnological scholarship

1853 **John Curwen** founds Tonic Sol-Fa Association to teach reading music using his *Grammar of Vocal Music* (1843) and, later, his *Standard Course of Lessons on the Tonic Sol-fa Method of Teaching to Sing* (1858) that impacts quality of church music

1854 **Nikolas Grundtvig**'s "Built on a Rock" coupled with tune **Ludvig Lindeman**'s KIRKEN

1854–69 **Katherine Winkworth** publishes translations of German chorales into English ("Now thank we all our God," 1858; "Praise to the Lord, the Almighty," 1863)

1855 **Caroline Sandell-Berg**'s "Children of the heavenly Father"

Joseph Scriven's "What a friend we have in Jesus" (coupled with **Charles Converse**'s tune CONVERSE, 1868)

Henry Ward Beecher and musical editors **John Zundel** and **Charles Beecher**'s *Plymouth Collection of Hymns for the Use of Christian Congregations* for Plymouth Congregational Church, Brooklyn

1858 Widespread revivals in England, Northern Ireland, Wales, Scotland

Union Prayer Meeting Hymns published by Sunday School Union for use in Manhattan noon-day prayer meetings begun in 1857 (sometimes called Second Great Awakening or New York Prayer Revival)

George Duffield Jr.'s "Stand up, stand up for Jesus"

1861 Seminal collection *Hymns Ancient and Modern* (musical editor **William H. Monk)** contains J**ohn B. Dykes**' MELITA (for "Eternal Father, strong to save"), NICEA (for "Holy, holy, holy"), **William Monk**'s DIX (for "As with gladness men of old"), EVENTIDE (for "Abide with me"), **Joseph Barnby**'s LAUDES DOMINI (for "When morning guilds the skies"); with supplements and new editions produced into

	twenty-first century (*Common Praise*, 2000; and *Ancient & Modern: Hymns and Songs for Refreshing Worship*, 2013)
1861–65	American Civil War
1862	Salvation Army *The Revival Hymnbook* (and many revisions)
	Julia Ward Howe's "Mine eyes have seen the glory" ("Battle Hymn of the Republic") sung to folk tune JOHN BROWN'S BODY
1864	**William B. Bradbury**'s *Devotional Hymn and Tune Book* for American Baptists (Northern)
1865	Founding of Salvation Army by **William Booth**, initially relying on appeal of popular gospel hymnody and brass bands
1866	**Katherine Hankey**'s "I love to tell the story" (for **William Fischer**'s tune HANKEY)
1867	**Henry Smart**'s tune REGENT SQUARE (for "Angels from the realms of glory")
	Formation of The National (Campmeeting) Association for the Promotion of Christian Holiness, promoting collections such as *Beulah Land* (1870) and *Songs of Triumph* (1882) including tunes by **William J. Kirkpatrick** (TRUST IN JESUS for **Louisa Stead**'s "'Tis so sweet to trust in Jesus")
1868	*Church Book* hymnal published by Evangelical Lutheran Church
	Joseph Hillman and **Louis Hartsough** compile *The Revivalist*, reflecting American holiness movement
1869	**John Goss**' tune LAUDA ANIMA (for "Praise my soul, the King of heaven")
	Ocean Grove Camp Meeting Association establishes Holiness campmeeting grounds at Ocean Grove, NJ, featuring famous organ and great meetings of congregational song led by **John R. Sweney** (tune BEULAH LAND to **Edgar Page Stites'** "I've reached the land of corn and win," 1876) and others
1871	**Arthur Sullivan**'s tune ST GERTRUDE (for "Onward, Christian soldiers")
	Fisk University Jubilee Singers begin touring, popularizing Black Spirituals arranged for choral ensemble
1873–94	Gospel Song/Gospel Hymn publications: **Ira Sankey**'s British sixteen-page collection *Sacred Songs and Solos* expands to

1200 selections by 1903; **Philip Bliss**' collection *Gospel Songs* (1874); **Sankey** and **Bliss**' *Gospel Hymns and Sacred Songs* (1875) expands through six volumes to *Gospel Hymns Nos. 1–6 Complete* (1894)

1873–99 Nineteenth century Gospel Song/Gospel Hymn movement includes **Philip Bliss**' "Sing them over again to me/Wonderful words of life" to his WORDS OF LIFE (1874), "Man of sorrows, what a name" to his HALLELUJAH, WHAT A SAVIOR (1875) and tune VILLE DU HAVRE to **Horatio Spafford**'s "It is well with my soul" (1876), **James McGranahan**'s tunes EL NATHAN and SHOWERS OF BLESSING to **Daniel Whittle**'s "I know not why God's wondrous grace" and "There shall be showers of blessing" (1883), **Daniel Towner**'s tune TRUST AND OBEY to **John Sammis**' "When we walk with the Lord/Trust and obey" (1887), **William Kirkpatrick**'s tunes JESUS SAVES and TRUST IN JESUS to **Priscilla Owens**' "We have heard the joyful sound/Jesus saves" (1882) and **Louisa Stead**'s "'Tis so sweet to trust in Jesus" (1882), **Will L. Thompson**'s text "Softly and tenderly Jesus is calling" and tune THOMPSON or SOFTLY AND TENDERLY (1880)

1875 **Charles Robinson**'s *Psalms and Hymns and Spiritual Songs* published for Southern division of Presbyterian Church

1885/6 **Carl Boberg**'s "O store Gud" becomes "How great Thou art" in **Stuart Hine**'s 1949 translation coupled with anonymous tune O STORE GUD (ca. 1888)

1890 Founding of Moody Bible Institute (Chicago), playing major role in Gospel Hymnody; Gospel Song composer **Daniel Towner** as head of music department (1893–1919)

1892 *Dictionary of Hymnology: Setting for the Origin and History of Christian Hymns of All Ages and Nations*, edited by **John Julian**, becomes the definitive reference work on subject (revised with Supplement, 1907; Dover Reprint, 1957)

1895 Presbyterian Church in USA (Northern) *Hymnal*

1897 Central Conference of American Rabbis (CCAR)—Reform Judaism—publish *Union Hymnal* (with constant revisions through 1960s)

1900–1945 Gospel Song/Gospel Hymn movement includes **Charles Gabriel**'s "When all my laborsand trials are o'er" to his tune

GLORY SONG (1900), "Lord, as of old at Pentecost/Pentecostal power" to his OLD TIME POWER (1913), **Adelaide Pollard**'s "Have Thine own way, Lord" (1907) to **George Stebbins**' tune ADELAIDE, **Julia Johnson**'s "Marvelous grace of our loving Lord" (1910) to **Daniel Towner**'s tune MOODY, **C. Austin Miles**' "I come to the garden alone" and tune GARDEN (1912) and **George Bennard**'s "On a hill far away" and tune OLD RUGGED CROSS (1913), **Albert Brumley**'s "Some glad morning/I'll fly away" to his tune I'LL FLY AWAY (1932), **Eugene Bartlett**'s "I heard an old, old story" to his tune HARTFORD (1939)

1901 **Maltbie Babcock**'s "This is my Father's world" to **Franklin Sheppard**'s tune TERRA BEATA (1915)

James Weldon Johnson's "Lift every voice and sing" to **J. Rosamond Johnson**'s tune LIFT EVERY VOICE (published 1921)

1902 Pianist **Robert Harkness** accompanies congregational singing on piano (rather than organ or pump organ) with an improvisatory style of playing in revival meetings for evangelists **Charles Alexander** (songleader) and **Reuben A. Torrey** (preacher), introducing an approach called "Evangelistic Hymn Playing"; piano becomes dominant instrument for congregational singing in revivalistically-oriented churches and meetings

"Land of Hope and Glory" ("Dear Land of Hope, thy Hope is crowned"), with music by **Edward Elgar** (from *Pomp and Circumstance No. 1*) and lyrics by **A. C. Benson**, becomes a popular unofficial English national anthem

1903 **Frank Mason North**'s "Where cross the crowded ways of life"

1905 **Charles Tindley**'s "Trials dark on every hand/We'll understand it better by and by" to his tune BY AND BY and "When the storms of life are raging, stand by me" to his tune STAND BY ME

1906 *The English Hymnal*, edited by **Pearcy Dearmer** (texts) and **Ralph Vaughan Williams** (music) for Church of England; **Vaughan Williams**' inclusion of his tunes SINE NOMINE (for **William Walsham How**'s "For all the saints," 1864), KING'S WESTON, and English folksongs KINGSFOLD,

	FOREST GREEN. New edition, 1933; successor, *The New English Hymnal*, 1986
	Holiness-Pentecostal revival movement begins in Azusa, CA
1907	**Henry van Dyke**'s "Joyful, joyful, we adore Thee" to tune HYMN TO JOY from **Beethoven**'s *Ninth Symphony* (1824)
1908	**John Oxenham**'s (real name: William Dunkerly) "In Christ there is no East or West"
1909	Independent publisher **Robert Coleman** produces first collection, *The Evangel*, popular among Southern Baptists and other revivalist churches; his 1911 *New Evangel* is one of first publications to include the migrant text "When we've been there ten-thousand years" with **Newton**'s hymn "Amazing grace, how sweet the sound"; it was included in future collections, boosting its popularity in that form
1911	**William P. Merrill**'s "Rise up, O men of God" to **William Walter**'s tune FESTAL SONG (1912)
1912	*The Psalter* published by nine Presbyterian bodies in Canada and US—becoming most successful twentieth century psalter
	Pairing of **Katherine Lee Bates**' "O beautiful for spacious skies" (ca. 1895) with **Samuel Ward**'s tune MATERNA (ca. 1888), becoming popular during World War I
1914–17	World War I (America enters in 1917)
1915	**Louis Benson**'s study on *The English Hymn*
1916	**Sydney Nicholson**'s tune CRUCIFIER (for "Lift high the cross")
	Hubert Parry's tune JERUSALEM (coupled with "And did those feet in ancient time")
1920	*The Hymnal: Army and Navy* (also 1942 edition)
1921	Important African-American collection, *Gospel Pearls*
1922	The Hymn Society of America founded; name changed to The Hymn Society in the United States and Canada, 1991
1925	Lillenas Publishing Company founded as important publisher of Wesleyan-Holiness music including Church of Nazarene's *Glorious Gospel Hymns* (1931), *Praise and Worship* (1953), *Worship in Song* (1972)
1926	Stamps-Baxter Music Company founded, issuing annual "convention songbooks" featuring shape-note songs

popularized by male quartets of Southern Gospel fame (**Cleavant Derricks**' "I once was lost in sin/Just a little talk with Jesus," 1937; **W. B. Stevens**' "Tempted and tried, we're oft' made to wonder/Farther Along," 1937)

Beginnings of American liturgical movement (with publication of *Orate Fratres*)

1927 Scholar **Louis F. Benson**'s *The Hymnody of the Christian Church*

1928 *The Oxford Book of Carols*

1929 Beginning of economic Great Depression

1930 **Harry Emerson Fosdick**'s "God of grace and God of glory"

1932 **Thomas Dorsey**'s "Precious Lord, take my hand" to his tune PRECIOUS LORD, and

"I am tired and weary/There'll be peace in the valley" (1939)

1933 **George Pullen Jackson**'s *White Spirituals in the Southern Uplands: The Story of the Fasola Folk, Their Songs, Singings, and "Buckwheat Notes"*

1934 *Psalter Hymnal* of Christian Reformed Church

1935 Hammond Organ Company markets electronic instrument as alternative to pipe organ or piano

Three major branches of Methodism compile *The Methodist Hymnal* edited by **Robert G. McCutchan** who pairs **Harry Emerson Fosdick's** "God of grace and God of glory" with CWM RHONDDA tune

1937 **Robert Guy McCutchan**'s *Our Hymnody*, scholarly companion to *The Methodist Hymnal* (1935)

1939–45 World War II (American enters in 1942)

1940 **B. B. McKinney** compiles *The Broadman Hymnal*, popular among Southern Baptists, including his "Take up thy cross and follow Me" ("Wherever He Leads I'll Go," 1936) to his tune FALLS CREEK

Founding of monastic Taize Community (Burgundy, France); spoken and sung prayer (chants) supplied by **Jacques Berthier** and **Joseph Gelineau**

1941 Seventh-day Adventist popular, *The Church Hymnal*

Scholar **Henry Wilder Foot** publishes *Three Centuries of American Hymnody*

Alexander Burns' chorus "Christ for me, yes it's Christ for me" published and becomes theme song of Youth for Christ that publishes series of *Youth for Christ Songbooks* featuring popular choruses such as "Do Lord, O do Lord, do you remember me"

1943 Publication of Episcopal Church's *The Hymnal 1940;* serves until *The Hymnal 1982*

1945–80 Post WWII Gospel Hymnody includes **John W. Peterson**'s tune TORONTO (1954 for **Margaret Clarkson**'s "So send I you," 1938), words and music for "Marvelous message we bring/Jesus is coming again," to COMING AGAIN (1957), "O what a wonderful, wonderful day/Heaven came down," to HEAVEN CAME DOWN (1961); **Bill Gaither**'s "Shackled by a heavy burden/He touched me" to HE TOUCHED ME (1963) and with **Gloria Gaither**'s "The marketplace is empty/The King is coming" to KING IS COMING (1970), "God sent His Son/Because He lives" to tune RESURRECTION (1971)

1949 *The Hymn: A Journal of Congregational Song* quarterly journal of The Hymn Society in the United States and Canada begins publication

1950 World Library of Sacred Music/World Library Publications founded

1951 English collections *Congregational Praise* and *The BBC Hymn Book*

1954 **Georgia Harkness**' "Hope of the world"

1955 Four Presbyterian groups publish *The Hymnbook*

1956 Beginning of *Dictionary of North American Hymnology* project (DAH or DNAH); merged with hymnary.org (2009)

W. Hines Sims edits official Southern Baptist collection, *Baptist Hymnal*

1957 **Eric Routley**'s *The Music of Christian Hymnody* (revised as *The Music of Christian Hymns*, 1981)

Geoffrey Beaumont's *Folk Mass*

1958 Eight Lutheran groups publish *Service Book and Hymnal*

1960 Beginning of charismatic renewal movement (Roman Catholic renewal, 1967) popularizes songs of experiential nature and focus on Holy Spirit; strongly impacts non-Charismatic worship practices

Beginnings of explosion of Global Hymnody: World Lutheran Federation *Laudamus* (six editions, 1952–90), Christian Churches of Asia *Sound the Bamboo* (1963), WCC multilingual *Cantate Domino* (1974), United Methodist series of *Global Praise* (beginning 1996), International Council of Ethnodoxologists (ICE) formed (2003)

1961 **Albert F. Bayly**'s "Lord, whose love through humble service" Roman Catholic *People's Mass Book* of vernacular (non-Latin) hymns, with later editions in 1964 (containing **Omer Westendorf**'s "Where charity and love prevail" to **Paul Benoit**'s tune CHRISTIAN LOVE, 1959), 1970, 1984, 2003 (containing **Tom Colvin**'s "Jesu, Jesu, fill us with your love," 1969 to Ghanian folk melody CHEREPONI, 1963; Zulu song "Siyahamb' ekukhanyen' kwenkhos' [We are marching in the light of God]" to Zulu tune SIYAHAMBA; Doris Akers' "I am weak and I need your strength," 1953 to tune LEAD ME, GUIDE ME, 1953)

British Broadcasting Company (BBC) begins Songs of Praise popular TV program featuring congregations (and choirs) singing hymns in various church locations

1962 **Maurice Frost**'s *Historical Companion to Hymns Ancient and Modern*

Beginning of twentieth century "Hymn Renaissance" or "Hymn Explosion" with Dunblane (Scotland) Consultation on church music and hymns resulting in *Dunblane Praises* (1964) and *Dunblane Praises 2* (1966) with **Erik Routley**'s "All who love and serve your city" (1966). The (Anglican) Jubilate Group's *Youth Praise I* (1966) and *Youth Praise II* (1969). Hymns by **Carl Daw**, **Timoth-Dudley Smith**, **Brian Wren, Fred Kaan,** and **Fred Pratt Green**'s "When in our music God is glorified" (1972) to **Charles V. Standford**'s tune ENGELBERG (1904). Also results in flood of denominational and non-denominational hymnals [see 1978]

1963 Roman Catholic Second Vatican Council (1962–65) issues *Sacrosanctum Concilium*, the Constitution on the Sacred Liturgy that encourages congregational song, allowing singing in the vernacular, opening door for vast changes in Catholic musical practices **Sydney Carter**'s "I danced in the morning" ("Lord of the Dance") coupled with Shaker tune SIMPLE GIFTS (ca. 1848)

	Wyatt T. Walker's article, "The Soulful Journey of the Negro Spiritual: Freedom Songs," traces the development of Black "freedom songs" (e.g., "We shall overcome") popular during civil rights movement
1966	**Peter Scholtes**' "We are one in the spirit/They'll know we are Christians by our love" to his tune ST. BRENDAN'S
1967–75	Publication of Youth Musicals that impact congregational song: *Good News* (1967), *Natural High* (1969), *Tell It Like It Is* (including "It only takes a spark/Pass It On," 1969), *Celebrate Life* (1972)
1968	**Brian Wren**'s "Christ is Alive!" and "I come with joy to meet my Lord"
1968–80	"Jesus people" movement and popularity of Scripture choruses with guitar (**Karen Lafferty**'s "Seek ye first the kingdom of God" to her tune LAFFERTY, 1972)
1969	**Edwin Hawkins**' recording of "O happy day" (**Philip Doddridge**, 1755) becomes secular hit song, popularizing Black Gospel Music and redefining the term Gospel Music to mean Black Gospel including **Andrea Crouch**'s "I've had many tears and sorrows/Through It All" to his THROUGH IT ALL (1971), "How can I say thanks/My Tribute" to his MY TRIBUTE (1971), "Soon and very soon" to his tune VERY SOON (1978); **Dottie Rambo**'s "The sky shall unfold" to her tune WE SHALL BEHOLD HIM (1980)
	(Old) Mennonite Church and General Conference Mennonite Church publish *The Mennonite Hymnal*
1970s	St. Louis Jesuits popularize folk-style songs among Roman Catholics in response to Vatican II
1971	Roman Catholic hymnal *Worship* with successive editions: 1975 (containing **Joseph Gelineau**'s psalmody), 1986 (with music from Taize community), and 2011
1974	Publisher Maranatha! Music releases *Maranatha! Praise* album that features beginnings of "Worship Music"
	World Council of Churches' hymnal, *Cantate Domino* (harmony edition, 1980) with multi-ethnic hymnody
1976	**Carlos Rosas**' "Cantemos al Senor" ("O sing unto the Lord"): example of Global Hymnody, popular in Catholic and Protestant churches

1977 Roman Catholic folk hymnal *Glory and Praise: Songs for the Worshipping Assembly, Vol. 1* (additional volumes, 1979/80 with **Michael Joncas**' "Ye who dwell in the shelter/On eagle's wings" to ON EAGLE'S WINGS, and 1982, 1983); *Glory and Praise Comprehensive Edition* (1987; further editions in 1990, 1998)

Consultation on Ecumenical Hymnody publishes its list of *Hymns and Tunes for Ecumenical Use*

1978–99 *Lutheran Book of Worship* (1978) considered first of modern hymnals: Church of God in Christ (COGIC) *Yes, Lord Hymnal* (1982), Ecumenical *Mission Praise* (1983 and many later editions), *AMEC Bicentennial Hymnal* (1984), Episcopal *The Hymnal 1982* (pub. 1985), Reformed Church in America *Rejoice in the Lord* (1985), non-denominational *Hymnal for Worship and Celebration* (1986), Anglican Communion's *New English Hymnal* (1986), Christian Reformed Church *Psalter Hymnal* (1987), *United Methodist Hymnal* (1989), non-denominational *Worshipping Church* (1990), Presbyterian (PCA and OPC) *Trinity Hymnal* (1990), *Presbyterian* (USA) *Hymnal* (1990), *Southern Baptist Hymnal* (1991), Disciples of Christ *Chalice Hymnal* (1995), United Church of Christ *New Century Hymnal* (1995), Covenant Church *Covenant Hymnal* (1996), non-denominational *Celebration Hymnal* (1997), ecumenical *Australian Hymnbook II* (1999)—addressing issues of language ("thee/thou"), gender (use of "he" for males and females), power terms ("king," "Lord," "master"), military language ("Christian soldiers, marching as to war"), inclusivity (ageism or physical limitations), plus inclusion of African-American spirituals and Global hymnody

1978–2009 Publication of *CCM (Contemporary Christian Music) Magazine* as the mouthpiece for pop-rock, performance-based Christian music (changed to digital format in 2009); some songs—**Michael W. Smith**'s text/tune "How majestic is your name," (1981), text/tune for "Great is the Lord" (1982), and tune THY WORD coupled with **Amy Grant**'s "Thy Word is a lamp unto my feet" (1984); **Michael Card**'s text/tune "El Shaddai" (1981); **Twila** Paris' text/tune "We will glorify" (1982) published in hymnals as congregational song

1979	Prolific hymnologist **Erik Routley**'s *A Panorama of Christian Hymnody*, one of his many publications on hymnody and church music
1981	**Marilyn Kay Stulken**'s *Hymnal Companion to the Lutheran Book of Worship*
1983	Publisher Maranatha! Music issues *The Praise Book* song collection (and subsequent editions)—becomes "bible" of Scripture-oriented worship choruses
1985	CCLI (Christian Copyright Licensing, Inc.) founded to facilitate efficient and legal use of copyright law as pertains to churches; membership allows a wide latitude of applications for congregational song—especially in digital age
ca. 1985	Beginnings of "Worship Wars": conflicts in church about traditional versus contemporary worship styles—especially as related to congregational song
1987	Union for Reform Judaism publishes *Sharai Shirah: Gates of Song—Music for Shabbat*
1988	Roman Catholic folk hymnal *Gather* with later editions, 1994, 2004, 2011 including **Marty Haugen**'s "Let us build a house where love can dwell" ("All Are Welcome," 1994), and songs by **David Hass**, **Michael Joncas, Dan Schutte**
1989	Recordings by Church of God in Christ (COGIC), *Saints in Praise Volume I, Volume 2* (1990), *Volume 3* (1992), provide model of African-American Praise/Worship music
1992	Publication of *Worship Leader* magazine with its SongDiscovery service (1997) shapes choices for congregational song
1992	Publication of *The Revised Common Lectionary* by ecumenical Consultation of Common Texts; annotated edition in 2012
1993	Beginnings of "praise and worship" movement, including projection of song lyrics onto large screens (replacing hymnals), led by rock-band styled musicians featuring guitars, drums, amplification, and physical movement (e.g., uplifted hands); generally singing recently composed "Praise Songs" like **Graham Kendrick's** text/tune "Shine, Jesus, Shine" (1987), **Matt Redman**'s text/tune "When the music fades/The heart of worship" (1997), **Paul Baloche**'s text/tune "Open the eyes of my heart, Lord" (1997), **Chris Tomlin**'s text/tune "We fall down" (1998)

	Kirk Franklin's "The Reason Why We Sing," "Behold the Lamb" (1995), and "Stomp" (1997) including hip-hop influences
1996	Website *Cyber Hymnal* established (address was http://www.cyberhymnal.org until 2009)
1997	United Methodist Global Praise Project: *Global Praise I, II* (2000), *III* (2004)
1998	**John Bell** and Iona (Scotland) Community's *Common Ground* collection
1998–2000	Publication of *The Garland Encyclopedia of World Music* with recordings that include Global Hymnody
2000	Praise and Worship style generally accepted as common medium of congregational song
	First Passion gathering, featuring songs of **David Crowder, Chris Tomlin**, and **Matt Redman** that become popular as congregational song
	Reformed University Fellowship (RUF) releases *Indelible Grace* CD, reflecting interest in reformulating traditional hymnody
2001	Attack on World Trade Center on September 11. Countless memorial services feature "Amazing Grace," which soon becomes America's unofficial hymn
2000–2013	Major twenty-first century hymnals, some in digital editions (e.g., Kindle) or with computer apps: Church of England *Common Worship* (2000), Christian Churches of Asia *Sound the Bamboo* (2000 edition of 1963 original), *The New National Baptist Hymnal 21st Century Edition* (2001), *African American Heritage Hymnal* (2001), Missouri Synod *Lutheran Service Book* (2006), ELCA *Evangelical Lutheran Worship* (2006), Southern Baptist *The Baptist Hymnal* (2008); *Celebrating Grace Hymnal* (2010); *Lead Me, Guide Me: An African American Catholic Hymnal* (2012), Reformed *Lift Up Your Hearts: Psalms, Hymns, and Spiritual Songs* (2013), Presbyterian (USA) *Glory to God: Hymns, Psalms, & Spiritual Songs* (2013), and *Glory to God: A Companion* (2016)
2002	**Keith Getty** and **Stuart Townend**'s "In Christ alone" to tune IN CHRIST ALONE, "Speak, O Lord as we come to you" to SPEAK O LORD (2005), "O Church, arise" to O CHURCH ARISE (2005)

Journal *Ethnodoxology* published by International Council of Ethnodoxologists (ICE) with global focus; published online as *Global Forum on Arts and Christian Faith*, 2013

2008 hymnary.org: free, searchable database of hymn-related material appears online

2013 *Canterbury Dictionary of Hymnology* (purported replacement for **Julian**'s seminal *Dictionary of Hymnology*) available online with membership: www.hymnology.co.uk

2017 The Hymn Society in the United States and Canada establishes Center for Congregational Song

Contributor Biographies for Volume 3

Alphabetical Listing

E. Byron (Ron) Anderson (PhD, Emory University; MDiv, Yale University Divinity School) is Styberg Professor of Worship and director of the Nelle B. Ebersole program in Music Ministry at Garrett-Evangelical Theological Seminary in Evanston, IL. His writing and research has focused on the intersection between Christian liturgical practice and spiritual formation.

Bruce H. Benedict (MDiv, Reformed Theological Seminary) is the Chaplain of Worship Arts at Hope College (Holland, Michigan) and the Creative Director of Cardiphonia Music, a fellowship of songwriters that crowd-source worship music for the joy and benefit of the church.

David Bjorlin (PhD candidate, Liturgical Studies, Boston University School of Theology; MDiv, North Park Theological Seminary) is an adjunct lecturer of worship at North Park Theological Seminary and pastor in the Evangelical Covenant Church. His areas of interest include hymnody, the connection between liturgy and ethics, and the incorporation of children in worship.

Carl P. Daw, Jr. served as Executive Director of The Hymn Society in the United States and Canada from 1996 to 2009, when their offices were housed at Boston University School of Theology. He has remained there as Curator of Hymnological Collections and Adjunct Professor of Hymnology. An Episcopal priest, he is also a widely published author of hymn texts.

Jeremy Dibble (PhD, Southampton University; MA, Trinity College, Cambridge; FRSCM, FGCM) is a Professor of Music at Durham University. He has published monographs on C. Hubert H. Parry (OUP), Charles Villiers Stanford (OUP), and John Stainer (Boydell), as well as numerous articles on church music, hymnody, and organ music of the Victorian and Edwardian eras. He is the musical editor of the *Canterbury Dictionary of Hymnology.*

Michael S. Driscoll (STD, Institut Catholique de Paris; PhD, University of Paris IV-Sorbonne; S.T.L., Sant Anselmo, Rome) is Professor Emeritus of Sacramental Theology and Liturgy at the University of Notre Dame, USA. He is the founding director of the graduate program in sacred music and the undergraduate minor in liturgical music ministry at Notre Dame.

James R. Goff, Jr. (PhD, University of Arkansas) is Chair and Professor of History at Appalachian State University in Boone, North Carolina. His research interests are related to American religious history, specifically the holiness-pentecostal movement and gospel music. He teaches courses on the American South, United States church history, and country and gospel music. He is the author of *Fields White Unto Harvest: Charles F. Parham and the Missionary Origins of Pentecostalism* (Univ. of Arkansas, 1988) and *Close Harmony: A History of Southern Gospel* (UNC, 2002) as well as coeditor of *Portraits of a Generation: Early Pentecostal Leaders* (Arkansas, 2002) as well as numerous scholarly and popular articles. He is currently authoring a religious biography of the life and times of Elvis Presley for inclusion in the Library of Religious Biography series for William B. Eerdman's Publishing Company.

C. Michael Hawn (DMA/MCM, Music Education and Voice, Southern Baptist Theological Seminary; BME, Wheaton College) is University Distinguished Professor of Church Music and Director of the Sacred Music Program at Perkins School of Theology, Southern Methodist University. Hawn conducts research in hymnody and publishes widely in this field, especially in the area of non-Western congregational song.

Lim Swee Hong (PhD, Drew University; MSM, Southern Methodist University) is Deer Park Associate Professor of Sacred Music and Director, Master of Sacred Music program, at Emmanuel College of Victoria University in the University of Toronto, Canada. He is also the Director of Research for the Hymn Society in USA and Canada.

Beverly A. Howard (DMA, Organ, University of North Texas; MM, Organ, University of Oklahoma; BMus, Organ, University of Oklahoma) is Professor of Music at California Baptist University in Riverside, California. She is former editor of *The Hymn: A Journal for Congregational Song* and served on hymnal committees for *Celebrating Grace* (Baptist) and *Glory to God* (Presbyterian).

Robert J. Morgan is the teaching pastor of The Donelson Fellowship in Nashville, Tennessee, where he has served for thirty-five years. Among his thirty-five books in print is his three-volume set of hymns and their history, *Then Sings My Soul*, Volumes 1–3. He also writes for Dr. David Jeremiah and has many articles published in Christian periodicals.

Stephen Michael Newby (DMA, Music Composition, The University of Michigan at Ann Arbor; MM, The University of Massachusetts at Amherst) is Professor of Music at Seattle Pacific University in Seattle, Washington. His recent publications include areas of theology of multiethnic music and worship, oratorio and musical theater works based upon the prophet Hosea, Civil Rights and Underground Railroad movements.

Joanna Pepple (PhD candidate, Musicology, The Florida State University; MM, Music Theory/Composition, East Carolina University; MM, Violin Performance, Appalachian State University) is a musicologist who researches the history of pedagogy and institutions, focusing on Americans at the Leipzig Conservatory. She is an active church musician, maintains a private violin teaching studio, and co-directs the Tallahassee Homeschool String Orchestra.

Iain Quinn (PhD, Historical Musicology, University of Durham; MM, Yale University; BM, University of Hartford) is Assistant Professor of Organ and Coordinator of Sacred Music at Florida State University. Publications include editions of Barber, Czerny, Elgar, and Goss and books *The Highest Walks of Art—The Development of an English Organ Sonata* and *Saint or Siren? The Organist in Victorian Literature.*

Jocelyn Russell Wallace (PhD, MAR, Westminster Theological Seminary; MBA, Wharton School of Business; BA, Princeton) is Professor of Business at DeVry University. She has served on numerous boards including the Princeton University Board of Trustees and the Philadelphia Chapter of the American Marketing Association. Her doctoral research focused on African American religious experience.

Lester Ruth (PhD, University of Notre Dame; ThM, Candler School of Theology; MDiv, Asbury Theological Seminary) is the Research Professor of Christian Worship at Duke Divinity School. Prior to Duke, he taught at Asbury Theological Seminary and Yale Divinity School. His current research explores the non-musical aspects of the history of contemporary worship.

Greg Scheer (MA, Music Composition/Theory, University of Pittsburgh) is a composer, cofounder of hymnary.org, and author of *The Art of Worship* (Baker Books, 2006), *Essential Worship* (Baker Books, 2016), and "Shout to the Lord: Praise & Worship from Jesus People to Gen X" in *New Songs of Celebration Render* (ed. C. Michael Hawn, GIA, 2013).

Kendra Buckwalter Smith (STM/MDiv, Pittsburgh Theological Seminary) is Minister of Word and Sacrament in the PC(USA), serving as the Director of the Worship Program at Pittsburgh Theological Seminary. Her research is in the areas of Christian liturgy and worship music.

Martin Tel (DMA, University of Kansas; MA, Calvin Theological Seminary; MM, University of Notre Dame) is the Director of Music at Princeton Theological Seminary where he directs the seminary choirs, facilitates the music ministry for daily worship, and offers courses in church music. Tel's research focuses on psalmody and congregational song.

Karen B. Westerfield Tucker is Professor of Worship at the School of Theology, Boston University, where she teaches courses related to liturgical studies and church music. She is the author of *American Methodist Worship* (Oxford University Press, 2001), and the editor for *The Sunday Service of the Methodists: Twentieth-century Worship in Worldwide Methodism* (Abingdon/Kingswood, 1996) and (with Geoffrey Wainwright) *The Oxford History of Christian Worship* (Oxford University Press, 2006; rev. and exp. ed. online).

Vernon M. Whaley (PhD, Oklahoma University; DMin/MCM, Luther Rice Seminary; MA, Middle Tennessee State University) is Dean of the Liberty University School of Music. His publications include *Called to Worship: From the Dawn of Creation to the Final Amen* (Thomas Nelson); *Worship Through the Ages* (Broadman-Holman); *The Great Commission to Worship* (Broadman-Holman); and *The Dynamics of Corporate Worship* (Baker Books).

Mel R. Wilhoit (DMA, Southern Baptist Theological Seminary) served as Professor of Music and Department Chair at Bryan College, Dayton, Tennessee, for over thirty years. His popular and scholarly works on music have appeared in numerous traditional and online publications.

Index of Scripture

OLD TESTAMENT

Exodus

Joshua

Psalm

Proverbs

Isaiah

Jeremiah

NEW TESTAMENT

Matthew

Matthew *(continued)*

Mark

Luke

John

Acts

Romans

I Corinthians

II Corinthians

Galatians

Ephesians

Philippians

Colossians

I Timothy

Titus

Hebrews

I Peter

Revelation

Index of Names and Subjects

Index of Hymns

Hymns and Hymnody
Historical and Theological Introductions

Volume I: From Asia Minor to Western Europe
Volume II: From Catholic Europe to Protestant Europe

Edited by Mark A. Lamport, Benjamin K. Forrest and Vernon M. Whaley

Hymns and Hymnody is an introductory textbook in three volumes describing the most influential hymnists, liturgists, and musical movements of the church. This academically grounded resource evaluates both the historical and theological perspectives of the major hymnists and composers that have impacted the church over the course of twenty centuries.

Volume 1 explores the early church and concludes with the Renaissance era hymnists. Each chapter contains five elements: historical background, theological perspectives communicated in their hymns/compositions, contribution to liturgy and worship, notable hymns, and bibliography.

Volume 2 begins with the Reformation and extends to the eighteenth-century hymnists and liturgists. Each chapter contains five elements: historical background, theological perspectives communicated in their hymns/compositions, contribution to liturgy and worship, notable hymns, and bibliography.

The missions of *Hymns and Hymnody* are to provide biographical data on influential hymn writers for students and interested laypeople, and to provide a theological analysis of what the cited composers have communicated in the theology of their hymns. It is vital for those involved in leading the worship of the church to recognize that what they communicate is in fact theology. This latter aspect is missing in accessible formats for the current literature.

Volume I:
Paperback ISBN: 978 0 227 17720 4 | PDF ISBN: 978 0 227 90721 4
Specifications: 229x153mm (9x6in), 368pp
Published: March 2020

Volume II:
Paperback ISBN: 978 0 227 17721 1 | PDF ISBN: 978 0 227 90722 1
Specifications: 229x153mm (9x6in), 336pp
Published: July 2020

BV - #0017 - 141122 - C0 - 229/152/21 - PB - 9780227177228 - Gloss Lamination